START A CAREER
IN
COMPLEMENTARY
MEDICINE

G. Maher, B.Sc.

START A CAREER IN COMPLEMENTARY MEDICINE

A Manual/Directory of Courses
in Alternative and Complementary Medicine

TACKMART PUBLISHING

Published by: Tackmart Publishing
P.O.Box 140,
Harrow
Middlesex HA3 0UY

Design and Origination: Tackmart Publishing

Second Edition 1992

British Library Cataloguing-in-Publication Data

Maher, G, *1955-*
  Start a career in complementary medicine.
  I. Title
  615.5

  ISBN 1-872-967-01-9

Printed in Great Britain by Staples Printers Rochester Ltd., Rochester, Kent.

CONTENTS

What Others Are Saying About This Unique Book

"The book has been a great eye opener for me and contains a wealth of knowledge - all very useful."

Miss E. Harzmeyer (reader)

"Thank you for producing this manual. I've been looking for something like this for years!"

Ms. S. Turner (reader)

"I would like to take this opportunity to compliment the author on a first-rate publication. I have a Diploma in Naturopathy, and wish to undertake further studies before setting up a practice, and this book is going to be of enormous help to me."

Ms. S. A. Balmer (reader)

"Maher (the author) has chosen to tabulate his subject which enables the reader to get a quick overview and prevents duplication... This manual is a useful reference point."

Journal of Alternative & Complementary Medicine, January 1991

"If you want to be on the giving rather than the receiving end of alternative treatments, this manual points the way towards 21 alternative therapies... Recommended."

Health & Fitness, February 1991

"I would recommend this book as a helpful resource for anyone thinking of embarking on training in an alternative therapy."

Nursing Times, November 14, 1990

"This new publication will be particularly welcomed as a course directory... The book is attractively laid out .... This book should prove to be useful addition to careers libraries."

Newscheck with Careers Service Bulletin, Vol.1, No.5, November 1990

"I found it a most interesting and very informative publication and certainly contains a large volume of comprehensive information, which should be invaluable for all interested parties."

Margaret Hills (The Margaret Hills Clinic, Coventry)

"An excellent publication ."

Ursula Markham (Principal, The Hypnothink Foundation)

"The amount of information included and the method of presentation and cross-referencing is excellent."

Stuart Gracie (The School of Homoeopathy)

"I found this book both informative and helpful and I only wish that something like this had been around when I was thinking of becoming a Shiatsu Practitioner."

Sally Billings (Honorary Secretary, Shiatsu Society)

"In general I find the book a worthwhile project well thought out and presented."

Peter Mansfield (The Bates Association of Great Britain

"The general presentation, clarity and quality of the book are very impressive and it seems a potentially very useful publication."

Thomas Attlee (Syphysis for the Study of Holistic Health SSHH)

"My congratulations on a fine publication."

Alf Fowles (The National College of Psychic Counselling)

A REQUEST TO ALL SCHOOLS

A. To the schools listed in this book

Since the profession of alternative medicine is undergoing rapid and continuous change, it is reasonable to assume that many of the details presented in this book will be obsolete in a matter of months. Hence any help you can give us to keep the information up-to-date would be much appreciated. Obviously we want to make sure that our information is as precise as possible in future editions. So do please give us a few minutes of your time to check whether the information given in this book regarding your school and the courses it runs is correct. If it is not, please do write to us, enclosing your prospectus and whatever other information that you think is necessary to rectify any inaccuracy.

B. To schools not listed in this book

If you run courses in one or more of the therapies listed in this book, and if you have a register for your graduates, then please write to us enclosing your prospectus plus any additional information needed to complete the entries in the indexes of this book.

C. To schools running courses in disciplines not listed in this book

If your school runs courses in disciplines that are not listed in this book - whether your other courses are listed, or whether your school is not listed at all - and you think that these courses should be listed in future editions, then please write to us about them. We shall be studying the relevance of other disciplines to this book, and your opinion would be very helpful to us in reaching any decisions in this respect.

IMPORTANT NOTICE

The information contained in this directory has been compiled from materials supplied by the schools running courses in the various therapies included in this book. Every effort has been made to ensure that the information given is accurate and up-to-date. But, the fact that there is an entry or an advertisement in this directory is in no way a recommendation of the school or the course(s) they run.

ACKNOWLEDGEMENTS

I would like to express my thanks to:

A. the following individuals for their help in compiling, typesetting, editing and designing the book:
Dia Azzawi, Wijdan Maher, Antony Mason, Haidar Ogaily and Reem Zakku.

B. the following individuals for writing the articles on the following therapies and methods:
Victoria Dawes of The Professional Association of Alexander Teachers for writing the article on Alexander Technique,

Donald Harrison of The Institute of Allergy Therapists for writing the article on Allergy Therapy,

Lesley Kelly of New Beginnings for writing the article on Assertiveness,

Peter Mansfield of The Bates Association of Great Britain for writing the article on Bates Eye Therapy,

Dr Harry Howell of The Howell College of Lymph & Colon Therapies for writing the articles on Colonic Hydrotherapy and Lymph Drainage,

Howard Sun of Living Colour for writing the article on Colour Therapy,

Dr Arthur Jonathan of the School of Psychotherapy and Counselling - Regent's College for writing the article on Counselling,

Thomas Attlee of the Symphysis for the Study of Holistic Health for writing the article on Cranio-Sacral Therapy,

Dennis West of The Academy of Crystal and Natural Awareness for writing the article on Crystal Therapy,

Eileen Oldfield of The School of Electro-Crystsal Therapy for writing the article on Electro-Crystal Therapy,

Dr Lawrence Plaskett and *Anna Foster* of The College of Nutritional Medicine for writing the articles on Dietary Therapy and Nutrition,

Dr Michael Lyon of The Association of Scottish Dowsers for writing the article on Dowsing,

Dr David Smallbone of The College of Healing for writing the article on Healing,

Brian Butler of The Academy of Systematic Kinesiology for writing the article on Kinesiology,

Simon Brown of The Community Health Foundation and The Kushi Institute of London for writing the articles on Macrobiotics and Shiatsu,

John Seymour of John Seymour Associates for writing the article on Neuro-Linguistic Programming,

Dr Michael Forster of The International Society of Polarity Therapists for writing the article on Polarity Therapy,

Alf Fowles of The National College of Psychic Counselling for writing the article on Psychic Counselling,

Jill Curtis of The British Association of Psychotherapists for writing the article on Psychoanalytic Psychotherapy,

Diana Di Pinto of Delawarr Laboratories Ltd for writing the article on Radionics,

Norma Williams of The Raworth Centre for writing the article on Sports Therapy,

Stephen Palmer of The Centre for Stress Management for writing the article on Stress Management,

Mohammed Salim Khan Director of Mohsin Institute for Higher Education in Tibb - Oriental Medicine for writing the article on Tibb,

Dr George Lewith of The Centre for the Study of Complementary Medicine for writing the article on Vegatesting,

and *Mira Mehta* of Iyengar Yoga Institute for writing the article on Yoga Therapy.

C. the following schools for providing photographs some of which were used in this book:

The Academy of On-Site Massage, Community Health Foundation, Crane School of Reflexology, Delawarr Laboratories Ltd, London Centre for Yoga and Shiatsu Studies, The London College of Massage, The London School of Acupuncture and Traditional Chinese Medicine, The Northern Counties School of Osteopathy, The Professional Association of Alexander Teachers and The Symphysis for the Study of Holistic Health.

PREFACE

The first edition of this book, then called "Start a Career in Alternative Medicine", was warmly welcomed by the public and by people active in this field. Clearly it answered a long-felt need. "I've looking for such a book for years"; "I wish something like that was available when I started training"; "Thank you for producing this manual, I have been asking for something similar for some time now": such comments are typical of the letters received following the first edition. This encouraged us to produce this new edition, and we plan to continue publishing this manual/directory, and on a regular basis.

Why the change of name from alternative to complementary?

Before telling you about the changes I have made to the first edition and the material added to it, I wish to say a word about why I have changed the name and have chosen to use the word "complementary" rather than "alternative". Personally, I have no preference to one over the other, nor to other names also used to describe this medicine, such as wholistic or natural. Each of them gives a good description of the subject, but none is complete in itself.

When you say "alternative" people immediately assume that it can be a substitute for conventional medicine in all cases and all the time, which is not true. When you say "complementary" people tend to relegate this medicine to a position inferior to that of conventional medicine, as they will understand from the name that it merely complements conventional medicine, and so could easily be dispensed with in most cases. This is not true either, and does an injustice to complementary medicine.

"Natural" might fool the hearer that everything used in the course of a "natural" treatment is in its natural state, or that all ingredients and tools used are available in Nature. This is not true because this medicine uses ingredients and equipment that could not justifiably be called natural.

"Wholistic" is a good umbrella name, as the approach used in all the complementary and alternative therapies is wholistic. This means that the practitioner does not see the problem affecting an individual organ as a local problem (i.e. that

treatment need only be applied to the affected organ or any closely related organs or tissues, as is normally the case in conventional medicine). Rather, the individual "as a whole" is treated - something that we discuss in Part I of the book. However, this wholistic approach is not always applied throughout the course of treatment in certain cases. For instance, a cut or a burn may call for a defined homoeopathic remedy immediately; and in certain cases the therapy may have to play a complementary role to conventional medicine, especially in the cases of accidents that inflict dangerous structural damage that calls for immediate surgery.

Moreover, wholistic, if written without the "w", is often inadvertently associated with holiness or spirituality. This can be misleading and may put some people off these therapies for misguided reasons.

Then why didn't we stick to "alternative", as in the first edition? Well, we, as well as many other people in this field, believe in building bridges between conventional medicine and alternative (or complementary!) medicine. It is better to promote cooperation rather than confrontation, especially as the government is still not only in favour of conventional medicine, which is understandable, but also still depends on the conventional doctor and expert for the evaluation of the alternative therapies. Given this situation, and the urgent need to safeguard the practice of complementary therapies in this country, we must do what we can to cooperate with the conventional circles of medicine.

In this context, the word "complementary" has been chosen as the most appropriate.

However, we have continued to use the word "alternative" extensively throughout the book - and even in the sub-title of the book on the front cover - because we believe that most of these therapies are a potent alternative to conventional medicine in the majority of cases. In fact, if these alternative therapies were to take their proper place in the healthcare of any nation as preventive medicine, conventional medicine would only be consulted later on when the alternative therapies fail. In such a situation it would then be conventional medicine that is playing the complementary role.

What is new in this edition?

The first edition was received in the very encouraging way, as we have mentioned, and so we decided to go ahead with this edition, and in response to enquiries we have decided to add more therapies to the book so as to make it really comprehensive. The therapies, teaching and diagnostic methods more than double those listed in the first edition; there were 21 disciplines in the first edition and there are 44 disciplines in this 1992 edition, an increase of 110%.

This inevitably raised the number of schools and courses, an increase of 82% in the former and 111% in the latter. This, plus the addition of Part VII and the increased space devoted to advertising, increased the volume of the book considerably.

Part VII was added to provide descriptions of various independent organisations so as to give more information about the work done in this field, and to provide details about points of consultation, enquiry and activity.

What changes have been made for this edition?

First of all the whole design of the book has been changed. Not because the old design did not work -

far from it. People from the public, organisations and schools were impressed by the layout and the design. However, this time the book has been prepared on an Apple Macintosh computer, rather than an IBM.

Some sections of the book have been rearranged. Part III was completely restructured in order to make the sections follow each other in a more logical way.

Also, various sections relating to the directory in Part IV have been moved. Sections on "How to Use the Directory" and "Abbreviations and Notation" that were at the beginning of the book, and the "Index by Page Number" that was at the end of the book have been brought into Part IV, at the beginning and the end respectively.

Two new sections and one sub-section have been added. "The Status of Complementary Medicine in Europe Now and After 1992" in Part II was added to provide a brief answer to people who have asked us about this point. "Charities and Trusts" in the section discussing the financing of training in Part III, and "Notes on the Course Details" in Part IV have been added to clarify some points regarding these issues.

Finally, various paragraphs have been edited and added in all the parts of the book, as more information had to be given following the addition of new therapies, as well as new information relating to developments in society, parliament etc.

INTRODUCTION

Making the decision to start a career, whether the first in one's life or a new one, is never easy. Quitting a career is much easier, since the reasons for doing so are established by existing circumstances. Choosing a new career presents a range of fresh problems. The new career must inevitably be appealing in order to have attracted you in the first place, but the most important thing is that it should provide the satisfactions that the abandoned career lacked.

Complementary medicine has many appealing aspects, one of which is no less than reducing other people's suffering. However, it also bears the significant disadvantage that it is still being discovered (and rediscovered in the case of many therapies), and the process of discovery is bound to take some time yet to complete. Before any therapy is fully recognized and acknowledged, it will be confronted by all sorts of discouragement, ridicule and doubt. Some of these negative responses are natural and quite understandable, while others may reflect unreasonable prejudices that can drive their bearers into becoming vehement opponents of complementary medicine. However, nothing can prevent such beneficial means of curing disease and alleviating suffering from becoming permanently established at some stage in the future.

This book is an effort to help bring this end-result nearer to realization. Its aim is to encourage people to train in alternative and complementary medicine, so enabling them to reap its numerous benefits, both to themselves and to their fellow human beings (and all living creatures for that matter). This book is both a manual and a directory. The directory lists and discusses courses in forty four alternative and complementary therapies, the details of which can be obtained through four simple procedures (see HOW TO USE THE DIRECTORY). The details given have been extracted from the prospectuses of colleges and schools, or from additional information which they have kindly sent to us, and reflect the key issues for deciding which course to enrol in.

The directory, which occupies PART IV of the book, is the first of its kind, and in fact represents the main purpose of the book as a whole. Many prospective students already possess a basic knowledge of the therapy which interests them, and so the only remaining step towards practising it is to sclect the most suitable course available. People in this position

will find the directory particularly useful, but will also benefit from the information given in the other parts of the book.

However, there are other prospective students who are attracted to a certain therapy, but their interest is founded on scant information. They need to know more about the various aspects of the therapy, details about how treatment is actually carried out, the scope of its healing powers etc. The brief descriptions of these important aspects of the various therapies given in this book will serve as an introduction to each of them. Such an introduction may well be sufficient for the needs of some readers; however, if you are still not quite sure that this or that therapy is suitable for you, you should find out more from more specialized literature or make further enquiries through a therapist who is already practising it.

This book will also serve the many people who want to leave an old career - be it for financial reasons, or out of boredom, or difficulties with, their present employment - in order to pursue something more fulfilling, and who may feel that alternative medicine holds out this prospect for them. By reading about the therapies described in the manual sections of this book, people in this position can obtain a clear idea of the choice available, and can learn what practising each of them entails, including their financial potential and their predicted future status in society.

This last category could include students who have just completed their O-levels or A-levels and have not yet chosen a career. Since most of these graduates are teenagers, they may find it difficult to enrol in some of the courses, as the schools and colleges are geared only to receiving mature candidates who have had some experience of life. However, anyone with great interest and ability in alternative and complementary medicine should not be discouraged, and should apply to the school or college and arrange to meet whoever is responsible so that they can discuss the matter.

In conclusion, the less you know about alternative and complementary medicine in general, and about the therapy that interests you, the more you will benefit from the manual sections of this book.

PART I provides a brief description of each therapy. The origin, idea, treatment and benefits are given, so the reader can obtain an overall picture. This part is useful for anybody who has merely heard about a certain therapy and has only limited knowledge of it. It is particularly useful for anybody who is thinking about a career in alternative medicine, but does not know which sort of therapy to choose.

PART II discusses complementary medicine as a profession and will help anyone who is interested in the subject and wants to practise it, but is not sure about the status of the various therapies in society and in the medical profession as a whole.

PART III discusses money matters. It provides estimates of how much you can earn from practising alternative medicine, and outlines the different ways of charging patients, the range of the fee structure, the proportionate effect on earnings of the number of patients seen etc. It also discusses the relative benefits of working from home or elsewhere, and of sharing a practice. The intention has been to provide the future practitioner with a realistic picture of his or her potential future income.

Part III also deals with the cost of training, and how to raise the money for training. This will provide useful guidelines for the prospective student who needs to know the costs involved, and who is not aware of the possibilities for financing training which are available.

The last section of Part III presents a detailed estimate of the cost of setting up a practice after graduation. Capital expenditure and running costs vary with each therapy; examples are given to provide a clear picture of the kind of outlay the future practitioner should expect to make.

Part IV is the directory, consisting of a general description of the syllabus and contents of the courses and five indexes. The first index deals with the course details: specific details of every course are listed to give a good picture of each course so as to make it easy for the reader to compare it with other courses.

The second index is the Schools Directory, which is similar to any usual directory of addresses and telephone numbers.

The third index is the Geographical Index where courses of each discipline are listed under the county of the UK where they are held.

The fourth index is the Type of Course Index, where courses of each discipline are listed according to their type (such as full-time, part-time etc).

The fifth index is a standard page index where you find the courses (course numbers only) listed and the relevant page numbers.

There are also two other sections: "How to Use the Directory", explaining how you can perform all sorts of cross referencing; and "Abbreviations and Notation", listing all the abbreviations that had to be used in the Course Details index because of space limitations, and the notation for the entry requirements of each course.

In PART V we answer the question of why many practitioners practise more than one therapy, and show the various combinations which are practised in the alternative and complementary clinics. In addition, the various courses offering a combination of therapies are discussed; this will enable prospective students to decide from the outset which therapies they want to be trained in, and hence to programme their training for the months or years ahead.

Although much will depend on circumstances, the difficulties and extra expenses arising from certain combinations are discussed, so reducing the likelihood of misunderstanding and consequent regrets.

PART VI provides a list of criteria that the reader might use to decide which course(s) to enrol in. Although some readers may be able to decide after browsing through the directory, most will benefit from the information and suggestions given in this part.

Part VII, the last part of the book, provides a brief description of the aims, objectives and activities, as well as membership details, of some of the organisations working in this field. This part is new to this edition and has been added to give information about the work done by people active in this field, as well as to provide additional reference and points of advice.

Read this book, browse through the directory, think about the potential that practising alternative and complementary medicine can have, and tell your friends about it. In doing this you will help yourself and others in many different ways, and will also help to make alternative medicine more available to the people who need it - that is to say, the entire human race.

I THE THERAPIES

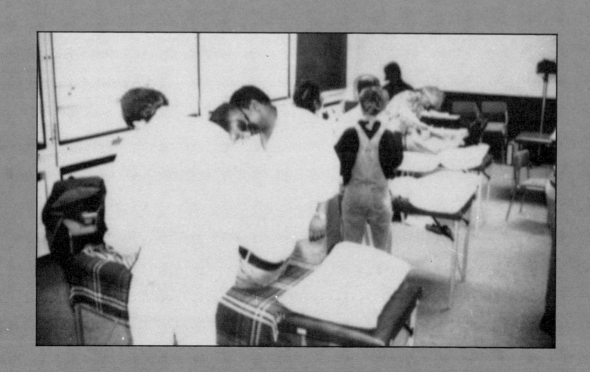

THE AIMS OF PART I

The main purpose of this manual/directory as a whole is to give details of the courses available in the discipline that the prospective student wishes to practise, and to give him or her useful information about the cost of training and of setting up a practice. However, after reading Part V in which the various possible combinations of therapies are discussed, prospective students might decide to enrol in another course of some other therapy that would work well in conjunction with the therapy they are already interested in. They might decide to train in both courses at the same time, or to leave the second until they have mastered the first, or until they have earned enough money from practising the first to finance the training in the second. They might even change their minds altogether and decide to train in another therapy.

For all these reasons we think that it is useful, essential even, to give a brief but informative summary of each of the therapies for which courses are listed in Part IV. Even if the reader does not use the directory again as a means of selecting a course, it will provide valuable reference work for future use.

Each section is devoted to an individual therapy and contains the following:

a basic definition;

the ORIGIN of the therapy (its early history only, and not its development over the decades or centuries);

THE IDEA, or group of ideas, which form the principles upon which the therapy is based;

the TREATMENT, describing what the practitioner of this therapy actually does. (Please note that in some disciplines, schools running courses prefer, or may even be bound ethically, not to think of the discipline as "treatment", but rather a "teaching method". These include, for example, kinesiology, Bates Eye Method and The Alexander Technique.)

WHAT ILLNESSES may be cured or alleviated by this therapy, and the BENEFITS that might be gained by the patient.

Although no certificate courses for them are listed in this directory, we have also included sections on Bach flower remedies, biochemic tissue salts therapy and magnetotherapy. A practitioner qualified in another discipline could practise both of these without extensive training, and both are totally safe. If you are interested in using them in your practice, you can attend a short course, or even teach yourself how they can be applied.

One word about the length of the articles. A shorter article does not necessarily imply a less important, less effective therapy, and a longer article does not necessarily imply a more important, more effective therapy. Rather, the articles are of the given length because this is how they were written by people who kindly contributed them. In the case of articles written by the author, some therapies seemed to need more space because there was more to say about them, or because they are more complicated to describe.

What I want to say is: firstly, homoeopathy should not be thought of as necessarily a more effective therapy than, for example, acupuncture simply because the article written about it is longer. Secondly, a longer article does not imply encouragement on our part to the reader to train in that discipline. After all, the results achieved by the therapist, any therapist, is determined not only by the nature and technique of the therapy he/she is practising, but by a mixture of factors of which technique is only one.

Moreover, person A could be a better homoeopath than person B, but person B could be a better reflexologist than person A. This, has nothing to do with the length of the articles in my book!

AM I RIGHT FOR THE JOB?

The therapies included in this manual/directory may be divided into seven main categories.

1. The first consists of the therapies that involve manual work by the practitioner, and so he or she must be in good physical shape, although the levels of exertion vary. This category includes **aromatherapy, chiropractic, cranio- sacral therapy, healing, kinesiology, lymph drainage, massage, osteopathy, shiatsu and sports therapy.** All these therapies demand that the practitioner is of normal physical health, for they all involve the full range of movements that the healthy human body is capable of doing. Sports therapy would also suit those who like to work with groups as many sports therapists work with teams rather than in a clinic.

2. The second category consists of those therapies that involve manual work by the practitioner, but with precision rather than physical exertion. **Acupuncture, auricular therapy, biomagnetic therapy and reflexology** all fall in this category. Of these, auricular therapy calls for the highest level of precision because of the large number of treatment points that are concentrated in a small area (the ears). Although the reflexology treatment points are also numerous, there are fewer of them scattered over a larger area (the feet). The reflexologist has to treat all the points, while the acupuncturist and the auricular therapist have to choose few treatment points among hundreds; the selection of these points alone is no easy task. Biomagnetic therapy can tolerate some deviation from the exact acupuncture points on which the biomagnet is to be placed, because the area of effect of the magnetic field is larger than the acupuncture point; thus this therapy demands less precision.

3. The third category consists of those therapies that do not involve any manual work, and hence could be practised by someone who has a physical disability. These therapies include **assertiveness, Bach flower therapies, Bates eye therapy, biochemic tissue salts therapy, colour therapy, dietary therapy, herbalism, homoeopathy, hypnotherapy, macrobiotics, naturopathy, nutrition and polarity therapy.** In all these therapies, the therapist can sit on a chair while facing the patient, who is also seated. Hence, the practice of any therapy in this category is more or less like that of conventional medicine. However, you might enjoy planting, collecting and drying herbs, and making your own `home-made' herbal remedies, all of which demands a certain amount of mobility.

Magnetotherapy may be added to the third category, if all that the therapist has to do is instruct the patient on which magnets to use, how, where and for how long, so that the patient can carry out the treatment at home. But some magnetotherapists do have to do some manual work, if no more than the actual application of the magnets for the duration of the treatment session, in which case they have to be reasonably mobile. The same applies to **crystal and electro-crystal therapies.**

4. The counsellor, hypnotherapist, psychic counsellor or psychotherapist has to be someone who will persevere in trying to discover the deep-rooted causes of a problem in the patient's past, and someone who can build up the patient's confidence, self-esteem, sense of comfort, or any virtue he or she might lack as a result of the problem, as well as develop a solution to a problem through sessions of discussions and analysis. The therapist should be someone who is clever enough to tell whether the patient is telling the full story. The patient's problem itself may push him or her to tell lies, or deliberately or otherwise to misrepresent or distort the case, making the job of the therapist even harder. It is an advantage if the hypnotherapist has a soothing, warm and comforting voice, as this is the media by which suggestions are made to the hypnotized patient.

5. Allergy therapy combines diagnosis and treatment. The allergy therapist tests the patient for all the possible allergens (either by muscle testing or vegatesting), then desensetises him or her by administering an oral dose of the allergen (see the article on Allergy Therapy) to give permanent or temporary relief from the problem.

6. Alexander Technique and yoga therapy do not involve any manual work, but the teacher has to be physically fit to demonstrate all the postures and movements (asanas etc). Hence, the people best suited to these disciplines are those who like physical work, but are not so drawn to the therapies which involve massaging and manipulating patients. Yoga therapy, however, has more in it than the physical postures (see the section Yga Therapy at the end of this Part).

7. Iridology is the opposite of yoga in this respect. It does not call for physical fitness; it would be quite possible for a disabled person to work from a wheelchair. However, it does involve some manual work, in that you need your hands to record your findings, and you need both your hands and your eyes to make your observations, whether you use the simple torch and magnifier method, or the more expensive camera.

Dowsing, radionics and vegatesting are other diagnostic techniques, using a range of equipment from a simple pendulum costing few pence to expensive electronic analysers and other machines. The results of dowsing and radionics can be affected by the practitioners energy, vibrations or state of the mind at the time he/she is working, while vegatesting is a procedure involving a series of steps which can only be mastered through months of practice. All of them could be used by any therapist; however, not every therapist would have the ability to dowse correctly, and not every therapist likes to exchange a simple pendulum for a complicated machine and procedure.

For all of the therapies, whether manual or not, and whether you, the practitioner, are able-bodied or disabled, you should have the desire to help others. You need to be sympathetic to the holistic approach to medicine, and you need to be able to work consistently to very high standards. You can earn a good living from alternative and complementary medicine: the better the results that you achieve, the better your reputation will be, and hence the more your practise will flourish.

COMPLEMENTARY MEDICINE

Complementary medicine is the group of therapies which deal with the sick person as a whole - and not the symptoms of a particular sickness only - and which, unlike conventional medicine, do not depend on chemical drugs.

WHY CHOOSE COMPLEMENTARY MEDICINE?

Many people, especially those who are not suffering from illness, wonder why some people use these complementary therapies and abandon the conventional medicine that is now practised in almost every corner of the world.

Is it because of the success of complementary medicine in curing the conditions that conventional medicine has failed to cure? The answer is yes (but there are also other reasons, as we shall see).

Complementary medicine has indeed succeeded in curing cases that have been deemed by conventional medicine as hopeless. It has also been successful not only in treating many conditions, but in preventing their recurrence. By contrast, only too frequently conventional medicine takes a shorter-term view of cure, and often does not recognize later recurrence as a failure of the earlier treatment.

THE BASIC IDEA

Alternative and complementary therapists believe that treatment cannot be successful if it does not deal with the patient as a whole. In other words, you cannot cure the problem simply by dealing with the part of the body in which the symptoms manifest themselves.

Asthma sufferers will not be cured by taking a drug that deals with the respiratory system only. Aspirin may bring temporary relief to the sufferers of chronic headache, but the problem will return. Even in the more difficult cases, such as cancer, treatment which deals with the affected area only can never be wholly successful. The evidence for this is overwhelming: drugs, chemotherapy or radiation treatment may stop cancer spreading for a time, but then the activity begins again. And even when surger is used as a last resort to remove the cancerous cells, there is no guarantee that the disease will not start again somewhere else.

So, what is the solution from the complementary medicine point of view? Or, to ask a broader question, what is disease?

Generally speaking, in complementary medicine the focus is not so much disease, but the diseased person. In the case of accidental injuries, such as bone fractures, symptoms strike the victim out of the blue; but in the case of disease, people are not affected and do not suffer its symptoms unless there is something already wrong within them that makes them prone to the disease. The problem therefore lies in the sufferer's defence system, or the natural internal balance of sufferer's body.

How else can one explain why, when two people visit somebody with influenza for instance, one of them may become infected but not the other? Why, in cases of food poisoning when all the members of a family have eaten the same food, may some be affected but not others? And why is it that when two people in similar physical condition catch cold, one of them recovers before the other?

Thus when the therapist using complementary medicine gives a particular kind of massage, or puts the acupuncture needle in a certain place, he or she is in fact trying to restore the natural balance to the patient's body, and to revive the body's own power to fight illness. When the therapist succeeds in that, the body's natural ability to fight illness will be back to its proper strength, and will be able to fight the disease and rid the body of it.

This explains why the common cold does not call for any medicine, but simply the appropriate conditions to allow the body to rid itself of the cold by it own resources. A cut, even if it is deep, does not need any help to heal. The surgeon only needs to put the ends of a fractured bone together for it to heal in a fairly short period of time.

The 'holistic' approach to health - in which the whole person, not just individual parts of the body, are treated - is the cornerstone of alternative and complementary medicine, and hence is the major difference between it and conventional medicine.

OTHER ASPECTS

Complementary medicine takes account of the human race's long experience of medicine. It does not reject the lessons of the past for the sake of thinking that is new - as in the case of much modern medicine, to its detriment.

Complementary medicine uses old therapies that have proved successful throughout the ages. At the same time, it does not reject any new method of treatment if there is a chance that it might benefit patients. Traditional Chinese medicine, for example, has successfully treated millions of people over thousands of years; treating with herbs (herbalism) can claim a similar record. It is simply blind folly to attempt to write them off as useless therapies. As we shall see in the sections on the various therapies below, some alternative and complementary therapies have been discovered and developed after the rise of conventional medicine - something that may be of interest to those who do not like anything old, for no reason but its age!

An attractive side to complementary medicine is the absence of strong drugs - and their dangerous side effects - on which conventional medicine depends for treatment. These drugs are effectively poisons which, while benefiting one part of the body, will harm another. Such treatment is quite unacceptable to the complementary therapies. This factor is one of the most important reasons why more and more people are turning to alternative medicine.

Another aspect of complementary medicine is the very low cost of treatment compared to the very high cost of conventional medicine - which sometimes reaches astronomical figures in the case of major operations. Many of these operations might actually be avoided if more patients consulted alternative medicine in the early stages of their illness.

In addition to this, alternative doctors and therapists will generally show far greater care and concern than the conventional doctor, something easily felt by the patient. One reason for this is that alternative therapy calls for an integral knowledge of the patients, their social circumstances, family, medical history, their life even before the manifestation of the symptoms, their psychological condition, occupation, and so forth. All of these details allow the therapist to build up a full picture of the patients and their problems, whilst the patients may also benefit from the opportunity to rid themselves of some of their frustration, anger, sorrow and other negative emotions which could stand in the way of their cure. Such opportunities are virtually nonexistent in conventional medicine.

Paradoxically, one of the most important aspects of alternative medicine is the lack of specialization. In conventional medicine there is one doctor for eye troubles, another for the heart, a third for the urinary tracts, and so on. Such division by specialists simply does not conform to the holistic approach to medicine. The therapist has to find out the basic cause of the problem, which lies deeper than the symptoms that show up in just one or more organs of the body.

UNLIMITED APPLICATION

Complementary medicine can treat all diseases (or diseased people, rather). These therapies are not just a selection of primitive ways to deal with simple illnesses, as some people think. They are potent effective medical systems, to which all sufferers can turn. If the body is given the right treatment, it will be cured. A basic belief of alternative and complementary medicine is that there are no incurable diseases, contrary to what conventional medicine would have us believe. Yes, there are difficult cases, some of which are advanced and complicated - but even here there exists a personal factor which differentiates each case from the next.

I would like to emphasize here that I do not mean to say that cure is guaranteed if the patient consults an alternative clinic, for cure depends on several factors. The most important of all is the ability of the therapist to use the curative powers of the alternative therapy to the level that can bring about the cure. Unfortunately, there are plenty of therapists who claim knowledge which they lack. The same situation undoubtedly occurs in the world of conventional medicine, but alternative medicine is more prone to false claims because of the comparative lack of strict regulations. The patient should, therefore, make sure that the doctor or therapist has gained the necessary knowledge from one of the established colleges, which only issue certificates to those who have completed the appropriate training.

However, there are other factors involved in successful cure. The patient must follow the advice of the practitioner. Patience and perseverance are always very important. These can be difficult to maintain, given that many patients go through healing crises, and may also find their treatment undermined by doubts sown by others who have little knowledge about complementary medicine, or even by those to whom alternative medicine represents professional competition!

THE SIDE EFFECTS OF CONVENTIONAL DRUGS

For the treatment of illness, conventional medicine essentially depends on chemical drugs in the form of tablets, capsules, fluids and injections. If these drugs fail, conventional medicine turns to surgery. Before, during and after surgery, the patient is given even greater amounts of these drugs.

Conventional medicine does offer some other forms of treatment - such as physiotherapy in the form of exercises and massages, radiation treatment, electric treatment, and so forth. But these represent only a

very small part of conventional medicine, and drugs continue to be the main choice. The ineffectiveness of drugs in the treatment of so many illnesses is now widely known. Every now and then great hopes are shared between sufferers of this or that illness following announcements by research establishments or drug companies that a new wonder drug will be available shortly. Only too often, however, after the drug has been released on to the market and doctors have prescribed it to the patients for a while, hopes begin to fade as people begin to realize that this wonder drug really is no great improvement on what was available previously. They may even discover that its side effects are actually more harmful.

It is a sad fact that many doctors prescribing these drugs are informed about the side effects (or at least some of them), yet nevertheless oppose alternative therapies that have proved their ability to cure disease without any dangerous side effects. I understand why conventional doctors prescribe these drugs, and appreciate that these are the basis of the medicine that they have studied and trained in; but I can not accept their attempts to discourage patients from seeking help from alternative medicine, and their inclination to disparage alternative therapists' claims about their indisputable success in curing or alleviating diseases where conventional medicine has failed. Such attitudes are shameful, given that the patients' well-being - whatever means are used to achieve it - should be the first priority of all doctors.

Nevertheless, there are quite a few conventional doctors who are convinced of the benefits of alternative and complementary medicine, and some have given up the orthodox medicine in which they trained to practise it. Undoubtedly their numbers will increase with time.

THE ATTITUDE IS CHANGING

In one study, the attitude to alternative and complementary medicine of a random sample of 200 general practitioners in the Avon area was assessed. The therapies under enquiry were acupuncture, homoeopathy, herbal medicine, manipulative procedures, faith healing and hypnosis. A total of 145 responses were received and analysis of these responses produced the following results:

● 59% thought that the alternative techniques being assessed were useful to their patients;

● 76% had referred patients over the past year to medically qualified colleagues who practise alternative medicine;

● 72% had referred patients to non-medically qualified practitioners;

● 41% observed benefits to their patients;

● 38% had personal or family experience of benefit;

● 93% of those who responded thought that alternative practitioners needed statutory regulation;

● 3% thought that they should be banned.

These results were published in the British Medical Journal 1986 (7 June:1498-1500).

A COMPARISON BETWEEN THE TWO SCHOOLS

1. As we have stated before, complementary medicine's attitude towards disease is different from that of conventional medicine. It approaches each case by looking at the patient as a whole, trying to find out the real cause of the disease, and not trying simply to relieve the symptoms in the affected part only. From this, it can be seen why it succeeds in treating the cases that conventional medicine fails to treat, because the real cause in these cases cannot be removed by a drug given to relieve the symptoms only. It can be seen as well why relief is permanent in cases cured by complementary medicine, whilst the problem may well return to the patient treated by conventional methods.

2. It follows that specialization is incompatible to complementary medicine. Specialization has become so established in conventional medicine that it has lost the wisdom of a holistic approach. Complementary therapists should be knowledgeable about all parts of the body, not only its anatomy, but also about the way in which the physical and psychological systems interconnect. Only in this way can the therapist find out the real cause of the trouble and put the patient on the correct path towards the solution.

In conventional medicine, a patient has to consult a specialist doctor for each different complaint of the various systems or organs. The patient may go to a general practitioner about pain in the abdomen, but may then be referred to a heart specialist; if the heart specialist finds nothing following standard diagnostic methods, the patient will be referred to yet another specialist. In the end this same patient may well end up in a psychologist's consultation room because the doctors could find nothing wrong, and hence concluded that the problem must be psychological. Nowadays, because doctors have used it so often, the phrase "the cause is psychological" has entered common parlance.

3. Doctors using conventional medicine rely upon chemical drugs in the treatment of cases. If these fail, they turn to other methods such as operations, radiation (especially for cancer), physiotherapy (including hydrotherapy), or the use of artificial means to replace the loss of a function (for instance, dialysis - one of conventional medicine's greatest contributions). Complementary medicine approaches the problems differently, and does not rely on drugs at all. Even in homoeopathy, which uses tablets, fluids or ointments for treatment, there is no place for the chemical drugs which conventional medicine uses so extensively.

4. There are no harmful side effects in alternative medicine. However, there is often a reaction which follows the commencement of treatment, be it in the form of tablets, an osteopathic session or whatever. This reaction lasts for a very short period, after which the patient should begin to feel the benefits of the treatment. As for conventional medicine, the side effects of drug treatment may be one if its most serious problems.

5. The conventional doctor has little time to discuss or look into anything other than the symptoms that the patient is complaining about, before writing out the prescription. This is because, with this kind of diagnosis-prescription treatment, the doctor does not have to look at or deal with any part of the patient besides that which bears the symptoms. This does not usually take a great deal of time. Furthermore, the conventional doctor, through the nature of the system, is always under pressure from an increasing number of patients, and simply cannot spare more time for them. This is not the case with the alternative practitioner, who has to spend much longer with the patient in order to fulfil the requirements of a holistic approach, taking into account the patient's psychological, social, environmental, intellectual background, as well as the actual physical complaint.

6. The cost of the two treatments do not compare. The fees of conventional doctors have become very high indeed, and could be some three or four times what the complementary practitioner charges. This ratio of 3:1 or 4:1 rises even more when you add the cost of drug treatment (injections, pills etc), some of which are very expensive indeed. Complementary medicine still only plays a very tiny part in government-funded medicine, and is hence not normally free (as the case in countries such as China or India), but people are willing to pay for it. The benefits which complementary medical consultation and treatment offer are generally considered good value for money, especially in view of the fact that the costs are not high.

The cost of operations in conventional medicine have no comparison in complementary medicine. People

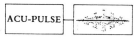

simply could not afford to pay real of most operations, which include the surgeon's fee and other wages, the hire and use of equipment and the operating theatre, the cost of drugs before and after the operation, and the cost of diagnosis (X-ray, scanning, blood tests). There is no doubt that these operations have saved the lives of a great number of people, and will continue to do so. We believe, however, that a large number of these operations, if not most, could be avoided if the holistic approach to medicine prevailed.

7. Complementary medicine pushes patients towards paying more attention to their own well-being. Thus, by encouraging them to think more about their way of life, including diet, rest, physical activity, environment and even relationships with other people, patients begin to bear some of the doctor's responsibility.

This sense of the responsibility of patients towards their own health has been marginalized in conventional medicine. Here, the patient's role is simply to take the medicine in the correct dosage at the times stated by the doctor. At most, the patient may also receive some additional advice about taking more rest, or which foods to avoid.

SOME STATISTICS

Some important statistics appeared in an article in the October 1986 issue of *Which?*, the magazine published in the U.K. by the Consumers' Association. The article was entitled "Magic or Medicine?", reflecting the common belief that some kind of magic is responsible when successful results are achieved by complementary medicine after conventional medicine has failed. We can summarize the conclusions as follows:

1. One out of every seven Britons consulted an alternative medicine clinic in 1985.

2. 15% of these had some sort of psychological complaint, and 71% were suffering from arthritis or pain in general.

3. 81% said that they had tried conventional medicine first.

4. 81% of these (i.e. 66% of the total) said either that the conventional doctor could do nothing to help them, or that they did not benefit at all from the treatment, or that they had only temporary relief.

5. 31% were completely cured by alternative medicine, and the condition improved in 51% of the cases.

From the number of the patients that consulted alternative and complementary medicine (one out of seven) it is clear that this form of medicine has established itself as an effective and valid way of treatment. That 31% of patients were completely cured by alternative and complementary medicine demonstrates the high level of its effectiveness, especially in view of the fact that these were cases which conventional medicine had failed to cure.

No doubt the rate of success (31% totally cured, and 51% better) would have been much higher if these people had used alternative and complementary medicine from the outset. The delay in doing so would have caused the condition of some of them to deteriorate beyond recall; as the disease proceeded unchecked cells would have become permanently damaged, and the patient's will to fight would have been increasingly impaired. Furthermore, it is impossible to quantify the damage inflicted by the side effects of the drugs administered during the course of treatment by conventional medicine.

More recently, in 1989 a poll done by MORI showed that:

1. 73% of the people asked said they would seriously consider using one or more of six alternative forms of medicine (33% acupuncture, 13% chiropractic, 37% homoeopathy, 19% hypnotherapy, 12% faith/spiritual healing, 32% osteopathy). 23% said none of these, and 4% had no opinion.

2. However, only a quarter of those who said they would seriously consider using these forms of

alternative medicines (25.6% to be precise) had actually used them before. This means that more people know about these therapies, and would use them, than actually do use them. No doubt the availability of a free NHS treatment (as opposed to private alternative medicine that has to be paid for) pays a major role in putting some people off using the latter (see 4 below).

3. In all the six alternative therapies in question, the majority of people who used them were very satisfied or fairly satisfied.

4. 74% of the people asked said they would strongly support or tend to support making these alternative forms of medicine available on the National Health.

5. In Scotland 76% of the people asked said they would seriously consider using one or more of the therapies in question. This showed a 38% increase of interest in these therapies over the poll of 1985, four years earlier.

This poll shows that people are becoming more aware of the benefits of alternative and complementary medicine, which should increase the pressure on the legislators to make these therapies available free under the NHS.

Alternative and complementary medicine involves a safe and successful treatment that does not cost much. Every encouragement should be given to it to allow it the opportunity to prove itself yet further, and thereby to help even more people. This will not be possible, in my opinion, in most parts of the world without government patronage and the support of medical authorities. Complementary medicine needs more qualified practitioners and clinics. It also needs to develop firmer links between different countries where different alternative and complementary therapies are practised. Above all it needs generous

funding to finance research and increase facilities for education and training. If this does not happen, patients will not be encouraged to try these therapies until they lose hope in conventional doctors, and this reduces drastically the potential rate of success of alternative and complementary therapies.

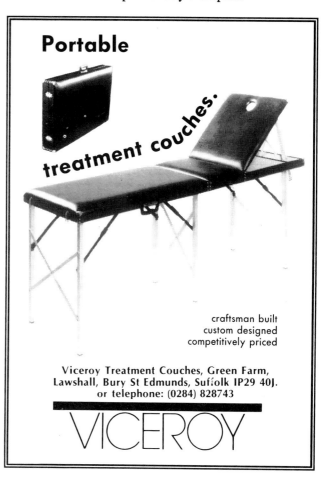

ACUPUNCTURE

Acupuncture is the therapy in which a number of specially-made needles are inserted into the body at specific points to bring back the energy balance of the body, hence effecting a cure.

ORIGIN

No one knows when this kind of treatment was first used, but the first book about it was written some time between 475 and 221 B.C. - although some people claim that a yet earlier book was written some 4,500 years ago. Acupuncture history can be traced by the development of the needle itself. Needles were first made of stone, then from wood, bones and ceramic. Gradually bronze needles began to replace the others at the time of Chang dynasty some 3,000 years ago.

THE IDEA

Chinese medicine, and indeed all the Far Eastern traditional therapy, is based on the philosophy of Yin and Yang. In brief, at the heart of this philosophy is a general concept of energy called Ch'i (or vital force, as in homoeopathy). Two energy levels, Yin and Yang, are present in every aspect of the universe - light and darkness, good and evil, day and night, life and death, cold and hot, etc - and they interact with each other as one, although they are opposites. They are not defined quantities, but rather a concept (see HERBALISM for more about this). To preserve good health, a person's Yin and Yang must stay in balance.

Early practitioners of acupuncture found that the forces of Yin and Yang circulate through the body along pathways similar to blood and lymph vessels. These pathways are called meridians. Nowadays they can be detected by certain electronic appliances. The absence of meridians indicates death.

There are 26 meridians, each of which is linked to a particular organ or function of the body. For the healthy body to stay healthy, it must keep the Yin and Yang in balance. This is done by expelling the excess

energy through the surface of the body at specific points on the meridians, and by redirecting energy to the areas that need it. About 800 points have now been identified, but more points are being discovered all the time.

Now, how does the needle work?

There are several theories. One is the `Gate Control' theory. It suggests that there are certain gates which permit the flow of the pain impulse from the fine nerve fibres to the brain. Other larger nerve fibres transfer the needle impulse to the brain through the same gate, and this shuts the gate, stopping the flow of the pain impulse, so no pain is felt.

Some experiments and studies have shown that stimulation by the needle increases the release of endorphins (natural morphines in the body) to the cerebrospinal fluid. Moreover, they revealed that the release of these endorphins only takes place at the spinal locations that were stimulated by the needles.

However, this theory fails to explain the reason behind the permanent effect of the treatment. Countless cases have been cured by acupuncture, with no recurrence of the symptoms even years after the original treatment. Such theories serve to demonstrate that we are still groping in the dark for a comprehensive explanation of the effects of the acupuncturist's needle. Acupuncture is not a miracle, but the laws upon which it is based have yet to be fully unmasked.

TREATMENT

First of all, you, the acupuncturist, have to diagnose the problem. You need to establish the patient's medical history, and all other details. You might have asked for a urine sample. The manual checking of the area in question, or any other area, should be carried out. But you would also perform the unique diagnostic technique of pulse testing. This is not the same as conventional pulse reading, but rather a test of Yin and Yang to see whether they are out of balance - which, if the patient is unwell, they will be. The pulses can inform you about future problems, and hence give a valuable warning to the patient. This might be the explanation why the Chinese, whilst paying a doctor when they are well, stop doing so when they become ill!

Another diagnostic method is the examination of the tongue. It is examined for its shape, colour, movement and coating. In addition, the patient's colour, face and body features are observed, so that any sign of abnormality can be taken into consideration.

After diagnosing the case, you have to decide upon the locations where the needles should be inserted. No more than six needles are normally used at a time. The needle is normally 5cm in length, half of which is the part to be inserted, while the rest is the part you hold as you manipulate the needle - by rotating, tapping or by other techniques.

You might even stick a small ball of a certain herb to the head of the needle and light it, so as to add heat to the treatment. This is called moxibustion. Some acupuncturists use other heat sources for the same purpose.

Other forms of needles which can be used include very small needles (no more than 9mm long) that are inserted in the upper layer of the skin and left there for days or weeks in order to provide a long-acting stimulus. Another piece of equipment is the small plastic hammer called the 'plum blossom needle', which has a two-sided head. On each of these sides there are fine spikes, which are used to stimulate an area rather than a point. This hammer is useful for treating children - or anybody for that matter - who may be afraid of the needles. Some acupuncturists provide electrical nerve stimulation by using an electrical generator, which has wires that connect with the needle-heads.

In all cases, the needles are inserted in a special manner, insuring the least possible pain, and are then left for 15-20 minutes. Needles are either used brand new from their box and then discarded for each patient, or they are sterilized with alcohol or by heat treatment before reuse.

The first five or six treatment sessions could be given weekly, then the periods between the sessions could be increased to three to six weeks, and later to three months. But this would depend on each individual case. The first session takes anything between 30 to 60 minutes, as it involves all the initial enquiries - medical history, diagnosis etc. The following sessions might take no more than 20 minutes each. However, the treatment would definitely take more time if some additional types of treatment (such as moxibustion or electrical stimulation) are used, or if it is necessary to leave the needles in for more than the normal time.

WHAT ILLNESSES AND BENEFITS?

Acupuncture is more successful in treating cases of tissue function (such as chronic headache, migraine, ulcers, digestive disorders, sciatica, dermatitis, hypertension and depression) than those cases in which a considerable tissue damage has occurred (such as an arthritic hip or brain damage). In cases of the latter, acupuncture may play a valuable subsidiary role to any other therapy, but cannot be the main therapy. We have cited here the conventional labels for diseases, but you should not be restricted by such labels in dealing with your patient. You should be a wholistic therapist, who recognizes that the symptoms from which your patient is suffering may be a manifestation of an imbalance which has some deeper cause. As in every other form of therapy, the personal and individual aspects of each case play a part in determining the efficacy of the treatment. Some patients suffering from problems not normally helped by acupuncture have greatly benefited from it, while other cases that are usually easily cured by acupuncture fail to respond to it.

Acupuncture is widely used in the East as an anaesthetic. Since 1958 more than one million operations have been performed in China using needles instead of the chemical anaesthesia. This makes acupuncture of vital importance to elderly patients, or to those suffering from diseases where the use of the conventional anaesthesia would endanger their lives.

NOTE: Chinese medicine combines acupuncture with herbal remedies. These are integrated in the syllabus of some schools, while others teach acupuncture only. (See also the section on HERBALISM.)

ALEXANDER TECHNIQUE

In the Alexander Technique, an improvement in balance and coordination, and conscious awareness, is promoted, through the medium of the teacher's hands. Simultaneously, the teacher gives instruction in how to maintain the improved state in actual engagement in everyday activity, allowing the pupil to enjoy a better quality of, and a fuller, life.

ORIGIN

The principles of the Alexander Technique were discovered by F. M. Alexander, an Australian recitor and actor (1869-1955). When Alexander was investigating the cause of his own hoarseness and voice-loss during performance, he obsereved a recurring pattern of distortion of his body. He went on to see that this pattern of distortion was a result of his own habitual neuro-muscular activity, and that it underlay and dominated everything that he did and thought. It was this pulling out of shape which was causing the vocal problems. When Alexander learnt how to stop pulling himself out of shape, not only his voice, but his whole quality of performance and level of well-being improved. He went on to apply the principles he had learnt in teaching others. Although his first pupils were other performers, and people with breathing and vocal difficulties, he later made the technique relevant to people in any walk of life who wished to bring about a change and improvement in their lives.

The

Professional Association of Alexander Teachers

For Private Lessons, Workshops, Talks and Training Course, please contact:

The Secretary,
P.A.A.T.,
14 Kingsland,
Jesmond,
Newcastle Upon Tyne,
Tyne and Wear.
NE2 3AL

Telephone: (091) 281 8032

THE IDEA

The underlying element that Alexander observed was one of use - the way that we put machinery (body and brain) into activity, which is a constant for us, waking or sleeping, for our whole lives. Mechanically, there is a best relationship between the structural elements - muscles, bones and ligaments - associated with good balance. This relationship will promote the best possibility for coordination and general functioning. When the framework is held out of shape by the over-contraction of some of the musculature, the whole range of functioning, mental and physical, will be influenced for the worse; although some people may compensate, many will find that their ability to perform even quite simple activities is being impaired and may disappear altogether. For the majority, the way we use ourselves is very much habitual; we have learnt one way of doing things (based on our one way of standing upright against gravity) and in order to change anything fundamental about ourselves we need to change our habitual use of ourselves. Alexander came to realise that we cannot think of use as either 'physical' or 'mental', since it includes the whole of ourselves. Therefore, to really change our mind about something involves us in a change of total use, i.e. of the way we remain upright against gravity. In the same way, changing the way we use ourselves to write, to walk, or to bend down and pick something off the floor, involves us in a change of thought about the activity. Use is, however, learned, so change is possible by learning not to operate in the old way and learning a new way of using ourselves that does not involve us in stressing the mechanism.

Learning good use involves us in learning to be consciously aware of our activity, and to choose consciously to put the new use into operation. This conscious activity opens up tremendous possibilities for choice of behaviour, enabling us to escape from limiting, harmful, unsatisfactory behaviour patterns learnt from the past.

THE "TREATMENT"

Alexander lessons are concerned with learning this conscious control. The work that a teacher does with his hands provides the basis for the speediest acquisition of good use, so that balance and coordination begin to improve from the first lesson.

A development of the understanding of the technique is also an on-going process, through time, so pupils are generally recommended to have regular lessons over a more or less extended period of time, depending on how far they wish to take the technique in their own lives.

WHAT ILLNESSES AND BENEFITS?

Basically, any illness or condition that is caused by misuse, has the possibility of improving through the Alexander Technique. However, the Alexander Technique cannot really be classed as a therapy - it is a re-educative process. It is undisputed that the Alexander Technique has therapeutic effects, which are a product of the technique, but its major aim is the development of understanding and control of our lives in whichever direction we choose. Often, the pulling out of shape has brought with it pain and discomfort - headaches, pains in the joints, 'muscular pain' and so on. It is not possible to distort the outer framework without placing the internal organs under stress, giving rise to problems, for example, with digestion. Perhaps most seriously, the 'out-of-shapeness' interferes with our breathing; this in itself will severely constrain our activities both physical and mental. It is worth emphasising that both mental and physical activities will be adversely affected by misuse, since mental activities normally have correlative physical activities, even if this is just the maintenance of present posture. The working of the brain and body must therefore be considered as an indivisible whole. Complaints such as being unable to pay attention, suffering from feelings of lack of confidence, and habitual worrying, are as much a product of bad use as 'writers cramp', or being tongue-tied.

In providing the means to overcome misuse, the Alexander Technique gives people a chance to explore their full potential, and achieve a level of functioning they have never enjoyed before.

ALLERGY THERAPY

Allergy, a word coined by Van Pirquet in 1906 means literally other work, and is intended to refer to an abnormal reaction by the body to substances to which it is exposed. Allergy therapy is directed towards modifying those responses so that they approximate as closely as possible to the normal.

ORIGIN

'One man's meat is another man's poison' the Roman writer Lucretius pointed out over 2000 years ago. Since this time it has been recognised that some people reacted badly to certain foods, to certain dusts, pollens, and fumes and became ill as a result.

THE IDEA

The allergic response is inflammatory. Sometimes it is caused by deficiencies in the immune system which operates at several distinct levels. This means that the lower levels are by-passed and the body's attempt to protect itself from allergens results in the antigen/antibody reaction which is the classic allergic response as seen in, for instance, hay fever, urticarial rashes, asthma and eczema. This deficiency is commonly the result of genetical predisposition to allergy known as Atopy.

In other cases, the body's response is cell-mediated, and the sufferer cannot tolerate eating certain foods or inhaling certain pollutants from the environment.

Common substances responsible for the antigen/antobody response are pollens of various kinds, shellfish, house dust and housedust mite, contact with petrochemicals, with animal hairs and danders. Building materials and household chemicals can be responsible for contact allergies or inhalant problems. A person whose immune system is inadequate may respond badly to foods such as cows milk and its products, eggs, wheat, soya, potato, tomato, onion, in fact, any or all of the common foods. When the offending substances are foods, in addition to directly obvious allergic reactions such as indigestion for certain meats, abdominal bloating when fermented products are eaten, the phenomenon of 'masked allergy' is often a problem. In this condition, the allergic response is seen almost as an addiction. When the patient needs a 'fix' such as his morning cup of tea or a snack of crisps or peanuts, he feels low, lacking in energy, tired, disinterested and listless. A little of his favourite food soon puts him on top of the world. Unfortunately, the trend is then to want and take more of the food that is causing the problem and the cycle of needy withdrawal symptoms followed by feeling better after taking the food develops.

THE TREATMENT

Since the allergy problem was first recognised, the search for satisfactory treatment has been unremitting. In the orthodox field attention has focussed on suppressing the symptoms with antihistamine drugs, using other drugs to prevent the antigen/antibody response occurring, or desensitisation injections against the suspected allergen. The non-antibody responses have largely been unrecognised or ignored.

The alternative approach initially was to avoid troublesome foods, reduce the build up of environmental pollutants, avoid the use of household chemicals and so on. In other words, to recognise that the immune system is not as efficient as it could be, and reduce the work it has to do. Later developments involved the administration of diluted allergens in liquid form, either by mouth or by injection in order to 'switch off' the reaction once it had occured. More recently treatments in various forms have developed aiming to deal with the allergies at source, improving the immune systems' effectiveness and promoting general good health.

One of the difficulties in treating allergy is the identification of those substances which the body cannot tolerate. Food allergies can be identified and treated by avoidance diets, many other allergens by skin scratch tests or laboratory blood test such as the RAST and cytotoxic tests.

However, two tests, based on changes in the body's energy fields when exposed to allergens have proved to be extremely effective. These are muscle testing and the Vega test.

In the writers opinion, the muscle test is the most useful. It has the qualities of effectiveness, simplicity, reliability and of low cost to the patient.

Once the allergens have been identified either avoidance or desensitisation can be practised. A form of desensitisation using specially homoeopathically potentised allergens taken in the form of drops by mouth is practised by many allergy therapists in this country. This has the advantage that it leads to permanent improvements in the immune system and rapid reduction of symptoms. The therapists use muscle testing to identify the suspected allergens then prepare a course of desensitisation treatment designed to lead to a steady improvement in health both in the short and long terms.

WHAT ILLNESSES AND BENEFITS?

Because the immune response is inflammation and can appear in any organ of the body, the range of illnesses that are caused by allergy is very wide indeed. Persistant tiredness, palpitations, under or over-weight, fluid retention, eczema and other skin problems, asthma, sinusitis, migraine, depression, anxiety, hay fever, muscle and joint pain, bowel problems, ulcers, irritable bowel syndrome, dizziness, fainting, persistant cytitis, M.E. In all these, allergy can be involved. It is becoming generally recognised that allergy is at the root of a very high proportion of previously undiagnosed illness, and as such assumes major importance in medicine in modern times. Often dismissed as a 'fad' or a 'popular illness' by those who do not understand it, its successful treatment has led to the restoration of good health for many whose illness had previously been considered to be 'all in the mind'.

AROMATHERAPY

Aromatherapy is the treatment in which the fragrance of plants is used in massaging the body to relieve ailments and improve health.

ORIGIN

Our ancestors, wherever they were in the world, used the oils of plants in the treatment of illness. There is evidence of this in religious texts, as well in the literature of various ancient civilizations, including Egyptian, Chinese and Greek.

In modern times a chemist called Gattefosse discovered that oil of lavender could heal burns when he immersed his hand in it after receiving a burn during an experiment. Carrying out further trials on soldiers of the First World War led him to the discovery of the healing properties of other oils.

THE IDEA

As the name implies, aromatherapy is the use of aroma - the fragrance of plants and other substances - in treatment. These oils, as the work of Gattefosse revealed, are able to penetrate the body through the skin. They can reach the blood and lymph, and hence can reach all the organs of the body. In addition to this, and while penetrating the skin, they can affect the skin itself in a favourable manner, improving its quality.

Essential oils, the basic substance of these fragrances, are obtained from the various parts of plants: roots, stems, barks, leaves and flowers. The essential oils are usually extracted by steam distillation. The amount which can be extracted varies from one plant to another.

TREATMENT

Aromatherapy treatment involves two or three different processes. The first is the blending or mixing of the oils needed for a particular patient; the second involves massaging the body of the patient using these oils; and the third is any other way that the patient may use the essential oils at home, as taught by the aromatherapist.

In blending the oils the aromatherapist takes into consideration both the effects of the oils on the condition and the effects of the aroma on the person.

Each of the essential oils affects people in different ways. If the person to be treated does not like the aroma of the chosen oils, other oils of the same desired healing effect should be mixed and used. The oils are not in fact oily, as their name might suggest, and so the treatment mixture has to be combined with a carrier substance so that it can be used for massage. The carrier must be a pure oil, such as avocado, calendula, corn, grapeseed, hazelnut, olive and sunflower.

For the techniques of aromatherapy massage a training in proper therapeutic massage is necessary. This normally forms part of any aromatherapy course. All parts of the body may be massaged: the back, abdomen, head, arms, shoulders and legs. The acupressure treatment points may be also massaged during an aromatherapy treatment session, so knowledge of the location of these points (or at least those lying on the major meridians), as well as the proper acupressure techniques, is beneficial. (See the section on SHIATSU.)

Reflexology can be used alongside aromatherapy by applying the usual reflexology treatment of the feet, but finishing with the required essential oil. This should be used to massage the feet and legs up to the knees. Reflexology, furthermore, has a wonderful diagnostic technique which is widely used by aromatherapists. (See the section REFLEXOLOGY.)

The third part of aromatherapy treatment may be necessary as part of the whole treatment, or may replace the second part altogether. This part is the treatment performed by the patient at home. The aromatherapist may instruct the patient to take mixtures of oils internally, or to inhale them, or to add them to a bath, or to use them in a compress.

Taking the prescribed oils internally might be recommended for problems of the digestive system, or as a preventative measure against many diseases, including cancer. The oils are added to a mixture of honey and water, or to tea prepared from tea-bags of certain selected flavours. In prescribing this treatment, the aromatherapist must be absolutely sure that the oils used are pure oils. Not all essential oils are suitable for internal use, and not all ailments can be treated by this method.

The inhalation method is suitable for patients who cannot take the oils internally. They may simply put drops of the prescribed oil on a towel or handkerchief and inhale from it regularly; or put drops on their pillow, for instance when they have nasal blockage and need to free the nose to breathe comfortably. A further method involves putting drops of the prescribed oil into hot water and breathing the vapours.

Prescribed essential oils may also be added to a bath. This may be a full bath for the whole body, or a small

one just for the feet or hands. In the former case, drops of oil are added to a hand-hot bath, in which the patient should remain immersed for 15 minutes or more; in the latter case drops of oil are added to a bowl of hot water and then the hands or feet are placed in this for a similar period.

One further method is the compress, made up using the essential oils mixed with hot water and applied to a small or a large area of the body.

WHAT ILLNESSES AND BENEFITS?

Aromatherapy may be used to help alleviate all sorts of diseases and ailments. However, in some cases it gives better results when it is combined with other forms of alternative therapies, such as reflexology or dietary therapy.

In addition to the treatment given at the clinic (or instead of it), the aromatherapist can instruct the patient to take the oils internally - particularly beneficial in such cases as coughs and colds, headaches, painful periods, indigestion, constipation, kidney stones, depression, as well as others. Patients suffering from tension, sore throat, blocked sinuses or any disorder of the respiratory system can be helped by inhalation. Those with rheumatism, arthritis or dermatitis may be advised to use a hot hand- or foot-bath to which drops of the required essential oils have been added. But a full body bath may be prescribed for the patients complaining from insomnia, muscular disorders, circulation problems,

headaches, fluid retention and other such problems. For external problems, such as skin complaints, wounds, bruises, as well as for neuralgia, sprains, painful periods or muscular pains, a compress containing essential oils may be recommended.

Essential oils are also effective in emergency cases, such as burns, bites or stings, for they give relief from the discomfort and also have an antiseptic effect.

As applies to herbs or homoeopathic medicines, the same essential oil may be used to treat different conditions, while the same condition could respond well to more than one essential oil. This is very useful, since people differ in their reaction to the aroma of the oils: patients may reject an oil because of their strong dislike of its aroma, even though it may be the correct one for their complaint. In such cases, the aromatherapist can switch to another oil of different aroma, but with the same therapeutic effect.

ASSERTIVENESS

Assertiveness behaviour promotes equality in human relationships through honest, clear and direct communication. This fosters mutual respect, appreciation of rights and feelings of self and others, and retains a sense of worth and dignity.

ORIGIN

Assertiveness training was first used as a positive goal for clients of the behaviour therapist Andrew Salter in 1949. He worked from the view that if people have trouble expressing their feelings to others, frustrations arise which affect their behaviour. This in turn may then require therapeutic help.

Continued use and research highlighted its worth as a general social skill. This was boosted by its use by human rights groups to express their viewpoint effectively; and by the production of training packages for the general public.

By the 1970s its teaching was widespread in the USA and moving into the UK. Many of the first teaching packages were aimed at encouraging women to move out of their submissive stereotype and speak up for their rights. However other forward thinking asserters realised its value in other areas such as in teacher training, sales work and negotiation skills amongst other.

Today assertion training is widely available.

THE IDEA

Assertiveness training is based on the beliefs that in any situation the emphasis within the communication will be recognised by accepting that both parties have needs to be met, rights specific to that situation, and something to contribute. It does not guarantee happiness but it does offer a feeling of effectiveness. It empowers the asserter to decide whether or not to be bothered with the situation, and by focussing realistically satisfying conclusion. The main objective may not be reached, but self esteem is preserved and enhanced by the knowledge that the situation was handled to the best of the asserters ability. Training is therefore is an wholistic approach, rather than goal directed which it is sometimes thought to be.

THE APPROACH

The aims of assertiveness training is to increase confidence when dealing with people by unlearning old ineffective behaviours and replacing them with new assertive ones. Four considerations have to be taken into account:

Firstly, different people and different situations engender different responses in the asserter. By encouraging the person to examine the thoughts and feelings that arise at these times, personal strengths and weaknesses can be assessed and built on to aid them when a similar occasion arises. This facilitates a feeling of composure, dignity, and achievement.

Secondly, by learning and practising specific skills, the asserter producers clear and direct communication and so experiences the feeling of being understood.

Thirdly, exploring and comparing different types of common behaviour, (usually aggressive, passive and manipulative), the concept of respecting peoples' rights is introduced. Thus to assert your own rights without respect to the other people involved in the interaction is actually aggressive rather than assertive. There are no 'normal' behaviours and so there is no element of comparison, thus freeing the asserter to form their own decisions as to how they will use the skills.

The rights form the basis of the forth element - group work. They are mainly based around the asserter's concept of 'self' and what they believe is rightfully theirs. Through group discussion and sharing of experience a more wholistic approach can be formulated by the asserter and personal responsibilities clarified; e.g. I have the right to make mistakes providing that I learn from them. This encourage the asserter to carry on developing their own self concept, and not become complacent and so running the risk of becoming a skilled robot. The group also provides a safe environment for the asserter to practise and work through situations they would like to handle better. Assertion training can be taught on a 1:1 basis, but it is enhanced in a group.

Small successes are built upon until the asserter feels able to tackle larger issues that they feel they must address to allow themselves to live their lives with dignity.

WHAT BENEFITS AND APPLICATIONS?

If we communicate effectively we tend to feel good about ourselves and other people, thus anybody who feels they have difficulty in being heard will benefit from assertiveness training. The unfortunate confusion of assertion with aggression does deter some people directly, or indirectly through pressure from close associates as they may fear a change in the would be asserter, and see a ripple effect entering to their lives too.

The main benefits are that others know that the asserter is approachable and fair, which provides a good basis for all communications to work from. This in turn helps the asserter by feeling uplifted in this knowledge and so see that they have something definite to contribute and not feel that the world is passing them by. Psychological research has shown that the more the attainment of a desired outcome is seen to be under volitional control, the stronger is the person's desire to try. The asserter also then has the option not to be assertive if they think that that is the best route to follow.

Assertiveness training therefore has wide ranging benefits in both personal and private communications, and can readily be applied in business and training schemes where two or more people are required to talk.

AURICULAR THERAPY

Auriculartherapy is a method of treating the diseased by stimulating specific points on the ear, using acupuncture needles.

ORIGIN

See ACUPUNCTURE.

THE IDEA

In addition to what is discussed in the section on ACUPUNCTURE, auriculartherapists also believe that all the body organs are represented in the human ear, which is very similar in form to the human embryo. Hence, the earlobe represents the heart and the lungs, the part below it represents the neck, while the abdomen and feet are represented in the upper part of the ear. (See REFLEXOLOGY for a similar idea.)

TREATMENT

Auriculartherapists insert very short, fine needles into the ear at the points related to those parts of the body which will benefit from stimulation, leading to the desired outcome. If, for example, you wanted to treat an asthma case, you would have to insert a needle in the exact location on the earlobe which represents the lungs.

Some acupuncturists do not resort to auriculartherapy until ordinary acupuncture has been tried and has failed to give the desired result. This is partly because of the very small area of treatment in the ear, by comparison to the whole body, making the treatment on the ear much more difficult, and calls for far more precision. However, others will use auriculartherapy from the outset, especially in cases where experience tells the practitioner that this is more appropriate for the condition in question.

In cases of alcohol, drug, or smoking addiction, or of obesity, continuous stimulation over a long period of time is required, so needles are left in their chosen locations on the ear, fixed with a tape, until the treatment takes effect. In all these cases, the needles do not force the patient to abandon the habit or to become slimmer, they only reduce the withdrawal symptoms. If the patient does not want to quit smoking, alcohol and drugs, or to eat less, the needles are useless.

In cases of addiction, the needles are left in for two to three weeks in the first instance; when the patient no longer feels a desire for the subject of the addiction, the needles are taken out for a period. They are then inserted again for another stretch of time, then taken out for a longer period than before. This process is repeated several times. After a few months the patient should have beaten the addiction.

WHAT ILLNESSES AND BENEFITS?

Very good results have been achieved in cases of addiction and obesity: 50% success for obesity, 60% for smoking addiction, 70% for alcohol addiction, and 80% for drug addiction. However, auriculartherapy is not used to treat only these problems. It is a complete system of healing that may succeed in curing all kinds of conditions that do not respond to other types of treatment.

BACH FLOWER THERAPY

Bach flower therapy is the system of treatment in which a flower remedy - or a combination of many flower remedies - are given to the patient to act on the emotional levels which are considered to be the place where the problem, physical or otherwise, has originated.

ORIGIN

In 1930 Dr Edward Bach, a prominent bacteriologist and homoeopath, gave up his successful London practice in order to begin the search for simpler method of healing, one in which nothing should be destroyed or changed. During the short span of six years before his death, he established the system of treatment which now bears his name.

THE IDEA

Bach believed that the cause of disease was 'a means adopted by our own souls to point out to us our faults, to prevent our making greater errors, to hinder us from doing more harm and to bring us back to the path of Truth and Light from which we should never have strayed'. This explanation of disease led Bach to a new approach, a spiritual one, which a matter not just for the person suffering from illness, but rather for the whole universe and its relationship with God. Diagnosis and remedies deal with disharmony in the soul, and not simply with the physical symptoms, which are merely manifestations of this disharmony.

There are many explanations of how the Bach flower remedies work, one of which is Dr Bach's own. He wrote: 'The action of these remedies is to raise our vibrations and open up our channels for the reception of the Spiritual Self; to flood our natures with the particular virtue we need, and wash out from us the fault that is causing the harm.' And: 'They cure, not by attacking the disease, but by flooding our bodies with the beautiful vibrations of our Higher Nature, in the presence of which disease melts away as snow in the sunshine.'

Every one of us has a Soul, which is immortal, and which leaves the body when death occurs. We also have a Personality, the entity which the individual represents during this life. The Higher Self is the link between the Soul and the Personality. This Higher Self, or Higher Nature as Bach puts it, is prevented from conveying the ideals of the Soul to the Personality, and so these fine qualities, or virtues, are not brought to realization. Because of this, the opposites of these virtues develop, and in the end these manifest themselves as disease.

But why do these noble qualities of the Soul fail to reach the Personality? Bach believed that there are two reasons for this. The first is that the Personality acts as if it is totally separate from the Soul, and so does not realize that the Soul possesses the ideal qualities which it wants to transmit. It may even err to the point that it does not recognize the very existence of the Soul, and hence descends into a totally materialistic world. It may, however, recognize the Soul but misunderstand what is intended, which again puts it out of harmony with the Soul.

The second reason is that the Personality sins against God, the 'Principle of Unity', by trying to force its will on other people against their will. This not only harms the other people in question, but all mankind, for negative qualities affect the whole universal energy level. To conclude: people who are ill owe their condition to disharmony between their Personality and their Soul. Disharmony can manifest itself not only in sorrow, shock, abuse by others, and any other experience in which the person is a victim, but also in feelings which lead people to harm or victimize themselves or others, such as greed, envy, hatred, domination of others etc.

So, what can flowers do to remedy this? Bach called the plants from which the remedies are extracted 'plants of higher order'. Each of them has a certain soul quality, and each of these soul qualities is in tune with a certain quality of the human being. The number of these remedies totals 38, and so the number of the Soul's qualities must likewise be 38. The difference between the quality of the plant and that of the diseased person is that the former is not distorted. But, since it is of the same frequency (in tune with it) it can make contact with it, and can flood the negative state with its higher, harmonious, undistorted waves - so that the negative qualities melt away 'as snow in the sunshine'.

TREATMENT

Bach wrote: 'No science, no knowledge is necessary, apart from the simple methods described herein; and they who will obtain the greatest benefit from this God-sent Gift will be those who keep it pure as it is; free from science, free from theories, for everything in Nature is simple.' These therapies do not call for a training in medicine or lengthy courses, but they do demand special feeling and sensitivity on the part of the therapist, and the ability to understand what lies behind the words and movements of the patient.

Your diagnosis as a therapist will be based on the negative soul states only, and not on any physical symptom by which the disease has manifested itself. In cases of fully established chronic illness, especially ones involving damage to the tissues, flower remedies may well not be sufficient to bring about a cure, as many factors are involved. However, these remedies can cure the negative states that might have caused the disease in the first place, and hence also cure any negative feelings that are associated with the disease, and so can help the patient.

Before you start to diagnose patients, however, you should know how to treat yourself successfully, firstly by knowing yourself and identifying any problems that you may have, and secondly by taking the correct remedies. Diagnosis will be based upon not only what patients tell you about their problems, or the feelings that are causing them suffering, but also upon the way in which they tell you this information - how relaxed or tense they seem; how their eyes look; how they behave towards you. You will be looking for signs which tell you more about their personality.

Moreover, what do the patients' answers about their family life, occupation, relationships with others, parents, children, friends, workmates reveal about them? What effect have major events in their lives, such as operations, accidents, the deaths of relatives or close friends, had on them?

Finally the patient has to respond to a series of direct questions. Are you a day dreamer? Do your thoughts prevent you from sleeping? Do you have specific fears or phobias? During these sessions, patients should not feel as though they are being interrogated, or that you are trying to force your views on them; rather they should be reassured that, through their cooperation, you will be able to identify the correct remedies which will allow their Personality to recognize their positive high virtues.

Your patient may experience healing crises. Old problems and past painful experiences may show up after the start of the treatment. This is a sign that the treatment is having the desired effect, bringing to the fore the energy blockages of the past, which can then be cleared away. You should assure your patients that this is good for them, and that whatever the severity of the healing crises, they will be able to cope with them and will emerge from them in better emotional shape.

In any case, patients may have complete confidence that these remedies can do no harm, even if the wrong remedies are chosen. If that should happen, the Higher Self is able to recognize that the remedies are not what is needed, and so they will be driven out of the system.

The 38 remedies are extracted from different parts of plants, and one is taken from pure, natural spring water. The names of the remedies are the names of the plants from which they have been extracted, such as Heather, Cherry Plum, Clematis, Olive. In addition, there is one remedy called Rescue Remedy, which is a mixture of five remedies. This is used in emergencies and in first aid.

The remedies are purchased in concentrated form, so you would use only two drops from each of those selected for use. The drops are then mixed with spring water in small glass bottles. These have attached pipettes, so the patient can take a few drops from this diluted mixture several times a day, according to your instructions.

Bach flower remedies can be applied in other ways. Compresses can be used for cases involving skin eruptions and inflammation. A few drops of a chosen remedy can be added to baths. Rescue Remedy ointment can be purchased, and can be used for external application, for instance for skin rashes, burns and cuts.

As a therapist, you might have to instruct your patient to back up a treatment using flower remedies with other measures, such as yoga exercises, positive suggestion, and so forth.

The length of the whole treatment depends on the nature of the problem. In chronic cases it could take some time before the negative qualities have melted away, but for recently contracted illnesses it could be a matter of days or a few weeks. Obviously for daily problems of stress, depression, sorrow and the like, or even for physical conditions such as wounds, burns or even difficulties in labour at childbirth, remedies may be effected with just one or two doses, or with a day or two of treatment.

WHAT ILLNESSES AND BENEFITS?

Generally speaking, people who have a materialistic outlook on life benefit less from Bach flower therapy than those who are interested in metaphysics. For some people the effect of the remedy is almost instant, as contact with the Higher Self is made immediately.

Whether the illness is physical or emotional, or even congenital, Bach flower remedies could be effective. Even if a physical case is labelled as incurable, or an emotional problem is deep rooted, the remedies can help. Degrees of success can range from simply relieving patients of the negative feelings associated with an illness to rescuing them from death. Emergency cases can be helped tremendously by the remedies, be they emotional trauma, or physical damage, such as burns and wounds - which are likely to be accompanied by emotional trauma. In such cases Bach remedies have known to perform real wonders.

Pregnant women can benefit from treatment during the months of the pregnancy as well as during the painful hours of labour. Infants can benefit as well, and so the remedies have much to offer mother and baby alike.

Even plants and animals have been known to benefit from the remedies - although dosages have to be scaled down accordingly!

NOTE: There are no certificate courses in Bach flower therapy listed in this directory.

THE BATES METHOD

The Bates Method is a re-educational approach to the problems of eyes and vision. It involves both a wholistic understanding of the nature of human vision and a practical approach based on relaxation and development of perception.

ORIGIN

Dr William Bates was an eminent American Opthalmologist who worked, mainly in New York, from 1880 until his death in 1930. His clinical experience raised doubts about the standard teachings on visual function, prompting him to research alternative ways of helping visual problems, and this in turn led to his utterly rejecting the orthodox teaching and describing visual function in a completely new way.

The Bates method has been taught in England since the early 1930s, and is currently experiencing something of a renaissance.

THE IDEA

To an optician or an orthodox doctor, vision should always be perfect, regardless of the time of day, state of mind, or general health of the patient. If this is not the case, there is a fault in the eyes, which must be corrected by glasses or surgery. Diseases of the eyes have nothing to do with the functional condition of the sight, and are incurable, except by drugs or surgery.

The Bates approach flatly contradicts every one of these ideas. The functioning of the eyes is seen as an expression of the inner life. Vision is inherently variable, and visual difficulties should be seen, not as a problem in themselves, but as indications of underlying problems - disturbances of mental, emotional or physical health. Seeing is a skill, normally learned to a high level in early childhood, but which can suffer from neglect or abuse in later life. The failure to appreciate and act on the true causes of poor vision leads to the habits of mental and visual strain and the permanent derangement of the visual mechanism. Visual re-education is then necessary to return eyes and mind to a proper co-ordination.

Dr Bates was particularly clear that spectacles, far from solving the problem of poor vision, are a major cause. Since glasses are completely adapted to the misuse responsible for the problem, they are not only incapable of bringing about improvement, but by confirming the eye in a bad habit, are likely to make it worse. Vision can only be improved by dealing appropriately with any underlying causes and learning to use the eyes properly so as to see without glasses. Eye disease should not be treated in isolation but as the consequance of strain and misuse, together with a constitutional predisposition to disease.

'TREATMENT'

The Bates Method is an educational technique - strictly speaking one is teaching a skill rather than giving a treatment and inevitably the results vary according to the aptitude of the pupil.

The teaching room should have space to move around in and be convenient for setting up wall charts, lamps etc as necessary. A sight line of 20ft (6m) is ideal although not indispensible. It is normal to begin by taking a fairly comprehensive history, paying attention to physical, mental and emotional problems as well as the state of the vision, and it will be necessary to carry out simple but comprehensive diagnostic tests.

On this basis the teacher will devise a course of work that best addresses the case. The techniques used range from simple matters of eye hygiene, to relaxation and visualisation methods, to quite complex studies in perception and awareness. At all times the responsibility for progress rests with the pupil, not only in conscientiously carrying out instructions but more importantly in making the whole-hearted decision to change their way of thinking and behaving. The teacher's job is to help and support them in this task by explaining, demonstrating, watching, correcting and above all listening and being able to change the approach to find what will help in an individual case. It is no good just handing out a book-learnt formula: teaching the Bates Method, like playing jazz, requires the ability to improvise that can only come from a thorough knowledge of every aspect of the process. Underlying causes must be dealt with as far as possible but there is no hard and fast separation. Emotional problems frequently surface later on in the course of apparently straightforward practical exercises so one needs to be simultaneously aware of all the different levels. It is also important to have a good knowledge of other natural therapies so as to be able to refer with confidence in the many cases which will benefit from a combined approach.

Cases of eye disease will normally remain under the care of a physician and/or receive appropriate supporting therapy: nonetheless the Bates teacher needs to have a thorough working knowledge of the nature and standard treatments of all these conditions, if only to explain to the pupil what is going on. Similarly, it is necessary to understand thoroughly the standard optical approach: although we are not interested in prescribing glasses, it is important to be aware of the basis on which this is done. One will have to advise pupils who have become dependant on glasses how to reduce their dependance: it is important that this takes account of their circumstances and in severe cases great flexibility and persistence may be needed.

In a proportion of cases severe emotional difficulties may underly the visual problem; the teacher will need both skills and personal qualities necessary to deal with these situations and the discretion to call on more specialised help when required.

WHAT CONDITIONS AND BENEFITS?

Because normal function is at the root of good health the Bates Method can be of great benefit in almost all visual problems and can also help in other conditions with a visual component, eg. headache and migraine, where these involve eyestrain, also ME, MS and other general conditions where there are visual symptoms. The techniques of relaxation and visualisation have application to other areas such as reading and learning difficulties and even to other sensory problems such as hearing loss.

The Bates Method can be used with benefit at any stage but it is always easiest to solve visual problems before they become habitual. Broadly speaking, the longer a condition has existed the more time and work will be needed to clear it up. From that point of view, the more 'trivial' cases one can deal with the better but one must be equally prepared to give long term commitment and support to apparently hopeless cases.

BIOCHEMIC TISSUE SALTS THERAPY

Biochemic tissue salts therapy is a treatment in which one or more of twelve tissue salts are administered to cure conditions that have arisen as a result of the imbalance of certain vital salts in the cells of the body.

ORIGIN

This system of healing developed as the result of the work of the nineteenth-century German doctor and homoeopath Dr Wilhelm Schuessler. In 1873 he published his theories on biochemistry. Another German, Dr Julius Hensel, published many works on the subject a decade later. However, the pioneer was Schuessler, and so the tissue salts have become known as 'Schuessler's tissue salts'.

THE IDEA

Dr Schuessler identified a total of twelve mineral salts that are vital for health. By taking one or more of these salts, someone suffering from illness can restore balance to the cells of the body, and hence conquer the disease, the symptoms of which originate from an imbalance.

Minerals are necessary for good health, and they are found naturally in the foods we consume. However, not all people have balanced diets containing all the vitamins and minerals that their bodies need, and in the required quantities. And even if they do have a good diet, there is no guarantee that the minerals will be absorbed properly and adequately. Without an adequate intake of all the minerals, the enzymes and proteins in the body will be deficient, the bones will be defective, and the balance of the body's fluids will be disturbed.

As it is, most minerals are not adequately absorbed by our bodies, and this - along with the harmful effects of non-organic farming, food refining and processing, and the addition of chemicals to the foodstuffs that are consumed by most people nowadays - will definitely ensure a shortage of these minerals in our bodies. Such shortage will be more threatening at times where the body's vital force is either low or involved in fighting a problem, which increases the demand for these minerals and so increases the shortages.

The twelve tissue salts are known by their Latin names or their abbreviations. They are:

1. Calc. Fluor. (Calcium fluoride)
2. Calc. Phos. (Calcium phosphate)
3. Calc. Sulph. (Calcium sulphate)
4. Ferr. Phos. (Iron phosphate)
5. Kali. Mur. (Potassium chloride)
6. Kali. Phos. (Potassium phosphate)
7. Kali. Sulph. (Potassium sulphate)
8. Mag. Phos. (Magnesium phosphate)
9. Nat. Mur. (Sodium chloride)
10. Nat. Phos. (Sodium phosphate)
11. Nat. Sulph. (Sodium sulphate)
12. Silica (Silicon dioxide)

TREATMENT

Although these biochemic tissue salts are prepared homoeopathically, in exactly the same way as homoeopathic medicine (see the section on HOMOEOPATHY), they are prescribed differently and work differently. The homoeopath diagnoses and then prescribes according to the symptoms picture of the patient and the change in these symptoms throughout the different stages of illness; the tissue salt therapist prescribes according to the illness, which has a defined set of symptoms. Thus, from the point of view of prescription, biochemic tissue salts therapy is similar to conventional medicine. It might therefore sufficient for the tissue salts therapist to know that a patient is suffering from varicose veins to prescribe Calc. Fluor. In homoeopathy, however, this is not enough: homoeopathists have to rely upon their own judgment, and not on the labels attached to specific illnesses. That said, biochemic tissue salts are on the syllabus of every homoeopathy course, and are used by every homoeopath.

Although there are different indications for each tissue salt, there is an overall benefit ascribed to each of them, and so this or that tissue salt would benefit any condition that is associated with its respective overall property. Calc. Fluor., for example, is used for maintaining tissue elasticity, whether the condition is varicose veins, piles or poor teeth. Calc. Phos. is for bony structures, and so is beneficial for bone deformities but also for cramps, chronic tonsillitis and other problems. Many manufacturers of tissue salts produce combination remedies made of three or four tissue salts. There are now 21 combination remedies, the first 18 of which are called combination remedies A to S, and the others are Elasto, Nervone and Zief.

As in homoeopathy, doses can be repeated very frequently, depending on the condition. For very acute conditions the remedy could be repeated every hour. And as in every other therapy, chronic conditions need to be given more time to respond to the treatment.

Taking the salts internally in tablet form is not the only way. They can be crushed and dissolved in water or milk. They can be used for external application, as an ointment. Ointments can be made by crushing a number of tablets and mixing them in a small amount of boiling water.

WHAT ILLNESSES AND BENEFITS?

Biochemic tissue salts therapy is suitable for the treatment of all conditions, for the intention is to readjust the imbalance in the body, whatever the causes. The salts cover a wide range of diseases; according to Schuessler, it is the shortage of these salts in the body that causes the onset of all conditions.

Some of the uses of Calc. Fluor. and Calc. Phos. are mentioned above. Calc. Sulph. is found in the connective tissue, blood and liver, and hence it is used to treat disorders of the connective tissue, such as skin eruptions, and liver complaints, among other problems.

Ferr. Phos. is found in all the tissues of the body, but particularly in red blood cells. It is indicated for haemorrhage, heavy periods and so forth, and is also a very important children's remedy.

Kali. Mur. is used for the second stage of all inflammatory conditions, while Kali. Sulph., which is found in the external layers of the skin, is used for the third stage of all inflammatory diseases.

Kali. Phos. is used for the disorders of the nervous system, while Silica affects the nervous system and is present in the coverings of nerve fibres. Because of its effect on the connective tissue in which it is also found, Silica is administered as a preventive measure against premature aging, as well as in the treatment of other conditions such as brittle nails, and chronic bronchitis (as it pushes pus out of the body).

Mag. Phos. is a soft tissue salt and is used for muscle cramps and spasms, enlarged prostate, crampy labour pains, teething and constipation in infants, rheumatic pains, and many other conditions.

Nat. Mur. is based on table salt. Excessive intake of this in the normal diet of many people has thrown the sodium in their bodies out of balance. Nat. Mur. is regarded as the most important of all Schuessler's salts.

Nat. Phos. is found in the intercellular fluids and body tissues; it controls acidity and helps in dealing with fatty acids. Nat. Sulph., on the other hand, has an effect on the water content of the body.

The combination remedies bring together the effects of the single remedies of which they are composed and are formulated to treat specific conditions. Elasto is used for the elastic tissues of the body and hence is indicated in varicose veins; Nervone is indicated for nerve troubles; and Zief is prescribed for the treatment of rheumatic conditions.

NOTE: There are no certificate courses in Bach flower therapy listed in this directory.

BIOMAGNETIC THERAPY

Biomagnetic therapy is a form of magnetotherapy; it involves treatment using very small magnets, which are placed on certain acupuncture points.

ORIGIN

This therapy combines acupuncture with magnetotherapy, and the origins of both of these can be found in the sections on ACUPUNCTURE and MAGNETOTHERAPY. The combination of the two as biomagnetic therapy (or biomagnetotherapy) originated from the work of a Japanese doctor, Osamu Itoh. Dr Terence Williams introduced the therapy to his clinic in England in 1976, when he found that it could cure problems which were not responding to other forms of treatment.

THE IDEA

The majority of disorders produce an irregularity in the body's structural alignment. By correcting this irregularity using the biomagnets, the flow of energy from the brain, which has been impeded by stress, returns to normal. After this the body can start healing itself naturally.

THE TREATMENT

As a biomagnetotherapist, you would first of all look for any abnormality in the body's structure, such as differences in the length of the legs, the length of the arms, and so forth. According to the abnormalities found, you would decide upon the points on which the biomagnets should be placed. There are several patterns to choose from, depending on the meridians and the acupuncture points on these meridians. Some precision is needed, but thanks to the fact that the magnetic field takes up an area larger than the size of the magnet itself, the magnetic effect can be obtained even if the biomagnets are not placed on the precise points.

Your patient might get relief from the very first treatment session. Differences in the length of the legs or arms might be corrected within seconds not minutes! However, the natural healing process takes some time, especially in cases of chronic, long lasting illnesses. The treatment sessions need not take longer than 10 to 15 minutes; the number of sessions depends on the case.

WHAT ILLNESSES AND BENEFITS?

In addition to those illnesses and disorders listed in the section on MAGNETOTHERAPY, biomagnetic therapy can be used to correct any structural abnormality before it has a chance to inflict long-term harm on the body. This is a very important preventive benefit of this treatment.

CHIROPRACTIC

Chiropractic is a system of treatment which focuses on mechanical problems of the joints, especially in the spine, and their effects on the nervous system, and hence on the organs of the body.

ORIGIN

Manipulative treatment was known in the days of the ancient Greek physician Hippocrates some 2,500 years ago. Chiropractic began with the work of Canadian-born Daniel David Palmer (1844-1913). His great desire was to discover the cause behind all illnesses. Since the art of returning misaligned vertebrae to their proper location was known to the ancient Egyptians some 3,000 years ago, Palmer claimed only to have re-discovered this type of treatment. Palmer performed his first chiropractic treatment in 1895. He replaced one vertebra in one single move for a man who had become deaf when he had exerted himself in a stooped position. Palmer succeeded in restoring his hearing. Similar success was recorded for another patient with a heart problem: chiropractic was born.

THE IDEA

After these experiences Palmer deduced that, since he could cure two different cases by replacing the vertebrae which were pressing on the nerves, he might be able to cure other problems by the same method. He then started to develop the theory that all illnesses were caused by nervous tension produced by the impingement of vertebrae on the spinal nerves. Chiropractors use the term 'subluxation' to describe the condition of the dislocated bone; it means that the bone is out of alignment with its neighbours. Subluxation is an abnormality in the function of the motor unit of that particular vertebra, and this abnormality results in either restricted mobility or excessive mobility. It could also be partial (one sided) or total.

Palmer believed that the energy transmitted from the brain to the bodily organs through the spinal cord can be affected by any pressure on the nerve leaving the misaligned vertebra. This pressure on the nerve either can lead to irritation and excitation, increasing the nerve force, or can impede the flow of energy, decreasing the nerve force.

This explanation is far too simple to explain the causes of all illnesses. Nonetheless, the feeling of pins and needles for instance, or numbness, or even paralysis in the case of great pressure on the nerves, bears witness to the fact that the impingement of vertebrae on the nerves can result in a multiplicity of disorders, even if not all of them.

Palmer's son Bartlett was responsible for the further development of chiropractic. He brought chiropractic to the attention of the world at large by opening the Palmer School of Chiropractic in 1905. He improved diagnosis by using X-ray. He also developed the Meric system, in which the body is divided into 31 zones corresponding to the pairs of nerves connecting the spine to the organs. Disorders in each organ can be traced to the nerve corresponding to that organ. Hence, brain, eyes, ears, pharynx and the thyroid gland are affected by the dislocations or subluxations of the first four cervical vertebrae, while the subluxations of the fifth, sixth and seventh cervical vertebrae affect the mouth, lungs, shoulders and arms. Thoracic vertebrae displacements affect the digestive organs among others, while lumbar vertebrae displacements affect the sex organs and kidneys and others. (See also OSTEOPATHY.)

This division of the body enables the chiropractor to search for displacements in the spinal vertebrae to find the cause of the disorder.

TREATMENT

As a chiropractor, you would first of all take the medical history of your patient, then look carefully at the patient to check the range of the joint movements, posture, feet curvature, and the length of the legs, the pelvis, and look for any abnormal curvature in the spine.

Then you would ask your patient to lie on the couch face down, and begin static palpation (touching and feeling). From this, you would assess the position, size, shape, resistance, tone, temperature and texture of the structures beneath your fingers, including the skin, fat, connective tissue, muscles, bones and joints.

You would then begin motion palpation to assess mobility at intervertebral motor units, by means of manipulation. Motion palpation involves many techniques for the various parts of the back. Before deciding whether chiropractic treatment is best for your patient's needs, you may also ask for some X-rays.

The basic treatment technique in chiropractic is a sharp thrust applied across a joint. This separates the joint surfaces, so opens the joint. The technique is called adjustment, and is performed in various ways. The first consultation may take anything between 20 to 45 minutes, or more if you have asked for X-rays. The following consultations should not take more than 10 to 20 minutes, depending on the case. The period of time between consultations varies; the average is about a week.

After the problem has been cleared, your patient should come back for further treatment over a period of up to a year, especially in chronic cases or those caused by habit. If the symptoms return, your patient should come to you for treatment immediately, but the problem will take a shorter time to resolve the second time round.

The number of treatment sessions varies, depending on the problem. If the problem has a long history, or if changes in the tissues have taken place, the condition will take longer to treat than those more recently acquired. On average 6 to 10 treatment sessions are all that your patient would need.

WHAT ILLNESSES AND BENEFITS?

Prevention is the first good reason for consulting a chiropractor. If the chiropractor can locate some subluxation or any other misalignment when it is still in its early stages, this can be put right before any serious symptoms develop. People would be well advised to go to the chiropractor for a check-up every six months, in just the same way as they are advised

to go to the dentist, or women are advised to pay regular visits to the gynaecologist.

Advantages can also be had by people who suffer from problems which are not caused by spinal disorders. An asthma sufferer, for example, would benefit from an increase in chest mobility; someone suffering from Parkinson's disease would benefit from improvement in the vertebral movements; someone with multiple sclerosis could benefit from relief from the pain caused by muscle spasms; even the cancer patient could benefit, and women in labour.

Chiropractic has been successful in treating fibrositis, abnormal spinal curvatures such as sway back and sideways curvatures, and round shoulders. The chiropractor can also provide a back-up treatment to be used in conjunction with other forms of medicine, whether alternative or conventional. Even if it fails to cure a problem, such as a slipped disc, and the patient has to resort to surgery, chiropractic could well prove valuable in clearing away any more minor abnormalities that remain after surgery.

COLONIC HYDROTHERAPY

Colonic hydrotherapy is a safe method of introducing warm, filtered water into the colon for the purpose of cleansing, detoxifying, and implanting friendly bacteria and electrolytes.

ORIGIN

Recorded history indicates this form of therapy to have arisen from enemas, which date back to at least 1500 BC. Hippocrates spoke about the use of enemas in the 4th and 5th centuries AD, and Pare (1600 AD) actually distinguished between colonic irrigation and enemas.

THE IDEA

A wide variety of disease conditions may develop in the colon, ranging from constipation to cancer. The underlying causes may be due to bad toilet training, inadequate diet, prolonged periods of stress, overuse of laxatives, and so on.

These, in turn, can lead to constrictions in the colon (making the passage of waste more difficult), the formation of 'pouches' or sacs (diverticulosis), reabsorption of toxins into the bloodstream, infections developing, etc.

In addition, the colon is a common breeding ground for a variety of parasites, including threadworms, pinworms, tapeworms, flukes, etc. The ascending colon (right side of body) normally houses a large community of intestinal bacteria which forms a slightly acidic environment which helps to control unfriendly micro-organisms as well as enabling production of B and K vitamins to take place. The widespread use of broad-spectrum antibiotics, however, has led to the killing-off of this friendly bacteria. As a result, the colon commonly becomes inhabited by 'unfriendly' bacteria, which instead create an alkaline environment encouraging the proliferation of undesirable micro-organisms, and is also unsuitable for the production of B and K vitamins.

This brief overview of the colon and some of its associated problems is only a tiny indication of the role of the colon, and its pathological (disease causing) conditions. The diagnosis, psychological factors of influence, nutritional involvement, an understanding of the colon as a reflex organ, and other aspects make the study and treatment of colon disorders fascinating and enlightening.

TREATMENT

An initial case-taking of history and symptoms, accompanied by a physical examination, may indicate the desirability of colonic hydrotherpy. The type of equipment used is important and gravitational tanks are regarded as safest because the water pressure (predetermined by height of tank above patient) is constant and not subject to quick and dangerous rises. Some types of mechanical equipment would be acceptable.

Of prime importance is the use of disposable tubing and specula. Not all therapists use disposables, preferring instead to use a stainless steel speculum and rubber tubing, which they claim to sterilise. Depending on the method or type of sterilising agent used and the length of time of immersion, it is often the case that only disinfection and not sterilisation takes place, in which case the patient's health could be at serious risk.

Of secondary importance, but not to be neglected, is the reimplantation of 'bowel flora' - the friendly bacteria. Many therapists refuse to do this, preferring instead to prescribe some acidophilus-type product.

A properly trained colon therapist will be able to recognise and treat most colon conditions, will be able to determine - through observation of bowel contents - the general state of the digestive tract and advise, where appropriate, on any treatments thereof, the presence and identity of most types of parasite (that knowledge will enable the therapist to gauge what damage might have been caused) - including candida albicans - and have a clear and informed picture of the general condition of the colon.

Many conditions will respond quickly and favourably to the infusion of herbs in the water. Because different herbs have different medicinal qualities there is a wide selection to choose from. The gentle soothing action of herbs <u>inside</u> the colon - where they can act quickly and directly - is so much superior to taking them orally.

WHAT ILLNESSES AND BENEFITS?

Colonic hydrotherapy is certainly the treatment of choice for all colon problems, including constipation, diarrhoea, haemarrhoids, intestinal toxaemia, irritable bowel syndrome, inflammatory bowel disease, ulcerative/mucous colitis, Crohn's disease, diverticulosis/itis, Myalgic Encephalomyelitis (ME), candida albicans, etc.

The build-up of plaque on the inner walls of the colon can be broken down and eliminated, parasites and harmful bacteria and gases can be washed away (thus reducing 'bloating'), and the replacement of the correct type of bacteria can have the most exhilarating, beneficial effects on the whole person.

COLOUR THERAPY

Colour Therapy is the art of introducing various colours into the system through different media. It is concerned with unblocking and rejuvenating the colour energy balance of the wholistic system to bring about good health. Colour Therapy can also be used as a prevention to ill health, while acting to maintain well-being.

ORIGIN

The art of Colour Therapy is not a new one, in fact records on the use of Colour has been documented as far back as Pythagoras, Aristotle and Hippocrates. Even before their time, prehistoric man used colour for wall painting and body painting for symbolic, religious and healing temples, the Egyptians worshipped the Sun God - Ra, while the Romans adorned themselves with brightly coloured precious stones to invoke the healing qualities associated with their pigmentation.

Since the discovery of the refraction of light made by Sir Isaac Newton in 1666, where light was found to be composed of different bands of colour (red, orange, yellow, green, blue, indigo and violet), the mystical style of thinking was replaced by a more scientific approach. Newton's discovery eventually led to people like Babbitt, Hunt, Steiner, Luscher and others. Such people became well known for using colour for constructive, therapeutic purposes.

THE IDEA

Colour Therapy works on various levels (physical, emotional, mental and spiritual) and is perhaps one of the most subtle forms of vibration available to us. It offers us the opportunity to reach areas deep within ourselves, as well as levels far beyond. It acts as a bridge between the known and the unknown. The medium of colour is like a wonderful language that can help us to understand ourselves better and bring healing in our lives.

Colours are essentially vibrations. The way in which these vibrations affect us, depends largely upon the way in which we are exposed to it. Colour primarily affects us emotionally. If we are exposed to its rays the effects are highlighted or lessened depending on the media used. For example, colour in dress has a mild impact on us as opposed to colour received through the optic nerve, through illumination. Along with the psychological (emotional and mental) impact of colour there are also the physiological ones. These are usually triggered by the influence of light working through the nervous system which influences the chemical reactions and chemical changes in the body. Such changes can also be influenced via a different channel, by using the power of visualisation, mental projection and meditation skills to heal the body.

All of these methods are effective ways in which colour can be therapeutic used and which aid us in making a difference in our lives.

HOW DOES COLOUR THERAPY WORK?

Just as the earth has its own electro-magnetic energy field around it, the human body is also surrounded by its own energy field known as the aura. Clairvoyants see the aura in colours with each person having their own distinctive pattern in much the same way each of us have our own unique fingerprint. When we live out of balance for any significant length of time, our aura records these imbalances in varying colour(s). The purpose of this is mainly two-fold. Firstly, to warn us of an imbalance so we may take corrective and preventative measures to avert disease manifesting in any part of our physical, emotional or mental being. The second reason is, by imprinting these colours in our subtle energy field, we can have access to information which can be used as an aid to understanding the deeper and more hidden aspects of ourselves, which we are for the most part unaware of. In this way colour can help to increase our awareness and therefore offer us enlightened life choices.

Each of the colours are transmitted through the aura to it's associated power centre or chakra. These are energy points situated within each of the different levels of the aura as well as within the physical body itself. These chakras absorb and transfer colour energy throughout the complete human system in order to maintain it's proper functioning. If disease is unavoidable, these power centres cannot absorb the correct colour and so become blocked and the aura loses it's vibrancy and vitality, hence it becomes 'washed out' and faded.

TREATMENT AND DIAGNOSIS

In Colour Therapy, Colour-Light treatment and Colour Counselling are usually used together. Combined, they offer treatment of the whole person, i.e., physical, emotional, mental and spiritual. Colour Therapy is very effective in treating psycho-somatic problems. That is, treating not only the physical ailment, but also considering the metaphysical associations and causes of the problem.

The very first session of Colour Therapy is one mainly to gather information about the patient regarding their medical history and to discuss the nature of their problem. No actual treatment with coloured lights is given on this first visit. Time is mainly spent assessing the problem and diagnosing the condition. It is quite normal in this session for the patient to complete an Application Form which the therapist keeps for his or her records.

To assess the patient's condition the Colour Reflection Reading is usaed to find out the overall state of the patient. In addition, the main areas of concern are highlighted thereby pointing the way to further treatment with Colour Counselling. Ideally this process is repeated every four to six months or as the sessions indicate. In the interim period Colour-Light treatment is given based on colours received through a method of dowsing a Colour Spine Chart. Using the energy field of a patient, the Colour Therapist locates the colour imbalances and associates them to particular organs and parts of the physical body. Colour-Light treatment is then administered using complementary colours according to the problems 'picked up' by the therapist.

Colour Therapy treatment sessions are usually given on a monthly basis, with follow-up sessions administered on a consecutive weekly basis, as required. It is usual to give a course of Colour Therapy treatment spreading over nine months to a year. A Colour Spine Chart is made prior to the patients arrival for each main Colour Therapy session and will indicate how many, if any, follow-up sessions are required. This session lasts for approximately one to one and a half hours, while follow-up sessions usually last for half an hour only.

BENEFITS

Colour Therapy is effective in treating emotional imbalances, e.g., depression, loss of confidence, assertion, drive and self worth. It is also very effective in bringing mental and emotional clarification and in understanding one's personal circumstances and situation in life. Physically, Colour Therapy has helped many people relieve eczema, psoriasis, stress, digestive problems, migraine, nervous disorders, sleeplessness etc.

Colour and Light treatment is undoubtedly going to be one of the medicines of the future. Certainly there is much need for further investigation and research into this powerful and fascinating subject. We are on the verge of a new dawning of understanding. A "New Age" of awareness lies ahead of us. The path is illuminated with a glorious future. There is indeed light at the end of the tunnel.

COUNSELLING

Counselling is the skilled and principled use of relationship to facilitate self-knowledge, emotional acceptance and growth, and the optimal development of personal resources (British Association of Counselling definition).

ORIGIN

Counselling has probably been practised in one form or another since time immemorial. However, its development as a profession in this country has only come about fairly recently. The British Association of Counselling grew out of the Standing Conference for the Advancement of Counselling inaugurated in 1970. There are now over 7000 individual and over 300 organisational members.

THE IDEA

The overall aim of counselling is to provide an oppurtunity for the client to work towards living more satisfyingly and resourcefully. Counselling sessions would therefore provide oppurtunities for the client, with the help and guidance of a trained and skilled counsellor, to explore, discover and clarify ways of living more resourcefully and of thus achieveing greater well-being.

People who seek counselling are invariably those who are in some degree of confusion, distress or crises. They may be feeling overwhelmed by the choices facing them, or indeed be unaware of the range and scope of choices and options open to them; they may be experiencing or anticipating internal or external changes which may be causing them great anxiety or distress; or they may be in such a state of confusion that they don't know where to turn. Whatever the specific problems, people who come for counselling are generally not living in a way which is wholly satisfying to them, nor are they using all their resources.

One of the first tasks of counselling, therefore, is to provide an oppurtunity for the client to explore, clarify and understand the problem and thereby reduce confusion. Such exploration would focus either simultaneously or consecutively on the experience, the feelings, the thinking and the behaviour involved. Very often this may be all that is needed from counselling.

The process itself should lead to the client being enabled to clarify personal meanings and to implement objectives for him or herself. Again, this may be a sufficient end of the counselling task.

In many cases, however, oppurtunities may be provided for the client to try out and experiment, both within the outside of the counselling sessions, with new ways of being, which would include new ways of relating as well.

TREATMENT

In counselling, there is no 'treatment' per se: it would be more proper to talk in terms of different approaches to the exploration and/or solving of problems. The most well-known counselling approaches used in this country are Person-centred Counselling; Rational Emotive Therapy (a cognitive approach); Behavioural Techniques; TA (Transactional Analysis); Gestalt Approach; Existential Counselling; and many others.

These approaches all adopt different focuses; some, such as the cognitive/behavioural ones, are very solution/problem orientated and incorporate set goals, directive techniques and homework being set; others work from the assumption that the client has the ability, if not to resolve then at least to come to some acceptance/management of problems. The focus in these approaches would be on exploration, description/clarification of problems, rather than on an attempted solution. In all approaches adopted, much also depends on the personal differences between counsellors.

From my personal standpoint, which is existential, work would generally proceed in the following way:

The existential approach, which has its roots in phenomonology and existential philosophy, is about our perception of the world, our awareness of how we relate to, and operate in, the world and the clarification of what it means to be alive. Very often people choose to come to existential counselling because they are faced with existential issues, which are indeed life issues. They may be confronted by immediate and pressing problems, or they may be very anxious or distressed, but underlying all this is a feeling of being lost; of not knowing where or how they are in the world; of not knowing where they are and who they are. Somehow or other along the way they have become untrue to themselves and have evaded facing up to life's realities. They could be said to be living an inauthentic existence.

The aims of existential counselling are, therefore, to enable people to become truthful with themselves again; to widen their persepective on themselves and the world around them; and to find clarity on how to proceed into the future whilst taking lessons from the past and creating something valuable to live for in the present.

Your task, as the counsellor, would be to venture along with the client into an exploration of their persepective of their world and into how their experience fits into the wider map of existence. Your task would entail guiding them through the disturbances they have become caught up in and to help them look at their assumptions, values and aspirations, so that they can take a new direction in their life. This will include an exploration of the decisions and choices they have made in their lives, as well as the options which were available to them.

WHAT ILLNESSES AND BENEFITS?

For many counsellors, the range of 'illnesses' is a widely-open one, ranging from the neurotic symptoms such as prolonged grieving after a death, to phobias, to issues of selfworth. Some counsellors would work with more extreme forms of mental disturbance, such as schizophrenia or clinical depression, whereas others would only work in very specific areas such as AIDS/HIV Positive counselling; sexual dysfunctioning counselling; multicultural oriented counselling; gender-related counselling, and so on.

In terms of benefits, success varies depending on the criteria of measurement. Undoubtedly, in some cases, various persistent symptoms do disappear as a result of counselling; equally some symptoms remain, but lose their strength of disturbance to the client. Various statistical tests have been reported which on the whole agree that there is some benefit to clients as a result of counselling, but it must be stated that measurement of success in counselling remains a controversial area.

CRANIO-SACRAL THERAPY

Cranio-Sacral Therapy is a comprehensive therapy which treats the whole person by very gently balancing the membranes, bones, fluids and fascia throughout the body, which together make up the Cranio-Sacral System, thereby bringing the person into balance on all levels.

ORIGIN

Cranio-Sacral Therapy is a development of Cranio Osteopathy, which was in turn developed over 50 years ago by Dr. William Sutherland. Although an Osteopath, Sutherland developed this exceptionally gentle therapy after discovering and observing the very subtle rhythms, pulls and twists throughout the body which reflect the movement of the Cranio-Sacral System.

THE IDEA

The Cranio-Sacral System consists of the bones of the cranium and sacrum, the Dural Membranes surrounding the brain and spinal cord and enclosing the Cerebro-Spinal Fluid, and the Fascia enveloping every organ, muscle, nerve and blood vessel thourghout the body. All of these pulsate together in a symmetrical rhythmic movement associated with the rhythmic secretion and absorption of the Cerebro-Spinal Fluid.

Cerebro-Spinal Fluid surrounds and bathes the brain and spinal cord providing nutrition and drainage for the Central Nervous System and creating the medium within which the Central Nervous System develops, grows and functions. It is vital to Central Nervous System function.

Activity throughout the body, healthy or unhealthy, is mediated through nerves; all nerves are enveloped in Fascia; and all nerves penetrate the Dural Membrane as they enter and leave the Central Nervous System.

Consequently, all activity throughout the body is reflected into the Dural and Fascial structures which make up the Cranio-Sacral System causing imbalance or asymmetry in the system. Similarly, imbalances or restrictions anywhere in the Cranio-Sacral System will be reflected out to cause stresses, strains and dysfunction in associated areas throughout the body.

Dysfunctions can therefore be monitored and influenced by tuning into the Cranio-Sacral System and by doing so the Cranio-Sacral Practitioner can learn to assess every abnormality in a patient's condition, every stress and every strain, every injury recent or chronic and ultimately every qualitative change of any kind, from whatever cause, in any part of the body.

TREATMENT

Treatment is exceptionally gentle. The practitioner simply places his or her hands very gentle on the patient's head, sacrum or other appropriate part of the body and by application of the softest pressures, balances the subtle twists, pulls and asymmetries reflected through the system. The pressure is often so slight that the patient may not even be aware that anything is happening - at least until the beneficial effects are felt.

By tuning-in this way the Cranio-Sacral Practitioner can make a detailed diagnosis of the patients condition and the root cause of any problems. The gentle treatment will then correct imbalances at the very core of the system and this, in turn, will reflect out to remove restrictions, asymmetries and imbalances and restore proper function to all parts of the body.

Cranio-Sacral Therapy never imposes on the body; it works with it, stimulating its inherent self healing powers. In this way the gentlest of treatments can achieve profound releases and enable the body to

return to a more balanced and freely mobile state in which energy flow, fluid flow, blood flow and tissue physiology can all function more efficiently and harmoniously.

WHAT ILLNESSES AND BENEFITS?

Cranio-Sacral Therapy treats the whole person; it can therefore help in almost any condition from physical injuries and functional disorders (digestive, menstrual, nervous etc) to emotional disturbances and persistent symptoms of obscure origin.

Because of its gentleness it is very valuable in acutely painful or delicate conditions and also for babies, children and the elderly. As it works on a very profound and subtle level, influencing the Central Nervous System, it can penetrate to deep rooted causes.

Cranio-Sacral Therapy has a very special role to play in the treatment of Birth Trauma, which probably affects all of us to some degree but which is particularly important in long and difficult births. Excessive compression of the cranium at birth can lead to many severe problems (often not recognised until many years later, if at all) from Cerebral Palsy (spasticity), learning difficulties, dyslexia, autism, epilepsy, squint and hyperactivity to less debilitating effects such as reduced general mental ability, poor memory, headaches, susceptibility to allergy, or general constitutional weakness. Other injuries to the head, particularly the subtle effects of major head injuries are also effectively treated by Cranio-Sacral Therapy.

Another area of special importance to Cranio-Sacral Therapy is conditions affecting the Fascia such as adhesions and other post-operative effects, frozen shoulder or persistent problems arising from sprained ankles, knees and other traumatic twists to the joints or body fascia.

The after effects of Meningitis (from which patients often feel they have never fully recovered) are another important area for Cranio-Sacral treatment, since Meningitis affects the meninges, which are the very same thing as the Dural Membranes of the Cranio-Sacral System.

Ultimately, Cranio-Sacral Therapy treats the person as a whole and so can treat anything from simple back pain and sciatica to complex conditions such as, asthma, period pains, whiplash injuries, ME and other severely debilitating conditions. Because it treats the whole person at a fundamental and profound level it is very effective, not only in eradicating the root cause of major conditions, but also in promoting general improvement in health and energy, re-integrating following illness, accident or injury, and integrating the whole person on many levels.

CRYSTAL THERAPY

Crystal therapy is the therapy in which crystals are used as an aid for healing in different ways according to the needs of the client. The most basic of these methods is to have them in close proximity to the body.

ORIGIN

Crystals have intrigued man since he walked on this earth and he has always used crystals, rocks and gemstones to survive. They were used to build houses, to build roads; they used them to make weapons and tools; they were also used to make medicines. Also they were used as a medium for writing and recording, the most famous being the Ten Commandments! They were also used as talismans and amulets for healing and protection. As then they are still used for their beauty and great value is placed on many of them. They are all around us and the world is made of them. Crystal Healers will see crystals, rocks and gemstones as universal tools of healing.

There is evidence that crystal healing has been in use in many parts of the world for thousands of years.

Legend says that they were extensively used as the main healing source in the lost continent of Atlantis. Historical evidence has also proved that they were used in the times of ancient Egypt, China, India, Australia and also the continent of America where even today many of the Red Indians are still using crystals.

IDEA

Crystals have intrigued man since he walked on this earth and he has always used crystals, rocks and gemstones and their properties for survival by using them to build houses, roads, medicines and unfortunately weapons as they do today. They also used them for their beauty and they placed great value on many of them. They are all around us and the world is made from them.

Within their structure they contain every mineral that life on this earth needs to exist and unlike man their vibrational energy levels are constant. Crystals are usually formed due to the immense pressures and heat within the earth and as they develop they entrap the surrounding minerals within their structure. When this happens they become energy and mineral in crystalline form.

Gems are composed mainly of the following elements: flourine, iron, potassium, sulphur, silicon, zinc, beryllium, carbon, copper, hydrogen, manganese, oxygen, phosphorus, tin and many, many others. In fact all crystals and gemstones contain within their structure all the minerals that all organic matter needs to survive, flourish and live.

Perhaps it is because crystals contain all the chemical elements that our bodies need in its purest form that man has this close contact with them.

TREATMENT

Crystal therapists use crystals as an aid for healing in different ways according to the needs of the client. The most basic of these methods is to have them in close proximity to the body. Within the body's energy field, crystals tend to have an effect on the vibrational energy of the body, allowing it to rebalance itself so that it can begin to heal itself. Crystals tend to amplify not only the healing process but also any other healing method that the client may already be having.

Crystals can also have an effect by directing their energy towards the affected part of the body. As a healer you place crystals in various patterns around and on the client to aid the healing effect; you also use them for massage. You make use of their many colours as this is a strong healer of the body system and with the amplification of colour combined with the vibration of sound, it can be quite a powerful and beautiful healing process.

You use crystals in meditation and to help to relieve tension and stress and to bring relaxation to the body. Crystals are powerful releasers of blocked up emotions that often cause physical conditions to manifest. You use crystals to energise massage oils in order to allow deep penetration of their vibrational healing energy. Crystals are also used for making gem elixirs and remedies for the internal use of the client to aid the healing. With crystals you tend to reach more for dealing with the cause of the condition rather than just treating the effect. A crystal therapist treats the whole person by balancing, realigning, and harmonising the mind, the body and the spirit.

BENEFITS

Besides being a therapy, in their own right crystals will complement all other forms of healing. They can be used to release and clear all negative energies within the client's thought system or even in his environment by releasing negative energies within the walls of the house in which he lives. This can make the home a more comfortable environment to live in. Because crystals work at such a vibrational level, crystal healing knows no boundaries; this makes it a very powerful tool for absent healing.

Crystal Healing can aid and benefit in the healing process of all physical, mental and emotional conditions.

DIETARY THERAPY

Dietary Therapy is a system of treatment in which an individual diet is prescribed for the patient, often along with a purpose-directed programme of nutritional supplements, with or without additional cleansing procedures, in order to restore normal health where it has been disturbed by complexes of symptoms or disease.

ORIGIN

Please see the Section on Naturopathy.

THE IDEA

Part of the idea is that bad diet is one of the major causes of disease. This idea is common to both Dietary Therapy and Nutrition (q.v.) and the reader is referred to the entire section headed "The Idea" under "Nutrition", in which the aspects of poor diet, toxic exposure and drug suppression, which lead to poor health, are fully discussed.

To illustrate how a person becomes ill through wrong diet or toxic abuse one can draw upon the work of the German Doctor and writer Hans-Heinrich Reckeweg, who writes extensively about "Homotoxins", meaning substances toxic to Man. Quite simply, as these accumulate in cells and tissues progessively, the tissues move from a healthy state, downwards towards the depths of illness. They do so in six perceptible stages.

In phase 1 (excretion phase) there is expulsion of toxins through physiological orifices. In phase 2 (reaction phase) toxins are removed through inflammation. In phase 3 (deposition phase) there is deposition, followed by inactivation in tissues.

These are three different grades of condition, but active excretion and detoxification are an essential part of all three of them. At none of these three levels are the structures and enzyme systems of the cell severely damaged. Complete recovery of the affected tissue is very possible in all three of these phases.

However, in phase 4, (impregnation phase) local concentrations of toxins occur in the weakest organs which cause severe disease locally. In phase 5 (degeneration phase) the organ is severely and irreversibly damaged, with alteration of cellular

enzymes and of organic structure. In phase 6, the name of which means 'cancer phase', even the genes of the cells are damaged, so new but degraded types of cell are now formed.

At the same time as these deteriorative processes are going on, the disease is also moving from more superficial structures of the body towards deeper ones, and from organs and systems of lesser importance towards the vital organs. Hence, one can state a 'law of Disease', to the effect that "Disease progresses from below upward, from the outside to within, from the least important to the most important organs, and from the acute towards the chronic until degeneration and death ensue".

This gives us the picture of the onward march of a process of progressive deterioration. Yet it is very far from being a cause for despair, since it may so very readily be reserved, especially in the earlier stages.

Hence, Hering's "Law of Cure", which is the complete reverse of the above stated "Law of Disease" says "Cure proceeds from above downward, from within outward, from the most important organs to the least important organs, and in the reverse order of appearance of symptoms". This states that the whole process can be thrown into reverse by corrective action and that the patient can recover and, in doing so, progressively passes through the stages by which he or she arrived at their present poor condition. This tracing back of stages is thought to be absolutely necessary, because it represents reversal of the various stages in toxic accumulation and the tissue conditions which go with them and, by definition really, there is no alternative pathway by which one can proceed favourably.

Some people question the connection between illness and pollution and bad diet because they see that not all people fall ill even though they are exposed to these dangers. But there will always be some people who have a stronger constitution than others. Perhaps they have inherited this from their ancestors, who have fed themselves better through the generations; perhaps they built healthier bodies for themselves in early life by good diet and exercise. Perhaps they have been less affected than others, down their family tree, by the disease 'taints' known as *miasms*.

TREATMENT

Diagnosis in Dietary Therapy involves making a naturopathic-type assessment of the patient's present condition and how he or she arrived there. It involves plotting the course or history of his or her particular disease and understanding how the present condition was reached from the presumably far more favourable condition the patient enjoyed long ago. It therefore necessitates tracing the progress of the increasingly toxic condition from stage to stage, year by year, understanding which specific events marked a crucial or adverse turning point between one stage and the next. There will usually be periods in the history when the patient was taking a rapid downward slide - which can be linked to aspects of life-style, diet, occupational exposure or to orthodox medical treatment. At other times, typically, the patient will have been marking time, having reached a temporary stability and being, for the time being, on a plateau. At still other times, in some patients, one sees a period or periods of reversal when, just temporarily, some progress was being made back towards health, only to be dashed later by some other adverse development, and so continuing the downward slide again towards ill-health.

Of course, the objective of all treatment is to halt the progress of the disease process and to reverse it to regain improving health. The factors which always accompany the progression from stage 1 to stage 6 of the disease process are (1) progressive toxin accumulation (2) inadequacy of key nutrients (3) inadequacy of cell energy production.

Toxins exhaust the body's supplies of key nutrients and interfere with cell energy production. Availability of key nutrients helps to eliminate toxins and to maintain better levels of cell energy production. Adequacy of cell energy production helps the body to expel toxins. This is an interactive, three-way relationship.

In these circumstances it is obvious to give a diet which has a very good nutrient content, minimizes both endogenous and exogenous toxins, encourages good absorption, encourages toxin elimination from the tissues, facilitates toxin removal from the body via the organs of excretion and encourages excretion of out-of-balance nutrients which the body has in excess. It is also obvious to give extra nutrients as necessary to reverse deficiencies and to facilitate additional toxin removal, to use bowel flora bacteria and non-nutritional naturopathic cleansing procedures where appropriate, and to increase production of cell energy. All the above must be done in a way which takes fully into consideration the patient's idiosyncrasies and the details of his or her case-history.

These tasks represent a highly professional and skillful job and should only be done by people with an excellent understanding of diet and nutrition, combined with the principles of naturopathy and pathology. It is inherently very satisfying work to the practitioner, reversing the disease processes in this way.

Any of the many available measures relating to diet, supplements and cleansing may be used in a variety of permutations to give the diet which is the very best diet for each particular patient at a particular time. When diet and nutrition are used as a Prime Therapy, we seek after optima for the patient, in order to design specific well-thought-out treatments, rather than just providing something which will be "generally favourable for him".

Supplementary nutrient prescriptions should be made against the background of as much understanding as possible of the patient's biochemistry. Specific nutrient deficiencies are likely to be noted from the detail of the diagnosis, and efforts have to be made to correct these. Correction of such deficiencies involves not only giving an adequate level of the nutrient, but also overcoming the various barriers which exist in the unwell or imbalanced person, to absorption and assimilation of the nutrient and to actual entry of the nutrient into the deficient cells. That is not all, however, because the mere correction of nutrient deficiencies will only sometimes be enough to stimulate a recovery of the patient. The nutrients must also be used to initiate the body's efforts at toxin elimination and tissue repair. This requires other specific skills from the practitioner. A clear understanding of the relationship between the supply of minerals on the one part and toxic elimination on the other is fundamental to this part of the art of the Therapy. In this way, the nutrients, and, in particular, the minerals, become tools in the therapeutic process of naturopathic cleansing. The roles of the individual micro-nutrients in the body have to be thoroughly grasped for this to be possible and the balances between them have to be well understood, together with the means of their control.

If, on top of all this specifically nutritional skill and understanding, the practitioner has also an understanding of some extra non-nutritional cleansing procedures as used by naturopaths, then he or she has significant armoury available for dealing with difficult cases. Most people who undertake such training grow personally in the process, because of the maturing effect of the educational experience that is involved, because of the development of the ability to help others very effectively, and because of the deep understanding that is generated of the factors which determine health and disease and the progression from one to the other.

Nonetheless, training to practitioner level in this discipline is perfectly possible for persons with no prior medical or scientific background.

One should note that all the above relates to the provision of an initial prescription for the patient. But the practitioner's role thereafter is to pursue the treatment of the case with both sensitivity and insight. In particular, the practitioner:

1) Develops or designs a sequence of treatment stages suited to the condition and nature of the individual.

2) Observes the patient's responses to treatment over a period of time, and adjusts the eliminatory pressure according to the patient's needs.

WHAT ILLNESSES AND BENEFITS?

Generally, Dietary Therapy principles teach "the unity of all disease" in which all chronic states reflect the same adverse changes, to various degrees, with different tissues affected. The naturopathic Laws are always obeyed and hence there is no condition which fails to benefit from better nutrition and alleviation from toxicity.

It is obvious that any disease process which has progressed only as far as stages 1-3 above, is fairly readily reversed. Once tissue damage has started to occur, as in its fourth stage, then the body has not only to carry out a process of elimination and detoxification, but must also carry out some active processes of repair. In stages 5 and 6 complete recovery becomes more difficult to effect due simply to the amount of tissue and organ damage already done and varying levels of body repair and regeneration are possible. On the whole, the potential for success is great, even in these late stages, but will call for a very thorough-going application of the available measures. Conditions presenting include allergic, auto-immune, gastrointestinal, rheumatic, musculo-skeletal, urino-genital, skin, nervous, mental/emotional and respiratory disorders, and many others.

DOWSING

Dowsing is the way by which an object, a problem, a cause of a problem and the solution is found/determined by the movement of an object (normaly, the pendulum for medical dowsing).

ORIGIN

The history of Dowsing is not exactly clear, but is believed to be an extension of ones own intuitive self. As we all have latent powers hidden in our subconscious which, due to the development of civilisation and sophistication, have been driven deeper and deeper inward, which can be traced back to very early man. If we look at some of the more primitive races, still alive in our present day, they seem to have a deep sense of intuition and know where to look for water and what plants or leaves are required to relieve certain ailments. They do not have books or manuals on herbs, nor compasses to guide them when it is too cloudy to see the sun or the moon.

During the middle ages it was very popular in the simpler peasant classes. However, those who did not use or understand it became frightened and they persecuted dowsers, saying it was "against the church" and therefore evil, unbiblical.

It seems in ancient times "Dowsing" was known everywhere, as there are accounts of it from earliest of recorded history. It is generally believed that the pendulum evolved out of Jacob's rod which he held over the water to detect if it was safe for the cattle to drink. In 1949 a group of French explorers discovered wall paintings in the caves of Taesili. One of the giant murals depicted a dowser surrounded by other figures and it is believed he was dowsing for water. It was discovered the paintings were 8,000 years old.

Originally it was known as RHABDOMANCY, from RHABDOS - a rod, and MANTELA - a prophet. It meant the ritualistic practice of searching for springs, wells and metals.

Moses rod is a startling example of how one could detect things, or casue them to happen. With it he found water, caused it to flow, made the Red sea to dry up and cause the armies to vanquish their foes. The list is endless.

THE IDEA

One must realise first and foremost that there is nothing in the colour, design, material or suspension of the pendulum which has any magic in it. NO magic at all. It all lies in the latent force, that we all have the ability to tap, which sets off a message from the subconscious to the arm muscles which cause the vibrations which puts the pendulum into motion.

There are three basic, different, disciplines which come under the heading of dowsing. These are: Land Dowsing, Water Dowsing and Medical Dowsing (commonly called Healing Dowsing). But under those three headings there are sub-headings. However, it is difficult to separate them. Medical dowsing is the one we want to discuss here.

DIAGNOSIS

Medically, "Dowsing", can be used in diagnosis, in this way a lot of time and expense can be saved. The patient can be fully clothed, lying on a plinth and a scan over the body with a pendulum in the hand of a skilled, trained dowser can quickly determine the root cause of a symptom, or a damaged muscle, organ or bone, etc.. Another way to dowse for a medical problem is to use a detailed anatomical atlas. This way the cause of an illness or disease can be quickly detected, because the examiner is not confused with the symptoms. Once the cause is detected, the type of cure, therapy or medicine can be assertained using the pendulum.

It is not only bodies and minds that require healing, but often buildings, land and water also. That is why it is difficult to separate the disciplines. For example, in over 90% if not 100% of cancer cases it can be detected that patients have slept over geopathically stressed areas. Now it is no use trying to cure or treat a cancer patient and not either move them to a safe spot or cure the affected area. If you choose to move to a safe area how can you be sure it is safe? By dowsing, either with rods or a pendulum. When working indoors the pendulum is easier to handle. If you wish to cure (heal) the area then you require to dowse the spot or area to determine the exact location and direction of stressed EMF flow. Then using of the pendulum again one can determine which method would be the most efficacious to clear it. No hit and miss idea here. No need to say: "try this and see how it goes, phone me right away if things go wrong or get worse". You CAN expect results straight away and experience them.

WHO CAN AND HOW TO?

Now everyone who has full use of their mental powers can dowse. Very few indeed who cannot. However, the first or second attempt may be frustrating. But it is important to realise that a clear uncluttered mind, steady hand and very good gentle breathing techniques along with a relaxed, patient attitude are paramount to good successful dowsing.

Many highly educated and organised professionals, professors, engineers and ministers of religion, to name but a few, use the pendulum on a regular basis. Quite a number of doctors now use pendulums in their practices.

To dowse one can use forked twig, a single twig, a springy piece of wire, a length of fibre glass rod, a corset bone, a button on a thread, or a tradesmans plumb bob. In fact almost anything that comes to hand. However, if one is dowsing over food, a wooden dowel about 2" long with one end pointed, suspended on a thread is most ideal. When dowsing for health, then a clear crystal pendulum is best (a round or pearshaped cut glass crystal one would do). Brass is favourite for general dowsing.

TRAINING IN DOWSING

There are not many training opportunities and most people start off training themselves and become very proficient, but this takes time and discipline. It is essential, however, that those who can dowse, or are interested in dowsing, should join an association or society for dowsers. That way they will learn about lectures and training programmes and not be out in the dark, fumling along. They will learn and be made aware of the pitfalls and dangers, and find out how to overcome them.

BENEFITS

All these aspects of "Dowsing" are aspects of diagnosing in health and healing. Gas leaks, electricity, geopathic stress, underground current/energy, stagnant water in, under or around a house which is a serious health hazard, can be detected and cured by dowsing. It is quick, efficient and very successful as well as accurate.

It is clear for you now, that dowsing can be used in diagnosis for whatever the problem, illness or condition of a patient, human or otherwise. The dowsing instrument, the pendulum, can tell you what is the problem, where is the problem and what should be the solution.

The important thing is that everyone can learn to use the pendulum to detect food and chemical allergies for their families and this would relieve a lot of suffering for the person and family and expensive health bills. Using the pendulum over a glass of freshly drawn water, from the tap, one can quickly detect the presence of electricity and/or heavy metals and other chemicals, then determine the type of water filter would best be suited for clearing the water. It can also be determined if the water straight from the tap is the root cause of any illness or disease, or even if it is aggravating an illness or hampering recovery from an illness.

Likewise, by using the pendulum one can find out if an egg is free range or not, or the avocado is organic or not. In fact, one can find out whether this or that food is good for him or not.

ELECTRO-CRYSTAL THERAPY

Electro-Crystal Therapy is a wholistic and non invasive therapy which combines natural crystals and gem stones in a scientific way, stimulated by pulsed high frequency electricity, from a battery operated generator, to balance energy fields.

ORIGIN

Biologist, Harry Oldfield pioneered Kirlian Photography as a medical research tool in the U.K. and abroad from 1978. From this he developed a three dimensional method of scanning the body using electrical fields, known as Electro Scanning Method (E.S.M.). After discovering that diseased states manifest first in the body's enegy fields, he went on to develop methods with which to treat these energy imbalances. These methods became known as Electro-Crystal Therapy, which now include crystal sound therapy and crystal optical therapy.

THE IDEA

Quartz crystal has piezo-electric properties, which are the ability to respond in a definite and unique vibratory pattern when electrically or mechanically stimulated. These properties are due to the alignment of positive and negative charges within the crystal molecule and lattice structure. This alignment results in a stable and ordered electro-magnetic field. The energy field surrounding a human being is extremely complex and variable. When the energy fields of a crystal and a human interact, the focused pattern of the crystal has a stabilizing effect on that individual's energy field. Other crystals which have piezo-electric properties are topaz and tourmaline. Quartz crystal has the ability to amplify, transform, store, focus and transfer energy. In Electro-Crystal Therapy the crystals are placed in a sealed glass tube filled with a saline solution. This is so that the specimens are surrounded by a conductive electrolyte. The stones are then electrically stimulated at various pulse repetition rates. Whilst pulsed high frequency treatment can be effective on its own, research has shown that, when it is combined with these crystals the spectrum of healing increases.

TREATMENT

As an Electro-Crystal Therapist you will scan a patient by E.S.M. using a special diagnostic meter. The only items of dress you will ask to be removed are large pieces of jewellry and metal belts etc. You will then be able to assess the extent of energy imbalance and therefore to decide upon treatment. Past, present and future disease may be picked up in the scanning. Electro-Crystal works with the energy centres in the body known as the chakras. The use of sound or optical therapy or both is then decided. Treatment takes place with the electrode containing the crystals, being placed over the site of the problem and also against the chakra to which it relates. The settings used relate to the body's natural harmonics. Initially you will sit with the patient to discuss their details. Later, a patient can be left for a period of time to relax and absorb the electro-magnetic forces. Each treatment session usually takes one hour. Several sites may be treated during a session. If a patient is a good subject, improvement in symptoms and/or general well being are noticed within the first few sessions. Once a week treatment is usual, but seriously ill patients may be seen 2-3 times each week at the beginning.

WHAT ILLNESSES AND BENEFITS?

All known disorders have been helped by Electro-Crystal Therapy. Cats, dogs, horses, and fish have also been successfully helped. Acute problems respond very much quicker than chronic illness. Research indicates that most people respond better to regular short treatments rather than to isolated long treatments. There have been no recorded adverse effects due to this therapy.

Note: it must be emphasised that Electro-Crystal Therapy does not take the place of medical diagnosis and treatment.

HEALING

The process of making whole - although all forms of activity that promote wholeness are healing - has, come to mean, specifically, the use of energies present in creation being channelled towards individuals, groups or places either by direct contact or by distant thought transmission.

There is, therefore, a very wide base and variety of techniques that have developed under the term 'healing', many groups not accepting the validity of other groups. But, just as in religions, the basic concepts are the same for all religions, so with healing, the energy used comes from the same source whatever we call it.

ORIGINS

The origins of healing are as old as human kind itself. Wherever compassion for fellow individual's needs was felt, here was the basis of healing. Compassion, that is, without will. All have the ability to heal and we all do in various ways, but it can also be done consciously and be developed and hightened.

In the past this has resulted in a healer, shaman, priest or any one of a hundred different titles being accepted as something special. Now the 'common man' is realising that we have all these archetypes within us, especially the healer archetype.

THE CONCEPT

The basic idea of all healing techniques is to rebalance the inharmonious energies associated with disease states, which then releases and stimulates the body's own healing agencies to rectify the situation. All gentle complementary techniques have this aim in common and, therefore, all can be said to be a form of healing.

The healing most commonly practised is the "laying on of hands", even though no direct contact may be made between healer and receiver. Energy correction can be made through specific interaction points known as chakras or by general methods through single point contact or whole body contact. Choice of the various different techniques that fall under the broad heading of healing is best left to the individual, whether healer or recipient.

It is, therefore, important that a grasp of the available techniques, how they interact and which is best for a given person, is fully understood along with potential pitfalls and problems. Hence, although we all have the potential to heal; developing, guiding and enhancing it is an important role and responsibility of the healer.

TREATMENT

Healing both direct and absent, can be performed anywhere, but preferably in a quiet, pleasant environment.

The process of healing is brought about by allowing oneself to become a channel or vessel for energies

that are capable of activating or moderating the natural energy patterns of the individual. For some this may be purely a thought process, no physical contact being made as occurs in absent healing, particularly. For others a direct physical contact is necessary as in "laying on of hands" and cranial osteopathy. For others still, interaction between the recipient and the healer occurs on a subtle plane with physical contact not being quite made, as occurs with auric and energy balancing healers. Or, a combination of all three techniques may be employed, together with other complementary forms of medicine. Indeed, it is said that inevitably people who practise any complementary methods are using healing, even if subconsciously.

The inner work of the healer is of paramount importance and ongoing, that they strive to understand and heal their own imbalances, thus becoming an ever clearer and more harmonious channel for the inflow of universal energy.

WHAT ADVANTAGES AND BENEFITS?

At no time should the recipient feel uncomfortable with or discomfort from any technique used by a healer, although there is sometimes an initial mild aggravation of the condition following healing. This is the body's attempt to re-adjust.

There is no invasiveness, providing the healer is not attempting to use will-power. Healing is given as an offering and can be rejected consciously or unconsciously by the recipient. The rate of response is left entirely to the recipient; but it does require he or she having enough vital energy to respond, although not necessarily to co-operate knowingly, or even to believe in the process.

It can be carried out from a distance.

It is compatible with most complementary forms of medicine and with orthodoxy.

It should be gentle in its action and produce no antagonism.

HERBALISM

Herbalism is the therapeutic system based on the use of herbs, often taken as teas, in the treatment of the various conditions. Treatment is based on a wholistic approach to health, in common with all the alternative therapies.

ORIGIN

Some people believe that early human beings had an innate knowledge of how to use herbs. They lost this, however, when their societies underwent the various changes leading to the development of civilizations. So to preserve their knowledge of the therapeutic powers of herbs, people had to turn to the animals and observed what they ate when they were ill.

I doubt if there has ever been a society or human community which has not at some stage used herbal treatment as the centrepiece of its system of medicine. As time progressed, people began to write down their findings, recording details of which herbs had been used successfully for which illness. Some of these writings have survived to this day, such as those by the Persian philosopher and physician Avicenna (980-1037), bearing witness to ancient skills in this field.

THE IDEA

Herbalism has long been known as the 'art of simpling'. Herbs were known as simples because one herb can cure many different conditions. There are three basic principles here. The first is that the types of disease found in a certain geographical area to some extent depend on the environmental conditions of that area, and so similarly the herbs that grow in a particular area may well treat the problems contracted in it. This principle may be a bit difficult to put into effect, so most people using herbal treatments will use ready-made remedies prepared by a herbalist.

The second principle is that only mild herbs should be used, because these can be taken freely, and have a gentle effect on the body. The third principle is that high doses of these mild herbs may be used in order to produce the required effect.

Any herb has three functions when it is used in medical treatment. The first is to detoxify the body and to eliminate waste; the second is to strengthen the body to help it heal itself; and the third is to build up the organs.

Herbs are categorized according to their effects on the body. The effects are as follows:

Stimulation: stimulating the vital forces to fight illness.

Tranquilization : for the restless, irritable and nervous patient whose restlessness is an impediment to healing.

Blood purification: and neutralizing its excess acidity.

Tonification: to build up energy, especially for those weak and exhausted, and for those suffering from chronic illnesses.

Diuresis: for balancing the quantities of the body fluids.

Sweating: to induce sweating from the skin in conditions caused by external factors, such as influenza.

Emesis: to induce vomiting, helping the body get rid from the stomach contents, when symptoms of food poisoning or overeating are apparent.

Purging: especially in cases of constipation.

TREATMENT

The idea of Yin and Yang is discussed in the section on ACUPUNCTURE. Further details are relevant here.

Yin and Yang are the essential opposites that form the basis of all opposites. Their physiological roots are found in the integral work of the adrenals. The adrenal cortex (outer part) controls more Yin, which is present in the parasympathetic nervous system responsible for the maintenance of the body, in particular digestion, circulation, and resistance to inflammation. The adrenal medulla (inner part) controls more Yang, which is found in the sympathetic nervous system responsible for resisting stress, for the immune system, and for the protection and stimulation of the primary bodily reactions.

There are a number of rules governing Yin and Yang, some of which give a clear insight into this idea and thus show the way in which the herbalist chooses from the wide range of herbal remedies available. For example, for every condition there exists an opposite, and the extreme of any condition will produce signs of its opposite. Another rule states that Yin attracts Yang, and Yang attracts Yin; also Yin and Yang are relative and so large Yin attracts small Yin, and large Yang attracts small Yang. But Yin also repels Yin, and Yang also repels Yang. Also, all phenomena are constantly changing their Yin and Yang constitution; nothing is solely Yin or Yang, but everything has a polarity; nothing is entirely neutral. As a herbalist, you should look to the Yin and Yang qualities of the body and the whole being, and also the Yin and Yang qualities in the nature of the complaint. Since it is essential that Yin and Yang are balanced if the body is to remain healthy, it is the goal of all herbalists (and indeed of any wholistic therapist for that matter) to restore balance to these two opposites in the diseased person.

Generally, a person whose constitution and diet is Yang (rich in red meat and fatty foods) tends to suffer Yang diseases, while someone whose constitution and diet is Yin (little or no meat and low-protein foods) tends to suffer from Yin diseases.

If the disease is a Yin one, the herbalist will prescribe Yang herbs and will advise the patient to change to a more Yang diet, and vice versa. The foods should be cooked in a way that brings out its Yin or Yang quality. Heat, age, pressure or salt would bring out the Yang qualities of Yin food, such as citrus fruits and leafy vegetables; water, honey, sugar and not cooking bring out the Yin qualities (or rather, neutralize the Yang qualities) in Yang foods, such as meat and root vegetables.

The detailed knowledge of the herbs is obviously very important. All colleges and schools offering courses on herbalism will try to teach you about the individual qualities of herbs: their shapes, tastes, toxicity, when and where to find them, and how to plant, collect, dry and store them. Some schools may also show you how these herbs grow in the wild, and will also teach specific techniques, such as how to make herbal tablets.

Most people think that herbal tea is the only way in which herbal remedies can be taken. In fact there are many other forms and methods: suppository, douche, electuary, enema, fomentation, gelatin capsule, liniment, oil, pill, poultice, salve, smoking, syrup and tincture. Each of these obviously has its own specific application, suited to certain sorts of complaint.

As for the period of treatment, generally the medicinal effects of the remedy are achieved within three days, even in acute cases. However, the patient must continue the treatment for a week or two after the disappearance of the symptoms, so as to ensure a complete cure.

In chronic cases, where the patient has been suffering for years, no cure can be expected in such a short time: it could take months to conquer the disease. As a general rule of thumb, the patient will need a month of treatment for every year of illness previously suffered.

HOMOEOPATHY

Homoeopathy is a treatment system in which the patient is given a specially-prepared medicine. If this medicine was given to a healthy person in high doses, it would induce symptoms similar to those suffered by the patient.

ORIGIN

The word 'homoeopathy' was used for the first time in 1796 in an article by the German doctor, Samuel Hahnemann (1755-1843), who was the founder of this therapy.

This followed numerous experiments by Hahnemann and his colleagues, in which over a period of six years they had injected themselves with different substances, carefully recording every symptom which they subsequently felt. This series of experiments had been initiated by Hahnemann after reading an article by an English doctor, who claimed that quinine was effective in treating malaria because of its bitterness. Hahnemann was not convinced by this, and started injecting himself with high doses of quinine. He soon began to suffer the symptoms of malaria, a result exactly contrary to the prevalent understanding of the way remedies worked, both then and today. It would have been easy to dismiss the results of Hahnemann's experiment as odd and unrepresentative. But he saw further than this: he concluded that the substance which cured a patient of a disease actually induced the same symptoms of the disease in the healthy person. Or put another way, the substance that induced a given symptom in a healthy person could be used to treat a patient suffering from the same symptom. This concept is often summarized as: 'Like cures like.'

THE IDEA

In his first book on homoeopathy Hahnemann laid down the principles of the science on which it is based. To summarize, the principles are: that cure occurs in line with specific laws of nature, and that it is not possible to effect a cure outside these laws; that there are no diseases, but diseased persons; that disease is by nature dynamic, and hence the treatment must also be dynamic; that only one remedy is needed in any one stage of illness, and cure is not possible if that remedy is not given. These principles imply that any treatment should involve strengthening nature's own powers to heal, and thus cure cannot be separated from nature.Furthermore, we should not lay too much emphasis on categorizing diseases in order to apply diagnosis. It is quite possible that two patients could suffer from two different diseases but show similar symptoms, or they could show different symptoms for the same disease. Also, if cure is to be accomplished, the prescribed remedy has to be 100% correct, otherwise no positive results - or only partial success - will be achieved. And for a cure to work, remedies should be changed whenever symptoms change throughout all the stages of illness.

Homoeopathy, in common with other alternative therapies, is based on the understanding that, within

LONDON COLLEGE OF CLASSICAL HOMOEOPATHY

INTRODUCTORY - POST GRADUATE
FULL AND PART TIME
PROFESSIONAL TRAINING COURSES

ALSO

HOMOEOPATHIC CLINICS

FOR PROSPECTUS PLEASE SEND £1 AND S.A.E. TO:

**The Registrar (CAR) L.C.C.H.,
Morley College,
61 Westminster Bridge Road,
London, SE1 7HT.
Tel: 071-928 6199**

*Disabled Access

the body, there is a force which Hahnemann called the 'vital force', and that this force is essential to the correct functioning of the organs. If the natural state of this force is changed or disturbed, the symptoms of disease will appear. Evidence of this force is the reaction of the body to a cold (fever), or to bad food (vomiting).

Contracting an illness is an indication that a change has taken place in the vital force. When that change is total, i.e. when the vital force ceases to exist, death occurs.

We all feel this vital force in everyday life, when our bodies adjust to changes in the weather or in our diet, or when we travel, or in illness or deep sorrow. In all these circumstances we feel the presence of a force which allows us to adapt to new conditions. Although homoeopathy takes disturbance and change in the vital force to be the cause of disease, it recognizes the possibility of outside causes as well. However, these outside causes could not harm the body unless there was a disturbance in the normal state of the vital force, which allows the body to fall prey to sickness.

Homoeopaths believe that suppressive methods of treatment used by conventional medicine have produced an ever-increasing weakness that has been building up gradually over generations. Children have begun inheriting certain sensitivities in specific organs, resulting in defects which are passed on from one generation to the next. This argument applies also to vaccination against disease, which conventional medicine, and the world at large, is so proud of.

So how do homoeopathic cures work?

The remedy is known to produce similar symptoms to the patient's symptoms, and indeed it does so when the patient takes the remedy. This stimulates the vital force to resist the symptoms of the disease whilst also resisting the symptoms produced by the remedy. What stimulates the vital force is the strength of the dose: the remedy induces symptoms stronger than the disease symptoms, and hence this provokes a stronger reaction from the vital force.

TREATMENT

As no two cases are the same from the wholistic point of view, the correct approach here is to study each case without referring to similar cases. As a homoeopath, you would not look at symptoms alone, but consider all aspects of each case, including your patients' physical and psychological characteristics, how they speak and move, their medical history and that of their families, their social and professional circumstances, and everything that might affect the case.

The methods for describing symptoms in homoeopathy are totally different to those employed in conventional medicine, or indeed in any other therapy. Nothing is missed: as the remedies are tested, everything is recorded. Depression occurs between 5pm and 9pm; chronic headache comes on every other day between 10am and 3pm; the patient experiences a fear of sleeping, of not waking up again; pain is felt when you press this or that area; the patient feels a great urge to eat a certain kind of food; a patient with rheumatism likes to leave his leg uncovered when in bed. These are the kind of things that fill the homoeopath's notebook, an essential tool of homoeopathy.

To identify the medicine which relates to the symptoms, you have to ask your patients for full details of what they feel. It is important to know if the pain comes on one side or both sides, or if it is a shooting pain,intermittent or continuous, sharp or dull, when and for how long and in which areas it is felt. Does the patient like to drink hot or cold drinks? Is he or she bothered by high-pitched noises, or irritable? And so forth. Since homoeopathy places a great deal of emphasis on the individuality of the human being, you might prescribe two different remedies for two patients suffering from the same symptoms - or the same remedy for two patients suffering from different symptoms.

After starting the treatment, you should monitor the changes that take place. In general, the symptoms should either move from the centre of the body to its perimeter, or move from the top of the body to the base, or move from the most vital organs to the less vital ones. The symptoms should disappear in reverse order, so that the symptoms that appeared at the beginning of the illness should disappear at the end, and the last to appear disappear first.

Since homoeopaths believe that the cause of illness is a disturbance of the vital force, they normally gives the patient one remedy only, even if the patient is suffering from what in conventional medicine would be categorized as several diseases. Somebody suffering from asthma, constipation and rheumatism, for instance, will be given three drugs by conventional doctors. But if this same patient consulted you, the homoeopath, you would prescribe just one remedy, because you would see that just one problem was the root cause of all three groups of symptoms.

What form do homoeopathic remedies take? Like other medicines, homoeopathic remedies come from a variety of sources: it is the method of preparation that is unique. The sources are plants (about 60%); salts, such as sulphur, sodium and chloride; animal products, such as cow's milk, cat's fur and dead ants; diseased tissues, such as tuberculosis abscesses; substances that induce sensitivities, such as pollen or house dust;substances taken from conventional drugs (in order to overcome their side effects), such as salicylic acid, which is used to make aspirin.

Hahnemann called the method of preparation of homoeopathic medicine 'potentization'. The aim is to reveal the natural essence of the source material, which ought to be in harmony with the essence of the patient. To start with, the extract from the source substance is crushed into powder, then soaked in alcohol, water or lactose for some time to obtain the first solution, which is called the `mother tincture'. One drop is taken from the mother tincture and mixed with 9 drops of alcohol, then it is shaken well and hit firmly against a hard surface to obtain the 1:10 solution. One drop of this solution is then mixed with 9 more drops of alcohol and shaken and hit to obtain the 1:100 solution. This is how the decimal series is made up.

For the centesimal series, 99 drops of the fluid are mixed with one drop of the mother tincture to obtain the 1:100, and then a second time to produce 1:10,000 and so on.

The least diluted 'potency' of a preparation is normally 1:1,000,000 (one in a million), but 1:1,000,000,000,000, the sixth centesimal potency, which is far more diluted, is widely used. But, can you imagine what is left from the original substance, if any, in the 100 and 200 potencies which are widely used in practice, or even the 1,000 potency. It is understandable to think that what tiny amounts are left in such highly diluted solutions will have no effect. But, the startling fact is that these highly diluted solutions are not only effective, but the more diluted they are, the more effective they are! This is in total contrast to the thinking behind the conventional medicine.

As mentioned earlier, homoeopathic medicine is tested on human beings; they are known as 'provers', and the experiments are called 'provings'. Since no animals are involved in testing the remedies, no suffering is inflicted on them for the benefit of other creatures. But, more important, testing on human beings gives far more reliable results: the differences between us and animals make it impossible to justify

claims that a medicine tested on animals would have definite, positive, long-lasting results and with no side effects when used for human beings. The failure of a number of conventional medicines provides some alarming evidence of this.

As a homoeopath, you would take care in choosing the correct remedy, deciding on the correct potency when you have selected the appropriate medicine. Potencies differ in their effect. The general rule here is to prescribe a remedy with high potency (i.e. highly diluted, with more zeros!) for a short period for an acute condition, and a remedy with low potency for a long period for a chronic condition.

Patients taking homoeopathic treatment have more responsibilities than is the case with other therapies. You, the homoeopath, will instruct your patients on how to take the medicine (which should not be touched by human hand), and how to record all the changes and feelings experienced through the various stages of the treatment. You need this information to assess the efficacy of the medicine, and whether it needs to be changed. Two other important points: people undergoing homoeopathic treatment need to have patience, and they need to persevere during the healing crisis, which indicates that the body is responding to the treatment (a common feature of most alternative treatments).

The length of the treatment varies according to the case: the longer that a patient has been suffering, the longer the treatment will last. If the patient's vital force is weak, it is bound to take longer for his or her condition to be cured than would be the case with the patient with a stronger vital force.

There is also the psychological factor which can elongate the time needed for the treatment to be successful. But as in some other alternative therapies, just one consultation, or even one dose, may be all that is needed to clear away the problem.

WHAT ILLNESSES AND BENEFITS?

Homoeopathy is a wholistic treatment which tries to cure diseased people (and animals as well) by restoring and strengthening their vital force, with which their bodies normally and naturally resist illness. Hence, homoeopathy could tackle and cure any case, provided that the rules are abided by. If the correct remedy of the correct potency is given during the matching stage of the illness, and for every stage, a cure could be expected.

Because the correct selection of the remedy is of vital importance, the question of which homoeopath to consult is a crucial matter for the patient. Also, given the fact that there are more than 2,000 remedies to choose from (and the numbers are always increasing with new provings), homoeopathy is far more difficult to practise than conventional medicine, where the specialist usually has no more than a dozen or so medicines to choose from.

HYPNOTHERAPY

Hypnotherapy is the treatment in which hypnosis is used to help the patient get rid of an emotional problem, a harmful habit, an unpleasant condition, or even a physical problem.

ORIGIN

Hypnosis might well have been used by ancient civilizations - the Egyptians, Greeks, Persians and Romans. In more modern times, the Austrian physician Anton Mesmer (1734-1815) used a sort of hypnotism involving magnets to cure problems. Then Marquis de Puysegur pursued Mesmer's techniques further and discovered what was called somnambulism. In the 1840s a British doctor, James Braid, first proved that hypnosis could work without the use of magnets. Despite its early beginnings, hypnotherapy did not advance with each succeeding decade. In fact, it was replaced by psychoanalysis by Freud in the early 1900s after he found he could achieve little by it. Fairly recently, however, hypnotherapy has begun to gain ground again, and to become recognized as a potent form of therapy.

THE IDEA

Hypnosis is a state of heightened suggestibility, and is reached by accessing the link between the mind and the body. Although the conscious mind is relaxed in the state of hypnosis, it is present; meanwhile the words and suggestions of the hypnotherapist work on the subconscious mind. Since the subconscious mind is the one which has been programmed by past experiences, the effect of hypnosis on any condition in which such past experience plays a part can be appreciated.

Hypnosis itself is not the medicine, but is the trance-like state in which the increased awareness of the patient allows the cure to be achieved. The autonomic nervous system is receptive, and so is the subconscious mind which is part of it, and hence, any suggestion by the therapist can reach it without the interference of the conscious mind. Any past experience which is recorded in the subconscious mind can be brought out and dealt with.

The effect of hypnosis on pain remains uncertain. People can be hypnotized - either by themselves in self-hypnosis, or by a therapist - to control pain. If the pain is in your legs for instance, and under hypnosis it is suggested that you do not have any legs, then you may get total or partial relief from pain. By another suggestion, you could be made to imagine that you are taking morphine or any other analgesic drug to remove the pain, and so on.

One theory says that hypnosis works in several ways. It produces relaxation, and so any pain that is caused by tension can be banished or at least reduced; it removes anxiety, which is another cause of pain; and it distracts the patient from pain, and so provides some relief in that way too.

TREATMENT

In any other therapy, all that the patient has to do is to abide by the instructions of the therapist: how to take the medicine, what diet to follow, what exercises to do, and so forth. In hypnotherapy, the cooperation of the patient during the session itself is a very important; without this no positive result can be achieved.

Patients are involved in every part of the hypnotherapy treatment. If they cannot relax fully as instructed, or if they cannot concentrate as required on what the therapist is saying, the therapy cannot be successful. Many people think that in hypnosis a patient is like a toy in the hands of the therapist, and that the patient can be made to do whatever the therapist likes. This is not true, for hypnosis is an intermediate state between deep relaxation and light meditation, and so the patient is fully aware of what is going on: stage hypnosis, as seen on TV, is something else.

If a patient was suffering from a painful condition, and the goal of the treatment was the removal of pain, then you, as the therapist, should consider the matter thoroughly before commencing the treatment. This pain could be an important signal to your patient that the disease needs to be tackled, and the pain may in fact be the best monitor of the patient's condition. By contrast, however, chronic pain is normally useless pain which has done its job, but which has remained behind to hurt, discomfort and depress the sufferer; this kind of pain is best removed.

As a hypnotherapist, you would normally teach your patients self- hypnosis to practise at own home. The reason for this is that most conditions cannot be treated by hypnotherapy sessions at the clinic alone; these sessions need the support of homework. Without techniques of self-hypnosis at their disposal, patients who are being treated for habits or addiction are liable to fall prey to temptation in the interval between sessions. Furthermore, in self-hypnosis patients have a useful tool with which to fight off any relapse that might occur at some future date.

Self-hypnosis is also a must for certain specific cases. The asthma sufferer, for example, may well need to carry out self- hypnosis during an asthma attack, and cannot afford to wait for the therapist to

arrive. Women in pregnancy can also benefit from self-hypnosis, which can be used both when the labour pains begin, and later in the labour ward.

In the first stage of hypnosis, patients are put into a state of deep relaxation. As the hypnotherapist, you then start the suggestions by using one of several techniques. You could tell your patients to visualize in their minds an image or a scene and to incorporate their problems, with their solutions, into this image. Obviously, the image should be beautiful and positive, such as a waterfall, a river, or walking in a beautiful garden, or lying in the warm sun on a soft, sandy beach, or listening to the sounds of birds and the rustle of leaves in the trees, and so on.

For problems of a physical nature, a useful technique is the inner search, in which patients are asked to go to the location of their illness - be it a cancer or a stricken liver, an arthritic knee or a prolapsed disc. Patients are then asked to imagine the disease and its effects on that area, and then to try to fight the disease with their white blood cells, or with the remedies they are taking, or even by imagining external help, such as an army or a pack of animals, entering the area and setting about destroying the diseased cells.

Hypno-analysis is another technique which is used for cases where the problem is a deep-rooted emotional one. Patients are taken back into their past to find the roots of their problems, which they can no longer recollect in the conscious mind.

The length of the whole treatment depends on the case. By the case, we mean here not only the problem, but also the personality and circumstances of the patient, and the relationship between therapist and patient. The sooner confidence is built in you, the therapist, the sooner positive results may be expected.

Some therapists believe that if, after the fourth session, things are not improving, then it might be advisable for the patient to consult another therapist; for if they have not built up the necessary rapport between them by this time, they are unlikely to do so in future sessions. Some problems, however, such as most phobias, smoking, nail biting etc, would not require as many as four sessions.

The length of each session is around 45 minutes, but the hypnosis part should not exceed 20 minutes, as people begin to lose their concentration after that time.

WHAT ILLNESSES AND PROBLEMS?

Any emotionally-based problem may be treated by hypnotherapy. All physical problems would also benefit from hypnotherapy, either by conquering the patient's negative state of mind, which is an obstacle to recovery; or by reducing or removing pain; or by actually destroying diseased cells and building up new, healthy ones by concentrating the power of mind on the body's vital force.

One of the great achievements of hypnosis is its indisputable success as an anaesthetic in surgery. Operations are carried out in many places around the world using hypnosis alone; the hypnotist may sometimes not even be in the same room as the patient, but present only on a television screen. Dr Esdale, a nineteenth-century Scottish physician working in India, performed more than 3,000 operations - including limb amputations and abdominal surgery - using hypnosis alone. Moreover, his mortality rate was between 5% and 10%, while in Europe the rate was about 50%!

There are, however, a few cases where hypnotherapy is unlikely to succeed, or should not even be attempted. Patients suffering from epilepsy should never be treated by hypnotherapy, as they might have a fit during hypnosis, which could be harmful.

Hypnotherapy has little effect on alcoholics or anyone addicted to strong drugs. The former group will always be under tension from the inner conflict which will have been induced by the therapist in the treatment. This will surface subsequently, when the patient encounters the temptations once more in the streets, in public houses, and off-licenses; the treatment is thus likely only to exacerbate the problem, and has a low probability of success. With those addicted to strong drugs, the withdrawal period will prove too hard, unless the therapist has experience of dealing with withdrawal symptoms. In the case of both groups, however, hypnotherapy could form part of the treatment given by a specialized clinic, where patients are kept in during the period of treatment, or at least during the first, crucial stage.

Finally, hypnotherapy is unlikely to work for the mentally deficient or for very young children, for the simple reason that they are not capable of following the instructions of the hypnotherapist.

IRIDOLOGY

Iridology is a diagnostic method in which the eye iris is observed in order to look for one or more of the signs which indicate disorder in the bodily organ corresponding to that part of the iris.

ORIGIN

One day in the latter part of the nineteenth century, a Polish boy called Ignaz Peczely had a battle with an owl and, in the fight, the owl's leg was broken. The boy took the owl home and, while he was bandaging its leg, he noticed a black dot in the owl's eye. By the following morning this had become a black line between the pupil and the edge of the iris. After a while the leg healed, but the black line turned into a white line. This was the first iridology observation.

When he became a doctor, Peczely had the opportunity to study the irises of his patients' eyes. The experience with the owl never left him. Other researchers, then and later, developed this science further, and knowledge in it continues to expand all the time as more is revealed by observations. As each year passes the growing bank of photographs recording patients' irises enable iridologists to compare more data, and hence diagnose more precisely and effectively.

THE IDEA

The iris is the coloured part of the eye. This part of the eye can be divided into sections, each of which represents an organ in the body. When particular, distinctive markings are present on the iris, the location and nature of these markings indicate specific disorders in the corresponding organs. The markings are the work of reflexes carried from the brain to the iris by the sympathetic nervous system.

The iridologist of today can identify about 200 iris markings as a result of the work done by the researchers over the years. The lacuna - open, closed or circular - is the most common of the iris markings. Pale flecks indicate a skin problem. The daisy iris is an effect which results from many markings, giving the iris the look of a daisy, and which indicates a variety of disorders. The tulip sign, in which a thick fibre splits into the tulip shape, may indicate a problem in the sinuses, depending on its location on the iris. The honeycomb sign appears as small, hexagonal clusters and indicates degeneration of the organ corresponding to that location on the iris.

TREATMENT

The first thing that the iridologist observes is the colour of the eyes. There are, you may be surprised to learn, only two proper colours: brown and blue. All other colours are false and indicate abnormal conditions of the body. Green eyes were originally blue, but they turned green because of yellow pigmentation, which may indicate liver or gall bladder problems.

Similarly, most of the brown-coloured eyes of Europeans or Americans were originally blue, but turned brown because of brown pigmentation. As an iridologist, you would study the irises through a magnifier, aided by a small light, recording any sign that shows on your patients' irises on the iris chart.

You would then ask your patients about their medical history and their particular complaints, comparing this information with your iris observations. This is very important, for the iris continues to show signs of disorder even years after that problem has been sorted out, by an operation, for example. Also, some kinds of medication alter the colour of the iris; it is thus very important for the iridologist to know if a patient is taking any medication.

In order to keep a record of the case, the iridologist may take photos of the irises with a special camera. Enlargements of up to 20 times the size of the iris can be produced on X-ray-like film. Photographs and charts are used to compare the patient's markings in the future, and during subsequent reassessment sessions after treatment.

Some iridologists do other tests to back up their iris observations: for instance, they may take the patient's blood pressure to be sure about the function of the adrenals if the iris indicates some disorder. Underarm temperature, taken on three consecutive mornings upon waking, may reaffirm thyroid disturbance indicated by a sign on the iris. A nylon thread can be swallowed by the patient to check stomach acidity, or to see if there is any bleeding. Physical tests can be used to check heart condition, should the iris indicate some problem with the heart.

WHAT ILLNESSES AND BENEFITS?

The most important benefit of iridology is early warning. Through iridology tests, patients can learn if there is something wrong in a certain organ even before illness has manifested itself. By paying attention to this early on, the patient may be able to prevent the disorder from becoming a fully-developed illness. Some diseases take years before they indicate their presence through pain and discomfort.

Many conditions are caused by the accumulation of toxins in one or more parts of the body as a result of defective elimination of body waste, or gland dysfunction, or other causes. They advance surreptitiously, month after month, year after year, until one day they may appear as cancer of the colon, or arthritis of the joints, or diabetes. When illness has reached such advanced stages, even alternative therapists face a difficult task (conventional doctors offer no cure for these conditions). But the iridologist can identify disease in its early stages, and through therapy its advance can be thwarted.

Many people go to the dentist for a regular check-up every six months, even though dental problems are seldom that dangerous or fatal. They should adopt the same habit for iris diagnosis. The iridologist, after diagnosis, could advise them if treatment is necessary, and if so, what kind of treatment. Iridologists know from experience which therapy will be appropriate, and can usually advise patients where to seek it. However, many iridologists are themselves practitioners of one or more other therapies. Indeed, very often the iridologist is primarily a homoeopath, herbalist or reflexologist who has trained in iridology in order to make use of the power of iris diagnosis.

KINESIOLOGY

Kinesiology is the muscle response testing and energy balancing techniques that are performed to detect and correct the minor imbalances caused by the failure of the body's self-righting power to handle the daily minor stressors.

ORIGIN

In 1964, an American chiropractor, Dr. George Goodheart D. C. discovered that specific muscles when gently tested could reveal a great deal about the state of health of the body. He called this new science "Applied Kinesiology". Kinesiology because it relates to energy and movement, and "Applied" because it is information put to practical use.

He found that each muscle could reveal information about the mental, chemical, structural and energy status of associated parts of the body. He asked many colleagues to check his findings, who together formed the International College of Applied Kinesiology (I.C.A.K.). Many more dicoveries are continuously being made by this method of muscle testing.

THE IDEA

The effects of most minor stressors we experience each day are handled by the body's automatic self-righting procedures. Some are not handled so well, they may cause a slight imbalance, which gives rise to the need for the body to make some sort of compensation.

The muscle response testing procedures of Kinesiology can detect and correct these minor imbalances. Each muscle relies on a nerve to activate it, blood supply to oxygenate it, lymph to feed and clean it, and the acupuncture energy meridian which energises it. These in turn rely on energy connections at spinal level. These electrical energy "circuits", largely ignored by conventional approaches, link muscles to organs, to mental activity and nutritional factors.

All disease is the result of stressing the body more than it can adapt to. If enough of these stresses remain unsolved, they can cause changes in function. These functional changes, in time, may give rise to symptoms, which if still unresolved - disease, and ultimately death.

If the Kinesiological "balancing" of imbalanced "circuits" is performed on a regular basis, aches, pains and other minor symptoms are relieved. Everyday small imbalances are resolved as they occur. The accumulation of functional changes is addressed and steps taken to prevent a reoccurrence.

Kinesiological balancing not only solves health problems, but it raises the general health level of the individual. The soundest protection against any form of discomfort or disease is radiant health. The most powerful function of Kinesiology is prevention.

THE TREATMENT

When a person presents for the first time, the Kinesiologist will listen carefully to the reasons which have brought the person for help. They will ascertain whether the individual has consulted a medical practitioner, and whether other forms of therapy have been tried. The practitioner, without prying, will encourage the client to give as much background information about home life, work, food intake, sleep rest and exercise patterns, as is necessary to form a fair picture of possible lifestyle causes.

Then follows the muscle testing analysis procedure which is both gentle and non-intrusive. Any muscle weaknesses or energy imbalances are recorded, and structural compensations noted.

Kinesiological procedures enable the practitioner to determine what needs correcting from the individual's responses to the various muscle tests. One of the great advantages of Kinesiology is that the muscle tests reveal the priority order in which corrections should be made.

It has been observed that corrections made out of priority order may help for a short while, but the problem usually returns quite quickly. This may account for the fact that many people who seek help from various therapies and get relief, find that the beneficial effect is only short lived.

In practice, these priority testing procedures mean that the Kinesiologist does not have to guess at a diagnosis, or form an openion as to what treatment is required, they merely follow the detailed specific corrections procedure by the results of the muscle tests. Everyone gets a different, individual treatment.

Corrections are made in a number of ways. Kinesiology offers techniques to give profound relief to emotional disturbances simply by touching certain points on the head very gently.

Some firm massage of specific reflexes is also used to restore balance to muscles which have tested weak. This can be uncomfortable for a few seconds, but this quickly passes, and full muscle power is quickly restored.

Nutrition has a very powerful effect on balancing muscles and their related organ functions. This fact is used to great value by actually "feeding" the circuits whilst other corrections are being made. A person may be asked to chew a nutrient whilst the relevant balancing points are being touched or massaged.

Lifestyle changes in the four realms of mental

activity, nutrition, exercise and rest, and exposure to electrical factors will be recommended where it is felt they will speed recovery.

East treatment usually takes between fifteen and forty minutes. Research shows that is unwise and unnecessary to give prolonged treatments. Treatments often promote profound changes in bodily functions which may have been impaired for years. It is wise to allow the body to adjust to these changes before more correction are made.

It is preferred to give several treatments in short succession, say two in the first week or two, then once a week, then maybe once a fortnight. The preventive power of Kinesiology can keep people in better health if they have maintenance treatments at whatever spacing they decide, certainly not less than monthly.

The valuable effects of balancing are cumulative provided the benefit of the previous treatment has not been completely lost because too long a time has elapsed.

WHAT ILLNESSES

Kinesiologists do not address disease unless they are professionally and medically trained to do so.

Kinesiology promotes a strengthening and balancing of the immune system, the endocrine and digestive systems and all bio-chemical and bio-energetic systems. It also facilitates mental strength, positivity and balance. In rebalancing the individual, the bodies' own self healing resources are empowered better to deal with any long term functional impairment.

BENEFITS

Kinesiology does not offer "cures". However, remarkable and sometimes seemingly miraculous results do occur from appropriate regular Kinesiological balancing.

Kinesiology has helped many people who had "tried everything", sometimes over many years, to resolve problems they had been told they had to live with.

Lay people can learn safe and simple Kinesiology procedures to help themselves. This can mean less cost for professional help, and faster relief from distressing problems, particularly in the realms of emotional strain and phobias, physical aches and pains, nutrition and weight control.

Kinesiology is easy to learn. In a relatively short time, trainees can achieve remarkable results, safely. The practice of Kinesiology actually benefits the practitioner as well as the subject. Somehow, the balancing of the energies of the one, gives a benefit to the other.

Kinesiology has been quickly recognised as a valuable adjunct to other therapies by professionals in all branches of health care. The American olympics teams use Kinesiologists to tune athletes for peak performance.

There is no doubt that the greatest benefits from using Kinesiology regularly are the defusing of everyday imbalances before they can cause problems, the maintenance of good health, aviodance of injury, and the prevention of disease.

LYMPH DRAINAGE

Lymph drainage, or lymphatic irrigation, is a gentle form of fingertip manipulation/massage that encourages the free flow of lymph, releases blockages in lymph nodes, and generally stimulates and strengthens the immune system.

ORIGIN

Knowledge of the existence of the lymph can be traced to Ancient Greece and the writings of Herophilus. It was not until the 1600s, however, that substantial progress was made in charting the lymph system, and it was Thomas Bartholin, a Danish scientist, who first described the entire system and gave it the name 'lymph' derived from the Latin limpidus, meaning 'clear'.

Considerable progress was made over the next few hundred years, leading Professor Cecil Drinker, a great American researcher, to declare in the mid-1950s that in time the lymphatic system would become recognised as the most important organic system in humans and animals.

THE IDEA

Lymph is a colourless liquid which circulates around the entire body (much as blood does) through a network of veins called 'vessels'. It carries nutrients, fatty acids (essential for good health), white blood cells, and antibodies (which together make up the major part of the immune system), and also drain toxins from the tissues.

Interspersed at strategic points in this network of vessels are lymph nodes (over 650 throughout the body). These nodes are miniature organs, manufacturing and storing lymphocytes and antibodies, and acting as filters to remove toxins from the lymph as it passes through. It is in these nodes that most lymphatic problems arise. Sometimes the nodes are unable to get rid of toxins they have filtered out of the lymph, and they become blocked. As this occurs, following lymph is effectively unable to progress and begins to build up, causing a condition called oedema - or water retention. In extreme cases, serious consequences can ensue, like the loss of a limb.

If blockages occur, it also means that circulating lumphocytes and antibodies are not able to travel freely around the body dealing with bacteria or antigens that have invaded the body. Thus disease - after causing 'flu-like' symptoms - can quickly develop, leading to fever or worse.

Breast cancer (the number one killer for females) is usually caused by enlarged lymph nodes in the breasts which, due to lack of recognition and treatment, may become cancerous. It requires proper training to differentiate the types of lymph node that can be easily treated and those that may require thorough medical examination and treatment.

Many of the more serious illnesses today are related to the immune system, e.g. cancer, Aids, rheumatoid arthritis, lupus erythematosus, Epstein Barr virus, myalgic encephalomyelitis (ME), glandular fever, and so on. Since the lymphatic system makes up the major part of the immune system it becomes imperative to treat the lymph through nutrition, herbs, and irrigation.

TREATMENT

Treatment always begins with a meticulous history and symptoms case-taking, including diet and elimination details. This is followed by a thorough examination of any parts noticeably affected. Very often, the patient will become distressed by swollen 'glands' (nodes) in the throat (particularly left side), under the arms, breasts or chest, groin, the inside of thighs, and behind the knees. There may be water retention - puffy ankles, wrists, abdomen, breasts, etc. - or heavily swollen legs or arms. There may be 'lumps' somewhere in the body. Or there may be a constant weariness, fatigue or lethargy - often ascribed to ME.

A worm, derived from eggs thrust into lymphatic vessels by mosquitoes, can develop to a full 10 cm, with a lifespan of 5 years, and can move around the body - particularly into the lungs, causing problems there (like airborne allergies) - weakening the immune system and creating chronic fatigue. In addition, a circulate in the lymph system, where it sets about overwhelming and weakening the immune system.

Treatment may begin by giving herbal infusions (in the form of a tea to be drunk) for up to a month, to allow obstructions in the lymph to be broken down and eliminated. If this is completely successful, as it frequently is, no further treatment may be required. If lymphatic irrigation is indicated, this is preceded by the application of specially developed lymphoils that penetrate the skin and gently stimulate the flow of lymph. Fingertip and palm-rolling massage and manipulation will usually unblock congested nodes, though in severe cases electro-stimulation might be used.

Lymph irrigation is a pleasant, relaxing experience that occasionally leads to emotional as well as toxic releases.

WHAT ILLNESSES AND BENEFITS?

The list of symptoms is extremely long, and includes the following: poor memory/concentration, mental confusion, irritability, moodswings, itchy scalp, headaches, hair loss/thinning, general fatigue and lethargy, acne, boils, carbuncles, hives, itchiness, oedema/water retention, muscle fatigue, arthritis (some types), cancer (some types, e.g. leukemia, Hodgkin's disease, Kaposi's sarcoma, etc.), ME, glandular fever, allergies, adenitis, bloating, and so on.

Lymphatic treatment invloves looking at all aspects of the patient's condition, including lifestyle, diet, stresses, etc. A complete understanding of the anatomy and physiology of the lymph system is essential before any sort of treatment can be given. *But one thing is clear: one cannot have good health and a congested lymph system.* Treatment is uncomplicated, pleasant, and leaves you feeling and being so much better.

MACROBIOTICS

Macrobiotics is an approach to health in which each individual studies how food, exercise and lifestyle affect their health and matches them to suit their own needs.

ORIGIN

In 1897 Dr. Ishizuka published his conclusion after years of clinical research into the effect of natural foods when applied to various health problems. The basis for his work was the "Yellow Emperors Classic of Internal Medicine" which was said to be dating back to 2600 BC. From 1923 George Oshawa built on this work and gave this approach the name macrobiotics meaning large life. He was acknowledged with re-introducing the characteristics of Yin (calm, relaxed, cool) and Yang (alert, active, hot) in a practical way that can be used in everyday life.

THE IDEA

Macrobiotics is based on the principle that outside influences will affect the internal condition on the body and that these effects can be predicted with a good understanding of yin and yang. In this context yin and yang are seen as two opposing forces whose characteristics can be applied to anything such as people, food, exercise, jobs, activities, sports and so on.

Macrobiotics focusses on food as this is something that is acknowledged as having a deep influence on health; people eat daily anyway and practically there is now a great choice. The principle being that food is absorbed primarily by the small intestine into the blood, which via the liver will largely determine the blood quality. This blood will then nourish all the body's cells. Food therefore is the foundation for good health.

By observing different cultures and eating habits and levels of health, and by observing the effects of a change in diet in a society and the effects on their health macrobiotic practitioners claim to have developed a framework for a diet that is safe, contains all the required nutrients and has been shown to consistently improve health. This is a diet based on grains, vegetables, beans, fish, fruit, seeds, nuts, oils, natural beverages, seasonings, sea vegetables and many other natural foods.

As each person is unique and has individual requirements the balance and uses of these basic foods will vary. The aim is to eat the foods that most suit the individuals health needs and helps them lead the lifestyle they enjoy. Someone who likes to lead a more active, demanding lifestyle would benefit from a more yang diet with a large proportion of root vegetable stews, fish and grains like porridge. Conversely, to relax leafy green vegetables, salads and fruit (all yin) would be increased. In the same way yang foods would have a warming effect whilst yin foods a cooling influence.

TREATMENT

As a macrobiotic consultant your first job is to make an assessment of the person's nature in terms of yin and yang. This is achieved through a range of oriental diagnosis skills including physiognomy, skin diagnosis, sclera diagnosis, tongue diagnosis, pulse diagnosis along with feeling the condition of the various organs and listening to your patient's testimony. The main purpose is to educate the patient to understand their own condition, the likely causes of the symptoms they have and to provide a clear advice. The advice is focussed on their dietary needs along with recommendations for external compresses and exercise.

The macrobiotic practitioner will balance the foods in terms of yin and yang and be able to create special dishes based on a traditional understanding of the healing effects of specific foods.

The patients will often require ongoing advice, cooking classes and follow up consultations to adapt the foods to their changing needs and complete the educational process.

WHAT ILLNESSES AND BENEFITS?

As diet appears to have such a profound effect on health macrobiotics can be applied to almost any illness. It has over the years been mostly applied to disorders of the digestive system. The application of a well balanced diet that is high in natural fibre, low in fat and simple sugars and moderate in terms of acidity has been claimed to help many common problems.

For the disorders of the respiratory system the absence of diary food, sugars and acidic fruits and juices will according to macrobiotic practitioners have a beneficial effect on the lining of the lungs. Improvements have been claimed for asthma, allergies and shortness of breath.

The skin, being one method of elimination, appears to respond quickly to dietary changes. Common problems are treated such as eczema, dry skin, oily skin and acne.

MAGNETOTHERAPY

Magnetotherapy is a treatment system in which magnets are applied to parts of the body as a means of curing disorders.

ORIGIN

In the past, magnets were thought to have magical qualities. The wealthy wore them to prevent aging; Cleopatra wore them on her forehead to maintain her beauty. In some parts of the world magnets were thought to have divine power. One philosopher went as far as to claim that magnets must embody spirits, for only that could explain how they were capable of moving iron. The therapeutic effects of magnets are mentioned in certain religious texts.

But the pioneer of modern human magnetism was the eighteenth- century Swiss-born doctor, Franz Mesmer, who studied in Vienna and developed the idea that man is affected by various forces found in the universe. He was influenced by the theories of the sixteenth-century Swiss physician Paracelsus, who believed in the therapeutic power of magnetism, and Father Hall, a Viennese physician who used magnets to treat patients with nervous disorders.

THE IDEA

The earth is a huge magnet, and the human body is another magnet. The head and upper part of the body are the north pole, and the feet and lower part of the body are the south pole. The right hand is another north pole, and the left is another south pole; similarly the front of the body is north, and the back is south. If these magnetic forces - the earthly and the human - are out of balance, negative effects could occur; if they are balanced, the resulting good effects will bring relief to disturbances and disorders. Insomnia, for example, might be caused by lying with the north and south poles of the body opposing those of the earth. The sufferer might be cured by sleeping with the body's north pole (the head) pointing in the same direction as the earth's north pole.

Numerous experiments in magnetism have been performed on animals, plants and also live tissue. Such experiments have established that living creatures are not harmed by exposure even to strong magnetic forces. This has encouraged the use of magnetic force in treating disorders. Experimental work has also led to the following conclusions: that the magnetic field affects the middle brain, which controls the endocrine system; that it has an effect on every cell in the body; that magnetism has a positive effect on the healing of wounds; that there is a certain interaction between the work of the central nervous system and external magnetic fields, and that exposure to magnetism reduces the sense of pain; and that magnetic fields have an effect on aging. Further experiments have shown that changes in the blood picture occur if the body is exposed to a constant magnetic field, and that the magnetic effect may be retained in the body for several hours after the removal of the field.

In other experiments the life-span of the domestic fly was doubled when it was fed with magnetized sugar, and the live-span of mice was increased by 50% when they were exposed to magnetic fields. Some scientists have projected that the human life-span could be increased to 400 years by using magnetism.

The magnetic fields of the various bodily organs have differing strengths; these can be measured, and this enables the doctor to check if a particular organ is performing normally. If an organ's magnetic field has decreased, it is not functioning properly. If, for instance, the heart shows a comparatively low magnetic field, the patient could take preventive measures against possible heart attack.

But how does magnetism in the human body work?

The most accepted theory is that magnetism affects the substances in the body which contain iron, such as haemoglobin. Scientists have found that, when exposed to magnetism, many chemical and physical properties of water change; that the sedimentation rate of a fluid - and blood is a fluid - changes; and that a weak electric current is generated when a magnet touches the human body, increasing the number of ions in the blood, which has a positive effect on the body as a whole.

In brief, the beneficial effects of magnets on the human body are as follows. Pain may be alleviated as a result from the increase in temperature due to collisions between the secondary currents of the magnetic waves and the magnetic waves themselves. Haemoglobin movement in the blood vessels increases, and this brings down the calcium and cholesterol levels; this also helps to remove waste products on the vessels walls, and so reduces high blood pressure. Magnetism regulates the function of nerves; increases hormone release; increases the movement of blood and lymph; and renews and increases the number of cells; strengthens inactive blood cells and increases the number of the new ones. Magnetism generally improves health and brings increased energy. People receiving magnetotherapy often feel that they can work more without becoming tired. It also has remarkable therapeutic powers, particularly for certain diseases and ailments such as toothache, wounds, arthritis, eczema and asthma.

THE TREATMENT

For a patient with a localized complaint only one pole would be used; two poles would be used for a patient with a general disease. For example, the north pole is used for cases of inflammation, such as arthritis and bronchitis, cancer, bleeding, bone fractures, hypertension, ulcers, kidney stones, and disorders of the liver, prostate, teeth and gums, and kidneys (kidneys suffering partial failure have been restored to normal in some cases). The south pole is used for pain, stiffness, indigestion, flatulence, hair colouring, low insuline production, heart problems, headache and weak muscles.

As a magnetotherapist, you would touch the problem area with the pole in localized cases. But in the case of a general disease, you would put the two poles under the palms of the hands if the problem is in the upper part of the body, and under the feet if it is in the lower part of the body. If the ailment affects the whole body, such as arthritis, both palms and feet should be used.

If the case calls for carrying out the treatment twice daily, or for longer periods, making it impractical to do it in the clinic, you might instruct your patient to use the poles at home.

The two poles used should be of the same power, size and shape. There are several types of magnets: shapes include bars (straight or U-shaped), solid cylinders, hollow cylinders, spheres, crescents, horse shoes and cups.

Magnetized water is used either in addition to the magnets, or as a therapy in its own right. Applications include treatment for kidney stones and digestive disorders. The preparation is simplicity itself. Two tumblers or bottles of water are put on the north and south poles of a large magnet, one on each pole. After 10 to 12 hours you mix the contents of both containers and start using it!

Each treatment session should not take more than 10 minutes daily. However, in chronic cases such as polio, rheumatism and arthritis, the session should be increased gradually to 30 minutes daily, or 15-20 minutes twice daily. The treatment session should take even less time in the case of children, depending on their age.

The complete treatment can last for any length of time, without limits: it should continue until a cure has been achieved. And as in all other therapies, chronic cases take longer to cure than recently contracted diseases.

WHAT ILLNESSES AND BENEFITS?

Since magnetotherapy involves applying magnetic fields to specific parts of the body, or to the whole of the body, and since these magnetic fields affect the blood, the brain and all the cells of the body, it could be considered appropriate for the treatment of any disorder, without exception. Magnetotherapy can help chronic and acute cases, and could start yielding benefits from the very first treatment session.

Magnetotherapy improves blood circulation, induces warmth, and increases strength and endurance. Its greatest benefit may be its power to relieve pain, which is such a common symptom of so many ailments and diseases; it offers quick and effective relief in cases such as toothache or muscular tension, and this can be achieved in one session only.

Restoring the original colour to hair after it has turned grey in old age is one interesting application of magnetotherapy. Another strange phenomenon was spotted by a foreman in an Indian factory producing magnets: he noticed that the married male workers at the factory produced only male offspring!

An important advantage of this therapy is its preventive role. Using magnets regularly helps the body to rid itself of toxins, stimulates its energies and strengthens it. This reduces your chances of contracting infectious illnesses, such as influenza.

Besides the therapeutic value of magnetotherapy, it has many advantages over other therapies. You can carry out treatment whenever and wherever you like; and once you have invested in the magnets, no additional costs for equipment need be incurred.

NOTE: No certificate courses in magnetotherapy are listed in this directory.

MASSAGE

Therapeutic massage is a system of treatment in which the body is manipulated, rubbed, tapped and kneaded by a qualified masseur or masseuse.

ORIGIN

Since the basis of massage is touch, it must be as old as mankind. The ancient Greek physician Hippocrates called it anatripsis, and the Greeks and Romans found it beneficial for the treatment of various conditions such as asthma and digestive disorders; the ancient Chinese, Indians and Egyptians also appreciated the therapeutic effects of massage.

THE IDEA

In addition to the physical manipulation involved in massage, there is another important aspect to it: massage brings with it warmth, comfort, the nearness and company of another person. To touch and be touched means that you are no longer alone; you are in actual physical contact with somebody who can help you, comfort you and appreciate your difficulties. The desire for such comfort is instinctive, originating perhaps from the way that the foetus touches the walls of the womb. The process continues after birth, when the mother cuddles, kisses, holds and touches her baby.

The beneficial effects of touch have now been confirmed by studies. Children become healthier when members of their family are used to touching each other; they sleep better and are more sociable. Touching is a good antidote to many family

problems, helping to prevent the kind of strife that can lead to divorce.

TREATMENT

The treatment room should be very comfortable, welcoming and warm - since the patients will be partially naked. Massage can be performed on a special treatment couch, or on the floor.

To massage the body easily you have to use oil; this should be pure oil, to which a few drops of an essential oil could be added. There are numerous essential oils, and they have a multitude of therapeutic benefits, so their use in massage enhances its healing powers. In fact, massaging with essential oils is also a technique of aromatherapy (see the section on AROMATHERAPY).

Massage consists of a variety of different movements; above all, they should be rhythmic. Stroking is the most common movement, but there arc many forms of stroking, some light, some involving considerable pressure, some with the whole hand, some with just the fingers and thumbs. Other movements include kneading, applying pressure, knuckling and pummelling. Each of these movements has a different effect, and a particular movement should not be used unless its effect is desired. If you want to relax the body, you should not use a motion that has the effect of stimulating it, and so on.

A massage of the entire body (i.e. the feet and legs, hands and arms, abdomen and chest, back and shoulders, head and face) takes one to one-and-a-half hours. Obviously a massage that concentrates on just one area will take less time.

WHAT ILLNESSES AND BENEFITS?

Massage is very effective in relieving physical and mental stress because it relaxes the muscles, and hence the body. Massage can be so relaxing as to send the patient to sleep: it is thus a helpful form of treatment for insomnia.

Headaches can be cured by massage. If the headache is caused by the constriction of a blood vessel on account of muscle spasm, then massage can cure the condition by relaxing the muscle.

Similarly, if muscle spasm is the cause of backache, the problem can be relieved by massage. However, if the backache is caused by spinal problems, such as a prolapsed disc, then massage is not a suitable treatment for your patient.

The pain of varicose veins can be reduced by gently massaging the areas around the affected vein - but not

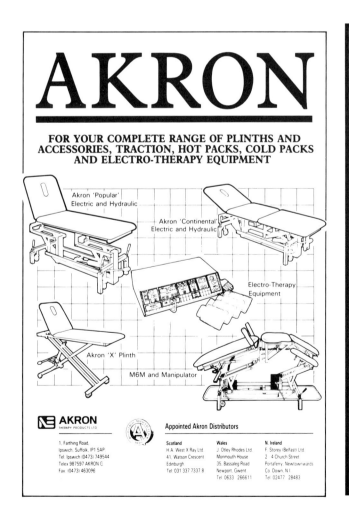

the vein itself. With arthritis, massage around the swollen joint can be of great benefit, but the joint itself should be left alone.

Patients with more serious conditions, such as heart problems and cancer, will also find massage helpful. The pain of angina can be alleviated by massage; and patients recovering from heart surgery can benefit from the relaxing movements of massage, which help to reduce blood pressure. Cancer patients benefit from the physical relaxation of massage as well; and here the other aspects of massage are perhaps more important, the company, warmth and the concern of other human beings.

It surprises many people to learn that babies' ailments can be successfully treated by massage. Colic, constipation and diarrhoea, coughs and colds, and other conditions can all be alleviated by massaging the babies' soft-skinned bodies.

Other areas where massage can be beneficial include drug rehabilitation, pregnancy and childbirth, and slimming. Massage, using the technique of manual lymph drainage, can help rid the body of waste substances faster. The body is massaged very gently following the lymphatic vessels, moving up towards the lymph nodes, which are responsible for the expulsion of toxins from the body. This is something that would benefit anyone, sick and healthy alike; toxins can have a harmful effect on the body and, if allowed to build up, can manifest themselves in various disorders. Manual lymph drainage is useful for any case involving swelling or injury, as well as for dealing with problems of fluid retention, acne and eczema. (See the section Lymph Drainage for detailed description of this discipline.)

FULL PROFESSIONAL TRAINING IN BODY PSYCHOTHERAPY

at the
Boyesen Training Centre
for Biodynamic Psychology

The training is offered in three modules

Module one is a ten-week part-time pre-training course in Bio-release. Bio-release is an experiential educational programme based on the principle that the body-mind has an inherent capacity to regulate itself organically and can thus, if we follow its signals, restore itself to well-being even after severe traumas. The course also has an anatomy, physiology and massage content which leads to ITEC certification in holistic massage. The pre-training courses start in January, April and September each year.

Module two is a two-year basic course in Biodynamic physiatry (physical therapy) with clinical practice. This course is a certificated module (entitling practice) within the four-year psychotherapy course. It runs parallel to the first two years of the four year course and leads to the Satisfactory Completion Certificate in Biodynamic Physiatry. This qualification entitles the graduate to practice the Gerda Boyesen massage methods as a Biodynamic Physiatrist.

Module three is the third and fourth years of the four-year training course in Biodynamic psychotherapy. Satisfactory completion of this course will qualify the graduate to practice as a registered Biodynamic Psychotherapist.

Basic Principles

Biodynamic theory asserts that life itself is an energetic force that pervades all living tissue and forms an energetic field around each person. In the fully healthy person, the life force (also referred to as bioernergy) circulates continuously in ever changing patterns. The circulation changes according to its own laws of harmony and rhythm, and in response to stimuli from the environment, thus giving us a rich variety of moods, sensations and feelings—and joy to be alive. The circulation of bioenergy also fulfils the important function of finely cleansing the body tissue of hormonal and organic waste. This action is similar to the action of an electrical current which, when passed through water laden with organic waste, will purify the water by breaking up the organic material into its component parts.

When we are under stress, or in conflict with our feelings and try to stop them by holding our breath or tightening our muscles, we interrupt the natural circulation of the life force. When feelings are unexpressed and conflicts about them are unresolved, the energy of these feelings becomes trapped in the body and the hormonal and metabolic wastes are trapped in the tissue also. These waste products cause further barriers to the streaming flow of bioenergy. Chronic distortion or inhibition of the bioenergy circulation results. This leads to the development of physical, emotional and behavioural problems.

Biodynamic therapy ranges from treating physical symptoms, psychosomatic symptoms, emotional symptoms, psychological symptoms – right through to helping to resolve spiritualconflicts. As it follows the life force it can be as wide as life itself.

Biodynamic Physiatry

Biodynamic physiatry focuses on physical and psychosomatic symptoms while being aware that the physical, emotional and psychic structures are all inter-functioning. Students of Biodynamic physiatry learn Biodynamic massage and other techniques to free the circulation of the life force. They learn how to encourage and support it in its function of cleansing the body tissue. In this way they are able to relieve many kinds of symptoms which do not respond satisfactorily to conventional medicine; and help their clients to regain their joy in life.

The treatments that they learn to give can have a psychological effect because when the energy of an old mental or emotional conflict is released, the memory and feeling of that conflict can be released also. The course therefore has an essential psychotherapy component. Students are taught the basic theory of psychotherapy processes and how to manage a client's recall of past events. They are required to have regular massage and psychotherapy treatments in order to undergo a process of restoring their own life force circulation to optimum functioning.

<table>
<tr><td>

INTRODUCTION TO BIODYNAMIC PHYSIATRY
Ten-week part-time course in
BIO-RELEASE AND MAP
Leads to ITEC certification in holistic massage.
Starts January, April and September.

</td><td>

LOW COST
HOLISTIC MASSAGE
TREATMENTS
From Biodynamic physiatry students (ITEC qualified)
For appointments phone 081-993 6351

</td></tr>
</table>

For further information contact Alice Jacobus,
178 Acton High Street, London W3 9NN.   Phone: 081-993 6351

NATUROPATHY

Naturopathy is a system of medicine in which different natural methods are administered to promote health and to achieve cure by stimulating the vital force of the body.

ORIGIN

Although the term naturopathy is relatively new, its basis and some of the methods used in treatment are more than 2,000 years old. Indeed, it could be said that the basis of naturopathy is as old as life itself; the first human beings lived in harmony with nature, and it is this harmony that naturopathy seeks to restore to us. It was the ancient Greek physician Hippocrates who first laid down the laws of this therapy.

THE IDEA

Hippocrates' laws of natural medicine state that nature alone can heal, provided that it is given the opportunity to do so; that food should be the medicine; that disease is an expression of purification; and that all disease is one.

The principles of naturopathy are as follows. Firstly, the body has the ability to heal itself by its vital force; secondly, disease is nothing but the resistance by this vital force to abnormal conditions in the body, disturbing the normal functioning of its organs and tissues; thirdly, naturopathy, in common with other alternative therapies, is a wholistic treatment which approaches the patient as a whole, and not merely the symptoms of the complaint.

One of the major causes of disease is bad diet (see the section on DIETARY THERAPY). The other cause is pollution, the spoiling of nature by mankind. The Earth has been polluted by the excessive and continuous use of insecticides and pesticides (poisons used to kill insects and plant diseases on farms), and by chemical fertilizers (used to increase crop yields). It has also been polluted by the poisonous wastes dumped by factories into the rivers. Worse is yet to come with the problem of the disposal of nuclear waste.

The air is being polluted by insecticides and frivolous inventions such as air fresheners, as well as by the massive wood-burning that follows the ever-accelerating destruction of the world's tropical forests, which furthermore reduces that portion of the world's vital supply of oxygen which is produced by living trees. The Earth is now threatened by a consequent increase in temperature which could mean, as specialists predict, a dramatic rise in sea-levels as the ice-caps melt, flooding thcoasts and coastal cities of the world.

The human race has destroyed the balance of nature by interfering with it for the sake of fulfilling short-term desires. It is not yet possible to assess the extent of this destruction; to give just one example, we can cite what happened in Malaysia during the 1960s. The government decided to use D.D.T. in the forests and marshes as a way of controlling the mosquitoes which transmit malaria. The mosquitoes died and were eaten by cockroaches. These became sick and so were easily caught by lizards, which in turn easily fell prey to cats. As the poisoned cats died, the mouse and rat population increased. These attracted plague-carrying fleas. As a result, an epidemic broke out and had soon claimed more victims than malaria would have done over a much longer period.

The poisons which our bodies take in, whether in food, air or in water, are one of the main causes of disease. Add to this the stress of everyday life and we are looking at the basis of most of the conditions for which people seek treatment in our world today.

TREATMENT

As a naturopath, you would seek the real causes of disease. These may be chemical, acquired through pollution in food, and through the failure of the bowels, kidneys, lungs and skin to expel waste efficiently. Or they could be mechanical, arising from muscular tension, joint stiffness or the misalignment of the spinal vertebrae, which would affect the functioning of the nervous and musculo-skeletal systems. Or they could be psychological, brought on by stress or the like.

The naturopath uses a whole variety of measures in the treatment of patients. These include the prescription of a specially- formulated, balanced, natural diet, which might also involve some fasting (see the section on DIETARY THERAPY).

Another important method of treatment is cleansing. Since a basic belief of naturopathy is that most disease is caused by toxaemia, naturopathy relies upon inner cleansing to rid the body of these harmful toxins, and also to correct the body's natural balance, so that natural, continuous cleansing will go on after the treatment has been completed. The naturopath therefore gives the patient natural laxatives at the beginning of treatment to help the intestine to function efficiently; enemas or, more effective still, colonic irrigation, may also be used to cleanse it directly.

In addition to those formed in the digestive tract, naturopathy takes care of waste products expelled by the other systems. Drinking sufficient quantities of water or a prescribed herbal tea, opening the pores of the skin regularly, and promoting sufficient intake of pure air are some examples of the natural ways used to help the kidneys, skin and lungs to function more effectively.

Hydrotherapy is perhaps the second most important category of treatment in naturopathy. By this we mean the use of water or solutions in treatment, including the application of water- or fluid-soaked packs to specific parts of the body. In this way, patients can benefit from the wonderful healing qualities of water and other solutions in their own homes; this may be simply convenient for some, but it may be the only way in cases of severe disability or for those living far way from such facilities as swimming pools or saunas.

Patients of naturopathy receive instructions in how to prepare hot baths to rid their bodies of poisons, fungi and dirt, or to reduce stiffness in their joints; cold baths, by contrast are used to raise energy levels and to stimulate the heart and metabolism; and warm baths are used for relaxation and weight reduction.

The sitz bath is a type of bath in which only the lower body is immersed. A cold sitz bath is prescribed for bad circulation and to release congestion of the glands and organs of the lower abdomen, and is beneficial for invigorating the sex organs; the hot sitz bath is good for relaxation and body warming, and for treating haemorrhoids.

Epsom salts are often used: this is the commercial preparation of hydrated magnesium sulphate, which is dissolved in a bath filled of very hot water, as hot as the patient can bear. This draws poisons, such as uric acid, out of the body through the skin pores. It is very beneficial for arthritis, paralysis, rheumatism, sciatica, injuries, neuritis, and other conditions. Foot- or hand-baths can also be prepared using Epsom salts.

Steam baths follow the same principle as Turkish baths or saunas; there are ways of preparing steam baths in the home. This treatment is recommended for those patients who are also undergoing one of the cleansing programmes. Steam baths draw out toxins through the lungs and skin, and are very effective for reducing the cholesterol level.

The other type of hydrotherapy treatment involves packs, hot and cold. Hot-water packs are used to relieve muscular pain, while the cold-water packs can help to cure headaches, insomnia, high temperature and first aid. Both are simple techniques that have been much valued over the centuries.

Non-water packs of various kinds are also used by naturopaths. One of these is the castor- oil pack, used by an American naturopath called Cayce for more than 50 different conditions, and dubbed by him "the palm of Christ". Others include the potato pack for the eyes; the turpentine pack for menstruation, cystitis and other vaginal pains; the Epsom salt pack for arthritis, colitis, gastritis, injuries, influenza, sinus problems, tumours, and many other complaints; the eucalyptus pack for tuberculosis; the grape pack for poisoning, flatulence, ulcers and colitis; the ice pack for fever; the onion pack for asthma; the pine-needle pack for epilepsy. There are many others.

Rubbing the body, or the affected parts, with oils is another method of treatment used in naturopathy. The oils themselves possess healing qualities; the effect of the massage itself is dealt with separately under the section on MASSAGE. Cayce and other naturopaths prescribed a wide range of oils for the different complaints. A mixture of peanut oil and olive oil, for example, is used for arthritis, Parkinson's disease, kidney disorders, accidents and menstrual problems. Peanut oil on its own can be used for polio, paralysis, low vitality, bad circulation, ulcers, gland disorders, and other complaints. Other oils include castor oil for sprains and arthritis; olive oil mixed with myrrh for varicose veins and fractures; camphor and peanut oil for prostatitis and incoordination of the nervous system.

Of course different mixtures are used for these same conditions in different parts of the world. People everywhere have benefited from the oils of trees, flowers, herbs and other plants. Whatever substances are to hand - even mud - have been tested for their beneficial qualities; gradually knowledge of these has been built up, representing a wealth of experience which is passed down from one generation to the next.

Several other techniques may be used by a naturopath. One of these is cupping, which dates back thousands of years. Blood is forced to flow into a specific area, usually the painful one, to relieve pain or to give general relief. The Chinese use cupping extensively. Another is bleeding, in which blood is released in order to bring (temporary) relief from pain. Modern conventional doctors have seen the potential of this natural method of treatment in dealing with certain conditions, such as high blood pressure and blocked arteries. It has been observed that younger women rarely suffer from such blockages, perhaps because they lose a certain amount of blood regularly every month during menstruation; but they start to experience this problem after the menopause.

The naturopath can now also make use of some of the electrical instruments that have begun to become available in recent years, such as the transcutaneous neuromuscular stimulator. This generates one or more electric currents which are applied to the parts of the body where the symptoms have appeared, or to those related to them (acupuncture points for instance), using pads made of rubber or a special kind of paper. This treatment might be used for paralysis, arthritis, sciatica and other similar problems.

Whatever the treatment that you, the naturopath, prescribe for your patients, you should be able to detect a pattern in the progress towards cure in most cases. First to be observed will be a gradual improvement in the patient's general health, accompanied by one or more healing crises, which indicate that the patient's body is responding positively to the treatment. Next, the old symptoms will be observed, appearing in reverse order usually. As in homoeopathy, the first symptom of the illness should be the last to reappear in during the treatment. Lastly, there will be a migration of the disease from the deeper organs and tissues to the more superficial ones, from the more vital organs to the less vital ones.

It is of utmost importance, in naturopathy as in most alternative therapies, that the patient is informed in advance about the healing crises and reassured that this is a good sign, not an indication that the therapy is wrong. It is sad indeed to see patients abandoning treatment simply because they think that the treatment is doing them even more harm than the disease. Educating the patient about this aspect of therapy, and encouraging patience and perseverance, are essential to the success of the treatment, and should not be overlooked.

WHAT ILLNESSES AND BENEFITS?

From the above examples of baths, packs and massage oils, and their application, it will be clear that naturopathy covers the whole range of diseases and ailments. Like other alternative therapists, the naturopath is a wholistic healer and so is not restricted to a specialized field, as specialists in conventional medicine are. The naturopath tries to cure the diseased person, regardless of whether that person suffers from what, in conventional medicine, would be labelled as several quite different diseases.

If the world followed naturopathic principles and philosophy, it would enjoy all kinds of benefits, not least of which would be a massive reduction in medical bills. A healthy and natural way of living is the best protection against all kinds of disease - and especially those chronic conditions which cause so much suffering to their victims.

NEURO-LINGUISTIC PROGRAMMING

Usually referred to as NLP, this rapidly growing discipline involves unusually sophisticated and effective communication skills. It is most often used in conjunction with other disciplines and is especially suited to improving relationships with patients, information gathering, and dealing with emotional or behavioural problems.

ORIGIN

The field originated at the University of California in the mid-seventies. Two researches, John Grinder and Richard Bandler, worked with three top psychotherapists, Fritz Perls (Gestalt Therapy), Virginia Satir (Family Therapy) and Milton Erickson (Hypnotherapy) to find out what they were doing that worked so well. They discovered that underlying their very different approaches, they used a shared set of powerful and effective skills and processes. They called these discoveries Neuro-Linguistic Programming to reflect their belief that human experience is made up of the processes of our nervous system and language and that it has patterns of both structure and sequence. They started teaching the skills and processes that they had discovered to other therapists. Because of the effectiveness of these skills, the field has grown very rapidly, both within health care and outside it.

THE IDEA

Some people are more gifted at living than others. They lead lives of greater health and wellbeing. They also enrich the quality of life of those that they come into contact with. And yet, there has been no way of describing just what it is that they do differently, most of which is out of their conscious awareness.

Another way of saying this would be to say that each person unconsciously constructs their own reality, their own model of the world. This personal reality, which we each live in, is all made up. Once we know how it is made up and what it is made up of, it becomes a lot easier to make it up more the way we would like it to be.

Gregory Bateson, the British writer and creative thinker, was a Regent of the University of California and had studied many different subjects including biology, anthropology, psychotherapy and cybernetics. His life work was a quest for the differences that make a difference to our quality of life. He encouraged John and Richard to work with top psychotherapists and he influenced the creative approach they took to this research work. Together, they created a new approach to their research work which they called modelling.

The basic idea is that what we have been taught to think of as inborn qualities, talents or attributes are simply learned skills. If somebody can do something, then, since we have all got the same nervous system, in principle anybody can learn to do the same thing. The question becomes, how specifically? Modelling is the process of discovering, testing, refining and passing on to others, the out of conscious skills and abilities that constitute excellence in any field.

One of the reasons why NLP has become so popular with many different professional health workers is because it provides an effective and rapid way of learning the skills that the best therapists have spent a lifetime learning intuitively. Increasing the effectiveness of therapy produces more satisfied clients, a better word of mouth reputation, and a more successful practice.

Probably the vast majority of NLP treatments are carried out by practitioners of other disciplines, for example acupuncture of hypnotherapy. In fact, one form of hypnotherapy, Ericksonian Hypnotherapy, is a blend of NLP and Milton Erickson's style of hypnotherapy. Perhaps the reason for NLP's rapid spread into other disciplines is threefold. It is effective. It is a very recent discipline and has only been around in the UK for 10 years. And finally, its name is not noted for its user friendliness!

TREATMENT

The first thing that the therapist does is to establish a friendly and relaxed atmosphere. This is essential since successful treatment depends on a good relationship within which to apply unusually effective communication skills. The therapist will assist the client in clarifying what specifically has brought them to see the therapist, and exactly what they want to get from the consultation. This includes the identification of how they would know if they had got it, and taking care of any undesirable side effects that the solution to the problem might have brought with it. This concludes the information gathering and diagnostic stage of the consultation.

The therapist then chooses whatever combination of skills and techniques is most appropriate for assisting the client in making the changes that they want to make. The typical NLP practitioner will have around twenty major change processes to choose from plus a large number of minor variants. These range from enabling the client to change a simple behaviour or emotional response, through to identifying and changing limiting core beliefs about themselves, others or the nature or reality. In all these cases they will be assisting the client to identify and apply their own resources until they have succeeded in making the changes that they wanted to make. The therapist will pay exquisite attention to the clients verbal and non-verbal communications and will tailor their own communications towards the style that works best for their client. They may work predominantly at a conscious level, or more intuitively using metaphor and the subtle techniques of Ericksonian Hypnotherapy.

To summarise, the therapists approach will be wholistic, varied, client-centred and effective in terms of enabling the client to create the results they want. The typical length of a consultation will be between one and one and a half hours. The typical number of consultations being about average.

WHAT ILLNESSES AND PROBLEMS?

Where emotional or behavioural problems are concerned, NLP is often extraordinarily effective. Some of the problems that it is most frequently used for include building self-confidence, eliminating phobias, healing traumas, sexual abuse and physical abuse, reponding positively to criticism, gaining independence in relationships, overcoming fear of public speaking, resolving grief, recovering from shame and guilt, positive parenting, overcoming stammering, resolving internal conflict, slender eating strategies, decision making and positive motivation.

Where mental problems are concerned like poor spelling, ineffective study habits or exam nerves, there are techniques and skills that can markedly improve performance.

Where illness and physical problems are concerned there are a few techniques for healing illnesses including allergies and addictions. However it is probably in the psychosomatic side of illness that NLP has more to offer. For example, modelling the qualities of exceptional patients enables others to learn the internal attitudes, habits and beliefs that the bodies natural ability to heal is made up of. Current NLP research is exploring areas such as AIDS, cancer and longevity.

With regard to matters spiritual, it offers processes for empowering people through exploration and clarification of their life mission and purpose.

It is perhaps a little ironic that NLP evolved not as a therapy, but from the modelling of human excellence, and, along the way, discovered a very elegant technology for resolving human problems.

NUTRITION

Nutrition is recognised by most workers in the field of Wholistic Medicine as being an important back-up and support to the health of any individual. It is therefore widely seen as a most important aid to health, as an essential step in *prevention* of illness and, in cases of sickness, as something that really needs to be attended to if there is to be an opportunity for full recovery.

There is wide recognition of the adage that "you are what you eat" and hence that the biochemistry of the body cannot be normal while the raw material being taken in is poor in quality or is grossly out of balance with regard to the proportions of the essential nutrients. These nutrients are needed for the enzyme systems which supply the cells of the body with energy, and hence are crucial to every aspect of the body's economy and function.

In this preventative and supportive role, nutrition is seen as promoting better health, of itself, and also under-pinning, in a most significant way, the beneficial actions of other therapies.

Persons qualified generally to advise about Nutrition are often referred to as 'Nutritional Counsellors'.

ORIGIN

The idea that food is very important to maintain and under-pin good health and to facilitate recovery from poor health is very ancient, indeed, and re-apperas in a multiplicity of cultures. Diet plays a very significant part in Chinese Medicine and in Ayurvedic Medicine and was re-stated by Hippocrates in the early days of European culture.

THE IDEA

Part of the idea is that bad diet is one of the major causes of disease. Much of the food consumed today is far from wholesome. Modern farm practices, the methods used for storing, processing and cooking foods, and the formulations used for 'convenience' packetted and canned food are all to blame for producing foods which are both deficient or out-of-balance with respect to nutrients and which are also heavily contaminated with additives and toxins. The worst, the so-called 'junk foods', contain little of nutritional value apart from empty calories and contribute badly to toxicity and imbalance.

The use of chemical fertilizers on farms is a direct cause of mineral deficiency and imbalance in crops. Unfortunately, for the sake of increasing quantity even at the expense of quality, this way of farming has become the norm in the last several decades. In addition, pesticides, hormones and drugs used on plant crops and livestock, enter our food-chain and represent agriculture's contribution to our toxic load. Food manufacturers contribute chemical preservatives, emulsifiers, bleaching agents, curing salts and artificial colours and flavours, as well as many more.

Modern choice of foods by the consumer has become terribly bad, having little regard for anything apart from instant gratification of the palate. This makes a really major impact upon development of health problems and is often especially bad in children. Cooking methods, both at home and in catering, often do much to spoil nutritional value. Moreover, the pace and complexity of modern life encourages hasty consumption of ready-made processed foods. Hence, many food specialists in Western countries have recognised that while the population have large quantities of food much of it is very low in quality and that the outward appearance of health in such populations is hiding serious deficiencies which express themselves in the very high incidence of chronic diseases.

Pollutants and toxins from non-food sources also contribute in a major way, including household and garden chemicals, occupational exposure to chemicals, atomspheric pollution (especially products of combustion), cigarett, smoke, hydrocabons, lead, oxides of nitrogen, aluminium in saucepans, copper in water reservoirs etc. Our orthodox medical services administer chemical drugs to the population, very widely indeed, (which are also synthetic pollutants of the body), which burden our systems, suppress the body's natural responses and often do very specific biochemical damage.

All this point to modern Man having a very nutritionally deficient and poisoned system. The cells of the body lack sufficient of the micro-nutrients they need to permit cell respiration to proceed at a good rate, and that results in a relative lack of cell energy that is required to provide for movement, thinking, digestion and scores of other body processes. We start to under-function and the immune system, which is particularly dependent upon good levels of micro-nutrients, under-functions or mis-functions. Allergies, over-sensitivity to the environment, weakness, confusion, emotional imbalance, indigestion or ineffective digestion are often the result. Problems of the liver, kidneys, skin, and reproductive problems are also liable to occur. Auto-immune diseases are particularly prone to occur, due to the special vulnerability of the immune system to conditions of nutrient lack or toxin burden.

TREATMENT

In its simplest form the treatment may consist of just replacing the patient's diet with a relatively toxin-free and 'balanced' diet, comprising whole-foods. Such a diet may also involve a calorie restriction where the subject is over-weight. Such work may sometimes invlove the use of a single standard diet or just a few standard diets and in this form, nutrition is often found used as a therapeutic adjunct to other therapies by practitioners of other disciplines who have only very limited training in the field of nutrition. Such practitioners do good work but always do well to deepen their knowledge and training.

However, diets of this kind can often be very useful in themselves because they help to make patients more aware of the dietary and nutritional dimension in their health. In some instances, a change of diet of this kind may be all that is necessary to make the difference between deteriorating health and gradually improving health. Therefore, we have plenty of examples of 'cures' being reported from simple changes of diet of this kind. For a great many other people, the adoption of a standard 'good' diet along the above lines, may prove itself as an effective preventive. People who would have otherwise succombed in the future to chronic complaints, can maintain themselves instead in a good state of health through simple adoption of dietary practices which avoid the worst excesses and abuses of the modern Western European or North American type of diet.

Restriction of fat, achieving a balance between fat types, inclusion of sufficient plant fibre, use of fresh fruit and vegetables, avoidance of packetted and processed foods, avoidance of the abuse of dairy products, wheat, sugar, salt and stimulant beverages can, in themselves, prove to be very potent measures for _prevention_ of future ill-health.

This shows that a great deal of good can be done by people with just a modest amount of knowledge, because they work in a culture in which even the simplest and most basic requirements for the nutrition of the body are routinely flouted.

Such practitioners may often also suggest the use of individual nutrients as supplements or the use of balanced multi-formulae which contain a spread of nutrients.

However, when nutrition is offered in the form of fully professional counselling, it is, and needs to be linked with additional expertise. this often takes the form of careful measurements and calculations, designed to ensure the subject's return to a more 'normal' nutritional status. At this point some form of diagnosis has to be used to indicate the nutritional measures that are needed. It is the application of these diagnostic measures, their interpretation, and the translation of the results into 'treatment' measures, on an individual case-by-case basis, which then dictates that Nutrition should be applied by fully trained people and in a fully professional way. This is true regardless of whether the diagnostic approach used is to be by ;

1) Analysis of diet.

2) Analysis of specimens of hair, blood, sweat etc.

3) Symptomatic (i.e. dependent upon medical condition or symptoms).

or 4) Naturopathic.

Diagnosis by analysis of diet is approached by taking full details of present or past diet and analysing it to assess its content of essential and important nutrients. From that the practitioner assesses the likely state of the patient's body in terms of excesses and deficiencies of specific nutrients. Diet and supplements are then prescribed which aim either (a) to restore a balance to the intake of nutrients or (b) to go further than this so as to provide excesses in the future diet of nutrients which were formerly deficient, and to eliminate of any excesses from the past diet.

The main limitations of the 'diet analysis' approach arise because it omits, in itself, to correct those factors which make for poor utilization of the diet eaten, both in terms of intestinal absorption and cellular uptake.

By analysis of samples of blood, hair, sweat etc. the aim is usually to detect any deficiencies or excesses in the sample material and to treat the patient with the respective nutrients until the levels in future samples are within the normal ranges. The main limitation of this approach, although it is quite widely used, is that the levels of *cellular* nutrition are not necessarily reflected at all accurately in the results obtained from body fluid or hair. It is, of course, the levels of the nutrients inside the cells which determines the activity and integrity of enzymes and hence the vitality of cell function. A name often given to this approach of concentrating upon normalization of analytical figures, is *orthomolecular nutrition.*

Prescription according to symptoms or illness, depends, of course, upon known relationships between individual medical conditions and specific types of nutrient imbalance. This approach has a certain validity, because illness conditions do have their own nutritional characteristics. But this approach should not really be applied without full reference to wholistic principles.

The use of Naturopathy diagnosis provides a great deal of information about the condition of tissues, organs and systems of the body. This approach leads on towards applying specific treatments that are aimed at the naturopathically diagnosed condition and hence towards Dietary Therapy (please see the section on this also).

WHAT ILLNESSES AND BENEFITS?

Healthy living is the best means of preventing disease. When it comes to reversing an already developed disease process, one uses the methods which are basic to healthy living, but takes them rather further. These principles apply to chronic states of health generally, and it is hard to pick out specific conditions that would benefit more than others from following good dietary and nutritional practice. Nutrition is very supportive to health across a very broad spectrum. More than anything else it serves to show us "the unity of all disease".

OSTEOPATHY

Osteopathy is a treatment system which tries to cure the various disorders, whether mechanical or otherwise, by treating the body's mechanical system of bones, muscles, joints, tendons, ligaments and the connective tissues with manipulation, massage and exercises.

ORIGIN

Manipulation and manual treatment are not new. The ancient Greek physician Hippocrates used such techniques, and all communities of the world have traditions of such treatment, but they are normally only used to deal with mechanical problems of the body.

The idea that manipulation can be used to cure disorders other than mechanical ones was first explored in the work of the American doctor Andrew Taylor Still. In 1874 he started to use the manual techniques of the treatment which he called osteopathy. The first osteopathic school was opened by Dr Still in Missouri after eighteen years of successful practice.

THE IDEA

Andrew Still believed that the body is able to heal itself, but that the blood and nerve supply to all the tissues of the body should be uninterrupted if they are to work properly. If any mechanical disorder affects the blood or nerve supply to the tissues, the self-healing process of the body is impaired and the tissues become diseased. Still therefore set out to form a system of manipulative treatment which could cure all mechanical problems, and hence any disease caused by them.

In common with chiropractic, osteopathy places great emphasis on the spine and its importance to the health of the whole body, for the nerve supplies to the various organs are channelled via the spinal cord. Any interference with the nerves to and from the brain through the spinal cord can affect the natural performance of the tissues to which these nerves are connected.

There are three principles for healing. The first is that the healthy body has its own capacity for defence and repair. The second is that the body is one unit, and any disorder or abnormality in the functioning of one part negatively affects the other parts. The third is that the body can defend and repair itself best when it is at its maximum mobility and flexibility.

The musculo-skeletal system, consisting of bones, muscles, ligaments, tendons and fascia (the layer of bands and sheets of fibro-elastic tissue which envelopes the whole body beneath the surface of the skin), forms one structural unit which, when disordered, can effect changes in the other systems of the body.

Dr Still laid considerable emphasis on the fascia, stating that the fascia was where the osteopath should look for the cause of disease, and that it was where the work of remedies for all diseases should start. As mentioned above, osteopathy pays particular attention to the relationship between the spine and the different organs of the body. This relationship centres upon the ingoing and outgoing nerves in the spinal cord, which lies in the spine, and the organs that these nerves supply. The osteopath, therefore, believes that a disturbance to an organ will inevitably occur if the nerves that link it pass through injured vertebrae.

However, the osteopath also believes that there are other factors which might cause, or contribute to, disease - such as dietary, genetic, environmental, psychological or bacteriological factors. Osteopathy makes no claim to be able to cure disorders caused by these factors.

In addition to the effect of the vertebrae on organs, on account of their effect on the nerve supply, osteopaths believe that disease can be caused by disturbance to any part of the nerve fibre. This includes what is called `osteopathic lesion' in the area adjacent to the nerve fibre, such as in a wrist, elbow or shoulder, in which the fascia has been inflamed. These disturbances are greater when the nerve fibre passes through bones, especially in the base of the spine. When the nerve fibre is impinged, a change in the harmony of the pulses that are sent through it occurs, and hence symptoms begin to be revealed.

Osteopathic lesion is a specific condition that could happen to any joint. If a joint moves in a way which is unusual for that joint, then a fixation may occur, and the joint will be held by the supporting ligaments, tendons and muscles in a position which is at the extreme limit of its normal range. Since it is held within its maximum range, however, the lesion will not be recognized as an abnormality by a doctor examining an X-ray. Osteopathic lesion could result in the entrapment of the nerves near to the joint where osteopathic lesion has occurred, or even in the inflammation of the nerve in a neighbouring area. It could interfere with the blood supply, or even cut it off completely. Damage to a vertebral disc may also occur, because if the condition is not treated the disc becomes less capable of absorbing water from the blood and lymph. The joint may also become worn.

Posture is an important matter for the osteopath; this could have a direct effect on the future health of the patient. One factor that might affect the posture of the patient is occupation: if certain muscles are used continuously in a specific way, this can force the body to adapt to the changes in the movement of the joints. Inherited factors have their effect as well; thin people seem to be more prone to disease than stocky people, but are easier to treat. Another factor is structural abnormality, such as what might be caused by dislocation of a joint during childhood.

TREATMENT

As an osteopath, before you even begin to take the medical history of your patients, you would observe their posture and movements, and how they walk and sit. You would look at the condition of all the joints, including the ribs, from which you could learn the patients' breathing habits. You would also look at the skeleton in general to observe its type of structure, and to see what abnormalities or occupational traits are present. You would also note the condition of the muscles: for instance, if you noticed a stoop, you would look at the large muscles supporting the spine to see whether there was anything here to be corrected, or whether the body had adapted to it.

Then you start with the surface of the body, carefully examining it using a special technique called palpation, which is unique to osteopaths. You should see if any structural changes, however minor, have occurred. With deep palpation you learn about problems at a deeper level: this is an important technique for examining the fascia.

Finally, you should examine the tendons and ligaments, and the way that they relate to the joints. The osteopath may not rely on X-rays for diagnosis, but may sometimes ask for them to make sure that osteopathic treatment is appropriate for the condition in question.

The treatment itself involves many techniques; the choice of which to use depends on many factors, such as the patient's size and posture, the nature of the problem, and the condition of the joint which is causing the problem. If the joint has been restricted

for a long time, the osteopath would not attempt to restore it to its normal position.

One of the most commonly used techniques is the high velocity thrust, which releases joint fixations. Other techniques include stretching and massage. The massage technique is not the same as that used by a masseur, or anybody practising massage at home. It is a soft-tissue treatment, in which the osteopath deals with the soft tissues lying immediately beneath the skin. This technique derives from Dr Still's advice to look first of all for the cause of the problem, and then to begin treating it at the level of these soft tissues or fascia.

An important part of your responsibility as an osteopath is to ensure that the problem will not return or get worse; you must therefore advise your patients about the correct way to use their bodies, and about the posture position that they should adopt, at work and in their leisure hours. You must also convince them of the importance of suitable exercises that will help them to maintain flexibility in the body and spine.

The duration of treatment depends very much on the case itself. The first treatment session might take an hour or so, during which the medical history is taken along with other pertinent information, and might include some treatment. In chronic cases, you would put the patient on a programme of short treatment sessions spanning a long period of time, with the periods in between getting longer gradually. If the problem was recently contracted, however, or if the patient's posture and movement needed to be improved, which would be mainly the patient's own responsibility, treatment sessions need be few.

WHAT ILLNESSES AND BENEFITS?

Although it differs in some of the basic ideas, in its general approach and in its treatment techniques, osteopathy's benefits are similar to those of chiropractic: it is very good as a preventive therapy; it is very effective as a means of relieving pain. Osteopathy can be used to cure problems that are not mechanical, but which are caused by a change in the normal condition of the structural system. Some cases can be cured in a single session by the high velocity thrust, a technique used in different ways by both therapies.

However, osteopathy does not limit itself to the spine, and its treatment extends to techniques that are designed for the various parts of the body, such as the soft-tissue massage. Thus osteopathy is capable of dealing with a wider range of problems, mechanical and otherwise.

POLARITY THERAPY

ORIGIN

Polarity Therapy is both old and very new in origin. The elements of Polarity Therapy were brought together by Randolph Stone, a Chiropracter, Osteopath and Naturopath who practised in Chicago from the early 1920s. He sought to discover the unifying factor behind the many systems of healing. This quest led him to investigate, among other things, the traditional healing arts of India and China. He also studied the early alchemical healing techniques of Europe and the Middle East. He synthesised his knowledge into the system that he named Polarity Therapy.

THE IDEA

The unifying factor behind Polarity Therapy is the concept of 'vital or life energy'. Randolph Stone recognised that a parallel could be drawn between the human body and an electromagnet, in that a magnet has a positive and negative pole with a magnetic field extending between them. Such fields are also produced by electric currents.

The body too can be viewed as an electromagnet or, perhaps more appropriately, as a biomagnet, with its own bioelectrical currents producing a field around it. In an ordinary ferric magnet, the atoms are aligned so each tiny individual magnetic field combines to produce one large field. The atoms of the human body too must be lined up or polarised with respect to each other or the biomagnetic field of the whole body will be disrecognised and the result will be ill health.

If a magnet is dropped onto a hard floor, the magnetic field weakens because the atoms are shaken out of alignment. The body reacts in a similar way to trauma, injury, stress, exposure to the electromagnetic fields of electrical appliances etc.

POLARITY HEALING COURSE

A short course of instruction for qualified practitioners or nurses who wish to use the gentle power of touch combined with Polarity principles to heal the human body.

For current details Tel **W. Douglas Bell on 0292-280494.**

THE SCOTTISH SCHOOL OF REFLEXOLOGY
2 Wheatfield, Ayr KA7 2XB   Telephone: 0292 280494
Principal: W. D. Bell

Polarity Therapists work to restore balance and to release obstructions to the free flow of life energy in the body in a complete and natural way. Once this is achieved the body-mind-spirit continuum that is a human being, will return to its natural state of balanced and harmonious functioning.

TREATMENT

Therapists use four different approaches to balancing the life energy: bodywork, nutrition, exercise and counselling. A typical session will consist of a bodywork treatment which might be combined with work in another of the three areas.

The bodywork consists of skilled, hands-on contact to free and balance the energy flow by using different kinds of touch, sometimes rocking the body, sometimes using a deeper touch to break congestion and sometimes just moulding the hands to the body and holding. The effects can be profound, affecting body tissue, mind and emotions.

Nutrition advice may be given, which is designed to have a purifying and energising effect. Exercises, sometimes called polarity yoga, may be recommended and these are also designed to encourage the movement of energy within the body. Finally, communication or counselling to facilitate greater self awareness and encourage more positive attitudes to the body and to life itslef, may be used.

Most sessions last between 30 and 60 minutes, at first, it is usual to have weekly sessions. After that, the number and timing of sessions depends on progress. There are three schools of polarity therapy in the UK, each with a different emphasis in terms of the four treatment modalities.

WHAT ILLNESSES AND BENEFITS?

Polarity Therapy can treat a full spectrum of conditions, from those realted to physical trauma to mental and emotional problems. It has been of benefit in the treatment of back pain, digestive disturbances, menstrual problems, headaches, arthritis, sports injuries and ME, amongst many other things.

Within the art of Polarity Therapy there is a whole system of balancing the structure of the body to alleviate stress put upon the spine, sacrum and internal organs by bad posture. Therapists can diagnose misalignments and then, with gentle manipulation, correct the alignment between the sacrum, spine and cranium, and their relation to other parts of the body. Once the body is correctly aligned many cases of chronic back pain are relieved.

PSYCHIC COUNSELLING

Psychic Counselling is a humanistic approach to therapy when the natural psychic abilities of the counsellor and a knowledge of various forms of healing, psychology and alternative medicine are used in helping a client to understand and deal with personal problems of both a physical and psychological nature.

ORIGIN

The origin of Psychic Counselling lies in an idea formulated by Ruby and Alf Fowles in 1984 when Ruby was practising as a Psychic Consultant and Alf as a Hypnotherapist and Psychotherapist. In both cases, it was felt that something more was needed and that the full potential of both forms of counselling were not being met.

After many hours of contemplation, Alf and Ruby felt that therapy in general was too entrenched in mechanical practices and, again generally, cures were too slow and expensive for most people needing therapeutic help. As a result they felt strongly that they were being physically impressed to form a therapy that would combine psychic awareness together with a more practicable means of helping a client to resolve problems in the shortest possible time.

Additionally they felt that work of a psychic nature must be presented to the public in a sensible manner and without the mystical trappings associated with psychic work. As a result only those people who have their feet 'firmly on the ground' would be permitted to train as a Psychic Counsellor.

Hence, the newest of all counselling techniques was born.

THE IDEA

The idea of Psychic Counselling is new to the many fields of counselling and psychotherapy available and it must not be confused with simple mediumship which is also sometimes wrongly described as Psychic Counselling. The difference being that in simple mediumship, a client is given messages, hopefully comforting, through the medium's contact with his or her 'guides' and that is often the sum total of the client's consultation.

However, in Psychic Counselling, the practitioner will give a client an in-depth psychic consultation which will involve counselling and valuable advice in how to deal with any personal problems which may arise during the consultation.

Again it is pointed out that Psychic Counselling should not be confused with mediumship as it goes much further than giving a psychic reading.

TREATMENT

A Psychic Counsellor is a caring person who has attended a course of instruction in Psychic Counselling. Development in various fields of

THE
NATIONAL COLLEGE
OF
PSYCHIC COUNSELLING
(Established 1986)

**DISCOVER YOUR PSYCHIC POTENTIAL
AND START A NEW CAREER**

On-going courses leading to a National Diploma in Psychic Counselling are held throughout the year.

Subjects taught include: counselling techniques; psychology; mediumistic development; alternative medicines; palmistry; numerology; stress management; dream interpretation; psychology of disease; colour healing; dowsing; spiritual healing.

For prospectus write to:

THE REGISTRAR
The National College
of Psychic Counselling
3 Broadfield, Harlow, Essex CM20 3PR
or telephone **(0279) 451402/425284**

The College is the official training organisation for registration with the Association of Psychic Counsellors.

psychic work, for example Clairvoyance, is an integral and important part of a Psychic Counsellor's training is instruction in counselling techniques, healing and, on a non-practitioner level, various fields of Alternative and Complementary Medicine.

As a result, the form treatment takes is similar in some respects to many other forms of counselling, but with one very important difference. Psychic Counselling uses the practitioner's developed sense of psychic awareness during the whole of the consultation.

At the beginning of the consultation, the practitioner will normally, but not always, use some form of tuning-in to the clients personal problems. This might be though the use of clairvoyance, palmistry, psychometry, numerology or using the tarot cards etc. This will represent the foundation stone of the consultation for it during this initial stage that in-depth problems reveal themselves.

The practitioner will then go one step further and psychically go deeper into the problem and look for its roots and then for a solution.

The final stage of the consultation is in the form of treatment and/or advice to resolve the problem, for example using Imagery Therapy and giving advice on other forms of treatment that may be considered of value to the client.

A full session can take up to two hours, at the end of which the client will always feel that they have benefited from the help, advice and treatment given. It is essential that a client never leaves a consultation feeling confused or dissatisfied in any way.

WHAT ILLNESSES AND BENEFITS?

As Spiritual Healing is part of a Psychic Councellor's training, most illnesses can receive some benefit Psychic Counselling, including chronic physical illnesses, although a Psychic Counsellor will never promise a cure.

However, the illnesses that best respond to this type of treatment are those of a psychological nature. Some psychological problems can be resolved in one treatment, where-as the more deep-rooted problems may take longer. However, it is not unusual for a serious problem, for example incest, to be dealt with successfully in one consultation. This is not a claim made lightly, as the effectiveness of Psychic Counselling, when carried out by trained practitioners, can reduce the exploratory time in therapy from weeks and months to only a few hours.

PSYCHOANALYTIC PSYCHOTHERAPY

Psychotherapy is a form of treatment for those who are experiencing difficulties within themselves or in their relationships with others, and for those prepared to examine the psychological origins of their distress,

ORIGIN

The roots of psychotherpy are firmly based in the thinking and discoveries of Freud and therefore of psychoanalysis. The first volume of his papers *Studies in Hysteria* published in 1895 gave an account of a new method of examining and treating patients. It was called the 'talking cure' because the method employed was verbal communication.

THE IDEA

Freud introduced concepts of unconscious ideas, ideas inadmissible to the consciousness. The method of treatment relies on the interpretation of what the patient says whilst the patient reports his thoughts and feelings without reservation. Freud also applied his new method to the study of dreams and published in 1900 *The Interpretation of Dreams* - thus began a theory of mental life. Thoughts and feelings previously seen as random, meaningless or accidental began to be explained by reference to past experiences. Freud demonstrated concepts regarding infantile sexuality, regression, Oedipus complex and wish fulfilment, all leading to internal exploration and understanding. Jung, a colleague of Freud pursued his own thinking and his work led to the development of the 'analytic psychotherapy'. Later thinkers such as Klein, Ferenczi, Fairbairn, Winnicott, Fordham and others, all have contributed widely to the development, understanding and application of psychotherapy.

TREATMENT

Psychotherapy is a process of exploration undertaken by two people, therapist and patient, in the context of a personal relationship between the two. In this exploration the patient takes the lead by relating thoughts, associations, feelings, memories and dreams. The therapist follows, clarifying what is happening by drawing the patient's attention to habitual modes of behaving and by making links between conscious and unconscious, present and past experience. All this has the aim of promoting the patient's self-understanding and capacity to view the world objectively and less coloured by personal wishes, fear and prejudices. Psychotherapy often means hard work and emotional stress for the patient. The psychotherapist undertakes to preserve complete confidentiality about patients and what is said. Part of the ethical code of the psychotherpist is to respect the autonomy of the patient, allowing development in the light of the patient's own beliefs and values. If the psychotherapist is not a doctor, the patient's general practitioner or a consultant psychiatrist will undertake medical responsibility.

The psychotherapist will offer a number of regular appointment times every week, each session lasting a customary fifty minutes. The patient makes a commitment to attend at the agreed times and to say whatever comes to mind as frankly and honestly as possible.

WHAT ILLNESSES CAN BE CURED?

Psychotherapy can be helpful to those troubled by feelings of depression, emptiness, futility and incapacitating fears, extreme mood swings or uncontrollable rage. It can also be helpful to those who experience dissatisfaction in their sexual, interpersonal, work and social relationships or to those who are unable to make relationships.

Others may seek psychotherapy because they work in professions such as psychology, social work teaching or medicine, which include a major involvement with people and where an understanding of oneself and others is a basic requirement.

RADIONICS

Radionics is defined as healing at a distance using specially designed instruments and the ESP faculty.

ORIGIN

The principles of radionics were first discovered by a distinguished American physician, Dr. Albert Abrams, AM. MD. Doctor Abrams was born in California in 1863 and studied medicine at Heidelberg, graduating with first class honours and the Gold Medal of the University. He became one of America's leading specialists in diseases of the nervous system, a respected teacher and writer of medical text books.

Various other people researched and developed Abrams work, including George W. de la Warr of Oxford, to the advanced form of Radionics of today.

THE IDEA

Abrams made a chance discovery during the examination of a patient and became convinced that a study of the energies emanating from the physical body could produce a system of medical diagnosis superior to that being used at the time and he undertook extensive research which provided the basis of all radionic treatment today.

Now nearly a century later we accept that all matter is energy radiating it's own particular energy patterns and that man and all life forms have their own electro-magnetic forcefield, which can become disturbed and result in disease and ill health. The science of Radionics is based on the recognition and measurement of energy, imbalances in the physical, emotional and mental levels of the patient.

These energy patterns can be reproduced on the Radionic Instruments - by the use of calibrated dials. Organs, diseases and remedies all have their own particular frequency or vibration which are expressed in numerical values, known as "Rates" which are used for diagnostic and treatment purposes.

A case history and details of the current symptoms from which the patient is suffering, together with a sample of hair or blood, will enable a trained and competent practitioner to carry out a Radionic Analysis to discover the basic cause of the problem, taking into account the physical, emotional, mental and in some cases the spiritual aspects of the patient. In doing this, the state of the flow of energy in the whole person, the predispositions to disease, the progression to certain major diseases and the causes of the total disharmony of the person are calculated.

The assessment of the patients problems as reflected in the analysis tests the practitioner's knowledge of physical anatomy and physiology and the depth of his study of subtle anatomy, psychology and the many aspects in our civilisation which affect health.

TREATMENT

The information revealed by the analysis forms the basis for radionic treatment which is given by directing corrective and balancing energy patterns to the patient through Radionic instrumentation or to place such energies into liquid or tablets which may be taken by the patient.

In considering treatment the practitioner has to decide what other forms of therapy as well as, or instead of radionics, will best suit the patient's problem at the time of the analysis.

The technique of selecting additional therapies or other energy medicine such as homoeopathy, or acupuncture, is part of the basic training of practitioners who are also required to have a sound knowledge of all forms of medical treatment. The practitioners aim is to bring each patient back to a high level of health which may be defined as balance in the physical, emotional, mental and spiritual, therefore it is obvious that great emphasis must be placed on the personal development of each practitioner of Radionics.

WHAT ILLNESSES AND BENEFITS?

Radionics seeks to restore harmony of mind and body systems by whichever way suits the patient best to cover all manner of diseases and conditions and works both in the normalisation, or curative, and the preventative fields as it assesses the individuals' personal reasons for their problems and endeavours to treat those reasons at source.

Unbalanced states can be pinpointed before they manifest as disease in the physical, thereby eliminating much future stress and suffering.

It is not essential for a patient to be in close proximity to the practitioner and the benefits of Radionic treatment can be and are experienced by the sick and suffering anywhere in the world.

STATUS IN THE UNITED KINGDOM

Energy medicine is gradually being accepted by the Western orthodox medical establishment and the Code of Conduct under which Radionic practitioners practise, has been accepted by the General Medical Council, the British Medical Association, the Royal Colleges and the Royal College of Veterinary Surgeons.

The major radionic professional organisations are members of the Confederation of Radionic and Radiesthetic Organisations which has links to practitioners of radionics throughout the world and is co-ordinating the training of radionic practitioners and other aspects necessary to provide an enhanced system for wholistic healing.

REFLEXOLOGY

Reflexology is a form of therapy that involves applying a sort of acupressure technique on the feet in a certain way in order to induce a therapeutic effect in other parts of the body.

ORIGIN

Reflexology might be as old as acupuncture. Some of the wall reliefs in Egypt show that the ancient Egyptians treated feet in a way that bears marked similarities to reflexology treatment.

Although some texts dating back to the sixteenth century touch on this subject, the therapy cannot really be said to have been founded until an American doctor from Connecticut, William Fitzgerald, started his research in 1913. Dr Fitzgerald observed that some of his patients who were undergoing treatment for ailments of the nose and throat appeared to feel less pain than others. He noticed that these same patients, while in the waiting room, pressed on their hands (hand reflexology is also used as explained below); it was no doubt an instinctive reaction to fear and anxiety, but they seemed to obtain some pain relief. Through further research he succeeded in establishing the basis for this treatment.

THE IDEA

The body is divided into ten longitudinal zones, five on each side of an imaginary longitudinal line which divides the body into two equal parts. The zones are of equal width and depth. There are reflex points on the feet corresponding to the organs lying in these zones. Hence, the kidneys lie in the second and third zones, and so do their reflex points on the feet, and so on. The reflex points do not cross, and hence change sides, as the nerves do when they reach the brain. This means that the reflex point of the right eye, for instance, lies on the right foot, and that for the left eye on the left foot.

In addition to the longitudinal zones, there are three transverse zones, with three corresponding reflex zones on the feet. Everything at shoulder level or above has its reflex point somewhere in the toe zone; what lies between the shoulders and the lower ribs has its reflex point somewhere in the middle part of the foot; and what lies on the hip line or below has its point somewhere on the heel zone.

This means that we have a two-dimensional definition for each organ: the first is the longitudinal,

and the second is the transverse. Reflexologists, in addition to the above divisions, divide the reflex points according to the bodily systems. There are nine such divisions: the head, the musculo-skeletal system, the endocrine system (the glands), the respiratory system, the heart and circulatory system, the lymphatic system, the digestive system, the urinary system and the skin.

Now, how does this work?

The accepted theory, among the many that have been put forward, is that reflexology treatment affects the circulation and the nerves. Everybody knows that blood is the vehicle by which nutrients are supplied to all the tissues of the body, and by which the waste products from these tissues are taken away. Most of the problems of the nervous system are caused - directly or indirectly - by nervous tension and stress. Reflexology treatment helps to relieve this stress, with the result that the bodily organs perform in a relaxed manner. Reflexology, therefore, helps the body to heal itself by stimulating its vital force through the improved functioning of the nervous and circulatory systems.

It has now been established that a flow of energy passes between the organs lying on the same longitudinal zone, but its exact nature remains a mystery. As in acupuncture, research continues to find the reasons behind the phenomena. It is, however, possible to see the amount of energy that surrounds these parts of the body by means of Kirlian photography; by photographing the feet before and after treatment, you can see how reflexology increases this energy.

As for the ability of reflexology to give relief from pain, this could be the effect of the technique itself (the pressure), which may cause the release of endorphins from the brain.

TREATMENT

As a reflexologist, you must first of all take down in detail the medical history of your patient. You then inspect the feet, noting the skin temperature and colour. Cold feet, for instance, indicate bad circulation, while feet that perspire a lot could indicate a dysfunction of the glands, and so on.

You then have to look for any corns, cracks, blisters, puffiness, and so forth. If there is any inflammation, no treatment should be given to that area in case the inflammation becomes worse. If this inflammation covers a large area, treatment has to be applied to the hands instead.

You should check whether your patient is flat-footed, which could mean a problem in the spine; or if any of the toes are connected, which could indicate a problem in the head, sinus or teeth.

The treatment itself involves a sort of acupressure technique, which is given in a special manner by applying the thumb in a circular motion. All the reflex points are treated, whatever the problem is, but

then you go back to those points that have shown tenderness, which is an indication of problems in the corresponding organs.

The patient should keep you informed about all the tender points; tenderness will be registered either as normal pain, or as piercing pain, or whatever. In general, the greater the pain (and this may be so great as to cause your patient to cry out), the more out of balance the corresponding organ is. As the body starts healing itself, and as the affected organ returns gradually to normal as the treatment progresses, the pain in the reflex area becomes weaker and weaker until it vanishes altogether.

The work calls for maximum precision, and no wonder since there are 7,200 nervous endings in the feet, each connected to the rest of the body through the brain and the spinal cord.

As mentioned earlier, if it is not possible to treat the feet for any reason, you can use the reflex points in the hands. These are similar to those of the feet, although there is a larger treatment area for those organs lying on the toe zone, and less for the others.

The hand reflex areas are also useful in that you can instruct your patient to press on chosen points in the period between treatments, if you think it is necessary to give more frequent stimulation to these specific points.

Reflexologists advise their patients on how to take care of their feet, and also on any other aspect of health that seems necessary in order to achieve the cure - such as, and most important of all, diet. You might, as therapists from other disciplines do, prescribe some vitamins and minerals, or give the patient a relaxing medicine from the Bach flower remedies available.

As a general rule, chronic cases need more time to cure than others. Also, the more complicated the problem, the longer it takes to put right. But generally six to eight treatment sessions are adequate for most cases. Once weekly, or twice weekly in some cases, is the norm. Even if the problem can be solved in a single session, the patient should be advised to continue for several treatments to make sure that the problem does not recur. There is no fixed time for each session. The average session probably lasts between 45 and 60 minutes.

WHAT ILLNESSES AND BENEFITS?

Since reflexology is a wholistic treatment, treating not just the disease but the diseased person, and also since by its very nature it treats all the parts of the body by massaging all their corresponding reflex points, reflexology is capable of tackling all health problems. Even in complicated and advanced cases of diseases such as cancer, reflexology can be very beneficial, firstly by strengthening the whole body (as it does with all the disorders it treats), and secondly by reducing stress and tension, relaxing the sufferer and thus enabling him or her to cope better.

SHIATSU

Shiatsu (or acupressure) is the therapy in which pressure is applied on the acupuncture points to cure disorders and give relief from pain.

ORIGIN

(See the section ACUPUNCTURE.)

THE IDEA

Shiatsu was developed on principles similar to acupuncture; it uses the same system of Ki (Chinese Chi) energy flowing throughout the body. This Ki energy is alleged to move along pathways called meridians, and may be influenced most easily at certain points along the meridians called Tsubos. It has been observed that by relaxing the body,

improving the circulation of blood and stabilising the flow of energy many common aches, pains and discomforts can be allevieted.

(On the idea of meridians, energy flow and how it works see the section ACUPUNCTURE.)

THE TREATMENT

Modern-day shiatsu in the West incorporates certain techniques such as chiropractic, osteopathy and Swedish massage. It is unique in that it combines the principles of acupuncture with physical massage. In the same way that acupuncture can be shown to relieve pain and discomfort, shiatsu has been seen to have these effects. Further, as the principles of acupuncture are applied in conjunction with relaxing

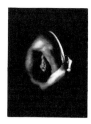

physical massage, stretching, and controlled, relaxed breathing, clients have also found shiatsu to be effective for stress relief.

The treatment is based on the practitioner's diagnosis, in which the following techniques can be used: Hara diagnosis, which is a slow and gentle palpation of the abdomen to identify areas that are tense, relaxed, painful, hard and so on; study of skin colour and condition; checking the structural alignment of the body; manual testing for sensitivity along the meridians; finding areas of tension or stiffness; and listening to the client's own testimony.

A typical shiatsu treatment lasts one hour. Normally the client sits or lies on a firm cotton mattress on the floor, wearing loose cotton clothing. The practitioner will start by looking for areas of tension or tightness, as well as areas that are loose or swollen. Any imbalance like this often cause muscular pain, as the muscles try to correct the posture.

The shiatsu practitioner uses a variety of techniques to relax areas of tension: stretching the limbs, kneading and squeezing the muscles, gently pounding the soft tissues with a loose fist or the sides of the hands, rubbing, and applying pressure with thumbs, fingers, elbow or foot. The practitioner usually covers the whole body area, and it is observable that relieving tension in one part of the body often relieves discomfort in another. For example, tension and stiffness around the sacrum and

lower back may develop a structural imbalance that causes discomfort in the upper back and neck.

WHAT ILLNESSES AND BENEFITS?

Shiatsu is a therapy suitable for use with clients of any age, from babies to old people. It works in many different ways. Physiologically, the stretching, squeezing and kneading of the soft tissues makes the muscles relax, improves the circulation of blood and lymph and increases the flexibility of muscles, tendons and blood vessels. Careful manipulation of the joints tends to reduce stiffness and increase mobility. Rubbing and stretching of the skin helps to open the pores as well as improve blood and lymph circulation. Pressing specific tsubos improves the flow of Ki energy.

Most clients will comment that after a shiatsu treatment they notice that they have more energy but feel completely relaxed. These effects may last for between several days and few weeks, depending on the client's lifestyle. Once in this state, clients feel better able to cope with what would normally be stressful situations, and they notice absence of stress-related symptoms. This is significant when so many health problems can be associated with stress like headaches, allergy, muscular pains, indigestion, insomnia and tiredness.

Although there are no absolute contra-indications to the employment of shiatsu, particular caution is exercised when treating clients with one of the following conditions: pregnancy, recent surgery, spinal injury, cancer and fever.

Like many other complementary therapies shiatsu takes a wholistic view of health. Practitioners often question and advise clients on their diet, regime of exercise, means of relaxation and, if appropriate, encourage them to adopt a healthier lifestyle. Correspondingly, many clients see shiatsu as part of their health maintenance plan.

SPORTS THERAPY

ORIGIN

Sports Therapy as a profession is relatively new, springing from changing patterns of living and leisure, and from a new awareness of the importance of a healthy lifestyle. This implies more than merely "getting fit" - we must now include a balanced diet and strategies for dealing with stress in considering the factors contributing to our total health and well-being.

IDEA

Clear proof of the importance now placed on developing and maintaining health and fitness is afforded by the increasing numbers of fitness clubs, sports and leisure centres and hotel leisure spas that have sprung up in the last decade. In addition, many large companies provide special fitness facilities and programmes, aware that fit employees are efficient employees.

Other forms of sporting activity have also shown an unprecedented surge in growth, whether group sports such as football, or individual sports such as tennis, running and golf.

However, the "fitness revolution" has its darker side - many injuries have resulted from rash, over-enthusiastic attempts by those who have not exercised for years to attain the perfect body they never had in the first place. Unfit or inexperienced "athletes" often take on too much too soon. They may take up a sport unsuitable for their body type and fitness level, bringing to the surface problems which may have been dormant for a long time. Thus, the first lesson to take to heart, often literally, is that you should "get fit to play sport rather than play sport to get fit". This means proper preparation, advice and training - a carefully sequenced conditioning programme, careful choice of equipment and a nutritional programme geared to the individual choice of sport and general level of health.

TREATMENT

The profession of Sports Therapy involves elements of a whole range of disciplines - the gym instructor, nutritionist, coach, masseur and psychologist, carefully balanced to provide the skills required to help the individual reach and maintain higher optimum level of health and fitness. Thus, the sports therapist's first key is role advisory, or EDUCATIONAL.

1. The therapist will test the individual's fitness level and devise and monitor an appropriate conditioning programme.

2. The therapist will advise on the proper choice of equipment - a vital element in the prevention of injury e.g. cheap, flimsy trainers, without proper cushioning, will not protect the foot, ankle or knee from injury.

3. Training in proper warming up and stretching before exertion is provided by the sports therapist.

4. The therapist will draw up an individualised nutritional programme.

5. The therapist will perform pre and post-event Sports Massage to prevent injury.

The second key role is more directly THERAPEUTIC: here the therapist may work in a complementary manner to medically qualified professionals, while never intruding on medical territory. The training of the sports therapist is geared to:

1) Safe handling and informed primary assessment of injury and other medical emergencies, whether in an aerobic studio or on a football field.

2) Sports massage and graduated rehabilitative exercise to bring the sportsperson back to full fitness.

The sports therapist is, therefore, equally as involved with the sportsperson when fit as well as injured or unfit.

TRAINING IN SPORTS THERAPY

From this brief overview of the various tasks involved in the practice of Sports Therapy it is clear that the professional training needs of the sports therapist are multi-disciplinary. The key elements are Anatomy and Physiology in considerable detail, an understanding of the way injuries occur, typical injuries relating to various sports-related situations.

The trained sports therapist may choose to focus on one or more of these elements in his or her professional life - maybe nutrition or massage - or utilise a broader range, in personal fitness training, for instance. Some may even incorportae a managerial function, but all will be secure in the knowledge that the health and well-being of the sportspeople in their care is safe in their hands.

STRESS MANAGEMENT

Stress management is an approach that uses a large range of techniques in a systematic manner to prevent or reduce stress or stress related symptoms in individuals or organisations.

ORIGIN

The word 'stress' is originally derived from 'stringere', a Latin word used three centuries ago to describe hardships. Later it denoted strain or effort. At the turn of this century the relationship between illness and busy individuals was noticed. In 1908, Yerkes and Dodson discovered that up to a certain optimum point, performance improved as pressure or stress increased. However, performance was reduced when stress increased beyond the optimum point. Research into stress was undertaken by Cannon and Hans Selye. Selye discovered a reasonably predictable sequence of psychophysiological reactions to stress. He called this the 'general adaptation syndrome'. Since then research has continued into stress and subsequently its management.

THE IDEA

Unlike most forms of complementary medicine, many thousands of research papers have been written on stress although less on its management. Stress is a real phenomenon. If an individual perceives that they are in a threatening situation, then their body gears up for action. The sympathetic nervous system, literally is sympathy with the individuals perceived environment, activates the release of stress hormones. Once the hypothalamus is triggered, it releases corticotrophin releasing factor (CRF) which sets this endocrine system in motion. Then the pituitary releases hormones that activate the thyroid and the adrenal cortex. The latter synthesises cortisol which increases blood sugars and helps speed up the metabolism. The CRF activates the adrenal medulla which then increases its output of adrenaline and noradrenaline. The heart beat and blood pressure is raised and finally almost immediately the individual is ready for either 'fight or flight'. The level of arousal is high, the muscles tense up. Blood is directed away from where it is not needed such as the stomach and intestines to where it is needed. When the perceived stressful situation is over, the body,

with aid of the parasymapthetic nervous system, returns to equilibrium. This explanation summarises briefly what happens, however, this is an oversimplification.

If the perceived stress does not disappear the individual may either attempt to adapt to it or stay in the aroused state. Research shows that both are likely to lead eventually to stress related symptoms or disorders such as insomnia, depression, headaches, phobias, twitches, essential hypertension and in some cases coronary thrombosis/heart attacks. This is not a complete list. About 2000 years ago Epictetus said that individuals "are disturbed not by things but the views they take of them". This early observation has affected how stress management has been applied by practitioners in this century. If accurate perceptions, dysfunctional thoughts or cognitions can be restructured, then the individual will become less distressed over present events or fears about the future. Sheakespeare's tragic character, Macbeth aptly summed this up when he said "Present fears are less than horrible imaginings". Disputing of thoughts and fears is known as a cognitive approach.

There are other approaches too that concentrate on different aspects of the stress response such as reducing muscular tension by using relaxation techniques or by using meditation to calm the mind. The main problem is that one person's stress is another person's joy. Thus, for any given individual, an approach concentrating on only one aspect of the stress response may not be the most effective help for that individual. This is where an important confusion arises. Different approaches such as hypnosis or relaxation are sometimes portrayed as 'stress management' whereas in fact this may only be a technique that a competent stress management practitioner may use or recommend. In addition, some 'experts' suggest that stress management can only be an educational approach, and therefore is not a therapy, as therapy concentrates on the relief of symptoms and not on prevention. They can not conceive a psycho-educational approach such as, for example, a cognitive-behavioural approach that is mainly concerned with a skills training model, and uses many different techniques to achieve this end. It is likely that this disagreement will not be resolved for some time.

TREATMENT

The stress management practitioner may choose to specialise in stress management training for groups as in adult education, organisational training or group therapy. Conversely the practitioner may decide to specialise in helping individuals on a 'one to one' basis. In stress management training generally the onus is on prevention whereas in group or individual therapy or counselling the onus may be on a cure of the stress related symptom such as anxiety as well as future prevention. However, such distinctions are unclear as often individuals join stress management training workshops wishing to learn about prevention and in addition reduce their existing psychological or physiological symptoms of stress. Thus this section on treatment is split into two parts: training and then therapy.

The table below illustrates the topics or combination of topics that are often looked at in stress management seminars, courses or training workshops. It is not complete. Counselling and listening skills are now often taught to health professionals and managers whereas prison officers may find anger management useful. The workshop facilitator may be directive or may allow the participants to decide upon the content and nature of the workshop. Often, when it is run in industry, then the human resources or training department may have an input on the contents too. It is very advisable in adult education or with industrial training not to venture into a psychotherapeutic approach. However, as participants may reveal personal experiences, good counselling skills are recommended. It is essential that the practitioner has a handout consisting of a referral list of organisations or qualified therapists that participants can use if the need be recognised. A goal of the stress management workshop may be for participants to devise their own individual stress management programme. In either group or individual therapy or individual training, a comprehensive assessment is advised. This can include why the client has chosen now to enter therapy, their expectations or anxieties about therapy, their stress related symptoms and disorders, if any, and/or discuss their emotional upset. If they are suffering from phobias, depression, obsessive compulsive disorders etc. appropriate questionnaires may also be used at the assessment stage if the therapist is experienced and qualified to treat these types of problems. Also at the initial interview a contract is negotiated. Over consecutive sessions an individual stress management programme can be designed. This involves explanations of the different techniques that can be used, eg exposure programmes for a phobia, relaxation or hypnosis for tension, time management for managing the personal work environment etc. Then the therapist/trainer negotiates with the client which techniques they wish to include in their own programme. It is important that the therapist/trainer has knowledge of the many techniques themselves, they are at least able to refer the client to a qualified specialist in the particular field. The client may still see the therapist/trainer to continue the programme that they can help with. Some practitioners are happy to work with both groups and individuals. It must be emphasised that appropriate in depth training and an ongoing supervision is recommended.

WHAT ILLNESSES AND BENEFITS?

If a comprehensive approach to stress management is practised then it can be successful in the prevention, management or cure of many disorders or stress related symptoms (such as: depression, anxiety, obsessions, phobias, muscle tension, palpitations, nausia, backache, headache, essential hypertension, heart disease, ulcers, migraines, skin disorders, allergies, insomnia etc). It has also been used to successfully treat schizophrenics in a family setting.

Stress management interventions can also be used in companies to reduce organisational symptoms of stress (eg reduce staff turnover, absenteeism, whilst increasing morale, for performance and quality control). The benefits to an individuals health is obvious. The research now shows that the benefits to organisations can be counted in financial terms, in addition to the enhanced well being of the staff. Stress management can empower individuals to take control of their lives and their health. The benefits can be enormous as well as prolonging life. In the USA health insurance companies are now reducing the premium to their clients who regularly practice transcendental meditation, as they have discovered lowered hospital admissions for this group. This is just one technique that may be used on a client's individual stress management programme. A systematic eclectic or multimodal approach to stress management shows real promise for the 21st century.

Table

Stress Management Training

Lifestyle, i.e. diet, exercise, smoking, weight, alcohol/drugs

Relaxation techniques

Coping techniques

Problem solving techniques

Life and time management

Commnication skills training

Assertion training

Role play

Awareness of healthy stress (eustress) and unhealthy stress (distress) or pressure versus stress

Recognition of stress in self and others

Psychological, physiological, and behavioural aspects of stress

Occupational, organisational, family and social issues

Changing maladaptive cognitions and behaviour

Constructive self-talk

Rational-emotive therapy

Stability zones and rituals

Stress mapping

Emotional outlets

Formulation of a personal action plan

TIBB

TIBB, which literally means medicine, is a tradition of medicine in which a range of techniques and methods are used in order to maintain health and restore it whenever lost.

ORIGIN

TIBB, is an Arabic word, which in different times and places has been referred to as Arabic, Unani, Islamic, Hikmah, Asian, and Sufi medicine. TIBB, as a tradition of medicine was synthesised in the Middle East about 1400 years ago and integrated elements from Egypt, India, China and Classical Greece.

THE IDEA

TIBB, in common with traditional Chinese medicine (TCM) and Ayurveda is based on the philosophy of elements, which are an expression of energy (Quwa, Prana, Chi). In TIBB, the central idea is that each individual has a unique MIZAJ - constitution and health for each person is the maintenance of the AITIDAL - Dynamic balance. When there is balance then all the functions are carried out in correct and whole manner. This balance and wholeness is maintained through observing and living according to natural laws. Disease is an outcome of deviation from FITTRA - Natural laws.

TREATMENT

As a practitioner of TIBB, a TABIB, you will need to understand and elicit causes of each persons imbalance or disease. From TIBBI perspective each individual is unique and you will have to understand the person. The imbalance may manifest itself on one or more of the four levels,

1. SPIRITUAL

2. MENTAL

3. EMOTIONAL

4. PHYSICAL

Diagnosis or evaluation of disease is arrived at through history taking, pulse taking as well as using tests such as urine tests etc. Treatment is planned using combination of TIBBI modalities.

The practitioner may select one or more modality from below,

Formentation

Diuresis

Hydrotherapy

Diaphoresis

Vomiting

Purgining

Cupping

Venesection

Massage

Manipulation

Or he may choose,

Diettherapy

Phytotherapy or

Psychotherapy

WHAT ILLNESSES AND BENEFITS?

Like most other natural medical systems, TIBB is extremely useful and effective in Chronic diseases. The range of diseases a TIBBI physician can deal with are extensive, except for cases of surgery.

The practitioner of TIBB, being wholistic practitioner, treats the whole person. However, TIBB is very successful in psychological, sexual, skin and joint disorders. It is safe for all age groups. Today TIBB is used all over the world to enable millions of people get back to health and well being. It is humane, ecologically friendly, safe and very economical. Given the increasing awareness of toxic side-effects of chemical drugs, TIBB is an ideal medicine for the future of human beings.

VEGATESTING

Vegatesting is not a therapy in itself, but rather a diagnostic system which is applicable to many areas of complementary medicine.

ORIGIN

The Vegatest technique is firmly grounded in the principles of functional or bio-electronic regulatory medicine. The first coherent use of this technique was within acupuncture. After the second world war Dr Voll began to take skin impedance measurements over a large number of acupuncture points. He worked on the principle that if the points gave an abnormal reading or were unable to hold their electrical charge then the points themselves were unhealthy. These points were said to reflect healthful illness in specific internal organs represented by particular acupuncture points. In this way measurements based on acupuncture points could be used to form some assessment of the way in which the body was balanced.

The initial technique was described as 'electro-acupuncture according to Voll' and involved the use of both functional diagnosis and therapy.

The concept of function diagnosis is of central importance within complementary medicine. Conventional medicine makes diagnosis based on proven functional change. For instance, a patient with abdominal pain will have a proven ulcer or just a tummy ache which may well be of emotional origin. There is therefore a strict division between illness and health, based on X-rays or endoscopic investigation of the stomach and upper part of the small bowel. Complementary medicine offers a completely different view. It does not concentrate on anatomy or structure as being of primary importance, but rather on function. A traditional acupuncturist measuring the pulses will be trying to assess functional imbalances and the pathogens responsible for those imbalances. Consequently their therapy will be directed at attempting to re-establish a normal energetic balance within the body rather than necessarily treating organic disease. In many instances the presence of organic disease is completely irrelevant to the acupuncturist or reflexologist, as they are simply treating functional imbalances.

THE IDEA

The Vegatest technique itself was developed by Helmut Schimmel and has its origins in electro-acupuncture according to Voll. Electro-acupuncture according to Voll required the individual practitioner to make individual point measurements with great accuracy and care. Originally Voll then went on to balance each of the acupuncture points with an appropriate electrical current. If the points were low and in need of tonification he charged them up, if they had excess energy and were in need of sedation he discharged them. Voll subsequently realised that, by placing an appropriate homoeopathic medication in circuit with the acupuncture point, he could balance the point. There are a number of different apocryphal stories about how he arrived at this somewhat surprising conclusion, but nevertheless he began to base a whole therapeutic approach on this assumption. By balancing a whole range of different remedies against the abnormal acupuncture points he could work out which was the best therapy for that individual and subsequently gave them the remedies which appeared most consistently to balance the majority of the abnormal acupuncture point readings. He called this 'medicine testing'.

Dr Helmut Schimmel, among many others, found this approach to be very time consuming. Furthermore Voll's technique involved giving patients very substantial doses of homoeopathic nosodes and this frequently produced adverse reactions, although, in the long run, it proved an effective therapy for many otherwise interactable problems. Schimmel began to use the concept of medicine testing both diagnostically and therapeutically. He simply used, as the basis for points measurement, one acupuncture point, and then tested a whole range of different homoeopathic medicines against this point. By using a complex protocol, involving a variety of test ampoules, he was able to ascertain a whole range of different functional ideas about what may be upsetting the body. The Vegatest protocol is primarily diagnostic in origin, and its main aim is to assess the important aspects of the individual's pathological terrain. For instance, is the primary problem a low grade toxicity from pesticides or a chronic infection? Does the patient have a particular focus in one of their tissues or organs - for instance a chronically infected set of tonsils may be acting as a focus and consequently may block and therapeutic intervention from producing a good, coherent, long term response. The Vegatest protocol also allows the practitioner to decide which organ is the most diseased. The term Vegatest originates from the name of the machine produced by Vega, a German company that makes a number of high technology engineering items including the Vegatest equipment.

TREATMENT/DIAGNOSIS

Vegatesting is primarily a diagnostic technique. Any number of different therapies can then be used in conjunction with it. If, for instance, you are a classical homoeopath then the functional diagnosis achieved through the Vegatest protocol can be cross checked against the particular remedy or remedies you feel are appropriate for an individual patient. Nutritional medicine, or indeed conventional therapies, can be used in conjunction with the Vegatest technique. It appears also that food intolerance can be diagnosed using this approach, so the Vegatest is a very useful tool in the context of clinical ecology or environmental mdicine.

WHAT ILLNESSES AND BENEFITS?

The technique itself, however, was developed specifically for use in conjunction with complex homoeopathy. Classical homoeopaths use single remedies in specific potencies, frequently using only one or, at the most, two remedies in any individual at a specific time. Complex homoeopathy involves the use of mixtures of low potency homoeopathics combined with herbal remedies. Furthermore these remedies are usually organ targeted and frequently used in association with nossodes (homoeopathic doses of bacteria, tissue, or acidophillis). Most of the Vegatest courses therefore involve an introduction of complex homoeopathy, but it is important to stress that the technique is primarily a diagnostic one which can be successfully applied to any field of endeavour. The therapeutic approaches are associated with the technique are a seperate issue, but they dovetail well into the diagnostic protocols developed by Helmut Schimmel.

The technique itself is conceptually straightforward and can give the individual practitioner great insight into how the body functions. This has enormous advantages for all complementary therapists. Prior to learning the Vegatest technique it is important to have some firm grounding in complementary medicine or conventional medicine, but ideally both. The technique does require some understanding of pathological processes.

The major disadvantage of the technique is that it requires some considerable degree of skill in order to become completely confident with the use of the probe. The Vegatest involves using a biological measurement and evaluating the body's response against a number of stimuli, using a specific measurement as its basis (i.e. skin impedence over an acupuncture point). In many ways this is similar to applied kinesiology, taking traditional Chinese pulses, or making a segmental diagnosis using osteopathic or chiropractic techniques. Initially it tends to be quite difficult and confusing until the practitioner has obtained the requisite manual skill. This usually takes between two and six months, depending on the expertise and skill of the practitioner, but, once obtained, Vegatesting is a powerful and very valuable diagnostic approach.

YOGA THERAPY

Yoga is a classical Indian discipline in which you work for your health. It is a systematic way for physical and mental self-improvement, based on the premise that the human being is an entity composed of physical, mental and spiritual attributes. The meaning of the word Yoga is union.

YOGA PRACTICE AND ITS BENEFITS

Yoga includes a system of physical exercises ("postures") which cover a wide range of body movement. It is a very effective, regenerative form of exercise which builds a firm foundation of health. Practice brings increasing mobility in the joints, strength, stamina and co-ordination. It improves circulation and the functioning of the inner organs.

Another important component of Yoga practice is breath control, which helps to concentrate the mind and calm the emotions. The combined mental well-being and physical health lead to a balanced personality.

There are no limits to this self-improvement: unlike many other physical activities, Yoga is not merely for the supple and young; nor does it require vast financial resources. All, regardless of age, sex or creed can practice and benefit from it.

Yoga is a powerful system of healing. For example, relief is felt from rheumatism and arthritis, back problems, menstrual disorders, migraine, circulatory and digestive disorders, and so on. The increased level of health ensures that diseases find it more difficult to take hold, are easier to stabilize and can also be shaken off quickly.

YOGA AS A THERAPY

The treatment of disease by means of Yoga is complex. It requires in the therapist a thorough knowledge of the postures (asanas) and their sequences, the individual and cumulative benefits of the postures, and of the relevant breathing techniques (pranayama). It also requires knowledge of anatomy and physiology and familiarity with the symptoms of the disease and the possible underlying causes. Further, the ability of the patient needs to be gauged in terms of his or her physical constitution. Other factors may complicate the treatment of the main problem, for example, a secondary condition or other temporary circumstances.

Minor complaints are often alleviated in the course of ordinary Yoga classes, through the general programme of postures. For instance, problems caused by structural defects, such as lower back pain, knee problems, stiff necks and shoulders, often disappear or can be quickly relieved by performing a series of postures with correct alignment and extension. Similarly, sluggish circulation, digestion and bowel movement almost invariably improve without a conscious effort to address these problems.

For serious or ongoing and intractable medical conditions it is necessary to follow specific regimes of asanas and/or pranayama, tailor-made for those conditions and the individuals concerned. This should be done with the guidance of an experienced and specially trained teacher.

An important aspect of Yoga therapy is that the patient should be physically helped to achieve the postures that are most beneficial for his or her particular condition, either by the teacher or by using a variety of 'props'. These latter are designed to allow the patient to stay for the maximum time in the postures, or to achieve the maximum intensity, without over-exertion. In this way the maximum benefit is gained.

There is an art to the placing of the props. It may be a bolster over which the patient lies to extend the liver; in this case the teacher must ensure the exact placing of the bolster so that the optimum extension is achieved. If standing poses are done using the wall for support, the teacher can adjust the patient to make him/her do the postures 'better', i.e. more effectively. The wall support means that there is no fear of overbalancing.

In all therapeutic work the onus is on the teacher to see that the patient works correctly and without strain, with maximum benefit. It is important to get feedback from the patient as to how they feel, so that adjustment, additions or substitutions can be made to the programme of asanas as necessary.

Another principle of Yoga therapy is that sequence of asanas must be performed. A single asana will not give a cure. The sequence will be a balance of postures that highlight the affected part, pump blood to it and allow the effect of this to be established. Depending on the problem, the cure or benefit may take weeks or months to effect, though some improvement should be felt straight away. In the case of serious illnesses, it is not so much a matter of cure but of stabilizing the condition so that it does not worsen and of helping the patient learn how to cope with it physically and mentally.

TYPES OF CONDITIONS TREATABLE

Yoga can help with a wide range of physical and mental problems. There is a high success rate in dealing with lower back pain, knee, neck and shoulder problems, gynaecological problems, arthritis, respiratory disorders, depression, anxiety and stress-related diseases, fatigue, insomnia, digestive problems.

Serious medical conditions can be helped, but there it is imperative to have the guidance of a specially qualified and experienced teacher.

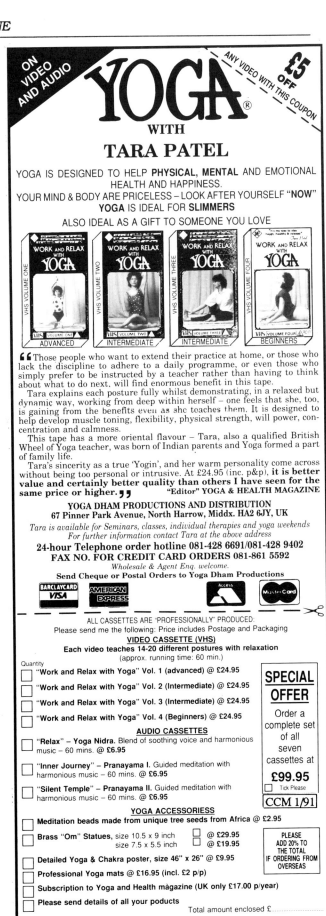

II COMPLEMENTARY MEDICINE AS A PROFESSION

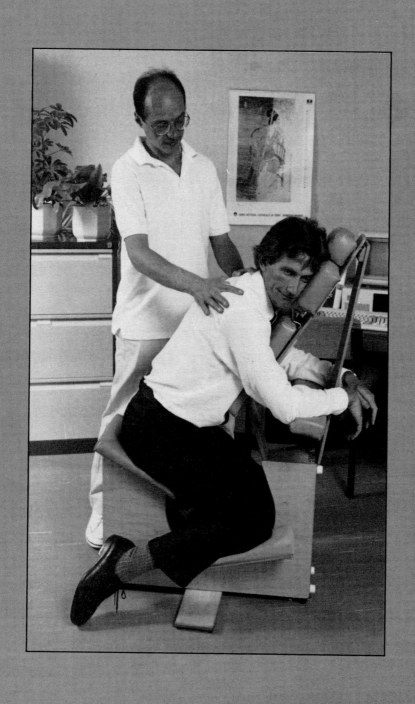

COMPLEMENTARY MEDICINE AS A PROFESSION

HELPING THE SUFFERER

People think that the prime motivation for everybody who works in the medical profession - or at least those who are involved in the direct care of patients, such as doctors and nurses - is the welfare of patients and the relief of suffering. But is this always the case? The medical profession, as any other profession, involves a whole variety of aspects, any of which might attract people to join it. Nevertheless, the fact that this is a profession which is devoted to helping people who are suffering, trying to cure their illnesses or rescue them from life- threatening danger, undoubtedly makes it one of the most noble, if not the most noble, occupations of all.

Medicine holds a unique position in the community, and with that comes an immense responsibility. Some people ascribe to doctors an almost god-like power as they wait to be cured. When the sick are in absolute despair, they may pray to God for help one moment, and then take the medicine that the doctor has prescribed the next. People believe only too readily in the doctor's authority; and if the doctor is able to cure them during illness, they might almost think that they are the beneficiaries of a great personal favour.

Yet there are two sides to this. Doctors are, after all, only doing the job for which they are being paid. People should not say: 'Doctor, please help me - I shall pay you whatever you want', but rather 'Doctor, I am paying you what you charge, and expect you to do your best to help me out of my suffering.'

Indeed, many of those who practise medicine see the financial aspects of the profession as a major attraction to this career. Some go into medicine specifically to join clinics established by their father or mother, to maintain the family's good name in this field and to keep a thriving business going. In any other profession these would often be cited as be the most important factors in attracting trainees. There is no shame for people in medicine to admit that it is a way of earning a good, and respectable living.

A RESPECTABLE PROFESSION

These issues apply to complementary medicine as well as to conventional medicine. However, since the financial and social benefits of practising alternative and complementary medicine are not yet as attractive as they are for conventional medicine, the dilemmas are markedly less acute. Nonetheless, as alternative and complementary therapies continue to flourish, these issues will become increasingly important, both to patients and to practitioners. As more and more people consult alternative therapists, they will inevitably start looking to them in the same way as they look to conventional doctors today, and gradually society will treat them all as one.

Regardless of this, alternative medicine is destined to play a vital role in maintaining public esteem in the medical profession as a whole, and as a practitioner you can be assured of the continuing respect of society.

A PROMISING FUTURE

In Part I we cited some statistics from *Which?* magazine, and figures from MORI poll in 1989 and from a survey of GPs in Avon published by the British Medical Journal. The figures show that alternative medicine is gaining ground on both fronts, both within the medical profession and with the general public at large. These changes in public and professional attitudes towards alternative medicine are not taking place because of some exceptional, temporary circumstances, but because of the very nature of both schools of medicine, their philosophies and how they work.

Recent opinion polls have shown that about 80% of the public would like alternative medicine to be available on the NHS. This would mean that many more people would consult alternative therapists if they did not have to pay the charges themselves. It is also an indication that people are becoming more aware of the benefits of alternative medicine, and of the disadvantages of conventional medicine. People who cannot afford the costs of treatment are not free to choose the treatment they prefer, and so they are stuck with what is available on the NHS - even though they may not be convinced that this is what is best for them. Many, out of past experience, have lost confidence in the ability of the NHS - and the kinds of medicine associated with it - to heal them, and that is very damaging to the prospects of achieving cure.

Media coverage of the various kinds of alternative treatments has increased public knowledge of them tremendously. Indeed there are seldom occasions when TV, radio, newspapers and magazines do not carry some kind of information on alternative medicine - be it alternative medicine in its own right, or as part of the alternative way of life which many countries and organizations are pushing for, as the need to save our planet becomes more urgent.

In short, as more information on alternative medicine becomes available, public demand for treatment will increase. And the more information people have, the more aware they will be of the power of alternative medicine, and the less susceptible they will be to the persuasions of those who are prejudiced against it. These developments are well under way.

THE FINANCIAL REWARDS

Complementary practitioners must earn good money to survive, and to improve themselves as therapists. Although the vast majority of alternative therapists charge less than private medical doctors, they are still able to earn a good and comfortable living. Paradoxically, the very fact that alternative medicine must suffer the presence of quacks in its ranks demonstrates that alternative practitioners can expect to earn a good living, for most of these ill-trained and unsuitable practitioners are attracted to the profession for no other reason but financial gain. (See also PART III, 'Earnings'.)

THE STATUS OF COMPLEMENTARY MEDICINE IN THE UK

The conventional medical profession is still at odds with alternative medicine. Its influence on the people making decisions in government, through the British Medical Association and the General Medical Council, has succeeded until now in keeping alternative medicine out of the NHS (except with certain, very limited exceptions), and hence in preventing the public from benefiting from the various alternative therapies. The General Medical Council is, however, more tolerant towards the ideas of alternative medicine, and has stated that doctors need not restrict their connections with complementary medicine, and so may refer patients to alternative therapists if they wish, provided that they retain overall responsibility.

The problem is that evaluation of the effectiveness of alternative medicine remains in the hands of conventional doctors. The conventional doctors serving in the various government-sponsored committees have not trained in the alternative therapies which they are evaluating. Since the philosophies of treatment in alternative and conventional medicine differ so widely, conventional doctors are the least suitable judges. In addition to this, professional competition - which is, after all, only human - undoubtedly has an effect on decision-making. And perhaps most influential of all, the giant manufacturers of conventional remedies strongly oppose any step that might affect their production and their profits.

One example of how inappropriate it is for a conventional doctor to judge alternative medicine concerns what is called the risk/benefit ratio. Conventional doctors believe that for every degree of benefit which a medicine offers, there will be a degree of risk (side effects). This thinking is perfectly logical, for this is their experience with the medications that they themselves prescribe. When these doctors come to evaluate the effectiveness of, say, a homoeopathic or a herbal remedy, and are told that it has no side effects, they immediately dismiss the remedy, ascribing any positive effect on a patient to a placebo effect. Such remedy cannot have any curative value (benefit), they think, because it has no side effects (risk).

But how long can such an attitude survive? The answer is that things are bound to change as the public becomes increasingly aware of the dangerous side effects of conventional drugs - and the impotency of a large number of them, especially when the criterion is long-term, lasting cure - whilst at the same time learning to appreciate the effectiveness and safety of alternative medicine. When 80% of the public wants alternative medicine to be made available through the NHS, the government cannot continue to ignore the issue.

But since the government depends largely on the opinion of conventional doctors, bridges have to be built between conventional and complementary medical circles so that research into the efficacy of alternative remedies and therapies are appropriately carried out.

That said, there are in fact no restrictions on practising any form of complementary medicine here in the U.K. Since practice is more restricted in other European countries, organizations representing the various alternative and complementary therapies are trying to establish a firm legislative basis for the practice of alternative medicine before the European Economic Community becomes a unified single market in 1992.

Ancient legislation and the Medicine Act enshrine the right to practise alternative and complementary medicine without restrictions. However, because the state does not recognize alternative and complementary medicine as conventional medicine, no form of alternative or complementary therapy has been available through the NHS until very recently. Acupuncture is used in hospitals mainly for pain control; reflexology is quite acceptable to medical doctors since it involves no medication taken internally; therapeutic massage and aromatherapy are becoming more widely used in hospitals and clinics alongside conventional medicine.

In 1991 the House of Lords discussed a bill concerning a proposal to let more of the alternative and complementary therapies into the NHS. In the subsequent vote the House failed to pass the bill by just three votes. This does however at least show that the legislators are increasingly in favour of giving recognition to alternative and complementary medicine. It is only a matter of time before such recognition becomes enshrined in Law.

When you decide to train in a certain course in a particular school, be sure to ask about the availability of the register in which all the graduates are entered; these graduates thereby form an association consisting of members who have graduated from that school. It is now becoming increasingly difficult to obtain insurance to cover public and professional liability unless you are a member of such an association. Although accidents very rarely happen in the practice of complementary medicine, it is wise to have insurance, and indeed most associations insist on it. In any case the insurance premiums are usually fairly low, sometimes as little as 1% or 2% of the premium payable by a conventional doctor - further evidence of alternative medicine's comparative safety. All the courses listed in this book are run by schools that have such an association, and all have qualifications which lead to an accepted status, for which insurance cover is easily obtainable. Nonetheless, this is something that you should look into before committing yourself to any course.

Just recently, the British Register of Complementary Practitioners has been formed. In the future training in the different alternative therapies will be standardised and, hence, alternative medicine will be placed in a better position than it is now. The National Consultative Council (NCC) is also working in this direction (see Part VII: Organisations).

THE STATUS OF COMPLEMENTARY MEDICINE IN EUROPE NOW AND AFTER 1992

Many people who bought the first (1990) edition of this book have contacted us to ask about the future after 1992, and in particular whether they will be able to practise the therapy they are interested in. Our answer was always "We don't know". Pesonally I don't think anybody knows what exactly will happen because existing legislations in the individual countries and the trends in the practice of complementary and alternative medicine vary widely from country to country, and from therapy to therapy.

If the European Parliament is to pass laws which take the middle road complementary medicine will suffer in the countries where it is more freely practised such as the UK and Denmark, while it would be encouraged in countries where practice is currently more restricted.

However, if it was the question of establishing the evidence of efficacy through clinical trials - as people opposed to complementary medicine want - and if the governments or the European Commission were ready to allocate funds for such research, then these therapies would not be subject to long term restrictions.

Since the effect of public demand should be felt in government through the work of MP's, pressure groups, the media and other channels, and since the demand for complementary medicine is on the increase in European countries without exception, a United Europe must give the people the freedom to choose the healing system they want, and must allocate the necessary funds for research and training on approved and standardised programmes. Complementary and alternative medicine will then be placed on a firm, permanent basis.

To give an idea of the status of complementary medicine - and the public demand for it - in Europe, here are several excerpts from "Complementary Medicine in the European Community" published in 'Complementary Medical Research' RCCM Journal, May 1991.

"The European Commission asked the Belgium Consumer Association to carry out a study on the market for alternative medicine among European consumers. This study, written by G. Sermeus, covers seven Community countries (Belgium, Denmark, Germany, France, Italy, Netherlands, United Kingdom) as well as Finland and Switzerland. It shows that a considerable proportion of the population makes use of alternative therapies."

"The author notes that it is generally adults between the ages of 40 and 60 with a high level of education who make most use of alternative medicine."

FRANCE

"In France there has been a steady increase in the use of alternative medicine since 1970. Alternative medicines are a mixed group of varying disciplines. While the validity of homoeopathy and acupuncture is being debated by the Academy of Science, prescriptions and consultations to which they give rise are reimbursed by Social Security payments."

"In a survey of 1000 people in 1985, 49% of the people questioned had already used alternative medicine. Homoeopathy is most widely used (32%) followed by acupuncture (21%)."

BELGIUM

"General practitioners offer most of the available homoeopathy and acupuncture. Physiotherapists provide most of the osteopathy.

Alternative health care is not reimbursed by the social security system although there is evidence that patients would like the cost of alternative health care to be reimbursed. About one in four Belgians consult a complementary practitioner, perhaps the highest use of alternative health care in Europe."

DENMARK

"Alternative treatment by alternative health practitioners is legal in Denmark. This practice is regulated by the Medical Act which governs the practice of medicine and the law concerning drugs, including natural remedies."

"Alternative treatments are used in combination with traditional health services, and not instead of those services, although alternative health care is costly. Rather than choosing an alternative treatment because of dissatisfaction with orthodox medicine, patients choose an alternative treatment for a specific illness."

"Alternative health care is seen by the population as a legitimate form of treatment. It is only the established professional groups who perceive 'alternative' care as 'alternative', ie., something with which they must compete."

FINLAND

"Finnish law do not recognise alternative medicines. Only medically qualified doctors are allowed to practise medicine, which is interpreted as the right to diagnose and take fees. Acupuncture, however, is accepted as part of orthodox medical practice and is included in the medical curriculum."

"Traditional medicines are used by the older, less well-educated rural population. Newer forms of alternative health care are used by a younger urban population."

NETHERLANDS

"Orthodox and complementary medicine are integrated in the Netherlands, and this has been actively encouraged by the Government."

"Complementary medicines are flourishing in response to public demand, with acupuncture, anthroposophical medicine, homoeopathy, manipulation, naturopathy and paranormal healing the most popular."

"The cost of complementary treatments is reimbursed by private and public health insurance when prescribed by a general practitioner. This includes homoeopathic and anthroposophic medicines."

III THE MONEY MATTERS

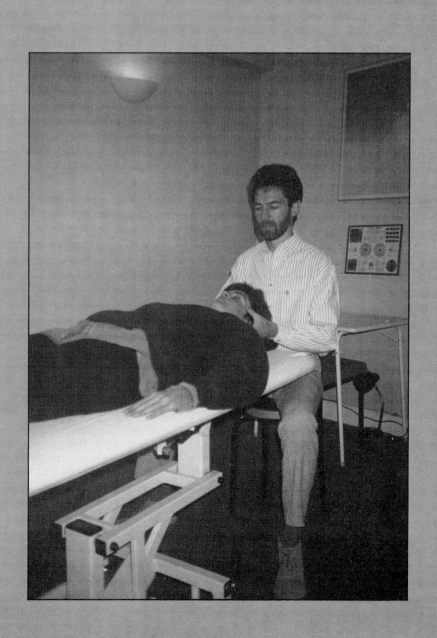

THE
COST OF TRAINING

Since the directory details do not show all the costs that have to be met upon enrolling in any course, this section has been written to minimize misunderstanding over this important matter.

COURSE FEES

The details of each course include, under FEES, the total fees of tuition plus the cost of any materials which are an essential part of the course - even if it is to be studied on a correspondence basis - before or during the course. Note, however, that books are not generally included in these costings.

OTHER COSTS

Any other costs mentioned in the college's prospectus, or in other information supplied by it, have been added up and entered under heading OTHER COSTS. These do not normally include books, but may include clothing or any other sundry items, and certainly includes any examination fees. Only in the rare exceptions do prospectuses list all conceivable costs - even the cost of a plastic skeleton in one case.

BOOKS

The cost of books should be taken into consideration; some courses will expect students to buy a considerable number. One homoeopathic college gave a figure of £200 per student as the normal budget for books. But, again, it depends on the course, the type of books, and even where they are purchased. Many of the standard homoeopathic texts are bought from India, where they are much cheaper. Generally, the longer the course, the higher will be the total cost of books. Short courses, and many part-time courses that do not involve extensive theoretical work, such as reflexology, aromatherapy and massage, often demand no more than a couple of books. You may also wish to purchase more books from the optional recommended reading list that is normally given out by the college at the beginning of the course.

Where we have experienced some confusion over details, or where details could not be given with certainty by the college or school (because of changes in the syllabus, etc), we have written A.F.D. (ask for details, from the college or school).

Please note that all course fees listed apply to 1992. These should remain valid if the course is no more than one year long. But if it is a full-time or part-time course that spans a period of years, then you should expect a possible increase of 5% to 10% per year, in line with inflation. Some colleges gave us more definite figures than others, and so we have been able to give an estimate of the increase to be expected in each year that the course runs. In any case, you should not find that course fees are markedly greater than those given in this directory, unless there is a radical change in the structure of the course.

ADDITIONAL COSTS

You should also take into consideration other additional costs, such as the cost of transportation, which could add up to a considerable sum if the course is held outside the area where you live. You may have to spend nights in a hotel, the cost of which might even exceed that of the course itself. Some courses require you to start practising from the start, so that you can present the cases you treat in a later stage of the course. If this is so, you might be obliged to buy some equipment even before you begin the course. A treatment couch, oil, charts, diagnostic equipment, or whatever might all add up to a bill in excess of £200.

If you have succeeded to getting a loan, such as the government's Career Development Loan (see the section below), remember that your living expenses could be added to the course costs for accounting purposes. Most of the colleges and schools offer easy methods of payment. Some allow the course fees be divided into two, three, four or even more instalments, but you will usually have to pay slightly more in these circumstances than if you settle the fee in one payment. Some allow you to pay as you study, for example paying monthly for a full-time or part-time course, or paying for each stage of a correspondence course as you reach it. In addition, some schools offer good discounts if you enrol in more than one course (see PART V about combining therapies).

FINANCING YOUR TRAINING

There are many ways in which you could raise the money needed to cover the course fees and all the other expenses (which could include your living expenses) that have to be met during your training.

A. CHEAPEST SOURCES

The cheapest way to finance your training is, obviously, from your savings, as there will be no interest to be paid. Also you can dispense with all the time-consuming form-filling and negotiations that accompany an application for a loan.

In a similar way, you may be able to borrow money from your parents, relatives or friends who are willing to help you start your first, or a new, career. In asking them, remember that you still have to present your case convincingly, so that they are sure that you know what you are doing. Tell them more about the kind of complementary medicine that you want to train in; they may have little knowledge about it, which may in any case be very much distorted, or no knowledge at all.

Selling your car to buy a cheaper one; selling any shares that you might have; using redundancy money - these are other possibilities. You are starting a new career which has prospects of good financial rewards, so you can comfort yourself that you will be able to recover the value of these assets in a matter of a year or two, or even within months
.

B. CAREER DEVELOPMENT LOANS

The government has a scheme called Career Development Loans in which one of three banks will lend you the money you need for your course, and will ask you to pay nothing until up to three months after your course has finished. One of the advantages of this loan scheme is that you do not pay interest on the loan for the whole period of the course (plus for the period of up to three months following the course); this interest is paid by the government.

The participating banks are Barclays Bank, Clydesdale Bank and the Co-operative Bank.

Conditions:

1. You have to be 18 years old or over.

2. You have to train in Great Britain.

3. The course should be job-related, though need not relate to your present or most recent job.

4. The course cannot last for longer than one year, or be shorter than one week. However, the final year of a longer course may qualify in certain circumstances; see the bank manager if you think this may apply to you.

5. The course should not be supported financially in any other way.

The bank will need to have full details about the course and about your personal circumstances in order to satisfy itself that you have chosen carefully and stand a good chance of succeeding - and that you will be able to repay the loan. Questions they may ask include the following:

Does the course lead to the qualification or level of skills you want?

Will the course help you get the level of earnings you need?

Can you afford the time to attend, study and complete the course?

Are there any other courses which would be more suited to your needs, such as a part-time one?

In choosing a course, have you taken account of any disability or health problems which might make it difficult for you to complete the course or get work afterwards?

Loan details:

1. The loan should not cover more than 80% of the course fees.

2. The maximum you can borrow is £5,000, and the minimum is £300.

3. You make no repayments at all to the bank during your course and for up to three months after you have finished it.

4. The Department of Employment will pay all the interest during the period of the course, plus up to three months following its completion.

5. Living expenses can be included in the loan if the course is a full-time course, provided that you are spending 21 hours or more a week in training, and

that you are working for less than 30 hours a week or not working at all.

Any other details, such as the repayment schedule, the length of the interest holiday that your course merits (the shorter the course, the shorter the interest holiday), the possibility of drawing the loan in instalments etc, can be supplied by the bank. The bank will of course be ready to provide you with a written quotation for the loan.

C. BANK LOANS

Every bank has a variety of loans to offer, and there must be one which will suit your needs. Some people think that banks are reluctant to give loans, and when they do, they think that the banks have done them a favour. In fact, if banks did not lend money they would be out of business. However, some banks, or indeed some branches, have stricter policies than others; the best way to find out is to pay a visit to your branch.

One kind of loan that all the banks offer is the Personal Loan. As with any other loan, it is not easily obtainable by somebody who is not working, such as a housewife. However, this should not stop you from going to your bank and asking for details.

The other possibility is a loan called a Reserve. The bank agrees to allow you to borrow any amount of money up to a certain maximum amount; your account will then be debited by the agreed monthly instalments as you repay the loan. Thus if you apply for this kind of loan and your application is accepted, then you can use it to pay the course fees either in one payment, or in instalments.

Another alternative is an overdraft facility, which your bank may agree to give you. The amount will vary according to your financial circumstances. Once this facility is made available to you, you will be able to draw money from your account up to the maximum that the bank has agreed to lend you, and you pay interest according to what you borrow.

D. GRANTS

Most Local Authority grants are discretionary (i.e. it is up to the Authority to decide whether they give them or not). This makes them very hard to get, but it is worth a try. The only way to know if this is a possibility is to apply to your Local Authority and to talk to somebody about it.

E. CHARITIES AND TRUSTS

You may be able to get a modest amount of funding through one of the few educational trusts which provide financial help for students. These trusts are usually set up for quite specific purposes - such as helping with the educational costs of people living in a certain locality.

You can find out more about these trusts through two publications which should be available in your local library: *The Directory of Grant Making Trusts* and *The Educational Grants Directory*. Your library may also be able to suggest other sources of information. Because of the limited resources of these trusts, and the great demand for them, you will have to produce a very good argument to support your case. Look very carefully at the criteria which they attach to funding: before applying, make quite sure that the trust does actually fund people in your position, and that you are eligible. This is not always clear from the documentation: if in doubt, ask.

As part of your application, you should attach a forcast of your financial needs for the duration of the course. This should show how a reasonable level of funding - in line with what the trust can offer - can help you. Present your case with a positive attitude, and do not exaggerate the financial hardships of undertaking the course: a trust is unlikely to fund you if you cannot demonstrate that you can control your finanical expenditure, and that your demands are realistic.

F. MORTGAGES AND REMORTGAGING

If you own a house or a flat and are not already paying for a mortgage, you can always take out a mortgage on it and use the mortgage money to pay for your course expenses. This solution is not recommended if your course fees and other costs are comparatively low. But if you are applying for a full-time or part-time course that takes many years to finish and will cost you thousands of pounds over the years, then mortgaging your house or flat is a possibility that you should consider.

Even if the property you own is already mortgaged, you may still be able to raise the money you need by remortgaging - provided that its market value is more than the maximum possible mortgage you can get. This is especially true if you have not mortgaged it for the maximum amount that the building societies or banks are prepared to lend; the maximums are calculated on the basis of your income and that of your partner, or could be related to the value of your house or flat if it has risen considerably since you first arranged the mortgage on it.

G. TEMPORARY EMPLOYMENT

Many people around the world work in part-time jobs to finance their training. Some work throughout the year, some take holiday jobs. You can do the same to raise the money for your course.

Working will of course be easier to accommodate if your course is a part-time one; full-time courses can consume all your time and effort. If both your work and your course are part-time, there should be no problem in managing to fulfil the responsibilities of both. Note, however, that in some cases, the college itself makes it a condition that you should not work at all while you are training.

One good way of working part-time is by doing work for your spouse, or for a relative or a friend. There may well be some useful work that you can do for them, and they may prefer to help you in this way rather than lend you money. As an additional incentive, the wages they pay to you should be tax-deductible.

CONCLUSION

If you can finance your training and the related expenses from your savings, or from interest-free loans from your parents, relatives or friends, then do it. This is the cheapest way, and involves no formalities. And if you can get a grant from the Local Authority so much the better. But if you seem to be unable to get free financing or an interest-free loan for your course, try a Career Development Loan. This is the next best choice - but you may not be able to fulfil the conditions.

Failing this, consider doing a part-time job, or even a full-time one if it does not conflict with your obligations towards the course. Earnings from such employment, even if not much, can help to finance your training and may even permit you to avoid any dependence on loans, with their accompanying interest.

If none of these possibilities are open to you, or if they provide only a partial solution, you should go to your bank and try to get a loan or an overdraft facility. Most banks offer Personal Loans of up to £10,000, which is double the maximum amount available through the Career Development Loan scheme, and may be considerably more that you can hope to borrow from a friend or relative.

The last choice is mortgaging or remortgaging your property, which may be the best solution if you need to raise more than any of the above options can supply.

THE COST OF SETTING UP A PRACTICE

Although this is a bridge you will cross after completing your course, many people like to know in advance the kind of expenses that they will incur when setting up their practice.

Some of the courses require their students to purchase equipment so that they can practise on cases during the course. If this applies to your course, you will have already paid for a certain amount of equipment for your clinic even before the course has ended.

A. BASIC EQUIPMENT

Most of the therapies require a treatment couch, on which the treatment is carried out. Indeed, the only exceptions are dietary therapy, herbalism, homoeopathy, yoga and iridology diagnosis. Some hypnotherapists, however, let their patients sit in a comfortable chair, instead of lying on a couch, when hypnotizing them. Treatment couches vary in make, size, model, and consequently in price. You should expect to pay anything between £150 and £300 for a good, brand-new couch, and less for a second-hand one.

Any clinic, whether a room in your house or a rented one, should have some furniture. You will need a desk and a chair for yourself, another for your patient, and a bookcase or some shelves for books and any materials that you use for the treatment. You should not refrain from buying any other item that makes your room look nicer and more welcoming. Obviously, the cost of these items very much depends on your taste and your ability to pay, but you can expect the costs to be in line with domestic furniture.

B. EQUIPMENT FOR TREATMENT

Some therapists need certain standard equipment for their treatment. Acupuncturists and auricular therapists use needles, moxibustion sticks and other items. Each needle costs around 10 pence when bought in bulk, and this should be calculated into the running costs.

Some acupuncturists also use electro-acupuncture, in which electric current is supplied to the needles through wires connected to the machine which generates the current. These machines cost somewhere in the region of £200 to £400; their cost is sometimes included in the cost of the course.

Acupuncture needles have to be sterilized after use, and the proper way to do this is by putting them in an electric autoclave. There are many makes of autoclave, and a range of prices, but you will not be able to purchase one for less than £200. More expensive autoclaves can cost £1,000 and more. Other small items that the acupuncturist may use are needle stands, needle saucers or dishes, charts and plastic models. An electric point-finder will cost anything between £50 to £300.

The biomagnets used by biomagnetic therapists cost around £70 for a set of two dozens (one dozen south poles and one dozen north poles). Magnetotherapists use a whole variety of magnets: big ones, small ones, electric ones, those embedded in leather for eye and throat troubles, small ceramic ones for the teeth, those sewn inside a back support or knee support, and those that form a part of a bracelet or a necklace. These may cost anything from few pounds for the small ones to £20 or £30 for a pair of big, strong magnets. However, if these are purchased from a country such as India the saving could be enormous: you might be able to purchase the whole set for a hundred pounds or so.

Iridologists use several items to do the iris diagnosis. A torch and a magnifier will cost around £30; this is the cheapest method. Those who can afford it will purchase a special camera which enables them to keep pictures of the patient's irises for future comparison as the treatment proceeds. These cameras cost hundreds of pounds, and are not normally purchased by practitioners who use iridology only as part of the treatment they practise

C. OILS, SALTS AND MEDICINES

Oils are used by therapeutic masseurs or masseuses to enable them to massage the body. Reflexologists use oils or talcum powder for the treatment of the feet. Aromatherapists keep a broad range of essential oils in their clinics to use in the treatment of various conditions.

Homoeopaths normally keep bottles of the most important homoeopathic medicines to use in acute conditions or in first aid. The same applies to any therapist using biochemic tissue salts.

A full set of Bach flower remedies is kept in the clinic of a therapist offering these, so that a remedy or mixture of remedies can be prepared for the patient on demand.

D. PROMOTIONAL AND ADMINISTRATIVE COSTS

Every therapist should prepare a business card bearing his or her name, the clinic name if any, address and telephone number, and the therapy he or she practises. The cards range from simple white cards to coloured and beautifully designed ones. A 100 of these cards could cost between £10 and £60 depending on design, quality and where they are printed, and the more you order the less will be the cost per card. You may also find appointment cards useful. This should show - in addition to the details of the business card - the appointment dates in the form of a table, or something similar.

Leave your card at the health food shops and chemists in your neighbourhood. Beauty salons and hairdressers are also good places at which to advertise your services.

Advertising in the appropriate publications and other outlets should have an important place in your budget. Although more than 70% of the people who consult you will probably come on the recommendation of other satisfied patients, advertising can attract a good number of additional patients. The ICM Report on Trends in Complementary Medicine suggests that more than 12% of the patients that consult you will do so after reading an advertisement.

Advertising is an art, and has to be done carefully to bring good results. You have to judge for yourself which outlet you should use - local newspapers or specialized health magazines - and for how long, what kind of design is most appropriate to your practice, and so on. You should be careful not to waste money in advertising, and should monitor carefully the success of each piece of publicity that you do.

It is not easy to give a cost for advertising, as there are so many factors that come into play. To give one example, advertising in the 'Practitioners' Announcements' pages in the magazine Here's Health for 6 months would cost around £150 for a standard 3cm box (3cm x 1/3 page column width), while a 3cm x 3cm box in the back page of the local paper would cost aorund £20 per week. However, you should normally qualify for a discount if you are booking a series, i.e., for several months.

Another way of paid advertising is by distributing leaflets in the neighbourhood of your clinic. These can be distributed on their own or as inserts in local papers. Using this method, you can say more not only about your clinic and services, but also about the therapy (or therapies) you practise.

Many people, for instance, do not quite understand what homoeopathy means; and many people hold mistaken beliefs about other therapies - for example, they think that they risk contracting the AIDS virus through acupuncture needles, or that they need to be mad to consult a psychotherapist, or that a hypnotherapist will manipulate them like a stage hypnotist on TV.

Local papers charge something like £15 - £20 per 1000 inserts, but will usually insist on a minimum number of inserts, such as 10,000.

You should not be shy of earning free publicity through giving speeches at health clubs, sports centres, gyms, and organisations such as women's groups. Also, tell your G.P. about your services. He/she might refer patients to you if he/she thinks it appropriate.

Other practitioners of alternative and complementary therapies should know about you so that patients maybe referred to you from them if they see fit, or if the patient asks for treatment by your therapy.

E. COST OF PREMISES

If you are working from home, there should be no (additional) rental costs. However, if you are paying rent a portion of the rent can be added to your total business expenses, which are tax- deductible. If you are paying a mortgage, a similar portion may be ascribed to your business in the same way. The same applies to the costs of electricity, gas, telephone and the community charge. Quite how you separate business costs from domestic ones for tax purposes depends on a number of factors, and you would be wise to take advice from a professional accountant.

If the clinic is a rented room, then the cost of this rent might be anywhere between £2.50 and £5 per hour. As we have mentioned earlier, this rental charge could be a fixed charge that you have to pay whether or not you have patients, or it could be a charge that you pay only for the hours that you see patients, which should work out cheaper. (See the section on EARNINGS.)

A very good source of information about all aspects of running a practice is a book called *Healthy Business* by Madeleine Harland and Glen Finn (themselves practitioners). It can be obtained from Hyden House Ltd, Little Hyden Lane, Clanfield, Hampshire PO8 0RU, Tel: 0705 596500.

EARNINGS

The main fee that is charged by any alternative practitioner is the consultation fee. This is normally slightly higher for the first consultation than that charged in the subsequent consultations, because in this first consultation the practitioner spends more time with the patient, to take his or her details and medical history, and to collect information relating to the complaint. For some therapies, especially homoeopathy, the first consultation is very lengthy, as the therapist needs to know a wide range of details in order to come up with the correct diagnosis and to treat the case successfully. Because of this, such therapists tend to charge more than others, especially for the first session.

Besides the length and nature of the treatment, the location of the practice plays a role in the fee-structure. More populated areas mean more patients, and also more fees to cover costs, but the costs may well be lower in rural areas. A newly-qualified practitioner, or a newly-opened clinic will normally charge less than a long-established clinic which has a large and established client-base.

CONSULTATION FEES

Consultation fees range from £10 to £30, with the first consultation costing around 50% more. However, the average fee usually ranges from £15 to £20. Some clinics are managed by a company, which takes a share of the fees charged by every practitioner working with them. Such clinics would, normally, charge more than the average.

The other factor affecting your earnings is whether you work from home, or from rented space. Working from home is cheaper. The alternatives are either to join an established, company-managed clinic, or to use a room in a clinic where you would have to pay a rental charge.

In a clinic, part of the fees you charge goes to the company; thus your earnings would be cut if you charged no more than you did when practising from home, yet you may well find that you lose patients if you charge more. On the other hand, if the clinic is well-established, you might well increase your number of patients as well as your earnings. But finding a place in a suitable clinic may well prove difficult.

RENTAL CHARGES FOR CLINICS

Renting a room in a clinic does not always mean that you have to pay a fixed amount of money. There are a number of possibilities, which will depend on the policy of the management. Some rent on hourly basis for fixed days of the week and/or for fixed times of the day. You could, say, rent a room for three days a week between 10am and 2pm, or from Monday to Friday in the afternoons only, and so on. The hourly rental charge (payable whether you see a patient or not) may be in the order of £2.50 to £5 per hour in London, and rather less in other areas of the country. Another alternative is to pay as you use a facility. As part of a clinic, you pay rent only if you have a patient, and so you pay from income.

Obviously the danger of rented facilities is that you could be paying for nothing if your patient does not show up, or if indeed you cannot fill the gaps between appointments. In any clinic, the efficient use of time and space is essential; the need to organize appointments, so that they do not clash or have long gaps between them, may call for a receptionist, whose job is to fix the appointments of all the practitioners using the clinic.

Working from home can be very convenient, especially for a practitioner with a young baby, or for the disabled practitioner, or for the practitioner working in remote parts of the country. You save both the expense and time involved in getting to and from a clinic, and avoid the stress, discomfort and pollution of the streets. There are no additional rental costs, and certainly no wasted rental charges when you have no patients. However, it usually takes longer to build up a practice when working from home, and so your earnings at the beginning would be lower. Indeed, you may have to charge a bit less to attract new clients to your practice. Whatever the circumstances, alternative medicine practices should be perfectly capable of bringing in healthy earnings - unless, of course, the therapist is incompetent.

Most of the people who come to consult a practitioner do so on the basis of reputation passed by word of mouth (73.5%, according to the Report on

Trends in Complementary Medicine by the Institute for Complementary Medicine - ICM). One satisfied patient will bring you further patients, and if they are satisfied, they will bring you more, and so your clientele can snowball. This same report suggested that over half the sample of practitioners in the survey were seeing between one and five new patients per week, and over a quarter of them between six and ten new patients every week. And that was in 1984, when the demand for complementary medicine was nowhere near what it is now. However, you should expect to wait for some time before you start to earn a satisfactory income.

SOME SAMPLE ESTIMATES FOR EARNINGS

So, suppose that you work from 10am to 6pm with a one-hour lunch break, and you work for five days a week only. Suppose also that all patients have sessions of one hour, from the time they knock on the door until the time they say good-bye. The total, maximum number of patients is thus 35 per week. If you charge £15 per session, you will end up with £525 per week - or anywhere between £375 and £525 allowing for gaps and for patients who have to cancel etc. If you work for 48 weeks a year, taking two holidays of two weeks each, your annual income will be between £18,000 to £25,000. But, suppose you work one hour more or charge 20% more, then your annual income will rise to somewhere between £22,000 to £30,000.

But not all therapists devote one full hour to every treatment session. Indeed, the ICM Report derives an average of 48 patients a week from a sample of more than 400 therapists. Using this figure, your annual income could be in the region of £25,000 to £35,000 if you charged £15 a session, or £30,000 to £41,000 if you charged 20% more, i.e. £18 a session. So your annual earnings, if you work from home, could be between £22,000 to £41,000, depending on the number of patients you see and the fees you charge.

Now, if you have to pay rent at £3.50 per hour, this will add up to about £5,000 per annum, assuming that you are renting for 6 hours a day. Your income after

rent would thus be anything between £17,000 to £36,000, depending on the number of patients you see and the fees you charge. So you see that working from home can save thousands of pounds a year - providing, of course, that the amount of work remains the same.

ADDITIONAL INCOME

In addition to the consultation fees, there are many other possible charges, depending on the therapy itself and the case being treated. Some aromatherapists, for example, sell the essential oils that are prescribed for home treatments. Homoeopaths, herbalists and naturopaths can sell homoeopathic medicine, herbal medicine or vitamins, minerals, proteins and other supplements to their patients. The sale of books, magnets, tapes and many other items could also form a part of your income. Tapes, for example, might be part of the hypnotherapy treatment, and hence would be sold either as part of the consultation fee, which would be higher to reflect this (in the region of £25), or as an additional charge to the normal consultation fee.

The sale of medicines, oils, equipment or any other item to your patients has many advantages, but also one disadvantage. This is that patients might think that you are making an unjustifiable profit in the sale, or even that you may be selling them items that are not really essential to the treatment. But the advantages to be set against this are persuasive. Firstly, you can make sure that your patients are getting exactly what they need - particularly when it comes to medicines, oils and other items of this kind, since there may be any number of makes on the market, some of which are less good than others. Secondly, you save your patients time and effort by providing them with the necessary items, so that they can start the treatment right away; this is sometimes vital. Lastly, you have the advantage of the additional income, to which you are perfectly entitled, given that you will have spent time selecting, buying and storing these products, and have furthermore saved your patients the time and effort they would have needed if they had had to buy these things from elsewhere.

IV THE COURSE DIRECTORY

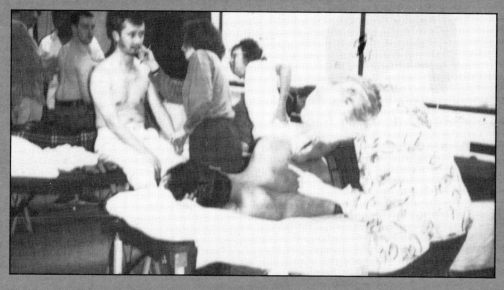

GENERAL ASPECTS OF THE SYLLABUS

Since the syllabus is not included in the information given in the directory, a brief account here will give an elementary idea of what the prospective student should expect.

THEORETICAL AND PRACTICAL

Every course consists of a theoretical part and a practical part. The theoretical part deals with the philosophy and principles of the therapy, providing detailed information about all the aspects of the therapy, including its professional aspects, and involves assessments in the form of exams, quizzes, essays and so forth. The practical (or clinical) part consists of practical tuition, such as blending herbs and making herbal medicine, practising the techniques of acupuncture on life-size plastic models, or practising manipulation on plastic spines in osteopathy and chiropractic courses; and it also involves real practice with real patients in the college's clinic or in some other clinic affiliated to the college. Obviously, the proportion to the total work done that is taken up by the practical side will differ from course to course. Some of the therapies, such as homoeopathy, need extensive theoretical study, while others need more practical work, to the extent that in some courses, such as yoga, the tuition is almost entirely practical.

ANATOMY AND PHYSIOLOGY

With the exception of Bach flower therapists, counsellors, hypnotherapists and psychotherapists (who deal primarily with the spiritual and emotional side of human life), every practitioner must have studied human anatomy and physiology. Anatomy and physiology courses can be taken on their own, either as short courses or as correspondence courses. In either case, the students must, after completing the studies, sit an examination to obtain the necessary qualifications. If they get anatomy and physiology qualifications from a nationally or internationally recognized body, such as the International Therapy Examination Council (ITEC), they will not usually need to take the anatomy and physiology part of the course and examinations in most of the courses.

HOME STUDY

Since most of the courses are part-time, with a considerable number of correspondence courses and some short ones, home study would represent a major part of the work that the student has to do.

PART TIME COURSES

Part-time courses, as you will find out from the course details, require no more than one, two or four weekends of attendance a month; hence a substantial amount of time for home study will be expected, in the order of 15 to 20 hours a week. This applies to acupuncture, homoeopathy, dietary therapy, osteopathy and the like.

However, in some courses where the ideas behind the therapy do not demand a great deal of formal tuition or home study, but where the treatment relies on good manual techniques, some practical clinical work between the tuition weekends may be all that is needed. Aromatherapy, biomagnetic therapy, massage and reflexology all fall into this category.

There are some part-time courses that span both these categories, such as some herbalism and iridology courses. Others, such as auricular therapy and cranio-sacral therapy, belong more to the second category than to the first; although the principles and philosophy involved require a fair amount of work, many of the courses are designed for qualified practitioners who already have a sound knowledge of this part of the subject.

FULL TIME COURSES

Full-time courses require no less work from the students than part-time courses, since the same material is covered. The main difference is simply that the total duration of the course is shorter, since the tuition is condensed into a shorter period.

SHORT COURSES

Short courses normally demand a certain amount of homework prior to the start of the course, especially if course time does not allow for anything other than the practical application of the therapy.

CORRESPONDENCE COURSES

Correspondence courses require no attendance, except either for a short concluding examination period (which may be no longer than a day), or for clinical sessions at the end of the course. In some, even the examination can be taken on a correspondence basis, especially if it can assess satisfactorily the student's individual command of the therapy through written essays or recording tapes during the course.

The clinical part of a correspondence course normally requires attendance at a clinic connected to the college. In most cases, you will be acting as an assistant to a practitioner in the clinic, gradually taking on more responsibility until you are able to perform the therapy on your own.

CASE STUDIES, PROJECTS AND PLACEMENTS

Many courses, the majority even, require you to submit case studies. This means that you will have to start working on patients (or volunteers, friends and relatives) while you are still in training. Some schools have their own clinics, which you would be asked to attend as a student-practitioner, under supervision, for a specific number of hours or days.

Some courses require students to submit projects and/or theses which form part of the basis for student assessment.

Some schools put students in placements in hospitals or other establishments as part of their training.

The Course Details in this directory should tell you about these aspects of any course.

HOW TO USE THE DIRECTORY

There are four indexes in the directory (Part IV). One is the main index, and the others could be thought of as indexes for cross-referring. There are four ways in which you can look up information in the directory in order to find the course that might be suitable for you. These indexes have been formulated in a way that makes it easy for you to move between them. Here are the four procedures:

A. *If you are looking for a course in a certain therapy and have no reservations about the location,* school or type of course, then you should look for the therapy in the main index, which is entitled COURSE DETAILS, and study the details of the various courses that are given under that therapy.

The therapies are listed alphabetically, and so if you are looking for a course in homoeopathy for instance, you have to locate the first course in homoeopathy which begins after the last course in herbalism. The list of homoeopathy courses ends before the first course in hypnotherapy, and so on.

After deciding that a certain course is perhaps suitable for you, read the name of the school running that course and turn to the SCHOOLS directory (cross index-1). The names of the schools are in alphabetical order. You will find here the name, address and telephone number of the school running the course that you are interested in, and so you can contact it and ask for the prospectus or details of the course.

Underneath the name, address and telephone number of each school, you will also find a list of all the courses that are held at that school. This will show you if the school is running any other courses that interest you. Arranging to train in more than one discipline at the same school is perhaps easier.

To summarize:

1. COURSE DETAILS (main index): Choose a course.

2. Read the name of the school running the course.

3. SCHOOLS (cross index-1): Note down the address and telephone number of the school.

4. Ring or write to the school for more details.

B. *If you are looking for a suitable course in a particular school* - such as a school that has been recommended by a friend, or one that is near to where you live - you should look through the SCHOOLS directory (cross index-1) to find that school. When you have found it, write down the course numbers of the courses that are held in that school.

Now, locate the courses by looking through the COURSE DETAILS (main index). The course numbers are listed from 1, which is the first course in acupuncture, onwards. If you could not find the course in question, turn to the end of the Part IV where an index of the course numbers and the pages they are listed in is provided.

If, after studying the details of all the courses that are run by that school, you are still interested in one of them, go back to the SCHOOLS directory to note down the address and telephone number of the school in question so that you can write to it or ring it for details.

To summarize:

1. SCHOOLS (cross index-1): Locate the name of the school you want.

2. Write down the course numbers.

3. COURSE DETAILS (main index): Locate the courses and study their details. If you fail look up the index at the end of Part IV.

4. SCHOOLS (cross index-1): Note down the address and telephone number of the school.

5. Ring or write to the school for more details.

C. *If you are looking for a course in a certain therapy in a certain area of the U.K.,* you should turn to the GEOGRAPHICAL index (cross index-2). Locate the county where you wish to train and then check if there are any courses in the therapy you are interested in. If you find some, note down their course numbers and repeat steps 3, 4 and 5 of B above.

However, if you do not find what you are looking for in that county, you may decide to see what courses available in the neighbouring counties. (Remember, of course, that a school in a neighbouring county may actually be nearer to you than a school at the other end of your own county.)

To summarize:

1. GEOGRAPHICAL (cross index-2): Locate the county where you want to train.

2. Write down the course numbers of the therapy(ies) you are interested in.

3. COURSE DETAILS (main index): Locate the courses and study their details. If you fail look up the index at the end of Part IV.

4. Read the name of the school running the course.

5. SCHOOLS (cross index-1): Note down the address and telephone number of the school.

6. Ring or write to the school for more details.

D. *If you are looking for a course of a particular type,* such as a part-time course, you should turn to the TYPE index (cross index-3) and look for the type of course you are interested in. If you find courses of that type in the therapy you want to train in, write down the numbers of these courses and repeat steps 3, 4, 5 and 6 above.

To summarize:

1. TYPE (cross index-3): Locate the type of course you want to follow.

2. Write down the course numbers of the therapy(ies) you are interested in.

3. COURSE DETAILS (main index): Locate the courses and study their details. If you fail look up the index at the end of Part IV.

4. Read the name of the school running the course.

5. SCHOOLS (cross index-1): Note down the address and telephone number of the school.

6. Ring or write to the school for more details.

COMBINATION COURSES

Some courses include more than one discipline (therapy) in their structure, syllabus or certification. These courses are listed under each of these disciplines (therapies) in the Course Details - the main index. However, the the way in which the course name is written is different in that the word relating to the therapy in question is picked out in bold, while the other therapies also included in the course are in a medium typeface.

To identify these courses at a glance, their course numbers are followed by (C).

ABBREVIATIONS AND NOTATION

Abbreviations

In the main index of the directory, there are some words that are abbreviated on all occasions, and some words that are abbreviated only sometimes. The reason behind this is the limitation in the space allocated to each course: space-saving has made some abbreviation inevitable.

The abbreviations, in alphabetical order, are as follows:

adv. = advanced

A&P = anatomy and physiology

A.F.D. = ask for details (from the school or college)

avail. = available

BAC = British Association for Counselling

cert. = certificate

CIBTAC = a qualification in beauty therapy

cl. = cli. = clin. = clinic. = clinical

corr. = corres. = corresp. = correspondence

dip. = diploma

equip. = equipment

equiv. = equivalent

eve = evening

exam. = examin. = examination

F/T = full-time

gradu. = graduation

hr = hour

ICM = Institute for Complementary Medicine

IFA = International Federation of Aromatherapists

indiv. = individual

int. = intens. = intensive

inter. = interm. = intermediate

introd. = introductory

IPTI = Independent Professional Therapists International

ISPA = International Society for Professional Aromatherapists

ITEC = International Therapy Examination Council

MAP = massage, anatomy and physiology

med. = medicine

min. = minimum

mth. = mnth. = month

N/A = not applicable

P = Part

PG = Post Graduate

physios. = physiotherapists

prelim. = preliminary

P/T = part-time

qualif. = qualifications

resid. = residential

S = Stage

TFH = Touch for Health

train. = training

U = Unit

vets. = veterinary surgeons

wk = week

wkday = week day

wknd = wkend = weekend

Y = yr = year

Notation

With Entrance Requirements (ENTRY REQ.), space does not permit anything other than giving the following notation:

a = age limit (with: = equal to; > more than; < less than)

b = O-levels

c = A-levels

d = O-levels and A-levels

e = qualified practitioners and doctors

f = interview may be necessary

g = entrance examination

h = nurses and physiotherapists

i = mature students with no qualifications

j = student therapists

* = desirable but not necessary

Notes:

1. For (a) above: e.g. a = 18 means 18 years old or more.

2. For (b), (c) and (d) above: the number and subjects (if there are desirable or compulsory ones) depend on the requirements of the school or college running the course. Ask them for details.

3. For (i) above: being a mature student is one of the following:

- a condition for acceptance if you have no qualifications, or

- preferable, or

- a condition in some cases.

4. A star between two alphabetical notations means that the first is the preferred condition, but if not held then the second condition has to be fulfilled. E.g., c*g means A-levels are desirable, but if an applicant does not have any, he or she may have to sit an entrance examination.

NOTES ON THE COURSE DETAILS

1. Where the Course Names for similar courses differ, this does not necessarily mean that the courses are in fact different, but simply that we are using the names of courses as supplied by the schools running them. For this reason you will find courses that bear the name of the school rather than the name of the therapy.

2. Fees have been entered either as totals for the full course, or per annum, per term etc, following the way in which fees have been presented to us by the schools. It is worth emphasizing what we said in "Earnings" Part III, that one should reckon on an annual increase of fees in line with inflation. Such an increase is not, however, inevitable.

3. The awards given may sometimes appear to be different for similar courses. This is either because the schools think of the same award (or qualification) in different ways, or because the syllabuses of the courses are different, although this may not be clear from the brief details given in this directory. Sometimes, however, the name of the award is no more than an expression of a school's preference for one title over another. For instance, a diploma or certificate can mean exactly the same thing. However, some schools rank a certificate below a diploma, and hence use a hierarchy of awards (certificate first, then a diploma for a more advanced course, and then possibly an advanced or post graduate diploma for yet another course).

4. If a course does not include information under the heading 'Notes', this does not mean that the notes given under other similar courses do not apply - but simply that the school in question did not supply any material for such notes.

COURSE DETAILS

ACUPRESSURE . ACUPUNCTURE (Including Electro-Acupuncture)

COURSE NO.: **1**   COURSE NAME: **Basic Acupressure**

SCHOOL: **GOOD SCENTS SCHOOL OF NATURAL THERAPIES**

TYPE: **P/T**   PERIOD: **5 weeks**

ATTENDANCE: **1 day a week**

VENUES: **West Sussex (Pulborough)**

FEES: **£150**   OTHER COSTS: **Nil**

COMMENCE: **February, June, October**   ENTRY REQ.: **None**

AWARD: **Certificate in Basic Acupressure**

COURSE NO.: **2**   COURSE NAME: **Acupuncture & Chinese Herbal Practitioners Training**

SCHOOL: **ACUPUNCTURE AND CHINESE HERBAL PRACTITIONERS TRAINING COLLEGE**

TYPE: **P/T**   PERIOD: **3 years**

ATTENDANCE: **Sundays (4 academic terms per year)**

VENUES: **Berkshire (Reading), London**

FEES: **£3,900**   OTHER COSTS: **Nil**

COMMENCE: **January, October**   ENTRY REQ.: **d, e, h, i**

AWARD: **Diploma in Traditional Chinese Medicine**

NOTES: **Membership of Acup. and Chin. Herbal Pract. Ass. and C.A.A. Hong Kong. Any extension of study free of charge.**

COURSE NO.: **3 (C)**   COURSE NAME: **Acupuncture, Homoeopathy and Naturopathy**

SCHOOL: **ASSOCIATION OF NATURAL MEDICINES**

TYPE: **P/T**   PERIOD: **3 years**

ATTENDANCE: **Y1 & Y2 = 1 weekend per month, Y3 = 1 weekend per month + 4 Saturdays + 10 days clinical**

VENUES: **Essex (Witham)**

FEES: **£640 per year**   OTHER COSTS: **Books**

COMMENCE: **September**   ENTRY REQ.: **f**

AWARD: **Certificate in Acupuncture OR Homoeopathy OR Naturopathy**

COURSE NO.: **4**   COURSE NAME: **Electro-Acupuncture**

SCHOOL: **BERKELEY COLLEGE OF NATURAL THERAPIES**

TYPE: **Correspondence**   PERIOD: **1 year approx.**

ATTENDANCE: **N/A**

VENUES: **N/A**

FEES: **£495**   OTHER COSTS: **Nil**

COMMENCE: **N/A**   ENTRY REQ.: **a>=18**

AWARD: **Diploma in Electro-Acupuncture**

NOTES: **Student can become a member of the Association of Complementary Acupuncture. Fees include machine.**

ACUPRESSURE . ACUPUNCTURE (including Electro-Acupuncture)

COURSE NO.: **5**	COURSE NAME: **Electro-Acupuncture**
SCHOOL: **BERKELEY COLLEGE OF NATURAL THERAPIES**	
TYPE: **P/T**	PERIOD: **1 year approx.**
ATTENDANCE: **Weekends**	
VENUES: **A.F.D.**	
FEES: **£995**	OTHER COSTS:
COMMENCE: **A.F.D.**	ENTRY REQ.: **a>=18**
AWARD: **Diploma in Electro-Acupuncture**	
NOTES: **Student can become a member of the Association of Complementary Acupuncture. Fees include machine.**	

COURSE NO.: **6**	COURSE NAME: **Acupuncture**
SCHOOL: **BRITISH COLLEGE OF ACUPUNCTURE**	
TYPE: **P/T**	PERIOD: **2-3 years according to qualifications**
ATTENDANCE: **Y1=14 wknds, Y2=1 wknd a month October to June, Y3= as Y2 + 200 hours clinical**	
VENUES: **London**	
FEES: **£3,100**	OTHER COSTS: **£180 books**
COMMENCE: **October**	ENTRY REQ.: **e, h (A.F.D. to see exemptions from Y1)**
AWARD: **Licentiate Diploma in Acupuncture**	
NOTES: **Diploma Chinese Herb. Med. (2 years P/T + Clinical at £1,000) is available for Members of Britsh Acup. Ass.**	

COURSE NO.: **7**	COURSE NAME: **Acupuncture**
SCHOOL: **THE COLLEGE OF NATURAL MEDICINE-LONDON**	
TYPE: **F/T - P/T**	PERIOD: **4 years**
ATTENDANCE: **Y1 = 3 days a week for 40 weeks, Y2 - Y4 = 15 hours a week for 40 weeks per year**	
VENUES: **London**	
FEES: **£1,800 for Y1, for rest A.F.D.**	OTHER COSTS: **Nil**
COMMENCE: **September**	ENTRY REQ.: **b*, f**
AWARD: **Diploma in Acupuncture**	
NOTES: **1st year is foundation course. Auriculotherapy course is available afterwards.**	

COURSE NO.: **8**	COURSE NAME: **Acupuncture & Oriental Medicine**
SCHOOL: **THE COLLEGE OF TRADITIONAL CHINESE ACUPUNCTURE, U.K.**	
TYPE: **P/T**	PERIOD: **3 years**
ATTENDANCE: **Y1=5 days in 1st wk+14x2-day sessions, Y2=as Y1, but 15x2-day sessions+extra 5 days,Y3=(10 1/2-day int., then 24 vistis of 1 day per wk + 11 days) for 1st 6 months, AND 2-day visit per month for 2nd 6 months**	
VENUES: **Warwickshrie (Leamington Spa)**	
FEES: **£1,895 for 1st year**	OTHER COSTS: **Approx, £200 for entire course**
COMMENCE: **March, September**	ENTRY REQ.: **d, f, i**
AWARD: **Licentiate in Acupuncture**	
NOTES: **Fees less if exempted from A, P or Biology. Advanced training available afterwards.**	

COURSE NO.: **9**	COURSE NAME: **Acupuncture**
SCHOOL: **INTERNATIONAL COLLEGE OF ORIENTAL MEDICINE**	
TYPE: **F/T**	PERIOD: **3 years**
ATTENDANCE: **30 weeks per year in 3 terms**	
VENUES: **West Sussex (East Grinstead)**	
FEES: **£9,400 approx.**	OTHER COSTS: **£150 books, materials etc**
COMMENCE: **September**	ENTRY REQ.: **b, c**
AWARD: **Licentiate of Acupuncture**	
NOTES: **Bachelor and Masters degrees are available afterwards**	

ACUPUNCTURE (Including Chinese Herbal Medicine)

COURSE NO.: **10**   COURSE NAME: **Acupuncture & Chinese Herbal Medicine**

SCHOOL: **LONDON COLLEGE OF CHINESE HERBAL MEDICINE & ACUPUNCTURE**

TYPE: **P/T**   PERIOD: **4 years**

ATTENDANCE: **Y1=16 long wknds+3 days clinical observation, Y2=16 long wknds+10 days clinical practice, Y3=14 long wknds+17 days clin. practice, Y4=10 long wknds+ 25 days clin. practice**

VENUES: **London (some clinical work can be outside London)**

FEES: **£2,400 per year**   OTHER COSTS: **Books**

COMMENCE: **September**   ENTRY REQ.: **b, f, i**

AWARD: **Diploma in Acupuncture & Chinese Herbal Medicine**

COURSE NO.: **11**   COURSE NAME: **Acupuncture and Chinese Herbal Medicine**

SCHOOL: **LONDON SCHOOL OF ACUPUNCTURE AND TRADITIONAL CHINESE MEDICINE**

TYPE: **F/T**   PERIOD: **4 years**

ATTENDANCE: **3 days a week + some evenings**

VENUES: **London**

FEES: **£3,250 per year**   OTHER COSTS: **Books**

COMMENCE: **October**   ENTRY REQ.: **d, f, i**

AWARD: **DipTCM (Diploma in Traditional Chinese Medicine)**

NOTES: **1 month intensive clinical practice in China at Graduation (optional).**

COURSE NO.: **12**   COURSE NAME: **Acupuncture and Moxibustion**

SCHOOL: **LONDON SCHOOL OF ACUPUNCTURE AND TRADITIONAL CHINESE MEDICINE**

TYPE: **F/T**   PERIOD: **3 years**

ATTENDANCE: **3 days a week + some evenings**

VENUES: **London**

FEES: **£3,250 per year**   OTHER COSTS: **Books**

COMMENCE: **October**   ENTRY REQ.: **d, f, i**

AWARD: **DipAc (Diploma in Acupuncture)**

NOTES: **1 month intensive clinical practice in China at Graduation (optional)**

COURSE NO.: **13**   COURSE NAME: **Practitioner Training Program**

SCHOOL: **NORTHERN COLLEGE OF ACUPUNCTURE**

TYPE: **P/T**   PERIOD: **3 years**

ATTENDANCE: **Y1=16 wknds, Y2=16 wknds + 10 clinical days, Y3=12 wknds + 20 clinical days**

VENUES: **Yorkshire (York)**

FEES: **£4,740 in 5 installments**   OTHER COSTS: **Books, materials**

COMMENCE: **October**   ENTRY REQ.: **d, i**

AWARD: **Diploma in Acupuncture**

NOTES: **Those with medical sciences training are exempt from western medicine part of the course**

COURSE NO.: **14**   COURSE NAME: **Electro-Acupuncture & Laser Therapy**

SCHOOL: **THE SOCIETY OF ELECTRO-ACUPUNCTURE & PHOTONIC MEDICINE**

TYPE: **P/T**   PERIOD: **4 months**

ATTENDANCE: **4 weekends**

VENUES: **London, Manchester**

FEES: **£1,250**   OTHER COSTS:

COMMENCE: **January, September**   ENTRY REQ.: **e**

AWARD: **Membership of the Society of Electro-Acupuncture & Photonic Medicine**

NOTES: **Open to those with general medical knowledge, orthodox or complementary. Electro-medical equipment included.**

ALEXANDER TECHNIQUE . ALLERGY THERAPY

COURSE NO.: **15**   COURSE NAME: **Alexander Technique**
SCHOOL: **ALEXANDER TECHNIQUE - THE NORTH LONDON TEACHERS TRAINING COURSE**
TYPE: **F/T**   PERIOD: **3 years**
ATTENDANCE: **4 days a week (16 hours), for 11 weeks a term, for 3 terms a year**
VENUES: **London**
FEES: **£950 per term**   OTHER COSTS:
COMMENCE: **Beginning of each term**   ENTRY REQ.: **a=<48, f, lessons with principal**
AWARD: **Diploma Certificate as Alexander Teacher**
NOTES: **Also Membership of Society of Teachers of the Alexander Technique (S.T.A.T.)**

COURSE NO.: **16**   COURSE NAME: **Alexander Technique Teacher Training**
SCHOOL: **THE CENTRE FOR TRAINING IN ALEXANDER TECHNIQUE**
TYPE: **F/T**   PERIOD: **3 years**
ATTENDANCE: **5 days a week (10am - 3pm) for 27 weeks per year**
VENUES: **London**
FEES: **£3,990 per year**   OTHER COSTS:
COMMENCE: **Jan, May, Oct**   ENTRY REQ.: **i, f (See NOTES)**
AWARD: **Certificate as Alexander Teacher leading to Membership of Society of Teachers of The Alex. Tech.**
NOTES: **Open to mature students with substantial experience in Alex. Tech., and several lessons with directors**

COURSE NO.: **17**   COURSE NAME: **Training Course for Teachers of the F. Matthias Alexander Technique**
SCHOOL: **THE CONSTRUCTIVE TEACHING CENTRE LTD**
TYPE: **F/T**   PERIOD: **3 years**
ATTENDANCE: **5 days per week, for 12 weeks per term, for 3 terms a year**
VENUES: **A.F.D. from S.T.A.T., 20 London House, 266 Fulham Road, London SW10 9EL, Tel: 071-351 0828**
FEES: **£3,525 per year**   OTHER COSTS: **£50 student membership fee in S.T.A.T.**
COMMENCE: **January, April, September**   ENTRY REQ.: **Course of instruction by individual lessons**
AWARD: **Certificate authorising teaching the technique, and eligible for election as Member in S.T.A.T.**
NOTES: **Students are encourged to remain for a PG term, free of charge, and receive nominal remuneration**

COURSE NO.: **18**   COURSE NAME: **Professional Association of Alexander Teachers Training**
SCHOOL: **THE PROFESSIONAL ASSOCIATION OF ALEXANDER TEACHERS**
TYPE: **F/T (for P/T A.F.D.)**   PERIOD: **3 years minimum**
ATTENDANCE: **4 attendances per week for F/T (15 hours) for 3 x 14 week terms per year**
VENUES: **Shropshire (Shrewsbury), West Midlands (Birmingham)**
FEES: **£500 per term for F/T (P/T pro rata)**   OTHER COSTS: **Textbooks**
COMMENCE: **By arrangement**   ENTRY REQ.: **a>=18 (See NOTES)**
AWARD: **P.A.A.T. Teaching Certificate**
NOTES: **There is considerable academic content. Normally, at least one year's private tuition is expected.**

COURSE NO.: **19**   COURSE NAME: **Food & Chemical Allergy - Diagnosis & Treatment**
SCHOOL: **INSTITUTE OF ALLERGY THERAPISTS**
TYPE: **Short**   PERIOD: **1 weekend**
ATTENDANCE: **1 weekend**
VENUES: **Avon (Bristol), London, Wales (Aberystwyth), West Midlands (Birmingham)**
FEES: **£105**   OTHER COSTS: **Test kits & Remedies**
COMMENCE: **A.F.D.**   ENTRY REQ.: **Nil**
AWARD: **For Membership of Institute of Allergy Therapists Register**

AROMATHERAPY

COURSE NO.: **20**   COURSE NAME: **Aromatherapy Associates Diploma Course**

SCHOOL: **AROMATHERAPY ASSOCIATES LTD**

TYPE: **P/T**   PERIOD: **60 hours**

ATTENDANCE: **A.F.D.**

VENUES: **London**

FEES: **£610**   OTHER COSTS: **Nil**

COMMENCE: **A.F.D.**   ENTRY REQ.: **MAP**

AWARD: **AA Diploma in Aromatherapy - recognised by IFA**

COURSE NO.: **21**   COURSE NAME: **Diploma Training in the Principles & Practice of Aromatherapy**

SCHOOL: **THE AROMATHERAPY SCHOOL**

TYPE: **F/T**   PERIOD: **3 months**

ATTENDANCE: **5 days a week for 12 weeks (9am to 1pm)**

VENUES: **London**

FEES: **£1,763**   OTHER COSTS: **Nil**

COMMENCE: **April, Sept, Oct, Nov**   ENTRY REQ.: **b***

AWARD: **The Aromatherapy School's Diploma**

COURSE NO.: **22**   COURSE NAME: **Post Graduate Clinical Aromatherapy Diploma Course**

SCHOOL: **THE ASSOCIATION OF MEDICAL AROMATHERAPISTS**

TYPE: **P/T**   PERIOD: **5 months**

ATTENDANCE: **5 weekends**

VENUES: **Strathclyde (Glasgow)**

FEES: **£350**   OTHER COSTS:

COMMENCE: **March, October**   ENTRY REQ.: **A&P**

AWARD: **Post Graduate Diploma in Clinical Aromatherapy**

COURSE NO.: **23**   COURSE NAME: **Aromatherapy**

SCHOOL: **ASSOCIATION OF NATURAL MEDICINES**

TYPE: **P/T**   PERIOD: **6 months**

ATTENDANCE: **Can be weekends, evenings or days (A.F.D.)**

VENUES: **Essex (Chelmsford)**

FEES: **Region of £200**   OTHER COSTS:

COMMENCE: **Throughout the year (A.F.D.)**   ENTRY REQ.: **f, Massage qualification**

AWARD: **Certificate in Aromatherapy**

COURSE NO.: **24**   COURSE NAME: **Aromatherapy**

SCHOOL: **AYLESBURY COLLEGE**

TYPE: **P/T**   PERIOD: **12 weeks**

ATTENDANCE: **3 hours once a week**

VENUES: **Buckinghamshire (Aylesbury)**

FEES: **£133**   OTHER COSTS:

COMMENCE: **Spring, Autumn**   ENTRY REQ.: **Massage qualification**

AWARD: **ITEC Certificate in Aromatherapy**

NOTES: **See other courses run by this college under LATE ENTRIES at the end**

AROMATHERAPY

COURSE NO.: **25**	COURSE NAME: **Postgraduate Course in Aromatherapy**
SCHOOL: **BEAUMONT COLLEGE OF NATURAL MEDICINE**	
TYPE: **P/T**	PERIOD: **10 weeks**
ATTENDANCE: **4 days + 1/2 day**	
VENUES: **East Sussex (Eastbourne)**	
FEES: **£280**	OTHER COSTS: **£40 exam**
COMMENCE: **April, Sept, Oct, Nov**	ENTRY REQ.: **MAP**
AWARD: **ITEC Diploma in Aromatherapy**	
NOTES: **Bed & Breakfast available from £10 per night**	

COURSE NO.: **26**	COURSE NAME: **Professional Aromatherapy Diploma (with reflexology techniques)**
SCHOOL: **BEAUMONT COLLEGE OF NATURAL MEDICINE**	
TYPE: **F/T**	PERIOD: **18 weeks**
ATTENDANCE: **4 days, then 5 days seperated by 8-week home study, then 1 day exam.**	
VENUES: **East Sussex (Eastbourne)**	
FEES: **£575**	OTHER COSTS: **£35 exam fee**
COMMENCE: **January, April, Sept, Oct**	ENTRY REQ.: **MAP**
AWARD: **Honours Diploma in Aromatherapy**	
NOTES: **Diploma recognised by ISPA**	

COURSE NO.: **27**	COURSE NAME: **Aromatherapy**
SCHOOL: **BERKSHIRE SCHOOL OF NATURAL THERAPY**	
TYPE: **P/T**	PERIOD: **2 months**
ATTENDANCE: **5 weekends (Saturday & Sunday)**	
VENUES: **Berkshire (Crowthorne)**	
FEES: **£350**	OTHER COSTS: **Nil**
COMMENCE: **February**	ENTRY REQ.: **ITEC in MAP or equiv., SRN & RGN**
AWARD: **ITEC Certificate in Aromatherapy**	
NOTES: **Advanced training available afterwards to I.S.P.A. membership**	

COURSE NO.: **28**	COURSE NAME: **Aromatherapy**
SCHOOL: **BERKSHIRE SCHOOL OF NATURAL THERAPY**	
TYPE: **P/T**	PERIOD: **2 months**
ATTENDANCE: **10 days (2 blocks Monday - Friday)**	
VENUES: **Berkshire (Crowthorne)**	
FEES: **£350**	OTHER COSTS: **Nil**
COMMENCE: **Jan, March, July, Oct**	ENTRY REQ.: **ITEC in MAP or equiv., SRN & RGN**
AWARD: **ITEC Certificate in Aromatherapy**	
NOTES: **Advanced training available afterwards to I.S.P.A. membership**	

COURSE NO.: **29**	COURSE NAME: **Advanced Aromatherapy**
SCHOOL: **BERKSHIRE SCHOOL OF NATURAL THERAPY**	
TYPE: **P/T**	PERIOD: **2 months**
ATTENDANCE: **4 days spread over 2 months**	
VENUES: **Berkshire (Crowthorne)**	
FEES: **£140**	OTHER COSTS: **Nil**
COMMENCE: **A.F.D.**	ENTRY REQ.: **ITEC in MAP and Aromatherapy or equiv.**
AWARD: **Diploma in Aromatherapy (I.S.P.A. accredited)**	
NOTES: **Accreditation by Internationl Society of Professional Aromatherapists**	

AROMATHERAPY

COURSE NO.: **30**   COURSE NAME: **Aromatherapy**

SCHOOL: **BOURNEMOUTH SCHOOL OF MASSAGE**

TYPE: **P/T**   PERIOD: **8 - 12 weeks**

ATTENDANCE: **4 days (9.45 - 5.30) + 4 evenings (6.45 - 10.00)**

VENUES: **Dorset (Bournemouth)**

FEES: **£195**   OTHER COSTS: **Nil**

COMMENCE: **January, May, November**   ENTRY REQ.: **f, ITEC MAP**

AWARD: **Diploma in Advanced Aromatherapy**

NOTES: **Also available to graduates of the school electro-therapies, basic colour healing and music therapy**

COURSE NO.: **31**   COURSE NAME: **Advanced Aromatherapy**

SCHOOL: **BOURNEMOUTH SCHOOL OF MASSAGE**

TYPE: **P/T**   PERIOD: **4 - 8 weeks**

ATTENDANCE: **4 days (9.45 - 5.30) + 2 evenings (6.45 - 10.00)**

VENUES: **Dorset (Bournemouth)**

FEES: **£195**   OTHER COSTS: **Nil**

COMMENCE: **February, August**   ENTRY REQ.: **ITEC Diploma Aromatherapy**

AWARD: **ITEC Diploma in Aromatherapy**

NOTES: **Candidates must have minimum of 3 months of experience in facial and body massage**

COURSE NO.: **32**   COURSE NAME: **Aromatherapy**

SCHOOL: **BRETLANDS BEAUTY TRAINING CENTRE**

TYPE: **Short**   PERIOD: **1 month**

ATTENDANCE: **4 weekends**

VENUES: **Kent (Tunbridge Wells)**

FEES: **£400**   OTHER COSTS: **Nil**

COMMENCE: **Twice yearly (A.F.D.)**   ENTRY REQ.: **MAP**

AWARD: **IFA Certificate/Diploma in Aromatherapy**

COURSE NO.: **33**   COURSE NAME: **IFA Aromatherapy**

SCHOOL: **CAMBRIDGE SCHOOL OF BEAUTY THERAPY**

TYPE: **P/T**   PERIOD: **5 - 10 weeks**

ATTENDANCE: **2 days a week for 5 - 10 weeks depending on qualifications already held**

VENUES: **Cambridgeshire (Cambridge)**

FEES: **£3,200-£4,200 depending on qualification held**   OTHER COSTS:

COMMENCE: **September**   ENTRY REQ.: **A.F.D., i**

AWARD: **IFA 'In-House' Diploma in Aromatherapy**

COURSE NO.: **34**   COURSE NAME: **Massage & Aromatherapy Intensive Course for Nurses**

SCHOOL: **THE CHALICE FOUNDATION**

TYPE: **Short**   PERIOD: **6 days**

ATTENDANCE: **6 consecutive days**

VENUES: **London**

FEES: **£195**   OTHER COSTS:

COMMENCE: **Every 3 months (A.F.D.)**   ENTRY REQ.: **Nurse/within caring or medical profession**

AWARD: **Diploma of course completion**

NOTES: **Following this course, students may enrole in the ITEC MAP course**

AROMATHERAPY

COURSE NO.: **35**   COURSE NAME: **Aromatherapy**

SCHOOL: **CHAMPNEYS COLLEGE OF HEALTH & BEAUTY**

TYPE: **Short**   PERIOD: **9 days**

ATTENDANCE: **4 days plus 4 days over two consecutive weeks**

VENUES: **Hertfordshire (Tring)**

FEES: **£562**   OTHER COSTS: **Nil**

COMMENCE: **Spring, Autumn**   ENTRY REQ.: **Minimum ITEC MAP or equivalent**

AWARD: **Champneys Diploma in Aromatherapy (IFA registered course No. 90/3/0104)**

COURSE NO.: **36**   COURSE NAME: **Aromatherapy**

SCHOOL: **THE EDINBURGH SCHOOL OF NATURAL THERAPY**

TYPE: **Short**   PERIOD: **1 week**

ATTENDANCE: **5 days**

VENUES: **Lothian (Edinburgh)**

FEES: **£130**   OTHER COSTS: **£40 reg. fee**

COMMENCE: **Throughout the year (A.F.D.)**   ENTRY REQ.: **Basic Massage (See under Massage) or ITEC MAP**

AWARD: **Certificate in Aromatherapy**

NOTES: **Graduates eligible to join I.P.T.I.**

COURSE NO.: **37**   COURSE NAME: **Aromatherapy**

SCHOOL: **FRANCES FEWELL (GEMINI INSTITUTE)**

TYPE: **P/T**   PERIOD: **60 hours**

ATTENDANCE: **1 weekend a month**

VENUES: **Essex (Chelmsford)**

FEES: **£500**   OTHER COSTS: **Exam fees**

COMMENCE: **January, March, June, September**   ENTRY REQ.: **MAP**

AWARD: **Association of Natural Medicines Diploma in Aromatherapy + IFA approved**

NOTES: **Advanced training available afterwards**

COURSE NO.: **38**   COURSE NAME: **Aromatherapy / Advanced Massage**

SCHOOL: **GABLECROFT COLLEGE**

TYPE: **P/T**   PERIOD: **4 - 5 months**

ATTENDANCE: **3 weekends**

VENUES: **Shropshire (Oswestry)**

FEES: **A.F.D.**   OTHER COSTS: **A.F.D.**

COMMENCE: **A.F.D.**   ENTRY REQ.: **ITEC MAP**

AWARD: **ITEC Certificate in Aromatherapy**

COURSE NO.: **39**   COURSE NAME: **Aromatherapy**

SCHOOL: **GOOD SCENTS SCHOOL OF NATURAL THERAPIES**

TYPE: **P/T**   PERIOD: **3 - 6 months**

ATTENDANCE: **1 day a week for 3 months, OR alternate weekends for 6 months**

VENUES: **West Sussex (Pulborough)**

FEES: **£300**   OTHER COSTS: **Essential oils**

COMMENCE: **April, September**   ENTRY REQ.: **MAP**

AWARD: **Diploma in Aromatherapy**

NOTES: **Students must sit the school's anatomy exam.**

AROMATHERAPY

COURSE NO.: **40**   COURSE NAME: **Aromatherapy**

SCHOOL: **GREENHILL COLLEGE**

TYPE: **P/T**   PERIOD: **6 months**

ATTENDANCE: **1 hour tutorial every fortnight + 6 x 3-hour workshops**

VENUES: **Middlesex (Harrow)**

FEES: **A.F.D.**   OTHER COSTS: **Essential oils**

COMMENCE: **January**   ENTRY REQ.:

AWARD: **ITEC Category 12 Aromatherapy**

COURSE NO.: **41**   COURSE NAME: **Aromatherapy Certificate Course**

SCHOOL: **HOTHS SCHOOL OF HOLISTIC THERAPIES**

TYPE: **P/T**   PERIOD: **9 months minimum**

ATTENDANCE: **Seminars and 6-weekend workshops**

VENUES: **Gloucestershire (Cheltenham), Leicestershire (Leicester)**

FEES: **£450**   OTHER COSTS: **Exam. fees**

COMMENCE: **A.F.D.**   ENTRY REQ.: **a>18, b**

AWARD: **Practitioners Certificate in Aromatherapy**

NOTES: **Eligible to enter the Association of Holistic Therapists and Register of Aromatherapy Organisation Council**

COURSE NO.: **42**   COURSE NAME: **Clinical Aromatherapy**

SCHOOL: **THE INSTITUTE OF CLINICAL AROMATHERAPY**

TYPE: **Short**   PERIOD: **8 days**

ATTENDANCE: **8 consecutive days (9am - 7pm approx.)**

VENUES: **London**

FEES: **£523**   OTHER COSTS: **Nil**

COMMENCE: **Approximately every month**   ENTRY REQ.: **MAP**

AWARD: **Diploma in Clinical Aromatherapy**

NOTES: **Course is IFA recognised**

COURSE NO.: **43**   COURSE NAME: **Aromatherapy for the Qualified Beauty Therapist**

SCHOOL: **THE INSTITUTE OF CLINICAL AROMATHERAPY**

TYPE: **Short**   PERIOD: **3 days**

ATTENDANCE: **3 consecutive days (9am - 7pm approx.)**

VENUES: **London**

FEES: **£218**   OTHER COSTS: **Nil**

COMMENCE: **Approximately every month**   ENTRY REQ.: **Beauty Therapist**

AWARD: **Certificate in Aromatherapy**

COURSE NO.: **44**   COURSE NAME: **Aromatherapy, Massage, Bodywork**

SCHOOL: **INSTITUTE OF TRADITIONAL HERBAL MEDICINE AND AROMATHERAPY**

TYPE: **P/T**   PERIOD: **12 months**

ATTENDANCE: **16 weekends, OR 30 week days**

VENUES: **London**

FEES: **£1,118**   OTHER COSTS: **Exam. fees £40, books**

COMMENCE: **January, May, October**   ENTRY REQ.: **None**

AWARD: **Diploma in Aromatherapy, Massage and Bodywork**

NOTES: **Those with A&P &/or massage are exempted from the relevant parts & fee reduction £125 for one or £250 for both**

AROMATHERAPY

COURSE NO.: **45**   COURSE NAME: **Aromatherapy**

SCHOOL: **LA ROSA SCHOOL OF HEALTH AND BEAUTY**

TYPE: **P/T**   PERIOD: **2 terms**

ATTENDANCE: **One evening per week for two terms (September-April)**

VENUES: **Devon (Brixham)**

FEES: **£250**   OTHER COSTS: **Nil**

COMMENCE: **September**   ENTRY REQ.: **ITEC MAP if seeking ITEC cat.12, or See NOTES**

AWARD: **Aromatherapy Diploma ITEC Category 12, or La Rosa Aromatherapy Diploma (see NOTES below)**

NOTES: **Those with massage experience but not ITEC MAP awarded La Rosa Diploma only**

COURSE NO.: **46**   COURSE NAME: **Aromatherapy**

SCHOOL: **LANCASHIRE HOLISTIC COLLEGE**

TYPE: **P/T**   PERIOD: **9 months**

ATTENDANCE: **1 weekend per month for 9 months**

VENUES: **Lancashire (Preston)**

FEES: **£110 per weekend approx. (£990)**   OTHER COSTS: **Exams, books, charts**

COMMENCE: **February, July**   ENTRY REQ.: **a=>18, b, i**

AWARD: **The College Diploma in Aromatherapy, ITEC Certificate or IFA Diploma**

NOTES: **Any part of Aromatherapy can be taken ad lib., but examination can only be passed upon attendance of all parts**

COURSE NO.: **47**   COURSE NAME: **Aromatherapy**

SCHOOL: **THE LEAVES INTERNATIONAL SCHOOL OF AROMATHERAPY, MASSAGE AND NATURAL THERAPY**

TYPE: **P/T**   PERIOD: **1 - 2 years**

ATTENDANCE: **3 x 5-day intensives + exam day (1 year), OR 8 weekends (1 - 2 years)**

VENUES: **Avon (Nr. Bath), Dorset, Wiltshire (Trowbridge)**

FEES: **£654**   OTHER COSTS: **Exam fee £33**

COMMENCE: **Twice yearly (A.F.D.)**   ENTRY REQ.: **ITEC MAP**

AWARD: **ITEC Diploma in Aromatherapy**

NOTES: **To prepare the students for the I.F.A. exam for full membership**

COURSE NO.: **48**   COURSE NAME: **Micheline Arcier Aromatherapy Diploma Course**

SCHOOL: **MICHELINE ARCIER AROMATHERAPY**

TYPE: **Short**   PERIOD: **8 days**

ATTENDANCE: **Thursday to Sunday in two consecutive weeks**

VENUES: **London**

FEES: **£510**   OTHER COSTS: **Nil**

COMMENCE: **A.F.D.**   ENTRY REQ.: **a=21, MAP with 2 yrs experience**

AWARD: **Diploma in Aromatherapy**

NOTES: **For nurses who have completed satisfactory facial and body massage course**

COURSE NO.: **49**   COURSE NAME: **Aromatherapy**

SCHOOL: **THE MILLFIELD SCHOOL OF BEAUTY THERAPY**

TYPE: **P/T**   PERIOD: **3 months**

ATTENDANCE: **7 - 8 days**

VENUES: **West Sussex (Rusper)**

FEES: **£350**   OTHER COSTS:

COMMENCE: **January, April, September**   ENTRY REQ.: **A&P**

AWARD: **ITEC Diploma in Aromatherapy**

AROMATHERAPY

COURSE NO.: **50**	COURSE NAME: **One Year Aromatherapy Diploma Course**
SCHOOL: **THE NATURAL CLINIC AROMATHERAPY SCHOOL**	
TYPE: **P/T**	PERIOD: **1 year**
ATTENDANCE: **8 blocks of 4 week days**	
VENUES: **Kent (Tunbridge Wells)**	
FEES: **£2,350**	OTHER COSTS: **Books up to £80, couch £200-£300**
COMMENCE: **March, September**	ENTRY REQ.: **a>18, f**
AWARD: **Diplomas in MAP and Aromatherapy**	
NOTES: **Qualify for external exam. to obtain diploma and membership of IFA**	

COURSE NO.: **51**	COURSE NAME: **Post Graduate Aromatherapy Course**
SCHOOL: **THE NATURAL CLINIC AROMATHERAPY SCHOOL**	
TYPE: **Short**	PERIOD: **9 days**
ATTENDANCE: **9 consecutive days**	
VENUES: **Kent (Tunbridge Wells)**	
FEES: **£500**	OTHER COSTS: **Books from £10 (optional)**
COMMENCE: **8 different days (A.F.D.)**	ENTRY REQ.: **e, h or MAP or massage**
AWARD: **Diploma in Clinical Authentic Aromatherapy**	
NOTES: **Another exam. to sit for diploma and membership of IFA**	

COURSE NO.: **52**	COURSE NAME: **Aromatherapy**
SCHOOL: **ON COURSE - PERSONAL AND PROFESSIONAL DEVELOPMENT CONSULTANCY**	
TYPE: **P/T**	PERIOD: **4 months**
ATTENDANCE: **12 evenings + 1 day theory and practical examinations**	
VENUES: **Hertfordshire (St. Albans)**	
FEES: **£290**	OTHER COSTS: **Nil**
COMMENCE: **April, July**	ENTRY REQ.: **ITEC Category 2,3,7,8 or 24**
AWARD: **ITEC Diploma in Aromatherapy**	

COURSE NO.: **53**	COURSE NAME: **Aromatherapy**
SCHOOL: **PARK SCHOOL OF BEAUTY THERAPY**	
TYPE: **Short**	PERIOD: **2 days**
ATTENDANCE: **1 weekend or 2 days minimum**	
VENUES: **Nottinghamshire (Retford)**	
FEES: **£235**	OTHER COSTS: **Exam fee, kit (optional)**
COMMENCE: **Every quarter (A.F.D.)**	ENTRY REQ.: **MAP, nursing qualifications**
AWARD: **ITEC Diploma in Aromatherapy**	

COURSE NO.: **54**	COURSE NAME: **Purple Flame Aromatherapy Diploma Course**
SCHOOL: **PURPLE FLAME SCHOOL OF AROMATHERAPY STRESS MANAGEMENT**	
TYPE: **P/T**	PERIOD: **3 months**
ATTENDANCE: **9 day intensive + 3 months practical assignments projects and home study**	
VENUES: **West Midlands (Warwick)**	
FEES: **£999**	OTHER COSTS: **Residential £266 (optional)**
COMMENCE: **April, July**	ENTRY REQ.: **None**
AWARD: **Aromatherapy Diploma**	
NOTES: **Graduates entitles to Membership of IFA and/or ISPA (International Society of Prof. Aromatherapy)**	

AROMATHERAPY

COURSE NO.: **55 (C)**   COURSE NAME: **Aromatherapy** and Reflexology

SCHOOL: **THE RADIX COLLEGE OF BEAUTY CULTURE**

TYPE: **Short**   PERIOD: **1 week**

ATTENDANCE: **5 consecutive days + 1 exam. day**

VENUES: **Strathclyde (Ayr)**

FEES: **£353**   OTHER COSTS: **Exam fee**

COMMENCE: **Throughout the year (A.F.D. & see Notes)**   ENTRY REQ.: **e, or allied professional with massage experience**

AWARD: **ITEC Diplomas in Aromatherapy and Reflexology (2 diplomas)**

NOTES: **Running a course depends on No. of candidates, but two definite commence. dates are May and October**

COURSE NO.: **56**   COURSE NAME: **Diploma Course in Holistic Aromatherapy**

SCHOOL: **RAWORTH COLLEGE FOR SPORTS THERAPY & NATURAL MEDICINE**

TYPE: **F/T**   PERIOD: **3 months**

ATTENDANCE: **4-5 days a week for 12 weeks**

VENUES: **Surrey (Dorking)**

FEES: **£1,320**   OTHER COSTS: **£150**

COMMENCE: **Jan, April, July, Sep**   ENTRY REQ.: **f**

AWARD: **Diploma in Holistic Aromatherapy**

NOTES: **Includes A&P, basic reflexology, TFH & clinical. ITEC diploma/MAP orAromatherapy could be taken at the end**

COURSE NO.: **57**   COURSE NAME: **Post Graduate Diploma in Clinical Aromatherapy**

SCHOOL: **RAWORTH COLLEGE FOR SPORTS THERAPY & NATURAL MEDICINE**

TYPE: **P/T**   PERIOD: **6 months**

ATTENDANCE: **2 days a week for 2 terms (11 weeks long each)**

VENUES: **Surrey (Dorking)**

FEES: **£1,350**   OTHER COSTS: **£40 approx.**

COMMENCE: **January**   ENTRY REQ.: **e**

AWARD: **Diploma in Clinical Aromatherapy**

NOTES: **Includs pathology, chinese med., nutrition, aromatherapy for sports injuries & clinical**

COURSE NO.: **58**   COURSE NAME: **Aromatherapy**

SCHOOL: **SCHOOL OF NATURAL THERAPIES AND ORIENTAL STUDIES**

TYPE: **P/T**   PERIOD: **3 months**

ATTENDANCE: **3 weekends**

VENUES: **Hampshire, London**

FEES: **£240**   OTHER COSTS: **£30**

COMMENCE: **A.F.D.**   ENTRY REQ.: **MAP Certificate**

AWARD: **The School Certificate in Aromatherapy**

NOTES: **ITEC Certificate available. Advanced course also available.**

COURSE NO.: **59**   COURSE NAME: **Aromatherapy Diploma (Post Graduate)**

SCHOOL: **SCHOOL OF PHYSICAL THERAPIES - BASINGSTOKE**

TYPE: **P/T**   PERIOD: **3 months**

ATTENDANCE: **4 day intensive + 100 hours clinical**

VENUES: **Hampshire (Basingstoke)**

FEES: **£160**   OTHER COSTS: **£20**

COMMENCE: **March, June, Sept, Nov**   ENTRY REQ.: **ITEC MAP**

AWARD: **ITEC Post Graduate Diploma in Aromatherapy**

NOTES: **Advanced ITEC aromatherapy course available afterwards**

AROMATHERAPY

COURSE NO.: **60**   COURSE NAME: **Advanced Diploma in Aromatherapy (Post Graduate)**

SCHOOL: **SCHOOL OF PHYSICAL THERAPIES - BASINGSTOKE**

TYPE: **P/T**   PERIOD: **2 months**

ATTENDANCE: **2 day intensive + 50 hours clinical**

VENUES: **Hampshire (Basingstoke)**

FEES: **£85**   OTHER COSTS: **£10**

COMMENCE: **January, June**   ENTRY REQ.: **ITEC Diploma in Aromatherapy**

AWARD: **ITEC Advanced Diploma in Aromatherapy**

NOTES: **Graduates are eligible for application to Membership of ISPA. Adv. Diploma Course avail. afterwards.**

COURSE NO.: **61**   COURSE NAME: **Aromatherapy Diploma (Post Graduate)**

SCHOOL: **THE SCHOOL OF PHYSICAL THERAPIES (GUILDFORD)**

TYPE: **P/T**   PERIOD: **3 months**

ATTENDANCE: **4-day intensive + 100 hours of clinical practice**

VENUES: **Surrey (Guildford)**

FEES: **£160**   OTHER COSTS: **£10**

COMMENCE: **March**   ENTRY REQ.: **ITEC MAP**

AWARD: **ITEC Post Graduate Diploma in Aromatherapy**

NOTES: **Graduates are eligible for application to Membership of ISPA. Adv. Diploma Course avail. afterwards.**

COURSE NO.: **62**   COURSE NAME: **Aromatherapy Diploma (Post Graduate)**

SCHOOL: **THE SCHOOL OF PHYSICAL THERAPIES (KINGSTON)**

TYPE: **P/T**   PERIOD: **3 months**

ATTENDANCE: **4-day intensive + 100 hours of clinical practice**

VENUES: **Surrey (Kingston)**

FEES: **£160**   OTHER COSTS: **£52**

COMMENCE: **March, June, Sep, Nov**   ENTRY REQ.: **ITEC MAP**

AWARD: **ITEC Post Graduate Diploma in Aromatherapy**

NOTES: **Graduates are eligible for application to Membership of ISPA. Adv. Diploma Course avail. afterwards.**

COURSE NO.: **63**   COURSE NAME: **Advanced Diploma in Aromatherapy**

SCHOOL: **THE SCHOOL OF PHYSICAL THERAPIES (KINGSTON)**

TYPE: **P/T**   PERIOD: **2 months**

ATTENDANCE: **2-day intensive + 50 hours of clinical practice**

VENUES: **Surrey (Kingston)**

FEES: **£80**   OTHER COSTS: **£45**

COMMENCE: **July**   ENTRY REQ.: **ITEC Diploma in Aromatherapy**

AWARD: **ITEC Advanced Diploma in Aromatherapy**

NOTES: **Graduates are eligible for application to Membership of ISPA**

COURSE NO.: **64**   COURSE NAME: **Shirley Price Aromatherapy Certificate (Includ. Foundation Course)**

SCHOOL: **SHIRLEY PRICE AROMATHERAPY SCHOOL**

TYPE: **P/T**   PERIOD: **3 - 6 months**

ATTENDANCE: **Foundation course = 5 consecutive days, Part I & Part II = 5 consecutive days each + exam day**

VENUES: **Cheshire, Hants, Herts, Leics, London, Norfolk, Strathclyde, Tyne&Wear, Wilts, N. Ireland, Eire, Overseas**

FEES: **Foundation = £306, Parts I&II = £646**   OTHER COSTS: **Nil**

COMMENCE: **Various (A.F.D.)**   ENTRY REQ.: **a=>18, A&P for Parts I & II**

AWARD: **Shirley Price Aromatherapy Certificate**

NOTES: **Higher studies available afterwards (see below)**

AROMATHERAPY

COURSE NO.: 65	**COURSE NAME: Shirley Price Clinical Practitioners Diploma in Aromatherapy**

SCHOOL: SHIRLEY PRICE AROMATHERAPY SCHOOL

TYPE: P/T	**PERIOD: 3 - 6 months**

ATTENDANCE: 5 consecutive days + 1 week experience in an approved clinic

VENUES: Leicestershire (Hinckley)

FEES: £306	**OTHER COSTS: Nil**
COMMENCE: A.F.D.	**ENTRY REQ.: a=>21, Aromatherpy Certificate**

AWARD: Shirley Price Clinical Practitioners Diploma in Aromatherapy

NOTES: Higher studies available afterwards (see below)

COURSE NO.: 66	**COURSE NAME: Shirley Price Post Diploma Course**

SCHOOL: SHIRLEY PRICE AROMATHERAPY SCHOOL

TYPE: Short	**PERIOD: 2 - 3 weeks**

ATTENDANCE: 2 weekends

VENUES: Leicestershire (Hinckley)

FEES: £229	**OTHER COSTS: Nil**
COMMENCE: A.F.D.	**ENTRY REQ.: Aromatherapy qual. to I.S.P.A. Membership**

AWARD: Will count towards the Higher Diploma

NOTES: First of series of short courses which form a Higher Diploma course the School is initiating in 1992

COURSE NO.: 67	**COURSE NAME: Holistic Aromatherapy**

SCHOOL: THE TISSERAND INSTITUTE

TYPE: F/T	**PERIOD: 6 months**

ATTENDANCE: 3 days a week (9.30am-5.00pm) for 2 x 9 week terms

VENUES: London

FEES: £2,808	**OTHER COSTS: Nil**
COMMENCE: May, September	**ENTRY REQ.: $21<a<55*$, b, f**

AWARD: Diploma in Holistic Aromatherapy

NOTES: See end of Course Details for courses in A&P and reflexology

---

COURSE NO.: 68	**COURSE NAME: Holistic Aromatherapy**

SCHOOL: THE TISSERAND INSTITUTE

TYPE: P/T	**PERIOD: 2 years**

ATTENDANCE: 52 class days (A.F.D.)

VENUES: London

FEES: £2,808	**OTHER COSTS: Nil**
COMMENCE: March, September	**ENTRY REQ.: $21<a<55*$, b, f**

AWARD: Diploma in Holistic Aromatherapy

NOTES: See end of Course Details for courses in A&P and reflexology

---

COURSE NO.: 69	**COURSE NAME: Aromatherapy**

SCHOOL: SOUTH WEST SCHOOL OF HOLISTIC TOUCH

TYPE: P/T	**PERIOD: 3 months**

ATTENDANCE: 1 weekend monthly

VENUES: Devon (Exeter)

FEES: £150	**OTHER COSTS: Nil**
COMMENCE: Twice yearly (A.F.D.)	**ENTRY REQ.: None**

AWARD: ITEC Certificate in Aromatherapy

AROMATHERAPY

COURSE NO.: **70**   COURSE NAME: **Essential Oil Therapy (Aromatherapy)**

SCHOOL: **WENDOVER HOUSE COLLEGE**

TYPE: **P/T**   PERIOD: **10 weeks**

ATTENDANCE: **1 evening OR 1 day a week**

VENUES: **London**

FEES: **£350**   OTHER COSTS: **Nil**

COMMENCE: **January, May**   ENTRY REQ.: **MAP or Beauty Therapy Certificate**

AWARD: **ITEC Diploma in Aromatherapy**

COURSE NO.: **71**   COURSE NAME: **Aromatherapy**

SCHOOL: **WENDY LORENS SCHOOL OF COMPLEMENTARY THERAPIES**

TYPE: **P/T**   PERIOD: **6 months (minimum)**

ATTENDANCE: **9 days usually over weekends**

VENUES: **Cornwall (Penzance), Devon (Plymouth)**

FEES: **£380**   OTHER COSTS: **£35 exam fee**

COMMENCE: **A.F.D.**   ENTRY REQ.: **a>18, MAP**

AWARD: **Diploma in Aromatherapy from the Association of Natural Medicine (Essex)**

NOTES: **Accomodation arranged if required**

COURSE NO.: **72**   COURSE NAME: **Aromatherapy Diploma Course**

SCHOOL: **THE WEST LONDON SCHOOLS OF THERAPEUTIC MASSAGE, REFLEXOLOGY & SPORTS THERAPY**

TYPE: **Short**   PERIOD: **2 days**

ATTENDANCE: **1 weekend**

VENUES: **London**

FEES: **£79**   OTHER COSTS:

COMMENCE: **A.F.D.**   ENTRY REQ.: **MAP**

AWARD: **ITEC Diploma in Aromatherapy**

NOTES: **Advanced course available afterwards**

COURSE NO.: **73**   COURSE NAME: **Aromatherapy**

SCHOOL: **THE WHITE ROSE SCHOOL OF BEAUTY**

TYPE: **Short**   PERIOD: **1 - 5 weeks**

ATTENDANCE: **Monday to Friday (9.30 - 4pm) for 1 week, OR 1 Saturday (9.30 - 4pm) per week for 5 weeks**

VENUES: **Greater Manchester (Huddersfield)**

FEES: **£300**   OTHER COSTS: **Book and exams. £65**

COMMENCE: **A.F.D.**   ENTRY REQ.: **a>17, MAP or nursing**

AWARD: **ITEC Diplom in Aromatherapy**

COURSE NO.: **74**   COURSE NAME: **I.F.A. Registered Aromatherapy Course**

SCHOOL: **THE YORKSHIRE COLLEGE OF BEAUTY THERAPY**

TYPE: **Short**   PERIOD: **2 weeks**

ATTENDANCE: **4 days a week**

VENUES: **West Yorkshire (Leeds)**

FEES: **£470**   OTHER COSTS:

COMMENCE: **August**   ENTRY REQ.: **A&P**

AWARD: **I.F.A. Diploma in Aromatherapy**

AROMATHERAPY . ASSERTIVENESS . AURICULAR THEAPY

COURSE NO.: **75**   COURSE NAME: **Aromatherapy Diploma Course**

SCHOOL: **ZIVA BELIC AROMATHERAPY INTERNATIONAL SCHOOL**

TYPE: **Short**   PERIOD: **66 hours**

ATTENDANCE: **3 hours daily, Wednesday, Thursday, Saturday and Sunday**

VENUES: **London, UAE (Abu Dhabi)**

FEES: **£200**   OTHER COSTS: **Nil**

COMMENCE: **A.F.D.**   ENTRY REQ.: **None**

AWARD: **The School's Diploma in Aromatherapy**

COURSE NO.: **76**   COURSE NAME: **Trainers Training in Assertiveness**

SCHOOL: **ON COURSE - PERSONAL AND PROFESSIONAL DEVELOPMENT CONSULTANCY**

TYPE: **P/T**   PERIOD: **2 months**

ATTENDANCE: **3 alternate weekends**

VENUES: **Hertfordshire (St. Albans)**

FEES: **£200**   OTHER COSTS: **Nil**

COMMENCE: **October**   ENTRY REQ.: **Assertiv. workshop, teaching, personal developm.**

AWARD: **Certificate for Trainers of Assertiveness**

COURSE NO.: **77**   COURSE NAME: **Advanced Course in Auricular Acupuncture**

SCHOOL: **THE ASSOCIATION OF AURICULOTHERAPY G.B. LTD.**

TYPE: **P/T**   PERIOD: **1-3 weekends depending on subject**

ATTENDANCE: **1 - 3 weekends depending on subject**

VENUES: **Bedfordshire, Lancashire, Scotland (central)**

FEES: **£100 per weekend**   OTHER COSTS:

COMMENCE: **February onwards**   ENTRY REQ.: **A.F.D.**

AWARD: **Accreditation to a Hons. Diploma in Auriculotherapy**

NOTES: **50% discount for Full Members of Association. Venues depending on response.**

COURSE NO.: **78**   COURSE NAME: **Auricular Acupuncture Therapy**

SCHOOL: **THE COLLEGE OF NATURAL MEDICINE-LONDON**

TYPE: **P/T**   PERIOD: **6 months**

ATTENDANCE: **2 days a week**

VENUES: **London**

FEES: **A.F.D.**   OTHER COSTS:

COMMENCE: **A.F.D.**   ENTRY REQ.: **e or g (see NOTES below)**

AWARD: **Diploma in Auricular Acupuncture Therapy**

NOTES: **Open to gradutes of the College's Acupuncture Diploma course, or others with recognised comprehensive training**

COURSE NO.: **79**   COURSE NAME: **Auricular Acupuncture**

SCHOOL: **THE MODERN TUTORIAL SCHOOL OF AURICULAR ACUPUNCTURE**

TYPE: **P/T**   PERIOD: **1 year for practitioners, 2 years otherwise**

ATTENDANCE: **1 wknd every 2 months + case histories**

VENUES: **Bedfordshire, Lancashire, Scotland (central)**

FEES: **£650-£700 depending on equipment (1 year)**   OTHER COSTS: **2 year with A&P at £600 approx.**

COMMENCE: **February**   ENTRY REQ.: **e, h for 1 year**

AWARD: **Diploma in Auricular Acupuncture**

NOTES: **On receipt of Diploma graduates are allowed entry into the Ass. of Auriculotherapy, G.B. Ltd.**

AURICULAR . AUTOGENIC TRAIN. . AYURVEDA . BATES METHOD . BIOMAGNETIC

COURSE NO.: **80**   COURSE NAME: **Auricular Therapy**

SCHOOL: **NATIONAL SCHOOL OF MASSAGE**

TYPE: **P/T**   PERIOD:

ATTENDANCE: **3 weekends**

VENUES: **Lancashire (Southport)**

FEES: **£180**   OTHER COSTS: **Nil**

COMMENCE: **A.F.D.**   ENTRY REQ.: **A course in Physical Therapy and practising**

AWARD: **Post Graduate**

COURSE NO.: **81**   COURSE NAME: **Teacher Trainers Course in Autogenic Training**

SCHOOL: **CENTRE FOR AUTOGENIC TRAINING**

TYPE: **P/T**   PERIOD: **2 years**

ATTENDANCE: **8 week P/T trainees + 3 weekends trainers + Tutorials (See NOTES below)**

VENUES: **London**

FEES: **£580**   OTHER COSTS: **Nil**

COMMENCE: **Trainees: Continuous, Trainers: April, May** ENTRY REQ.: **e, h, degree in clinical psychology, psychotherapy**

AWARD: **Membership of British Association of Autogenic Training and Therapy**

NOTES: **Students must attend as trainees (patients), then start their trainers training**

COURSE NO.: **82**   COURSE NAME: **Ayurveda**

SCHOOL: **AYURVEDA - (Science of Life) INDIAN MEDICAL SCIENCE**

TYPE: **P/T**   PERIOD: **1 1/2 years**

ATTENDANCE: **Introductory course= 2 days a week or weekends, Certificate course= as Introductory**

VENUES: **Leicestershire (Leicester)**

FEES: **£1,660 (£520 Introductory+£1,040 Certificate)**   OTHER COSTS: **Nil**

COMMENCE: **June or by appointment**   ENTRY REQ.: **None**

AWARD: **Certificate in Ayurveda**

COURSE NO.: **83**   COURSE NAME: **Professional Training in the Bates Method**

SCHOOL: **THE BATES COLLEGE**

TYPE: **P/T**   PERIOD: **22 months**

ATTENDANCE: **Y1 (foundation)= 10 wknds, Y2 (professional)= 10 wknds + 10 days clinical**

VENUES:: **London**

FEES: **£1,000 approx.**   OTHER COSTS: **Books & equipment**

COMMENCE: **October**   ENTRY REQ.: **f, assessment for Y2 also**

AWARD: **Certificate of Professional Competence to Teach the Bates Method**

NOTES: **Also eligible for Teaching Membership of The Bates Association and Bates section of the BRCM**

COURSE NO.: **84**   COURSE NAME: **Biomagnetic Therapy**

SCHOOL: **BRITISH BIOMAGNETIC ASSOCIATION**

TYPE: **P/T**   PERIOD: **5 - 6 months**

ATTENDANCE: **3 weekends introductory, intermediate and advanced**

VENUES:: **London**

FEES: **£480**   OTHER COSTS: **Biomagnets**

COMMENCE: **Spring**   ENTRY REQ.: **e**

AWARD: **Certificate in Biomagnetic Therapy**

NOTES: **Open to graduate practitioners only**

CHIROPRACTIC

COURSE NO.: **85**   COURSE NAME: **BSc Chiropractic**

SCHOOL: **ANGLO-EUROPEAN COLLEGE OF CHIROPRACTIC**

TYPE: **F/T**   PERIOD: **4 years**

ATTENDANCE: **36 weeks per year**

VENUES: **Dorset (Bournemouth)**

FEES: **£5,100**   OTHER COSTS: **£1,800**

COMMENCE: **September**   ENTRY REQ.: **a=>18, c (chemistry a must)**

AWARD: **BSc Chiropractic (CNAA)**

NOTES: **5 - year Masters programme in course of preparation**

COURSE NO.: **86 (C)**   COURSE NAME: **Osteopathy and Chiropractic**

SCHOOL: **THE COLLEGE OF NATURAL MEDICINE-LONDON**

TYPE: **F/T - P/T**   PERIOD: **4 years**

ATTENDANCE: **Y1 = 3 days a week for 40 weeks, Y2 - Y4 = 15 hours a week for 40 weeks per year**

VENUES: **London**

FEES: **£1,800 for Y1, for rest A.F.D.**   OTHER COSTS: **Nil**

COMMENCE: **September**   ENTRY REQ.: **b*, f**

AWARD: **Diploma in Osteopathy and Chiropractic**

NOTES: **1st year is foundation course. Cranio-Sacral Osteopathy course avail. afterwards.**

COURSE NO.: **87**   COURSE NAME: **McTimoney Chiropractic**

SCHOOL: **McTIMONEY CHIROPRACTIC SCHOOL**

TYPE: **P/T**   PERIOD: **4 years**

ATTENDANCE: **A.F.D.**

VENUES: **Oxfordshire (Oxford)**

FEES: **£1,487 p.a.**   OTHER COSTS: **£250 books & spine**

COMMENCE: **January**   ENTRY REQ.: **c**

AWARD: **M.C. McTimoney Chiropractic**

COURSE NO.: **88**   COURSE NAME: **Art & Science of McTimoney-Corley Chiropractic**

SCHOOL: **WITNEY SCHOOL OF CHIROPRACTIC**

TYPE: **P/T**   PERIOD: **4 years**

ATTENDANCE: **10 tutorials per year avoiding January & August**

VENUES: **Oxfordshire (Oxford)**

FEES: **£150 per tutorial**   OTHER COSTS: **£150 books**

COMMENCE: **September**   ENTRY REQ.: **a>21, b or c desirable but not compulsory, f***

AWARD: **Doctorate of Chiropractic**

NOTES: **Application is normally close end of May. 4th year clinical and venues for which will vary.**

COURSE NO.: **89**   COURSE NAME: **Art & Science of McTimoney-Corley Chiropractic for Animals**

SCHOOL: **WITNEY SCHOOL OF CHIROPRACTIC**

TYPE: **P/T**   PERIOD: **1 year (see NOTES below)**

ATTENDANCE: **For practical work as, when and where animal patients available**

VENUES: **Oxfordshire (Oxford)**

FEES: **A.F.D.**   OTHER COSTS:

COMMENCE: **After completion of human course**   ENTRY REQ.: **Completion of human course, vet. surgeons etc**

AWARD: **Certificate of Competence**

NOTES: **Takes less for veterinary surgeons. The treatment can be adapted for any domestic animals.**

COLON HYDROTHERAPY . COLOUR THERAPY

COURSE NO.: 90 **COURSE NAME: Colon Hydrotherapy**
SCHOOL: **THE HOWELL COLLEGE OF LYMPH & COLON THERAPISTS**
TYPE: **P/T** PERIOD: **5 weeks**
ATTENDANCE: **5 days over 2 wknds**
VENUES: **Dorset (Sherborne)**
FEES: **£590** OTHER COSTS: **£10 registration fee**
COMMENCE: **A.F.D.** ENTRY REQ.: **a=21, e, h**
AWARD: **Diploma in Colon Hydrotherapy**
NOTES: **Fees include accomodation and all meals. Leads to Membership of British Ass. of Lymph & Colon Therapists.**

COURSE NO.: 91 **COURSE NAME: Colour Healing & Psychology**
SCHOOL: **BRANTRIDGE FOREST SCHOOL**
TYPE: **Correspondence** PERIOD: **Open**
ATTENDANCE: **Nil**
VENUES: **N/A**
FEES: **£270** OTHER COSTS: **Nil**
COMMENCE: **N/A** ENTRY REQ.: **None**
AWARD: **Diploma in Colour Healing & Psychology**
NOTES: **Higher studies available afterwards**

COURSE NO.: 92 **COURSE NAME: Aura - Soma Colour Therapy**
SCHOOL: **DEV AURA ACADEMY**
TYPE: **Short** PERIOD: **1 year**
ATTENDANCE: **4 residential weeks**
VENUES:: **Lincolnshire (Tetford)**
FEES: **£370 per week** OTHER COSTS: **Nil**
COMMENCE: **Spring** ENTRY REQ.:
AWARD: **Diploma in Aura - Soma Colour Therapy**
NOTES: **Fees include residence**

COURSE NO.: 93 **COURSE NAME: Colour Therapy Certificate Course**
SCHOOL: **HOTHS SCHOOL OF HOLISTIC THERAPIES**
TYPE: **P/T** PERIOD: **6 months**
ATTENDANCE: **Seminars**
VENUES:: **Gloucestershire (Cheltenham), Leicestershire (Leicester)**
FEES: **£280** OTHER COSTS: **Nil**
COMMENCE: **On - Going** ENTRY REQ.: **a>18, b**
AWARD: **Practitioners Certificate in Colour Therpay**
NOTES: **Qualifies for Membership of the Association of Holistic Therapists**

COURSE NO.: 94 **COURSE NAME: Hygeia Colour Therapy**
SCHOOL: **THE HYGEIA COLLEGE OF COLOUR THERAPY**
TYPE: **P/T** PERIOD: **1 year**
ATTENDANCE: **2 weekends per month + 2-week residential**
VENUES:: **Gloucestershire (Avening), London**
FEES: **£104 per weekend + £900 residentials** OTHER COSTS:
COMMENCE: **February, September** ENTRY REQ.: **Introductory course, reading books**
AWARD: **Certificate - Diploma: H.cert.C.TH., H.Dip.C.TH.**
NOTES: **Not all courses have to be taken in order or in any one half year**

COLOUR THERAPY . COMPLEMENTARY M;EDICINE

COURSE NO.: 95   COURSE NAME: **The Living Colour Training Programme**

SCHOOL: **LIVING COLOUR**

TYPE: **P/T**   PERIOD: **3 years approx.**

ATTENDANCE: **Y1= 1 wknds+4 hr/month personal therapy+several eve. and days follow ups, Y2=4 days (2 hr)/ fortnight+clinical, Y3=3 day workshops+4 1/2 days (108 hr) clinical+supervision and endorsement in 1 year**

VENUES:: **London**

FEES: **£3,000**   OTHER COSTS: **£550 optional, recommended equipment**

COMMENCE: **Spring, Autumn**   ENTRY REQ.: **f**

AWARD: **Colour Therapy Diploma**

COURSE NO.: 96   COURSE NAME: **Mental Colour Therapy**

SCHOOL: **MAITRYA SCHOOL OF HEALING (Camberley Branch)**

TYPE: **P/T**   PERIOD: **March - June**

ATTENDANCE: **3 weekends**

VENUES:: **Surrey (Camberley)**

FEES: **£360**   OTHER COSTS: **Nil**

COMMENCE: **Spring**   ENTRY REQ.:

AWARD: **Certificate in Mental Colour Therapy**

NOTES: **Fees include books and vegetarian meals**

COURSE NO.: 97   COURSE NAME: **Colour Therapy**

SCHOOL: **THE PEARL HEALING CENTRE**

TYPE: **P/T**   PERIOD: **1 year**

ATTENDANCE: **6 - 7 days + practical work**

VENUES:: **Surrey (Croydon)**

FEES: **£180**   OTHER COSTS: **Books etc**

COMMENCE: **September**   ENTRY REQ.:

AWARD: **Certificate in Colour Therpay**

COURSE NO.: 98   COURSE NAME: **Univer. Colour Healers Research Foundation Spectro-Chrome course**

SCHOOL: **UNIVERSAL COLOUR HEALERS RESEARCH FOUNDATION**

TYPE: **P/T**   PERIOD: **2 years**

ATTENDANCE: **1 weekend per month**

VENUES:: **Berkshire, Buckinghamshire**

FEES: **£600**   OTHER COSTS: **Introd. course £20**

COMMENCE: **October**   ENTRY REQ.: **Introductory course**

AWARD: **Diploma UCHRF - Spectro-Chrome**

NOTES: **Eligible to enter the British Register for Complementary Practitioners - Colour Section**

COURSE NO.: 99   COURSE NAME: **British College of Complementary Medical Practices**

SCHOOL: **BRITISH COLLEGE OF COMPLEMENTARY MEDICAL PRACTICES**

TYPE: **P/T**   PERIOD: **4 years**

ATTENDANCE: **Y1 = 6 wknds, Y2 = 12 wknds+100 hours clinical, Y3 & Y4 = 24 wknds + 100 hours clinical each**

VENUES: **Manchester**

FEES: **£10,650**   OTHER COSTS:

COMMENCE: **Variable (A.F.D.)**   ENTRY REQ.: **None**

AWARD: **3 Diplomas awarded at: Basic, Interm. and Adv. levels (Doctorate after completion of course and thesis)**

NOTES: **Includes aromath. herbalism, hypnoth., iridology, kinesiology., massage, naturop., reflexology, osteop. and shiatsu**

COMPLEMENTARY MEDICINE

COURSE NO.: **100**	COURSE NAME: **Yoga Therapists Course**
SCHOOL: **THE BRITISH SCHOOL OF YOGA**	
TYPE: **Correspondence + Short**	PERIOD: **2 years (recommended)**
ATTENDANCE: **Parts 1, 2A and 2B are correspondence, Part 3 = 1 week**	
VENUES: **A.F.D.**	
FEES: **£650**	OTHER COSTS:
COMMENCE: **Anytime. Practical P3 = Twice a year.**	ENTRY REQ.: **None**
AWARD: **BSY Diploma and Associate Membership (BSYA(T))**	
NOTES: **The course is not a yoga course, but a general alter./complem. medicine course based on yoga principles (A.F.D.)**	

COURSE NO.: **101**	COURSE NAME: **Holistic Health**
SCHOOL: **THE HOWELL COLLEGE OF HOLISTIC HEALTH**	
TYPE: **P/T**	PERIOD: **1 - 3 years depending on qualification**
ATTENDANCE: **1 weekend per month**	
VENUES: **London**	
FEES: **£1,058**	OTHER COSTS: **£10 registraion fee**
COMMENCE: **Jan, June, Aug, October**	ENTRY REQ.: **a=18**
AWARD: **Certificate in Holistic Health (1 yr), Diploma in Holistic Health (2 yrs)**	
NOTES: **Fees can be on monthly basis. Scholarships available. Leads to Membership of professional association.**	

COURSE NO.: **102**	COURSE NAME: **Holistic Health Care in Practice**
SCHOOL: **LIFE FOUNDATION SCHOOL OF THERAPEUTICS**	
TYPE: **Correspondence + Practical**	PERIOD: **1 year**
ATTENDANCE: **4 residential weekends**	
VENUES: **West Midlands (Wolverhampton)**	
FEES: **£290**	OTHER COSTS: **£40 full board resid. each wknd**
COMMENCE: **September**	ENTRY REQ.: **None**
AWARD: **Certificate in Holistic Care (Does not entitle practice. Course is introduction before training in specific therapies)**	
NOTES: **Includes introduction to homoeop., osteop., herbal., stress man., reflex., aromath., Bach flower rem. and others**	

COURSE NO.: **103**	COURSE NAME: **Natural Health Practitioner's Diploma**
SCHOOL: **RAWORTH COLLEGE FOR SPORTS THERAPY AND NATURAL MEDICINE**	
TYPE: **F/T**	PERIOD: **1 year**
ATTENDANCE: **4-5 days a week for 3 terms each 11 weeks long**	
VENUES: **Surrey (Dorking)**	
FEES: **£3960**	OTHER COSTS: **£200**
COMMENCE: **July, September**	ENTRY REQ.: **b, i, f**
AWARD: **Natural Health Practitioner's Diploma**	
NOTES: **Includes A&P, aromath., reflex., TFH, acupressure, pathology, with many awarded ITEC Dip. & Cert.**	

COURSE NO.: **104**	COURSE NAME: **Natural Health Practitioner's Diploma**
SCHOOL: **RAWORTH COLLEGE FOR SPORTS THERAPY AND NATURAL MEDICINE**	
TYPE: **P/T**	PERIOD: **1 year**
ATTENDANCE: **By arrangement**	
VENUES: **Surrey (Dorking)**	
FEES: **A.F.D.**	OTHER COSTS: **A.F.D.**
COMMENCE: **July, September**	ENTRY REQ.: **b, i, f**
AWARD: **Natural Health Practitioner's Diploma**	
NOTES: **Includes A&P, aromath., reflex., TFH, acupressure, pathology, with many awarded ITEC Dip. & Cert.**	

COUNSELLING

COURSE NO.: **105 (C)**   COURSE NAME: **Counselling,** Hypnotherapy and Psychotherapy

SCHOOL: **ASSOCIATION FOR BODYMIND THERAPY AND TRAINING (AABTT)**

TYPE: **P/T**   PERIOD: **2 years**

ATTENDANCE: **1 evening (2 hours) per week + bi-monthly weekends + 6-day residential in the country**

VENUES: **London**

FEES: **£1,920**   OTHER COSTS: **Individual therapy**

COMMENCE: **January, April, September**   ENTRY REQ.: **i, some experience preferable**

AWARD: **Diploma of AABTT**

NOTES: **Completion entitles practice in counselling, hypnotherapy, psychotherapy and group facilitation**

COURSE NO.: **106**   COURSE NAME: **Counselling**

SCHOOL: **ASSOCIATION OF NATURAL MEDICINES**

TYPE: **P/T**   PERIOD: **2 years**

ATTENDANCE: **1 weekend per month**

VENUES.: **Essex (Witham)**

FEES: **£500**   OTHER COSTS:

COMMENCE: **September**   ENTRY REQ.: **f**

AWARD: **Certificate in Counselling**

COURSE NO.: **107**   COURSE NAME: **Counselling for Change**

SCHOOL: **BILSTON COMMUNITY COLLEGE**

TYPE: **P/T**   PERIOD: **1 academic year**

ATTENDANCE: **1 Monday evening per week (6pm - 9pm)**

VENUES: **West Midlands (Bilston)**

FEES: **£90**   OTHER COSTS: **R.S.A. reg. £60 + Cert. £15**

COMMENCE: **September**   ENTRY REQ.: **a>21, working in a job involving counselling**

AWARD: **Royal Society of Arts (R.S.A.) Certificate in Counselling**

NOTES: **Practical approach to counselling. Introduction to a number of approaches, but focusing on Humanist Theory.**

COURSE NO.: **108 (C)**   COURSE NAME: **Diploma in Counselling** and Psychotherapy

SCHOOL: **CENTRE FOR COUNSELLING AND PSYCHOTHERAPY EDUCATION**

TYPE: **P/T**   PERIOD: **4 years**

ATTENDANCE: **1 evening per week (7pm - 10pm) + 6 weekend training per year + 4 extra training days in Y1**

VENUES: **London**

FEES: **£950 per year**   OTHER COSTS: **Personal therapy**

COMMENCE: **January**   ENTRY REQ.: **Counselling Skills training + previous therapy**

AWARD: **Diploma in Counselling and Psychotherapy (accredited by British Association for Counselling BAC)**

COURSE NO.: **109**   COURSE NAME: **The Process of Counselling**

SCHOOL: **CENTRE FOR INTEGRATIVE PSYCHOTHERAPY & COUNSELLING**

TYPE: **P/T**   PERIOD: **3 years**

ATTENDANCE: **1 evening/afternoon per week over 30 weeks per year + 3 weekends per year & occasional seminars**

VENUES: **Somerset (Taunton)**

FEES: **£1,708**   OTHER COSTS: **Own counselling from year 2**

COMMENCE: **October**   ENTRY REQ.:

AWARD: **For national accreditation after appropriate clinical experience**

COUNSELLING

URSE NO.: **110** COURSE NAME: **Certificate in Counselling Skills**

SCHOOL: **CENTRE FOR STRESS MANAGEMENT**

TYPE: **P/T** PERIOD: **40 hours**

ATTENDANCE: **9 fortnightly daytime, OR 12 evening sessions**

VENUES: **London**

FEES: **£295** OTHER COSTS:

COMMENCE: **A.F.D.** ENTRY REQ.: **f**

AWARD: **Certificate in Counselling Skills. Accredited by the Institute for Complementary Medicine.**

COURSE NO.: **111** COURSE NAME: **Diploma Course in Holistic Therapeutic Counselling**

SCHOOL: **COLLEGE OF HOLISTIC MEDICINE**

TYPE: **P/T** PERIOD: **21 months**

ATTENDANCE: **Y1 = 10 x 2-day sessions (weekdays), Y2 = 8 x 2-day sessions + 4-day residential**

VENUES:: **Strathclyde (Glasgow), London**

FEES: **£1,780** OTHER COSTS: **£25 per annum for books**

COMMENCE: **September** ENTRY REQ.: **f**

AWARD: **Diploma in Counselling**

NOTES: **Y1 is complete in itself, suitable for practitioners wishing to incorporate counselling skills in practice**

COURSE NO.: **112** COURSE NAME: **Certificate in Counselling Skills**

SCHOOL: **DONCASTER COLLEGE**

TYPE: **P/T** PERIOD: **1 academic year**

ATTENDNCE: **1 evening per week**

VENUES: **South Yorkshire (Doncaster)**

FEES: **£420** OTHER COSTS: **Nil**

COMMENCE: **October** ENTRY REQ.: **None**

AWARD: **Certificate in Counselling Skills (issued by the AEB)**

NOTES: **Those completing this course and Cert. in Couns. (Theory) are eligible to apply for 1 yr AEB Dip. course in Couns.**

COURSE NO.: **113** COURSE NAME: **Biodynamic Physiatry and Counselling**

SCHOOL: **GERDA BOYESEN CENTRE**

TYPE: **P/T** PERIOD: **2 years**

ATTENDANCE: **20-day wknd intensives + 1 eve per wk + 1 eve per fortnight for 30 weeks/year + 5-10 hours supervised clinical per week for 36 wk/year + weekly psychotherapy for 30 wks per year minimum**

VENUES:: **London**

FEES: **£3,600** OTHER COSTS: **£60**

COMMENCE: **January** ENTRY REQ.: **a>21, Biorelease & MAP course**

AWARD: **Certificate in Biodynamic Physiatry and Counselling**

COURSE NO.: **114** COURSE NAME: **Certificate in Counselling Skills**

SCHOOL: **GESTALT CENTRE LONDON**

TYPE: **P/T** PERIOD: **1 year**

ATTENDANCE: **10 afternoons per term for 3 terms + 3 weekends + 4-day residential**

VENUES:: **London**

FEES: **£999** OTHER COSTS: **£8/session individual counselling - 30 hours**

COMMENCE: **October** ENTRY REQ.: **f, should engage in paid/unpaid counselling**

AWARD: **Certificate in Counselling Skills**

NOTES: **Diploma course, or Gestalt Psychotherapy training available afterwards**

COUNSELLING

COURSE NO.: **115**   COURSE NAME: **Certificate in Counselling Skills**

SCHOOL: **HALEY COLLEGE FOR COUNSELLING AND PSYCHOTHERAPY**

TYPE: **P/T**   PERIOD: **1 year**

ATTENDANCE: **2 weekends per term (6 weekends in total)**

VENUES: **Surrey (Burstow)**

FEES: **£280**   OTHER COSTS: **Nil**

COMMENCE: **September**   ENTRY REQ.: **Introductory wknd**

AWARD: **Certificate in Counselling Skills**

NOTES: **Practical and theoretical course. Carl Rogers Person Centred Therapy.**

COURSE NO.: **116**   COURSE NAME: **Diploma in Counselling**

SCHOOL: **HALEY COLLEGE FOR COUNSELLING AND PSYCHOTHERAPY**

TYPE: **P/T**   PERIOD: **3 years**

ATTENDANCE: **6 compulsory blocks per year of 3-4 days each + 8 optional courses over 3 years of 3 days each**

VENUES: **Surrey (Burstow)**

FEES: **£600**   OTHER COSTS: **Personal therapy and supervision**

COMMENCE: **September**   ENTRY REQ.: **1 yr Certificate in Counselling or others, i**

AWARD: **Diploma in Counselling**

NOTES: **Practical and theory all aspects of humanistic counselling. Students work with clients under supervision.**

COURSE NO.: **117**   COURSE NAME: **Diploma in Emotio-Somatic Therapy**

SCHOOL: **INSTITUTE OF EMOTIO-SOMATIC THERAPY**

TYPE: **P/T**   PERIOD: **4 terms**

ATTENDANCE: **4 weekends + 4 terms of one evening per week**

VENUES: **London (and home counties for wknds)**

FEES: **£1,090**   OTHER COSTS: **Residential if required**

COMMENCE: **January**   ENTRY REQ.: **Background in therapy/counselling, e**

AWARD: **Diploma in Emotio-Somatic Therapy**

COURSE NO.: **118**   COURSE NAME: **Psychic Counselling Diploma Course**

SCHOOL: **THE NATIONAL COLLEGE OF PSYCHIC COUNSELLING**

TYPE: **P/T**   PERIOD: **6 months - 1 year**

ATTENDANCE: **Minimum of 6 full weekends to be attended at student's discretion**

VENUES:: **Essex (Harlow) and other locations**

FEES: **£360**   OTHER COSTS: **£30 exam fee**

COMMENCE: **On - going**   ENTRY REQ.: **i**

AWARD: **Diploma in Psychic Counselling**

NOTES: **Subjects include psychology, mediumistic development, counselling techniques, dowsing etc**

COURSE NO.: **119**   COURSE NAME: **Psychic Counselling Diploma Course**

SCHOOL: **THE NATIONAL COLLEGE OF PSYCHIC COUNSELLING**

TYPE: **P/T**   PERIOD: **6 months**

ATTENDANCE: **6 full weekends held monthly**

VENUES:: **Essex (Harlow) and other locations**

FEES: **£395**   OTHER COSTS: **£30 exam fee, £20 books**

COMMENCE: **March, October**   ENTRY REQ.: **School's Diploma in Psychic Counselling**

AWARD: **Diploma in Advanced Psychic Counselling**

COUNSELLING

COURSE NO.: **120** COURSE NAME: **Counselling Skills for the Holistic Practitioner**

SCHOOL: **ON COURSE - PERSONAL AND PROFESSIONAL DEVELOPMENT CONSULTANCY**

TYPE: **P/T** PERIOD: **6 months**

ATTENDANCE: **5 weekends (1 weekend per month)**

VENUES:: **Hertfordshire (St. Albans)**

FEES: **£250** OTHER COSTS: **Nil**

COMMENCE: **May** ENTRY REQ.: **e**

AWARD: **Certificate in Holistic Counselling Skills**

COURSE NO.: **121** COURSE NAME: **Certificate in Counselling**

SCHOOL: **ON COURSE - PERSONAL AND PROFESSIONAL DEVELOPMENT CONSULTANCY**

TYPE: **P/T** PERIOD: **1 year**

ATTENDANCE: **6 evenings + 1 weekend per term**

VENUES:: **Hertfordshire (St. Albans)**

FEES: **£500** OTHER COSTS: **Nil**

COMMENCE: **September** ENTRY REQ.: **f, i**

AWARD: **Certificate in Counselling**

NOTES: **Graduates can enter into the 2-year Diploma in Counselling**

COURSE NO.: **122 (C)** COURSE NAME: **Pellin Diploma Course**

SCHOOL: **PELLIN TRAINING COURSES**

TYPE: **P/T** PERIOD: **3 years**

ATTENDANCE: **Weekly 4-hour group for 3 terms of 10 weeks each + 3 weekend workshops**

VENUES: **London**

FEES: **£950 per year** OTHER COSTS: **Nil**

COMMENCE: **January, September, October** ENTRY REQ.: **Appropriate work, prof. exper. preferred**

AWARD: **Pellin Diploma in Gestalt Therapy and Contribution Training**

NOTES: **Contribution Training is a counselling + therapeutic method**

COURSE NO.: **123** COURSE NAME: **Certificate in Counselling**

SCHOOL: **PROFESSIONAL DEVELOPMENT FOUNDATION**

TYPE: **P/T** PERIOD: **1 year**

ATTENDANCE: **1 evening per week + 4 weekend workshops**

VENUES: **London**

FEES: **£900 average (A.F.D.)** OTHER COSTS: **Personal supervision**

COMMENCE: **Continuous** ENTRY REQ.: **Voluntary experience, maturity, f**

AWARD: **Royal Society of Health Certificate in Counselling**

NOTES: **Higher studies (Diploma) available afterwards**

COURSE NO.: **124** COURSE NAME: **Diploma in Counselling**

SCHOOL: **PROFESSIONAL DEVELOPMENT FOUNDATION**

TYPE: **P/T** PERIOD: **2 years**

ATTENDANCE: **1 evening per week + 4 weekend workshops (450 hours in all)**

VENUES: **London**

FEES: **£900 per year average (A.F.D.)** OTHER COSTS: **Personal supervision**

COMMENCE: **Continuous** ENTRY REQ.: **Certificate course**

AWARD: **Royal Society of Health Diploma in Counselling**

COUNSELLING

COURSE NO.: **125**   COURSE NAME: **Certificate in the Fundamentals of Counselling**

SCHOOL: **SCHOOL OF PSYCHOTHERAPY AND COUNSELLING**

TYPE: **P/T**   PERIOD: **1 year**

ATTENDANCE: **Monday evening (5.30pm - 9.30pm) OR Thursday afternoon (2pm - 6pm) every week**

VENUES: **London**

FEES: **£990**   OTHER COSTS: **£50 reg. fee**

COMMENCE: **October**   ENTRY REQ.: **None**

AWARD: **The College Certificate in Counselling**

NOTES: **Higher studies (to Diploma, PG Diploma or MA degree) available afterwards**

COURSE NO.: **126**   COURSE NAME: **Diploma in Counselling**

SCHOOL: **SCHOOL OF PSYCHOTHERAPY AND COUNSELLING**

TYPE: **P/T**   PERIOD: **2 years**

ATTENDANCE: **1 day (Wednesday) every week**

VENUES: **London**

FEES: **£2,400**   OTHER COSTS: **50 reg. fee**

COMMENCE: **October**   ENTRY REQ.: **Prelim. study relevant to counselling**

AWARD: **The College Diploma in Counselling**

NOTES: **Higher studies (to PG Diploma or MA degree) available afterwards**

COURSE NO.: **127**   COURSE NAME: **Introduction to Counselling Skills**

SCHOOL: **SKILLS WITH PEOPLE LTD**

TYPE: **P/T**   PERIOD: **2 1/2 months**

ATTENDANCE: **1 evening per week for 10 weeks**

VENUES:: **London**

FEES: **£75**   OTHER COSTS: **Nil**

COMMENCE: **January, October**   ENTRY REQ.: **None**

AWARD: **Certificate (Institute of Complementary Medicine)**

COURSE NO.: **128**   COURSE NAME: **Certificate in Counselling**

SCHOOL: **TAMESIDE COLLEGE OF TECHNOLOGY - DEPT. OF CARING & PERSONAL SERVICES**

TYPE: **P/T**   PERIOD: **1 year**

ATTENDANCE: **1 afternoon or evening per week + 1 residential weekend**

VENUES: **Greater Manchester (Ashton-under-Lyne)**

FEES: **£155**   OTHER COSTS:

COMMENCE: **A.F.D.**   ENTRY REQ.: **2 yrs experience in an environment req. counsell.**

AWARD: **The College Certificate in Counselling**

NOTES: **Graduates eligible to apply for the Diploma course (see below)**

COURSE NO.: **129**   COURSE NAME: **Diploma in Counselling**

SCHOOL: **TAMESIDE COLLEGE OF TECHNOLOGY - DEPT. OF CARING & PERSONAL SERVICES**

TYPE: **P/T**   PERIOD: **1 year**

ATTENDANCE: **1 afternoon or evening per week on Thursdays + 1 residential weekend**

VENUES: **Greater Manchester (Ashton-under-Lyne)**

FEES: **£91**   OTHER COSTS:

COMMENCE: **A.F.D.**   ENTRY REQ.: **Certificate in Counselling**

AWARD: **The College Diploma in Counselling**

COUNSELLING

COURSE NO.: **130**   COURSE NAME: **Diploma in Interpersonal Counselling Skills**

SCHOOL: **TILE HILL COLLEGE OF FURTHER EDUCATION**

TYPE: **P/T**   PERIOD: **34 weeks**

ATTENDANCE: **1/2 day or evening per week + tutorials + supervised practice**

VENUES: **West Midlands (Coventry)**

FEES: **£350**   OTHER COSTS: **£70 validation fee**

COMMENCE: **September**   ENTRY REQ.: **See NOTES below**

AWARD: **Diploma of University of Warwick**

NOTES: **Open to those trained to a Cert. in Counselling level, and who have access to supervised prof. practice**

COURSE NO.: **131 (C)**   COURSE NAME: **Counselling, Hypnotherapy and Psychotherapy**

SCHOOL: **THE UK TRAINING COLLEGE**

TYPE: **P/T**   PERIOD: **3 years**

ATTENDANCE: **1 wknd/month for 12 months per year+personal therapy 20hrs in each of Y2&Y3+St. John's Ambul. course**

VENUES: **London, Eire (Dublin)**

FEES: **£5, 450**   OTHER COSTS: **£176 exam + St. John's Ambulance course**

COMMENCE: **May, September**   ENTRY REQ.: **Y1 = None, Y2 = Y1 completion, f**

AWARD: **Diploma in Counselling, Hypnotherapy and Psychotherapy**

NOTES: **Year 1 is a foundation course ending in Certificate of Attendance**

COURSE NO.: **132**   COURSE NAME: **Certificate in Counselling Skills**

SCHOOL: **UNIVERSITY OF DURHAM - DEPARTMENT OF ADULT EDUCATION**

TYPE: **P/T**   PERIOD: **1 year**

ATTENDANCE: **Monday daytime (OR evening) for 3 terms**

VENUES: **Durham (Durham), Tyne & Wear (Newastle-upon-Tyne)**

FEES: **£675**   OTHER COSTS: **Books**

COMMENCE: **October**   ENTRY REQ.: **Previous counselling training & experience**

AWARD: **University of Durham Certificate in Counselling Skills**

NOTES: **For Newcastle-upon-Tyne venue Monday daytime only**

COURSE NO.: **133**   COURSE NAME: **Advanced Certificate in Counselling Practice& Personal Development**

SCHOOL: **UNIVERSITY OF DURHAM - DEPARTMENT OF ADULT EDUCATION**

TYPE: **P/T**   PERIOD: **1 year**

ATTENDANCE: **Thursday evenings for 3 terms + occasional Saturdays**

VENUES: **Durham (Durham)**

FEES: **£850**   OTHER COSTS: **Books**

COMMENCE: **April**   ENTRY REQ.: **Previous counselling training & experience**

AWARD: **University of Durham Advanced Certificate in Counselling Practice & Personal Development**

COURSE NO.: **134**   COURSE NAME: **Certificate in Counselling Studies**

SCHOOL: **UNIVERSITY OF LEICESTER - DEPT. OF ADULT EDUCATION**

TYPE: **P/T**   PERIOD: **3 years usually (modular)**

ATTENDANCE: **1 x 2-hour session/wk for 6 terms + additional 2-hour sessions/wk for 2 terms (concurrent or consecutive)**

VENUES: **Leicestershire (Leicester), Northamptonshire (Northampton)**

FEES: **£100 per year approx.**   OTHER COSTS: **Books £10 per year**

COMMENCE: **January, April, September**   ENTRY REQ.: **None**

AWARD: **Certificate in Counselling Studies**

NOTES: **This course is not a qualification, but leads to Advanced Certificate (see below)**

COUNSELLING . CRANIO-SACRAL THERAPY

COURSE NO.: **135**   COURSE NAME: **Advanced Certificate in Counselling**

SCHOOL: **UNIVERSITY OF LEICESTER - DEPT. OF ADULT EDUCATION**

TYPE: **P/T**   PERIOD: **1 year usually (modular)**

ATTENDANCE: **1 x 2-hour session/wk for 2 terms + 2 x 3-hour sessions/wk for 1 term**

VENUES: **Leicestershire (Leicester), Northamptonshire (Northampton)**

FEES: **£100 per year approx.**   OTHER COSTS: **Nil**

COMMENCE: **January, April, September**   ENTRY REQ.: **Cert. in Couns. and Couns. under supervision**

AWARD: **Advanced Certificate in Counselling**

NOTES: **Can only be taken if a student has the Basic Certificate and has been counselling of at least 6 months**

COURSE NO.: **136**   COURSE NAME: **Certificate in Counselling**

SCHOOL: **UNIVERSITY OF MANCHESTER**

TYPE: **P/T**   PERIOD: **2 years**

ATTENDANCE: **1 afternoon (or evening) per week for 6 terms + 4 residentials**

VENUES: **Manchester**

FEES: **£725**   OTHER COSTS: **Nil**

COMMENCE: **September**   ENTRY REQ.: **Doing counselling in their job**

AWARD: **Certificate in Counselling**

NOTES: **Students must attend at least two thirds of the weekly meeting, and all the residentials**

COURSE NO.: **137**   COURSE NAME: **Cranio-Sacral Osteopathy**

SCHOOL: **THE COLLEGE OF NATURAL MEDICINE-LONDON**

TYPE: **P/T**   PERIOD: **1 year**

ATTENDANCE: **10 hours a week**

VENUES: **London**

FEES: **A.F.D.**   OTHER COSTS: **Nil**

COMMENCE: **A.F.D.**   ENTRY REQ.: **e or g (see NOTES below)**

AWARD: **Diploma in Cranio-Sacral Osteopathy**

NOTES: **Open to graduates of Osteopathy & Chiropractic Diploma Course, or other comprehensive training**

COURSE NO.: **138**   COURSE NAME: **Cranial Osteopathy**

SCHOOL: **CRANIAL OSTEOPATHIC ASSOCIATION**

TYPE: **Short**   PERIOD: **5 days**

ATTENDANCE: **Intensive 5-day intensive**

VENUES:: **London**

FEES: **£500**   OTHER COSTS:

COMMENCE: **February**   ENTRY REQ.: **Osteopathic, chiropractic, manipulative therapists**

AWARD: **Association Membership of Cranial Osteopathic Association**

COURSE NO.: **139**   COURSE NAME: **Craniosacral Therapy 1-year Post Graduate Training**

SCHOOL: **CRANIOSACRAL THERAPY EDUCATIONAL TRUST**

TYPE: **P/T**   PERIOD: **10 months**

ATTENDANCE: **9 x 3-day seminars + 5-day seminar**

VENUES:: **Devon, London**

FEES: **£1,250 non-resid. (London), £1,590 resid. (Devon)** OTHER COSTS: **£70 books**

COMMENCE: **September (London), October (Devon)**   ENTRY REQ.: **e, f, h, anatomy, physiology & pathology**

AWARD: **Certificate of Professional Practice**

NOTES: **Graduates eligible to join The Professional Association. Advanced courses available afterwards.**

CRANIO-SACRAL THERAPY , CRYSTAL THERAPY

COURSE NO.: **140** COURSE NAME: **Cranio-Sacral Therapy**
SCHOOL: **SYMPHYSIS FOR THE STUDY OF HOLISTIC HEALTH**
TYPE: **P/T** PERIOD: **2 years**
ATTENDANCE: **12 weekends (also see NOTES)**
VENUES: **London**
FEES: **£295** OTHER COSTS: **Nil**
COMMENCE: **November** ENTRY REQ.: **e, j**
AWARD: **Certificate in Cranio-Sacral Therapy**
NOTES: **Further training and alternative formats available**

COURSE NO.: **141** COURSE NAME: **Crystal Healing Certificate Course**
SCHOOL: **CRYSTAL 2000**
TYPE: **P/T** PERIOD: **1 year**
ATTENDANCE: **6 weekends + practical**
VENUES:: **London, Manchester**
FEES: **£500** OTHER COSTS: **Books & crystals**
COMMENCE: **March, October** ENTRY REQ.: **None**
AWARD: **Certificate entitling the graduate to the letters M.Crys. H.**

COURSE NO.: **142** COURSE NAME: **Crystal and Holistic Therapy Certificate Course**
SCHOOL: **HOTHS SCHOOL OF HOLISTIC THERAPIES**
TYPE: **P/T** PERIOD: **6 months**
ATTENDANCE: **Seminars**
VENUES:: **Gloucestershire (Cheltenham), Leicestershire (Leicester)**
FEES: **£290** OTHER COSTS: **Nil**
COMMENCE: **On - going** ENTRY REQ.: **b**
AWARD: **Practitioners Certificate in Crystal Therapy**
NOTES: **Qualifies for Membership of the Association of Holistic Therapists**

COURSE NO.: **143** COURSE NAME: **Vibrational Healing**
SCHOOL: **INSTITUTE OF CRYSTAL & GEM THERAPISTS**
TYPE: **P/T** PERIOD: **3 months**
ATTENDANCE: **1 weekend per month**
VENUES: **Dorset**
FEES: **£180** OTHER COSTS: **Nil**
COMMENCE: **September** ENTRY REQ.:
AWARD: **Certificate in Flower Essences / Gem Remedies & Crystals**

COURSE NO.: **144** COURSE NAME: **Crystal Therapy**
SCHOOL: **THE PEARL HEALING CENTRE**
TYPE: **P/T** PERIOD: **1 year**
ATTENDANCE: **6 - 7 days + practical work**
VENUES:: **Surrey (Croydon)**
FEES: **£180** OTHER COSTS:
COMMENCE: **September** ENTRY REQ.:
AWARD: **Certificate in Crystal Therapy**
NOTES: **Advanced courses available afterwards**

ELECTRO-CRYSTAL THERAPY . CRYSTAL THERAPY . DIETARY THERAPY

COURSE NO.: **145**   COURSE NAME: **Electro-Crystal Therapy**

SCHOOL: **THE SCHOOL OF ELECTRO-CRYSTAL THERAPY**

TYPE: **P/T**   PERIOD: **15 months**

ATTENDANCE: **1-day + 7 x 2-day sessions**

VENUES.: **London**

FEES: **£390**   OTHER COSTS: **Min. £433 for machine**

COMMENCE: **A.F.D.**   ENTRY REQ.: **A&P preferred but not compulsory**

AWARD: **Certificate in Electro-Crystal Therapy**

NOTES: **1-day introductory courses held in various areas around the country. Rest of the course held in London.**

COURSE NO.: **146**   COURSE NAME: **Gemstones for Healing & Transformation**

SCHOOL: **WHALE WHOLISTIC HEALTH AND LIFE EXTENSION**

TYPE: **Short**   PERIOD: **1 day**

ATTENDANCE: **1 day**

VENUES: **Middlesex (Hampton), other selected venues**

FEES: **£29**   OTHER COSTS: **Nil**

COMMENCE: **6 times yearly (A.F.D.)**   ENTRY REQ.: **None**

AWARD: **Certificate**

NOTES: **Using gemstons to correct and energise the Aura, Chakras & Channels. Overcoming serious illness & problems.**

COURSE NO.: **147**   COURSE NAME: **Dietary Therapy**

SCHOOL: **APPLIED SCIENCE - LEEDS POLYTECHNIC**

TYPE: **F/T**   PERIOD: **4 years**

ATTENDANCE: **Y1, Y2 & Y4 = 36 weeks over 3 terms, Y3 = placements**

VENUES: **Yorkshire (Leeds)**

FEES: **£1,675 per year**   OTHER COSTS: **£65 registration fee**

COMMENCE: **September**   ENTRY REQ.: **d**

AWARD: **BSc (Hons) Dietetics**

NOTES: **Y3 = 31 weeks clinical placement + 14 weeks industrial placement**

COURSE NO.: **148**   COURSE NAME: **Diet and Nutrition**

SCHOOL: **BRANTRIDGE FOREST SCHOOL**

TYPE: **Correspondence**   PERIOD: **Open**

ATTENDANCE: **Nil**

VENUES: **N/A**

FEES: **£270**   OTHER COSTS: **Nil**

COMMENCE: **N/A**   ENTRY REQ.: **None**

AWARD: **Diploma in Diet and Nutrition**

NOTES: **Higher studies available afterwards**

COURSE NO.: **149**   COURSE NAME: **Dietary Healing Diploma Course**

SCHOOL: **COLLEGE OF DIETARY HEALING**

TYPE: **P/T**   PERIOD: **15 months**

ATTENDANCE: **1 weekend per month**

VENUES: **London**

FEES: **£900**   OTHER COSTS: **Books**

COMMENCE: **September**   ENTRY REQ.: **Anatomy**

AWARD: **Dietary Healing Diploma**

DIETARY THERAPY

COURSE NO.: **150**　　COURSE NAME: **Correspondence Course in Dietary Therapeutics**

SCHOOL: **THE COLLEGE OF NUTRITIONAL MEDICINE**

TYPE: **Correspondence**　　　　　　　　PERIOD: **Variable (23 sessions)**

ATTENDANCE: **4 days at the end of the course**

VENUES: **Devon, Somerset**

FEES: **£1,213**　　　　　　　　OTHER COSTS: **Books**

COMMENCE: **N/A**　　　　　　　　ENTRY REQ.:

AWARD: **Diploma in Dietary Therapeutics (D.Th.D.)**

COURSE NO.: **151**　　COURSE NAME: **Correspondence Course in Nutritional Medicine**

SCHOOL: **THE COLLEGE OF NUTRITIONAL MEDICINE**

TYPE: **Correspondence**　　　　　　　　PERIOD: **Variable (29 sessions)**

ATTENDANCE: **4 days at the end of 23 sessions + 4 days at the end of 29 sessions (end of course)**

VENUES: **London**

FEES: **£1,733**　　　　　　　　OTHER COSTS: **Books**

COMMENCE: **Anytime**　　　　　　　　ENTRY REQ.:

AWARD: **Diploma in Nutritional Medicine (D.N.Med.)**

COURSE NO.: **152**　　COURSE NAME: **In-Class Course in Nutritional Medicine**

SCHOOL: **THE COLLEGE OF NUTRITIONAL MEDICINE**

TYPE: **P/T**　　　　　　　　PERIOD: **22 months**

ATTENDANCE: **1 weekend per month**

VENUES: **London**

FEES: **£1,313**　　　　　　　　OTHER COSTS: **Books**

COMMENCE: **October**　　　　　　　　ENTRY REQ.: **f**

AWARD: **Diploma in Nutritional Medicine (D.N.Med.)**

COURSE NO.: **153**　　COURSE NAME: **Clinical Nutrition**

SCHOOL: **THE HOWELL COLLEGE OF HOLISTIC HEALTH**

TYPE: **Correspondence**　　　　　　　　PERIOD: **1 year**

ATTENDANCE: **Nil**

VENUES: **N/A**

FEES: **£353**　　　　　　　　OTHER COSTS: **£10 Registration**

COMMENCE: **N/A**　　　　　　　　ENTRY REQ.: **Basic Nutrition or similar**

AWARD: **Diploma in Clinical Nutrition**

NOTES: **Fees can be on a monthly instalment. Qualification leads to Membership of National Guild of Clinical Nutrition.**

COURSE NO.: **154**　　COURSE NAME: **Clinical Nutrition**

SCHOOL: **THE HOWELL COLLEGE OF HOLISTIC HEALTH**

TYPE: **P/T**　　　　　　　　PERIOD: **1 year**

ATTENDANCE: **1 Saturday morning per month**

VENUES: **London**

FEES: **£353**　　　　　　　　OTHER COSTS: **£10 Registration**

COMMENCE: **January, June, August, November**　　ENTRY REQ.: **Basic Nutrition or similar**

AWARD: **Diploma in Clinical Nutrition**

NOTES: **Fees can be on a monthly instalment. Qualification leads to Membership of National Guild of Clinical Nutrition.**

DIETARY THERAPY . DOWSING . GENERAL (A&P)

COURSE NO.: **155**   COURSE NAME: **Dietary Therapy**

SCHOOL: **SCHOOL OF NATURAL THERAPIES AND ORIENTAL STUDIES**

TYPE: **P/T**   PERIOD: **2 months**

ATTENDANCE: **2 weekends**

VENUES: **Hampshire, London**

FEES: **£180**   OTHER COSTS: **£10**

COMMENCE: **A.F.D.**   ENTRY REQ.: **None**

AWARD: **School Certificate in Dietary Therapy (ITEC available)**

COURSE NO.: **156**   COURSE NAME: **Dowsing for Health - An Introduction**

SCHOOL: **SCHOOL OF PHYSICAL THERAPIES - BASINGSTOKE**

TYPE: **Short**   PERIOD: **1 weekend**

ATTENDANCE: **2 day intensive**

VENUES: **Hampshire (Basingstoke)**

FEES: **£80**   OTHER COSTS: **Nil**

COMMENCE: **February, August**   ENTRY REQ.: **None**

AWARD: **Dowsing Certificate (Basic) Society of Radionic Homoeopaths**

NOTES: **Advanced course is available afterwards**

COURSE NO.: **157**   COURSE NAME: **Dowsing for Health - An Introduction**

SCHOOL: **SCHOOL OF PHYSICAL THERAPIES (KINGSTON)**

TYPE: **Short**   PERIOD: **1 weekend**

ATTENDANCE: **2-day intensive**

VENUES: **Surrey (Kingston)**

FEES: **£80**   OTHER COSTS: **Nil**

COMMENCE: **May, November**   ENTRY REQ.: **None**

AWARD: **Dowsing Certificate (Basic) Society of Radionic Homoeopaths**

NOTES: **Advanced course is available afterwards**

COURSE NO.: **158**   COURSE NAME: **Anatomy & Physiology for Alternative Practitioners**

SCHOOL: **ALTERNATIVE TRAINING**

TYPE: **Correspondence**   PERIOD: **Open**

ATTENDANCE: **N/A**

VENUES: **N/A**

FEES: **£135**   OTHER COSTS: **Nil**

COMMENCE: **N/A**   ENTRY REQ.: **None**

AWARD: **Certificate in Anatomy and Physiology**

COURSE NO.: **159**   COURSE NAME: **Anatomy & Physiology**

SCHOOL: **GOOD SCENTS SCHOOL OF NATURAL THERAPIES**

TYPE: **P/T**   PERIOD: **3 months**

ATTENDANCE: **1 day per week, OR alternate weekends**

VENUES: **West Sussex (Washington)**

FEES: **£360**   OTHER COSTS: **Nil**

COMMENCE: **Jan, April, Sep**   ENTRY REQ.: **None**

AWARD: **Certificate in Anatomy and Physiology**

GENERAL (PHYSIOLOGY/DIAGNOSTIC, A&P, BIOLOGY)

COURSE NO.: **160**   COURSE NAME: **Physiology / Diagonstic Methods**
SCHOOL: **THE HOWELL COLLEGE OF HOLISTIC HEALTH**
TYPE: **Correspondence OR P/T**   PERIOD: **1 - 3 years**
ATTENDANCE: **1 Saturday afternoon per month**
VENUES: **London**
FEES: **£1,058**   OTHER COSTS: **£10 registraion fee**
COMMENCE: **Jan, June, Aug, October**   ENTRY REQ.: **a=18**
AWARD: **Certificate in Holistic Health (1 yr), Diploma in Holistic Health (2 yrs), Advanced Diploma (3 yrs)**
NOTES: **Fees can be on monthly basis**

COURSE NO.: **161**   COURSE NAME: **A&P**
SCHOOL: **THE LEAVES INTERNATIONAL SCHOOL OF AROMATHERAPY, MASSAGE AND NATURAL THERAPY**
TYPE: **P/T**   PERIOD: **3 months**
ATTENDANCE: **3 days**
VENUES: **Avon (Nr. Bath), Dorset, Wiltshire (Trowbridge)**
FEES: **A.F.D.**   OTHER COSTS: **Exam fee £33**
COMMENCE: **A.F.D.**   ENTRY REQ.: **ITEC MAP**
AWARD: **ITEC Certificate in A&P**

COURSE NO.: **162**   COURSE NAME: **Anatomy & Physiology**
SCHOOL: **LONDON COLLEGE OF MASSAGE**
TYPE: **P/T**   PERIOD: **15 weeks**
ATTENDANCE: **1 session a week (session = 3 hours)**
VENUES: **London, Ireland**
FEES: **£220**   OTHER COSTS: **Book**
COMMENCE: **4 times a year (A.F.D.)**   ENTRY REQ.: **None**
AWARD: **The College Certificate in Anatomy and Physiology**

COURSE NO.: **163**   COURSE NAME: **Human Biology O-level Practitioners of Alternative-Complementary Medicine**
SCHOOL: **THE MAPERTON TRUST**
TYPE: **Correspondence**   PERIOD: **6 months**
ATTENDANCE: **N/A**
VENUES: **N/A**
FEES: **£120**   OTHER COSTS: **Exam fee**
COMMENCE: **May, November**   ENTRY REQ.: **None**
AWARD: **Certificate**
NOTES: **Designed to meet the basic requirement for entry into many courses in alternative and complementary medicine**

COURSE NO.: **164**   COURSE NAME: **Anatomy & Physiology**
SCHOOL: **PURPLE FLAME SCHOOL OF AROMATHERAPY STRESS MANAGMENT**
TYPE: **Correspondence**   PERIOD: **12 months**
ATTENDANCE: **N/A**
VENUES: **N/A**
FEES: **£347**   OTHER COSTS: **Nil**
COMMENCE: **N/A**   ENTRY REQ.: **None**
AWARD:
NOTES: **In-depth study of A&P with deeper study of essential oils and cosmic law (approved by IFA, ISPA & IPTI)**

GENERAL (A&P, FIRST AID) . HEALING

COURSE NO.: **165** COURSE NAME: **Anatomy & Physiology**

SCHOOL: **SCHOOL OF NATURAL THERAPIES AND ORIENTAL STUDIES**

TYPE: **P/T** PERIOD: **3 months**

ATTENDANCE: **2 weekends + 1 evening**

VENUES: **Hampshire, London**

FEES: **£180** OTHER COSTS: **£10**

COMMENCE: **A.F.D.** ENTRY REQ.: **None**

AWARD: **The School Certificate**

NOTES: **ITEC A&P Certificate is available sitting their exam**

COURSE NO.: **166** COURSE NAME: **Shirley Price Anatomy & Physiology Correspondence Course**

SCHOOL: **SHIRLEY PRICE AROMATHERAPY SCHOOL**

TYPE: **Correspondence** PERIOD: **3 - 12 months**

ATTENDANCE: **N/A**

VENUES: **N/A**

FEES: **£176** OTHER COSTS: **£35 ITEC exam (optional)**

COMMENCE: **N/A** ENTRY REQ.: **None**

AWARD: **Certificate in Anatomy and Physiology**

COURSE NO.: **167** COURSE NAME: **Anatomy, Physiology and First Aid Life Support**

SCHOOL: **THE UK TRAINING COLLEGE**

TYPE: **P/T** PERIOD: **6 months**

ATTENDANCE: **4 weekends**

VENUES: **London**

FEES: **£280** OTHER COSTS: **Books**

COMMENCE: **June** ENTRY REQ.: **a=>18, Practitioners or others**

AWARD: **Certificate of Attendance from St. John's Ambulance and College's Certificate after optional exam.**

COURSE NO.: **168** COURSE NAME: **A&P**

SCHOOL: **THE WEST LONDON SCHOOLS OF THERAPEUTIC MASSAGE, REFLEXOLOGY & SPORTS THERPAY**

TYPE: **P/T** PERIOD: **8 weeks**

ATTENDANCE: **8 evenings**

VENUES: **London**

FEES: **A.F.D.** OTHER COSTS:

COMMENCE: **Monthly** ENTRY REQ.: **None**

AWARD: **ITEC Certificate in A&P**

COURSE NO.: **169** COURSE NAME: **Healing**

SCHOOL: **COLLEGE OF HEALING**

TYPE: **P/T** PERIOD: **1 year or longer**

ATTENDANCE: **3 x 6-day parts over 12 months, OR Part 1 over=3 wknds, Part 2=2 long wknds, Part3=6 days**

VENUES: **Hereford & Worcester (Malvern)**

FEES: **£415** OTHER COSTS: **£205 per part for full residential**

COMMENCE: **A.F.D.** ENTRY REQ.: **None (See NOTES below)**

AWARD: **Diploma in Healing: Associate of the College of Healing (A.C.O.H.)**

NOTES: **First Aid Certificate required before Diploma is rewarded. Part 4 post-graduate course availabe.**

HEALING . HERBALISM

COURSE NO.: **170**   COURSE NAME: **Healing**

SCHOOL: **THE LE PLAN INTERNATIONAL SCHOOL OF HEALING**

TYPE: **P/T**   PERIOD: **2 years**

ATTENDANCE: **4 fortnights**

VENUES: **Var, France (Le Plan Du Castellet)**

FEES: **£2,200**   OTHER COSTS: **Books**

COMMENCE: **February, December**   ENTRY REQ.: **a=23, f**

AWARD: **Diploma in Healing**

NOTES: **Course taught in English. Contact: Mrs S. Aubyn, 10 Irene Road, London SW6 4AL.**

COURSE NO.: **171**   COURSE NAME: **Healing**

SCHOOL: **PROMETHEUS SCHOOL OF HEALING**

TYPE: **P/T**   PERIOD: **18 months**

ATTENDANCE: **4 x 5 day courses with 2-3 months between each**

VENUES: **Yorkshire (Huddersfield)**

FEES: **£280**   OTHER COSTS: **Nil**

COMMENCE: **Three courses per year (A.F.D.)**   ENTRY REQ.: **None**

AWARD: **Diploma in Healing**

COURSE NO.: **172**   COURSE NAME: **Science and Practice of Esoteric Healing**

SCHOOL: **UNIVERSITY OF SEVEN RAYS (HEALING FACULTY)**

TYPE: **P/T**   PERIOD: **3 years**

ATTENDANCE: **2 x 6-day residential seminars per year + 1-day tutorial/clinical every 6 weeks + projects**

VENUES: **Dorset (Bournemouth), London**

FEES: **£2,400**   OTHER COSTS: **£300**

COMMENCE: **April, May**   ENTRY REQ.:

AWARD: **MSE Degree (USA), Certificate (UK)**

NOTES: **For our other 9 courses run in USA write to: USR, 128 Manhatton Avenue, Jersey City Heights, NJ 07307, USA.**

COURSE NO.: **173**   COURSE NAME: **Medical Herbalism**

SCHOOL: **ANGLO-EUROPEAN SCHOOL OF HERBALISM**

TYPE: **P/T (Correspondence + Seminars)**   PERIOD: **1 year**

ATTENDANCE: **1 day per month + 1 week residential + clinical days**

VENUES: **Dorset (Bournemouth)**

FEES: **£1,110**   OTHER COSTS: **£350 + £100 books**

COMMENCE: **September**   ENTRY REQ.: **a>=18, c**

AWARD: **Diploma in European Herbalism**

COURSE NO.: **174**   COURSE NAME: **Botanic Medicine (Herbalism)**

SCHOOL: **BRANTRIDGE FOREST SCHOOL**

TYPE: **Correspondence**   PERIOD: **Open**

ATTENDANCE: **Nil**

VENUES: **N/A**

FEES: **£270**   OTHER COSTS: **Nil**

COMMENCE: **N/A**   ENTRY REQ.: **None**

AWARD: **Diploma in Botanic Medicine**

NOTES: **Higher studies available afterwards**

HERBALISM

COURSE NO.: **175**	COURSE NAME: **Master Herbalist & Natural Healers Diploma**
SCHOOL: **THE COLLEGE OF HERBS AND NATURAL HEALING**	
TYPE: **P/T**	PERIOD: **1 year or more**
ATTENDANCE: **2 weeks solid + further weekends**	
VENUES: **Derbyshire (Buxton)**	
FEES: **£1,300**	OTHER COSTS: **Books**
COMMENCE: **2 week section in August**	ENTRY REQ.: **Primary Herbal Medicine (see above)**
AWARD: **Master Herbalist & Natural Healers Diploma**	
NOTES: **Diploma is EEC recognised**	

COURSE NO.: **176**	COURSE NAME: **Diploma Course in Herbal Medicine**
SCHOOL: **FACULTY OF HERBAL MEDICINE (GEN. COUNCIL & REGISTER OF CONSULTANT HERBALISTS)**	
TYPE: **Correspondence + Clinical**	PERIOD: **Open**
ATTENDANCE: **A.F.D.**	
VENUES: **Clinical training throughout the UK**	
FEES: **A.F.D.**	OTHER COSTS: **Exam fee**
COMMENCE: **N/A**	ENTRY REQ.: **f**
AWARD: **Diploma in Botano-Therapy (D.B.Th.)**	
NOTES: **Also Membership of the General Council & Register of Consultant Herbalists**	

COURSE NO.: **177**	COURSE NAME: **Chinese Herbal Medicine**
SCHOOL: **LONDON SCHOOL OF ACUPUNCTURE AND TRADITIONAL CHINESE MEDICINE**	
TYPE: **P/T**	PERIOD: **2 years**
ATTENDANCE: **1 day per week + 26 days clinic**	
VENUES: **London**	
FEES: **£1,550 per year**	OTHER COSTS: **Books**
COMMENCE: **October**	ENTRY REQ.: **e**
AWARD: **DipCHM (Diploma in Chinese Herbal Medicine)**	
NOTES: **For qualified acupuncturists, or other practitioners after a foundation course**	

COURSE NO.: **178**	COURSE NAME: **Primary Herbal Medicine & Natural Health**
SCHOOL: **OSHO SCHOOL OF HERBAL MEDICINE & NATURAL HEALING**	
TYPE: **P/T**	PERIOD: **1 year or less**
ATTENDANCE: **2 - 3 weekends**	
VENUES: **Suffolk (Nr. Ipswich)**	
FEES: **£225**	OTHER COSTS: **Books**
COMMENCE: **March, October**	ENTRY REQ.: **None, f (phone)**
AWARD: **None (see NOTES below)**	
NOTES: **Graduates eligible to apply for the EEC recognised Master Herbalist Diploma (see below)**	

COURSE NO.: **179**	COURSE NAME: **One Year Course**
SCHOOL: **SCHOOL OF PHYTOTHERAPY/HERBAL MEDICINE**	
TYPE: **Correspondence**	PERIOD: **12 months**
ATTENDANCE: **N/A**	
VENUES: **N/A**	
FEES: **£125 per quarter**	OTHER COSTS: **£10.95 textbooks**
COMMENCE: **Continuous**	ENTRY REQ.: **None**
AWARD: **Certificate in Herbal Studies**	
NOTES: **£75 additional fee for optional weekend seminar**	

HERBALISM . HOMOEOPATHY

COURSE NO.: **180**   COURSE NAME: **Full Time Course**

SCHOOL: **SCHOOL OF PHYTOTHERAPY/HERBAL MEDICINE**

TYPE: **F/T**   PERIOD: **4 years**

ATTENDANCE: **3 days per week + 500 hours clinical training**

VENUES: **East Sussex (Bodle Street Green), London**

FEES: **£3,000 per year**   OTHER COSTS: **£50 approx. for books**

COMMENCE: **September**   ENTRY REQ.: **c**

AWARD: **Certificate in Herbal Medicine**

COURSE NO.: **181**   COURSE NAME: **Tutorial Course**

SCHOOL: **SCHOOL OF PHYTOTHERAPY/HERBAL MEDICINE**

TYPE: **P/T**   PERIOD: **4 years**

ATTENDANCE: **1 week per year + 500 hours clinical training**

VENUES: **East Sussex (Bodle Street Green), London**

FEES: **£150 per quarter + £1.50 - £1.75 per hour clinical** OTHER COSTS: **£60 approx. for books**

COMMENCE: **September**   ENTRY REQ.: **c**

AWARD: **Certificate in Herbal Medicine**

COURSE NO.: **182**   COURSE NAME: **Specially Structured Course**

SCHOOL: **SCHOOL OF PHYTOTHERAPY/HERBAL MEDICINE**

TYPE: **P/T**   PERIOD: **Up to 2 years**

ATTENDANCE: **1 week per year + 50 hours clinical training**

VENUES: **East Sussex (Bodle Street Green), London**

FEES: **£175 per quarter + £1.50 - £2.00 per hour clinical** OTHER COSTS:

COMMENCE: **Continuous**   ENTRY REQ.: **e**

AWARD: **Certificate in Herbal Medicine**

NOTES: **Open to GP's and certain alternative-complementary practitioners**

COURSE NO.: **183**   COURSE NAME: **Planetary Herbalism**

SCHOOL: **SCHOOL OF PLANETARY HERBALISM**

TYPE: **P/T**   PERIOD: **2 years (See NOTES below)**

ATTENDANCE: **Y1= 3 weekends, Y2= 3 weekends + 5-day clinical residential**

VENUES: **Suffolk (Newmarket/Woodbridge) (See NOTES below)**

FEES: **£882**   OTHER COSTS:

COMMENCE: **Open ended**   ENTRY REQ.: **a=18, First Aid Certif. (See NOTES below)**

AWARD: **Diploma in Planetary Herbalism**

NOTES: **ITEC A&P required before issuing of Diploma. Period could be 3 years. Some clinical could be outside Suffolk.**

COURSE NO.: **3 (C)**   COURSE NAME: Acupuncture, **Homoeopathy** and Naturopathy

SCHOOL: **ASSOCIATION OF NATURAL MEDICINES**

TYPE: **P/T**   PERIOD: **3 years**

ATTENDANCE: **Y1 & Y2 = 1 weekend per month, Y3 = 1 weekend per month + 4 Saturdays + 10 days clinical**

VENUES: **Essex (Witham)**

FEES: **£640 per year**   OTHER COSTS: **Books**

COMMENCE: **September**   ENTRY REQ.: **f**

AWARD: **Certificate in Acupuncture OR Homoeopathy OR Naturopathy**

HOMOEOPATHY

COURSE NO.: **184**	COURSE NAME: **Homoeopathy**
SCHOOL: **BRANTRIDGE FOREST SCHOOL**	
TYPE: **Correspondence**	PERIOD: **Open**
ATTENDANCE: **Nil**	
VENUES: **N/A**	
FEES: **£270**	OTHER COSTS: **Nil**
COMMENCE: **N/A**	ENTRY REQ.: **None**
AWARD: **Diploma in Homoeopathy**	
NOTES: **Higher studies available afterwards**	

COURSE NO.: **185**	COURSE NAME: **British School of Homoeopathy Professional Diploma**
SCHOOL: **BRITISH SCHOOL OF HOMOEOPATHY**	
TYPE: **Correspondence + Clinical**	PERIOD: **Variable (A.F.D.)**
ATTENDANCE: **4-day introductory course in London or Swindon + Clinical**	
VENUES: **N/A**	
FEES: **£1,600**	OTHER COSTS: **Clinical fees depend on student's progress**
COMMENCE: **N/A**	ENTRY REQ.: **None**
AWARD: **Licentiate of British School of Homoeopathy**	
NOTES: **Progress throughout the course depends on continuous assessment. There are no formal examinations.**	

COURSE NO.: **186**	COURSE NAME: **British School of Homoeopathy Professinal Diploma**
SCHOOL: **BRITISH SCHOOL OF HOMOEOPATHY**	
TYPE: **P/T**	PERIOD: **4 years**
ATTENDANCE: **11 weekends a year**	
VENUES: **Wiltshire (Swindon)**	
FEES: **£3,500**	OTHER COSTS: **£200 approx. for books**
COMMENCE: **September**	ENTRY REQ.: **a=22, c, i**
AWARD: **Licentiate of British School of Homoeopathy**	
NOTES: **Y4 contains supervised clinical training under personal tutor**	

COURSE NO.: **187**	COURSE NAME: **Diploma Course in Homoeopathy**
SCHOOL: **THE BRITISH INSTITUTE OF HOMOEOPATHY**	
TYPE: **Correspondence (Open University - type)**	PERIOD: **3 years (variable)**
ATTENDANCE: **None (Tutorials and clinical optional)**	
VENUES: **Worldwide (30 countries)**	
FEES: **£600**	OTHER COSTS: **Nil**
COMMENCE: **Anytime**	ENTRY REQ.: **b**
AWARD: **Diploma of the Institute of Homoeopathy (D.I.Hom)**	
NOTES: **Includes video and audio materials. Clinical training arranged. Correspondence with personal tutor.**	

COURSE NO.: **188**	COURSE NAME: **Licentiate of the College of Homoeopathy**
SCHOOL: **THE COLLEGE OF HOMOEOPATHY**	
TYPE: **F/T**	PERIOD: **3 years**
ATTENDANCE: **3 days a week for 28 weeks + summer clinical (home study = 10 hours per week)**	
VENUES: **London**	
FEES: **£ 2,820 for 91/92 (instalments possible)**	OTHER COSTS: **Books £100/yr min., instruments approx. £100**
COMMENCE: **September**	ENTRY REQ.: **d, f, i**
AWARD: **Licentiate of the College of Homoeopathy**	
NOTES: **PG Membership of the College leads to registration with the Society of Homoeopaths**	

HOMOEOPATHY

COURSE NO.: **189**   COURSE NAME: **Licentiate of the College of Homoeopathy**

SCHOOL: **THE COLLEGE OF HOMOEOPATHY**

TYPE: **P/T**   PERIOD: **4 years**

ATTENDANCE: **1 wknd a year + regional tutorials if possible+clinical (home study=21 hr/wk)**

VENUES: **London**

FEES: **£ 940 for 91/92 (instalments possible)**   OTHER COSTS: **Books £100/yr min., instruments approx. £100**

COMMENCE: **September**   ENTRY REQ.: **d, f, i**

AWARD: **Licentiate of the College of Homoeopathy**

NOTES: **PG Membership of the College leads to registration with the Society of Homoeopaths**

COURSE NO.: **190**   COURSE NAME: **Homoeopathy**

SCHOOL: **THE COLLEGE OF NATURAL MEDICINE-LONDON**

TYPE: **F/T - P/T**   PERIOD: **4 years**

ATTENDANCE: **Y1 = 3 days a week for 40 weeks, Y2 - Y4 = 15 hours a week for 40 weeks per year**

VENUES: **London**

FEES: **£1,800 for Y1, for rest A.F.D.**   OTHER COSTS: **Nil**

COMMENCE: **September**   ENTRY REQ.: **b*, f**

AWARD: **Diploma in Homoeopathy**

COURSE NO.: **191**   COURSE NAME: **Professional Homoeopathic Training Course**

SCHOOL: **THE COLLEGE OF PRACTICAL HOMOEOPATHY**

TYPE: **F/T**   PERIOD: **3 years**

ATTENDANCE: **3 days per week for 28 weeks per year (10am - 5pm)**

VENUES: **London**

FEES: **£2,938 per year**   OTHER COSTS: **Nil**

COMMENCE: **September**   ENTRY REQ.: **f, i**

AWARD: **Certificate of The Midlands College of Homoeopathy (C.M.C.H.)**

NOTES: **Clinical training also available in Birmingham. Post-Graduate training available.**

COURSE NO.: **192**   COURSE NAME: **Introd. Int. Course on the Principles & Practice of Homoeopathy**

SCHOOL: **HAHNEMMAN COLLEGE OF HOMOEOPATHY**

TYPE: **P/T**   PERIOD: **3 years**

ATTENDANCE: **2 weekends a month + 1 day a week for 3 months clinical**

VENUES: **London**

FEES: **£ 2,250**   OTHER COSTS: **Exam fee**

COMMENCE: **September**   ENTRY REQ.: **c, introd. course in A&P for non-qualified**

AWARD: **Diploma in Homoeopathic Medicine**

NOTES: **A&P course runs for 3 months with an examination @£175**

COURSE NO.: **193**   COURSE NAME: **Diploma Course in Principles & Practice of Homoeopathy**

SCHOOL: **THE HOMOEOPATHIC FOUNDATION**

TYPE: **Correspondence + Clinical**   PERIOD: **Open**

ATTENDANCE: **Clinical sessions (A.F.D.)**

VENUES: **Practical workshops in London, Wales (Swansea). Clinical training throughout the U.K.**

FEES: **A.F.D.**   OTHER COSTS: **A.F.D.**

COMMENCE: **N/A**   ENTRY REQ.: **i**

AWARD: **Diploma in Homoeopathic Medicine (D.Ho.M., M.R.H.)**

NOTES: **Leading to Membership of the Register of Homoeopathic Practitioners. Instalment payment avail. Personal tutors.**

HOMOEOPATHY

COURSE NO.: 194   **COURSE NAME:** Homoeopathy

SCHOOL: LONDON COLLEGE OF CLASSICAL HOMOEOPATHY

TYPE: P/T   **PERIOD:** 4 years

ATTENDANCE: Y1-Y4=1 weekend a month for 12 weekends (Sept to June) + 1 day a week clinical for Y3 &Y4

VENUES: Devon (Tiverton)

FEES: £2,800   **OTHER COSTS:** Books

COMMENCE: September (late)   **ENTRY REQ.:** a>21, f, i

AWARD: Licentiate of College of Classical Homoeopathy (L.C.C.H.)

NOTES: Membership of the College (M.C.C.H.) after PG training of 12 months minimum supervised clinical work

---

COURSE NO.: 195   **COURSE NAME:** F/T Course in Classical Homoeopathy

SCHOOL: LONDON COLLEGE OF CLASSICAL HOMOEOPATHY

TYPE: F/T   **PERIOD:** 3 years

ATTENDANCE: 3 full days a week for 30 weeks per year + Clinical afternoons

VENUES:: London

FEES: £6,270   **OTHER COSTS:** Around £300 per year

COMMENCE: September   **ENTRY REQ.:** b, c, f

AWARD: Licentiate of The London College of Classical Homoeopathy

NOTES: PG & teacher training available afterwards. College charity clinic everyday.

COURSE NO.: 196   **COURSE NAME:** P/T Course in Classical Homoeopathy

SCHOOL: LONDON COLLEGE OF CLASSICAL HOMOEOPATHY

TYPE: P/T   **PERIOD:** 4 years

ATTENDANCE: 13 weekends per academic year + Clinical days. (Hope for evening tutorials as well.)

VENUES:: London

FEES: £4,200   **OTHER COSTS:** Book/paper costs

COMMENCE: September   **ENTRY REQ.:** b for a>21, c, f

AWARD: Licentiate of The London College of Classical Homoeopathy

NOTES: PG & teacher training available afterwards. College charity clinic everyday.

COURSE NO.: 197   **COURSE NAME:** Homoeopathy Diploma Course

SCHOOL: LONDON SCHOOL OF HOMOEOPATHY

TYPE: P/T   **PERIOD:** 4 years

ATTENDANCE: Y1-Y4= 11 weekend seminars + clinical for Y3 &Y4

VENUES: London

FEES: £3,900   **OTHER COSTS:** Small payments for Y3&Y4 clincial

COMMENCE: September   **ENTRY REQ.:** c, i

AWARD: Member of London School of Homoeopathy (MLSH) (Registration with Soc. of Homoeopaths recom.)

COURSE NO.: 198   **COURSE NAME:** Professional Homoeopathic Training Course

SCHOOL: THE MIDLANDS COLLEGE OF HOMOEOPATHY

TYPE: P/T   **PERIOD:** 4 years

ATTENDANCE: 1 weekend every 4 weeks + clinical in Y3 and Y4

VENUES: West Midlands (Birmingham)

FEES: £850 per year   **OTHER COSTS:** Nil

COMMENCE: September   **ENTRY REQ.:** f, i

AWARD: Certificate of The Midlands College of Homoeopathy (C.M.C.H.)

NOTES: Clinical training also available in London. Post-Graduate training available.

HOMOEOPATHY

COURSE NO.: **199**　　COURSE NAME: **Homoeopathic Professional Training Course**
SCHOOL: **THE NORTHERN COLLEGE OF HOMOEOPATHIC MEDICINE**
TYPE: **P/T**　　PERIOD: **5 years**
ATTENDANCE: **1 weekend per month for 10 months a year**
VENUES: **Tyne & Wear (Gateshead)**
FEES: **£4,750**　　OTHER COSTS:
COMMENCE: **September**　　ENTRY REQ.: **d, i**
AWARD: **Membership of the Northern College of Homoeopathic Medicine, Licentiate in Homoeopathic Medicine**

COURSE NO.: **200**　　COURSE NAME: **Homoeopathy**
SCHOOL: **NORTH WEST COLLEGE OF HOMOEOPATHY**
TYPE: **P/T**　　PERIOD: **5 years**
ATTENDANCE: **1 weekend per month for 11 months each year + tutorials and seminars**
VENUES: **Manchester**
FEES: **£4,500**　　OTHER COSTS: **Books, equipment, seminars & clinical**
COMMENCE: **September**　　ENTRY REQ.: **a=>21, d, f, i**
AWARD: **Licentiate of the North West College of Homoeopathy**
NOTES: **Clinical training with experienced homoeopaths**

COURSE NO.: **201**　　COURSE NAME: **Courses in Homoeopathy**
SCHOOL: **PURTON HOUSE SCHOOL OF HOMOEOPATHY**
TYPE: **Correspondence + Clinical**　　PERIOD: **4 years**
ATTENDANCE: **1 day a week for 36 weeks a year**
VENUES: **Buckinghamshire (Farnham Royal)**
FEES: **£3,780**　　OTHER COSTS: **Books**
COMMENCE: **September**　　ENTRY REQ.: **f**
AWARD: **Diploma in Homoeopathy**

COURSE NO.: **202**　　COURSE NAME: **Diploma in Homoeopathic Medicine**
SCHOOL: **SCHOOL OF HOMOEOPATHIC MEDICINE (DARLINGTON)**
TYPE: **P/T**　　PERIOD: **5 years**
ATTENDANCE: **Y1-Y4 = 1 weekend per month for 11 months each year + clinical, Y5 = Supervised Practice**
VENUES: **Durham (Darlington)**
FEES: **£4,750**　　OTHER COSTS: **£150 - £250 per year**
COMMENCE: **September**　　ENTRY REQ.: **d, i**
AWARD: **Diploma in Homoeopathic Medicine (Dip.Hom.Med.)**
NOTES: **Teaching clinics are available in Leeds, Newcastle-upon-Tyne and Sheffield**

COURSE NO.: **203**　　COURSE NAME: **Homoeopathy**
SCHOOL: **THE SCHOOL OF HOMOEOPATHY**
TYPE: **P/T**　　PERIOD: **4 years**
ATTENDANCE: **Y1 = Correspondence, Y2 & Y3 = 10 long weekends + clinical, Y4 = 4 long weekends**
VENUES: **Devon (Uffculme)**
FEES: **£2,830**　　OTHER COSTS: **A.F.D.**
COMMENCE: **Y1 = anytime, Y2,Y3 & Y4 = September**　　ENTRY REQ.: **None**
AWARD: **Diploma in Homoeopathy**
NOTES: **Y1 can be taken on its on. Professional practice starts at end of Y3, leading to R.S.Hom. after Y4.**

HOMOEOPATHY . HYPNOTHERAPY

COURSE NO.: **204**   COURSE NAME: **Homoeopathy-Professional Training**

SCHOOL: **SCOTTISH COLLEGE OF HOMOEOPATHY**

TYPE: **F/T**   PERIOD: **4 years + Supervisory year**

ATTENDANCE: **3 days a week for 30 weeks a year**

VENUES: **Strathclyde (Glasgow)**

FEES: **£3,000**   OTHER COSTS: **£10 per year**

COMMENCE: **October**   ENTRY REQ.: **c or equiv.**

AWARD: **Certificate of Scottish College of Homoeopathy**

NOTES: **No one is accepted straight from school**

COURSE NO.: **205**   COURSE NAME: **Homoeopathy-Professional Training**

SCHOOL: **SCOTTISH COLLEGE OF HOMOEOPATHY**

TYPE: **P/T**   PERIOD: **4 years + Supervisory year**

ATTENDANCE: **15 weekends per year**

VENUES: **Strathclyde (Glasgow)**

FEES: **£1,250**   OTHER COSTS: **£10 per year**

COMMENCE: **October**   ENTRY REQ.: **c or equiv.**

AWARD: **Certificate of Scottish College of Homoeopathy**

NOTES: **No one is accepted straight from school**

COURSE NO.: **206**   COURSE NAME: **Homoeopathic Medicine**

SCHOOL: **YORKSHIRE SCHOOL OF HOMOEOPATHY**

TYPE: **P/T**   PERIOD: **4 years**

ATTENDANCE: **10 weekends per year**

VENUES: **Yorkshire (York)**

FEES: **£2,240**   OTHER COSTS: **Books**

COMMENCE: **September every 4 years**   ENTRY REQ.: **f**

AWARD: **Next intake will be in September 1993**

COURSE NO.: **207 (C)**   COURSE NAME: **Hypnotherapy & Psychologist Training**

SCHOOL: **ACADEMY OF HYPNOTHERAPY**

TYPE: **P/T**   PERIOD: **Depends on frequency (A.F.D.)**

ATTENDANCE: **Once a week for 5 months (or shorter period if required) + 6 test revision lessons**

VENUES: **London**

FEES: **£840 (can be paid in installments)**   OTHER COSTS: **£256 for the revision lessons**

COMMENCE: **Anytime, continuous**   ENTRY REQ.: **i**

AWARD: **M.P.H.C. Diploma in Psycho. & Hypnotherapy**

COURSE NO.: **208 (C)**   COURSE NAME: **Hypnotherapy & Psychotherapy Certificate**

SCHOOL: **ARK COURSES IN HYPNOTHERAPY & PSYCHOTHERAPY**

TYPE: **P/T**   PERIOD: **1 year**

ATTENDANCE: **1 weekend per month**

VENUES: **Surry (Guildford)**

FEES: **£750**   OTHER COSTS: **Exam fee = £20**

COMMENCE: **February, July, October**   ENTRY REQ.: **a=21**

AWARD: **Certificate in Hypnotherapy/Psychotherapy**

NOTES: **Emphasis placed on supervised practical work. Diploma course avail. afterwards (see below)**

HYPNOTHERAPY

COURSE NO.: **209 (C)**   COURSE NAME: **Hypnotherapy** & Psychotherapy **Diploma**

SCHOOL: **ARK COURSES IN HYPNOTHERAPY & PSYCHOTHERAPY**

TYPE: **P/T**   PERIOD: **2 years**

ATTENDANCE: **1 weekend per month**

VENUES: **Surry (Guildford)**

FEES: **£950**   OTHER COSTS: **Exam fee = £20**

COMMENCE: **February, July, October**   ENTRY REQ.: **a=21, Certificate in Hypnotherapy**

AWARD: **Certificate in Hypnotherapy/Psychotherapy**

NOTES: **Emphasis placed on supervised practical work. Diploma Y2 can be started at any time of the year.**

COURSE NO.: **105 (C)**   COURSE NAME: Counselling, **Hypnotherapy** and Psychotherapy

SCHOOL: **ASSOCIATION FOR BODYMIND THERAPY AND TRAINING (AABTT)**

TYPE: **P/T**   PERIOD: **2 years**

ATTENDANCE: **1 evening (2 hours) per week + bi-monthly weekends + 6-day residential in the country**

VENUES: **London**

FEES: **£1,920**   OTHER COSTS: **Individual therapy**

COMMENCE: **January, April, September**   ENTRY REQ.: **i, some experience preferable**

AWARD: **Diploma of AABTT**

NOTES: **Completion entitles practice in counselling, hypnotherapy, psychotherapy and group facilitation**

COURSE NO.: **210**   COURSE NAME: **Hypnotherapy**

SCHOOL: **ASSOCIATION OF NATURAL MEDICINES**

TYPE: **P/T**   PERIOD: **9 months**

ATTENDANCE: **Weekends or days**

VENUES: **Essex (Witham)**

FEES: **£300**   OTHER COSTS:

COMMENCE: **Throughout the year (A.F.D.)**   ENTRY REQ.: **f**

AWARD: **Certificate in Hypnotherapy**

COURSE NO.: **211**   COURSE NAME: **Hypnotherapy Foundation Course**

SCHOOL: **AVON HYPNOTHERAPY (A.H.T.) CENTRE**

TYPE: **P/T**   PERIOD: **10 months (+ gap between Introduc. and Found.)**

ATTENDANCE: **Introduction = 1 day/wk for 3 wks, Foundation = 1 day/month for 9 months excl. Feb, Aug & Dec**

VENUES: **Avon (Bristol), Derbyshire (Derby), Nottinghamshire (Nottingham), West Midlands (Walsall)**

FEES: **£600 (Introduction=£180, Foundation=£420)**   OTHER COSTS: **Books**

COMMENCE: **Jan, March, May, July, Sep, Nov**   ENTRY REQ.: **Introd.: a=>18, f, Found.: Introduction or equiv., f**

AWARD: **Diploma in Hypnotherapy (Technique & Practice) (Certificate in Hypnotherapy after Introduc. course)**

NOTES: **These are 2 separate courses, but completing of both entitling practice. Adv. training avail. afterwards.**

COURSE NO.: **212**   COURSE NAME: **Hypnotherapy (Practical Work Experience)**

SCHOOL: **AVON HYPNOTHERAPY (A.H.T.) CENTRE**

TYPE: **Short**   PERIOD: **2 days (or 1 day if you prefer)**

ATTENDANCE: **2 consecutive days (week days)**

VENUES: **Avon (Bristol), Derbyshire (Derby), Nottinghamshire (Nottingham), West Midlands (Walsall)**

FEES: **£75 per day**   OTHER COSTS: **Books**

COMMENCE: **Jan, April, July, Oct**   ENTRY REQ.: **Previous training (e.g. correspondence), f**

AWARD: **Training Centre Certificate of Ability (if 2 days are attended)**

NOTES: **The 2 day course is ideal for those of little practical experience, e.g., from correspondence course**

HYPNOTHERAPY

COURSE NO.: **213 (C)**   COURSE NAME: **Ericksonian Hypnosis**, NLP and Cognitive Psychotherapy

SCHOOL: **BRITISH HYPNOSIS RESEARCH**

TYPE: **P/T**   PERIOD: **6 months**

ATTENDANCE: **6 weekends training + 6 days clinical supervision with hospital patients**

VENUES: **London**

FEES: **£1,225**   OTHER COSTS: **Nil**

COMMENCE: **March, October**   ENTRY REQ.: **Employm. in caring prof., 1st degree (see NOTES)**

AWARD: **Diploma (recognised by health authorities and social services). Leading to Membership of BHR.**

NOTES: **Those without formal entry req. are sometimes considered**

COURSE NO.: **214 (C)**   COURSE NAME: **Hypnotherapy** / Psychotherapy

SCHOOL: **THE HOWELL COLLEGE OF HOLISTIC HEALTH**

TYPE: **P/T**   PERIOD: **1 - 2 years**

ATTENDANCE: **1 Sunday morning per month**

VENUES: **London**

FEES: **£353 per year**   OTHER COSTS: **£10 reg. fee**

COMMENCE: **Jan, June, Aug, Nov**   ENTRY REQ.: **a=>18**

AWARD: **Certificate (1 year, Diploma (2 years) in Hypnotherapy / Psychotherapy)**

NOTES: **Fees can be paid on monthly basis in advance**

COURSE NO.: **215**   COURSE NAME: **Hypnotherapy**

SCHOOL: **THE HYPNOTHINK FOUNDATION**

TYPE: **Correspondence**   PERIOD: **Open**

ATTENDANCE: **N/A**

VENUES: **N/A**

FEES: **£260**   OTHER COSTS: **Nil**

COMMENCE: **N/A**   ENTRY REQ.: **None**

AWARD: **Diploma in Hypnotherapy**

NOTES: **Fees can be paid in instalments**

COURSE NO.: **216**   COURSE NAME: **Hypnothink**

SCHOOL: **THE HYPNOTHINK FOUNDATION**

TYPE: **Correspondence**   PERIOD: **Open**

ATTENDANCE: **N/A**

VENUES: **N/A**

FEES: **£145**   OTHER COSTS: **Exam fee = £40**

COMMENCE: **N/A**   ENTRY REQ.: **None**

AWARD: **Registered Hypnothink Counsellor (Certificate)**

NOTES: **A form of counselling used alone or in conjunction with other therapies. Fees can be paid in instalments.**

COURSE NO.: **217**   COURSE NAME: **Hypnotherapy**

SCHOOL: **LONDON COLLEGE OF CLINICAL HYPNOSIS**

TYPE: **P/T**   PERIOD: **1 year (see NOTES below)**

ATTENDANCE: **Basic Hypnosis = 3 consecutive weekends, Diploma Course = 8 weekends**

VENUES: **London**

FEES: **£690 (Instalments acceptable)**   OTHER COSTS:

COMMENCE: **November**   ENTRY REQ.: **None**

AWARD: **Diploma in Hypnotherapy**

NOTES: **The period from start to finish depends on the gap between the Basic and the Diploma parts**

HYPNOTHERAPY

COURSE NO.: **218**   COURSE NAME: **Hypnosis & Radical Hypnotherapy**
SCHOOL: **MERCURIAN SCHOOL OF HYPNOSIS & RADICAL HYPNOTHERAPY**
TYPE: **Correspondence**   PERIOD: **Open**
ATTENDANCE: **N/A**
VENUES: **N/A**
FEES: **£360**   OTHER COSTS: **Exam fee = £40**
COMMENCE: **N/A**   ENTRY REQ.: **None**
AWARD: **Diploma in Hypnosis & Radical Hypnotherapy**

COURSE NO.: **219 (C)**   COURSE NAME: **The National Association of Hypnotists & Psychotherapists: Training Faculty**
SCHOOL: **THE NATIONAL ASSOCIATION OF HYPNOTISTS & PSYCHOTHERAPISTS: TRAINING FACULTY**
TYPE: **P/T**   PERIOD: **15 months**
ATTENDANCE: **1 - 2 weekends per month (18 weekends in all) + 2 exam. days + supervision after qualification**
VENUES: **London**
FEES: **£70 - £85 per weekend**   OTHER COSTS: **Books, exam fee, supervision costs**
COMMENCE: **September**   ENTRY REQ.: **a=>25, d, i**
AWARD: **Diploma in Hypnosis and Psychotherapy**
NOTES: **Entitles Membership of the National Association of Hypnotists & Psychotherapists @£50**

COURSE NO.: **220 (C)**   COURSE NAME: Hypnotherapy and **Psychotherapy**
SCHOOL: **THE NATIONAL COLLEGE OF HYPNOSIS AND PSYCHOTHERAPY**
TYPE: **P/T**   PERIOD:
ATTENDANCE: **S1 = 4 weekends, S2 = 6 weekends, S3 = 4 weekends**
VENUES: **Cheshire (Cheadle), London, Strathclyde (Glasgow)**
FEES: **£1,575**   OTHER COSTS: **£75 exam fee**
COMMENCE: **A.F.D.**   ENTRY REQ.: **a=>25, d, e, i**
AWARD: **Diploma in Hypnosis and Psychotherapy**
NOTES: **A Certificate in Hypnosis and Psychotherapy is given upon completion of Stage 2**

COURSE NO.: **221 (C)**   COURSE NAME: **Diploma in Ericksonian Hypnosis**, Psychotherapy & NLP
SCHOOL: **NATIONAL SCHOOL OF HYPNOSIS & ADVANCED PSYCHOTHERAPY**
TYPE: **P/T**   PERIOD: **1 year followed by 1 year clinical supervision**
ATTENDANCE: **12 weekends during the year + clinical supervision to follow**
VENUES: **London (clinical supervision is not confined to London)**
FEES: **£1,269**   OTHER COSTS: **Exam fee, informal assessment £30**
COMMENCE: **April, October**   ENTRY REQ.: **PG background in the caring profession, i**
AWARD: **Diploma in Ericksonian Hypnosis, Psychotherapy & Neuro-Linguistic Programming**
NOTES: **Post-Diploma clinical supervision and advanced training available**

COURSE NO.: **222 (C)**   COURSE NAME: **Hypnotherapy** and Psychotherapy **Diploma Course**
SCHOOL: **'NEW LIFE' COURSES**
TYPE: **P/T**   PERIOD: **6 months**
ATTENDANCE: **1 full weekend per month**
VENUES: **Essex (Harlow)**
FEES: **£525**   OTHER COSTS: **£20 books, £30 exam**
COMMENCE: **March, August**   ENTRY REQ.: **a>25, reasonable education background**
AWARD: **Diploma in Hypnotherapy and Psychotherapy**
NOTES: **Entitles registration with the Association of Ethical and Professional Hypnotherapists**

HYPNOTHERAPY

COURSE NO.: 223 **COURSE NAME: Master Classes in Adv. Hypnotherapy Skills**

SCHOOL: NORMAN VAUGHTON SCHOOL OF HYPNOSIS AND PSYCHOTHERAPY

TYPE: P/T **PERIOD: 1 year approx.**

ATTENDANCE: 10 weekends

VENUES: Avon (Bristol), London, Manchester, Nottinghamshire (Nottingham)

FEES: £850 **OTHER COSTS: £30 exam fee (optional)**

COMMENCE: **ENTRY REQ.: e, basics (see NOTES below)**

AWARD: Certificate of Proficiency in Advanced Hypnotherapy Skills

NOTES: For those with basic training/counselling, psychoth., psychology or hypn. & those in caring professions

---

COURSE NO.: 224 **COURSE NAME: Master Hypnotist**

SCHOOL: PROUDFOOT SCHOOL OF HYPNOSIS & PSYCHOTHERAPY

TYPE: Short **PERIOD: 6 days**

ATTENDANCE: 6-day intensive

VENUES: North Yorkshire (Scarborough)

FEES: £395 **OTHER COSTS: Books**

COMMENCE: Feb, June, Oct **ENTRY REQ.: a>20**

AWARD: Diploma as a Master Hypnotist

NOTES: Hypnotherapy Diploma course available afterwards (see below)

COURSE NO.: 225 **COURSE NAME: Hypnotherapy**

SCHOOL: PROUDFOOT SCHOOL OF HYPNOSIS & PSYCHOTHERAPY

TYPE: Short **PERIOD: 6 days**

ATTENDANCE: 6-day intensive

VENUES: North Yorkshire (Scarborough)

FEES: £395 **OTHER COSTS: Books**

COMMENCE: Feb, June, Oct **ENTRY REQ.: Hynotist course (see above) or equiv.**

AWARD: Diploma in Hypnotherapy

NOTES: NLP Practitioner course available afterwards

COURSE NO.: 226 (C) **COURSE NAME: Hypnosis and Psychotherapy**

SCHOOL: PSYCHOTHERAPY AND HYPNOSIS TRAINING ASSOCIATION

TYPE: P/T **PERIOD: 2 years (or less A.F.D.)**

ATTENDANCE: 1 Sunday a month

VENUES: London

FEES: £1,500 **OTHER COSTS: Course texts £40**

COMMENCE: On-going, start anytime **ENTRY REQ.: None**

AWARD: Diploma in Psychotherapy and Hypnotherapy

COURSE NO.: 227 **COURSE NAME: Primary Cause Analysis by Hypnosis**

SCHOOL: SOCIETY FOR PRIMARY CAUSE ANALYSIS BY HYPNOSIS

TYPE: P/T (Clinical+Short) **PERIOD: Varies accord. to student**

ATTENDANCE: Weekly specific analysis for up to 6 months + Intensive course (100 hours) + Follow-up seminars

VENUES: Surrey (Croydon)

FEES: £40/2 hr analysis + £400 **OTHER COSTS: Nil**

COMMENCE: Course: April, Sep. Analysis: at convenience **ENTRY REQ.: e**

AWARD: Associate Membership of SPCAH leading to full membership after 1 yr of monitored practice

NOTES: Candidates to be practising hypnotherapists, psycho-analysis therapists and the like

---

HYPNOTHERAPY . IRIDOLOGY

COURSE NO.: **228**　　　COURSE NAME: **Diploma in Hypnotherapy**

SCHOOL: **SOUTH WORCESTERSHIRE HYPNOTHERAPY CENTRE**

TYPE: **Correspondence**　　　PERIOD: **Open**

ATTENDANCE: **2 x 1/2 days (can be same day)**

VENUES: **Middlesex (Feltham)**

FEES: **£500**　　　OTHER COSTS: **Books**

COMMENCE: **N/A**　　　ENTRY REQ.: **a>25, f**

AWARD: **Diploma in Hypnotherapy**

NOTES: **After passing the exam. graduates become eligible for Membership of professional organisation**

COURSE NO.: **229**　　　COURSE NAME: **Professional Course in Curative Hypnotherapy**

SCHOOL: **SOUTH WORCESTERSHIRE HYPNOTHERAPY CENTRE**

TYPE: **P/T**　　　PERIOD: **3 months**

ATTENDANCE: **Normally 10 Sundays**

VENUES: **Hereford & Worcester (Worcester)**

FEES: **£540**　　　OTHER COSTS:

COMMENCE: **Spring, Autumn**　　　ENTRY REQ.: **f, i**

AWARD: **Grade I Certificate in Hypnotherapy**

NOTES: **Training with actual patients. Recognised for entry into Instit. of Curative Hypnotherapists & Ass. of Natural Med.**

COURSE NO.: **230**　　　COURSE NAME: **Curative Hypnotherapy**

SCHOOL: **THERAPY TRAINING COLLEGE**

TYPE: **P/T**　　　PERIOD: **6 months**

ATTENDANCE: **6 weekends**

VENUES: **West Midlands (Birmingham)**

FEES: **£710**　　　OTHER COSTS: **Exam £50, Association £12**

COMMENCE: **March, September**　　　ENTRY REQ.: **None**

AWARD: **Certificate in Curative Hypnotherapy**

COURSE NO.: **131 (C)**　　　COURSE NAME: **Counselling, Hypnotherapy and Psychotherapy**

SCHOOL: **THE UK TRAINING COLLEGE**

TYPE: **P/T**　　　PERIOD: **3 years**

ATTENDANCE: **1 wknd/month for 12 months per year+personal therapy 20hrs in each of Y2&Y3+St. John's Ambul. course**

VENUES: **London, Eire (Dublin)**

FEES: **£5,450**　　　OTHER COSTS: **£176 exam + St. John's Ambulance course**

COMMENCE: **May, September**　　　ENTRY REQ.: **Y1: None, Y2: Y1 completion, f**

AWARD: **Diploma in Counselling, Hypnotherapy and Psychotherapy**

NOTES: **Year 1 is a foundation course ending in Certificate of Attendance**

COURSE NO.: **231**　　　COURSE NAME: **Iridology**

SCHOOL: **ANGLO-EUOROPEAN SCHOOL OF IRIDOLOGY (Formerly NCRIr)**

TYPE: **P/T**　　　PERIOD: **1 year**

ATTENDANCE: **1 day per month + 1 week residential + clinical**

VENUES: **Dorset (Bournemouth)**

FEES: **£1,110**　　　OTHER COSTS: **£350 residential, £100 books**

COMMENCE: **March, October**　　　ENTRY REQ.: **a=18, c**

AWARD: **Diploma in Iridology**

NOTES: **One week course for medically qualified £350**

IRIDOLOGY . KINESIOLOGY

COURSE NO.: **232**   COURSE NAME: **Iridology Course (Introductory)**

SCHOOL: **THE COLLEGE OF NUTRITIONAL MEDICINE**

TYPE: **Short**   PERIOD: **1 long weekend**

ATTENDANCE: **1 long weekend**

VENUES: **Devon, London**

FEES: **£90**   OTHER COSTS: **Equipment £25**

COMMENCE: **Twice a year (A.F.D.)**   ENTRY REQ.: **None**

AWARD: **Certificate of Attendance**

COURSE NO.: **233**   COURSE NAME: **Iridology Diploma Course**

SCHOOL: **THE COLLEGE OF NUTRITIONAL MEDICINE**

TYPE: **P/T**   PERIOD: **A.F.D.**

ATTENDANCE: **3 x 2 1/2 days**

VENUES: **Devon, Somerset**

FEES: **£310**   OTHER COSTS: **Equipment £25, books**

COMMENCE: **Twice a year (A.F.D.)**   ENTRY REQ.: **None**

AWARD: **Diploma in Iridology (D.Iridol.)**

COURSE NO.: **234**   COURSE NAME: **Opthalmic Somatology (Iridology) Certificate Course**

SCHOOL: **COLLEGE OF OPTHAMLIC SOMATOLOGY**

TYPE: **P/T**   PERIOD: **1 year**

ATTENDANCE: **1 Sunday per month**

VENUES: **London**

FEES: **£1,200**   OTHER COSTS: **Text and equipment £250 approx.**

COMMENCE: **January (A.F.D.)**   ENTRY REQ.: **A&P, f**

AWARD: **Certificate in Opthalmic Somatology**

COURSE NO.: **235**   COURSE NAME: **Opthalmic Somatology (Iridology) Diploma Course**

SCHOOL: **COLLEGE OF OPTHAMLIC SOMATOLOGY**

TYPE: **P/T**   PERIOD: **3 years**

ATTENDANCE: **1 Sunday per month**

VENUES: **London**

FEES: **£2,500**   OTHER COSTS: **Text and equipment £250 approx.**

COMMENCE: **January (A.F.D.)**   ENTRY REQ.: **A&P, f**

AWARD: **Diploma in Opthalmic Somatology**

NOTES: **Y1=Certificate course above. Students from other schools may be admitted to Y2&Y3 advanced studies.**

COURSE NO.: **236**   COURSE NAME: **T.A.S.K. Certificate Course (including Balanced Health Foundation)**

SCHOOL: **THE ACADEMY OF SYSTEMATIC KINESIOLOGY LTD**

TYPE: **P/T**   PERIOD: **Balanced Health=4 months, Cert.=9 months**

ATTENDANCE: **Balanced Health=4 wknds, Certificate course=4 wknds+1 x 8-day resid.+1 x 5-day intensive**

VENUES: **Balanced Health=All counties of the U.K., Certificate course=London, Surrey (Surbiton)**

FEES: **£1,625 - £1,725**   OTHER COSTS: **Books approx. £25**

COMMENCE: **A.F.D.**   ENTRY REQ.: **Balanced Health: None, Cert.: Balanced Health**

AWARD: **Certification to teach "Balanced Health", Certification as "Registered Kinesiologist"**

NOTES: **Two separate courses, but Certificate enabling practice only after completing both. Diploma course avail. afterwards.**

KINESIOLOGY . LYMPH DRAINAGE

COURSE NO.: **237**   COURSE NAME: **Touch for Health**

SCHOOL: **ASHTANGA CENTRE**

TYPE: **P/T**   PERIOD: **3 weekends**

ATTENDANCE:

VENUES: **Somerset (Frome)**

FEES: **A.F.D.**   OTHER COSTS: **Nil**

COMMENCE: **A.F.D.**   ENTRY REQ.: **None**

AWARD: **T.F.H. (Touch for Health) Certificate**

COURSE NO.: **238**   COURSE NAME: **Integrated Kinesiology**

SCHOOL: **THE HOWELL COLLEGE OF HOLISTIC HEALTH**

TYPE: **P/T**   PERIOD: **1 - 3 year**

ATTENDANCE: **1 Sunday afternoon per months**

VENUES: **London**

FEES: **£1,058**   OTHER COSTS: **£10 reg. fee**

COMMENCE: **Jan, June, Aug, Nov**   ENTRY REQ.: **a=18**

AWARD: **Certificate (1 year), Diploma (2 years), Advanced Diploma (3 years)**

NOTES: **Fees can be paid monthly. Qualification leads to Membership of "International Foundation of Kinesiologists".**

COURSE NO.: **239**   COURSE NAME: **Touch for Health (Basic Kinesiology)**

SCHOOL: **THE KINESIOLOGY SCHOOL**

TYPE: **P/T**   PERIOD: **3 weeks**

ATTENDANCE: **3 weekends**

VENUES: **All counties of the U.K.**

FEES: **£150**   OTHER COSTS: **Course manual £13**

COMMENCE: **Throughout the year (A.F.D.)**   ENTRY REQ.: **None**

AWARD: **Certificate of attendance only (see NOTES below)**

NOTES: **Diploma course (1-2 years) and award is available afterwards**

COURSE NO.: **240**   COURSE NAME: **Basic Applied Kinesiology (Touch for Health)**

SCHOOL: **SCHOOL OF PHYSICAL THERAPIES - BASINGSTOKE**

TYPE: **Short**   PERIOD: **2 months**

ATTENDANCE: **4 day intensive**

VENUES: **Hampshire (Basingstoke)**

FEES: **£160**   OTHER COSTS: **£14**

COMMENCE: **May, November**   ENTRY REQ.: **None**

AWARD: **Touch for Health Certificates Parts 1,2 &3**

NOTES: **Advanced studies and membership of Federation of Kinesiologists available afterwards**

COURSE NO.: **241**   COURSE NAME: **Dr. Vodder Manual Lymph Drainage Course**

SCHOOL: **BRETLANDS BEAUTY TRAINING CENTRE**

TYPE: **Short**   PERIOD: **5 days**

ATTENDANCE: **5 days**

VENUES: **Kent (Tunbridge Wells)**

FEES: **£300**   OTHER COSTS: **Nil**

COMMENCE: **May, November**   ENTRY REQ.: **MAP**

AWARD: **Dr. Vodder Certificate (Austria)**

LYMPH DRAINAGE . MACROBIOTICS

COURSE NO.: **242**   COURSE NAME: **Manual Lymph Drainage Course**
SCHOOL: **CLARE MAXWELL-HUDSON SCHOOL OF MASSAGE**
TYPE: **Short**   PERIOD: **5 days**
ATTENDANCE: **5 days**
VENUES: **London**
FEES: **£353**   OTHER COSTS:
COMMENCE: **Continuous (A.F.D.)**   ENTRY REQ.: **MAP**
AWARD: **The School Certificate in Manual Lymph Drainage**

COURSE NO.: **243**   COURSE NAME: **Lymphology**
SCHOOL: **THE HOWELL COLLEGE OF LYMPH & COLON THERAPISTS**
TYPE: **P/T**   PERIOD: **6 months**
ATTENDANCE: **1 weekend per month**
VENUES: **London**
FEES: **£705**   OTHER COSTS: **£10 reg. fee**
COMMENCE: **Febraury, August**   ENTRY REQ.: **e, h**
AWARD: **Diploma in Lymphology**
NOTES: **Fees can be paid monthly. Qualification leads to Membership of "British Ass. of Lymph & Colon Therapists".**

COURSE NO.: **244**   COURSE NAME: **Purple Flame Aromatherapy PG Workshop - Lymphatic Drainage I**
SCHOOL: **PURPLE FLAME SCHOOL OF AROMATHERAPY STRESS MANAGEMENT**
TYPE: **Short**   PERIOD: **2 days**
ATTENDANCE: **1 weekend**
VENUES: **Warwickshire (Kenilworth)**
FEES: **£141**   OTHER COSTS: **Residential if required**
COMMENCE: **Twice in 1992 (A.F.D.)**   ENTRY REQ.: **Aromatherapy Diploma**
AWARD:
NOTES: **Training in facial treatments and further lymphatic drainage techniques**

COURSE NO.: **245**   COURSE NAME: **Purple Flame Aromatherapy PG Workshop - Lymphatic Drainage II**
SCHOOL: **PURPLE FLAME SCHOOL OF AROMATHERAPY STRESS MANAGEMENT**
TYPE: **Short**   PERIOD: **2 days**
ATTENDANCE: **1 weekend**
VENUES: **Warwickshire (Kenilworth)**
FEES: **£141**   OTHER COSTS: **Residential if required**
COMMENCE: **Twice in 1992 (A.F.D.)**   ENTRY REQ.: **Attendance at Lymphatic Drainage I (See above)**
AWARD:
NOTES: **Training in advanced lymphatic drainage techniques**

COURSE NO.: **246**   COURSE NAME: **The Macrobiotic Healing Arts**
SCHOOL: **THE LONDON SCHOOL OF MACROBIOTICS**
TYPE: **P/T**   PERIOD: **2 years**
ATTENDANCE: **Foundation=8 wknds+4 day int. (or 4 wk int.), Y1= 17 wknds+6-day int.+3 x 8-day int., Y2=A.F.D.**
VENUES: **London**
FEES: **£4,690**   OTHER COSTS: **£150 approx. for books**
COMMENCE: **Found: Feb, May (or July), Y2: May, Sep**   ENTRY REQ.: **Introd. wknd and 1 day recommended (£103)**
AWARD: **Full Certificate of the School**
NOTES: **Successful graduates, after completion of field work, can apply to the Ass. of Mac. Practitioners and its Diploma**

MAGNETIC THERAPY . MASSAGE (Including MAP and On-Site Massage)

COURSE NO.: **247**   COURSE NAME: **Magnetic Therapy**

SCHOOL: **HOTHS SCHOOL OF HOLISTIC THERAPIES**

TYPE: **P/T**   PERIOD: **6 months**

ATTENDANCE: **Seminars and 3 weekend practical workshops**

VENUES: **Gloucestershire (Cheltenham), Leicestershire (Leicester)**

FEES: **£280**   OTHER COSTS: **Exam. fees**

COMMENCE: **On - going**   ENTRY REQ.: **b**

AWARD: **Practitioners Certificate in Magnetic Therapy**

NOTES: **Gives Membership of Association of Holistic Therapists**

COURSE NO.: **248**   COURSE NAME: **MAP**

SCHOOL: **ACADEMY OF NATURAL HEALTH**

TYPE: **P/T**   PERIOD: **6 months**

ATTENDANCE: **5 weekends + 5 supervised sessions + exam.**

VENUES: **London**

FEES: **£335**   OTHER COSTS: **Supervision £150, exam £55, books**

COMMENCE: **Monthly**   ENTRY REQ.: **None**

AWARD: **ITEC Certificate in MAP**

NOTES: **Can be taken in 3 flexible modules over a minimum period of 6 months and no maximum**

COURSE NO.: **249**   COURSE NAME: **On-Site Massage Training**

SCHOOL: **THE ACADEMY OF ON-SITE MASSAGE**

TYPE: **Short**   PERIOD:

ATTENDANCE: **2 1/2 days + minimum 50 practice treatments before assessment**

VENUES: **Avon (Bristol), East Sussex (Brighton), London, Manchester, South Glamorgan (Cardiff), and others**

FEES: **£115**   OTHER COSTS: **Nil**

COMMENCE: **Monthly**   ENTRY REQ.: **Bodywork qualif. OR (with pemission) student**

AWARD: **Certificate in On-Site Massage**

NOTES: **Follow up workshop in advanced techniques and marketing plus on-going review groups**

COURSE NO.: **250**   COURSE NAME: **Remedial Massage**

SCHOOL: **THE ALLIED SCHOOL OF REMEDIAL MASSAGE**

TYPE: **P/T**   PERIOD: **2 years**

ATTENDANCE: **1 weekend per month (24 weekends - first weekend in every month)**

VENUES: **Avon (Bristol)**

FEES: **£1,470 (By monthly direct debit)**   OTHER COSTS:

COMMENCE: **November**   ENTRY REQ.: **None**

AWARD: **Diploma in Remedial Massage**

NOTES: **In addition to Diploma, course to prepare students to enter Oxford & Northern Counties Schools of Osteopathy**

COURSE NO.: **251**   COURSE NAME: **Remedial Massage**

SCHOOL: **ASHTANGA CENTRE**

TYPE: **P/T**   PERIOD:

ATTENDANCE: **4 weekends + 1 day for exam**

VENUES: **Somerset (Frome)**

FEES: **£320**   OTHER COSTS: **Exam fee**

COMMENCE: **A.F.D.**   ENTRY REQ.: **a=>20**

AWARD: **ITEC Diploma in Remedial Massage**

194

MASSAGE (Including MAP and Massage and Aromatherapy)

COURSE NO.: **252**   COURSE NAME: **Therapeutic Massage and Aromatherapy Diploma Course**
SCHOOL: **THE ASSOCIATION OF MEDICAL AROMATHERAPISTS**
TYPE: **P/T**   PERIOD: **9 months**
ATTENDANCE: **9 weekends**
VENUES: **Strathclyde (Glasgow)**
FEES: **£750**   OTHER COSTS:
COMMENCE: **October**   ENTRY REQ.: **f**
AWARD: **Diploma in Therapeutic Massage and Aromatherapy**

COURSE NO.: **253**   COURSE NAME: **Massage**
SCHOOL: **ASSOCIATION OF NATURAL MEDICINES**
TYPE: **P/T**   PERIOD: **3 months**
ATTENDANCE: **Minimum 30 hours**
VENUES: **Cornwall, Devon, Essex (Chelmsford), London**
FEES: **£200 (region of)**   OTHER COSTS:
COMMENCE: **Throughout the year (A.F.D.)**   ENTRY REQ.: **f**
AWARD: **Certificate in Massage**

COURSE NO.: **254**   COURSE NAME: **MAP**
SCHOOL: **BEAUMONT COLLEGE OF NATURAL MEDICINE**
TYPE: **F/T**   PERIOD: **8 weeks**
ATTENDANCE: **5 consecutive days a week + 1 1/2 days assessment/exam**
VENUES: **East Sussex (Eastbourne)**
FEES: **£350**   OTHER COSTS: **£35 exam fee**
COMMENCE: **Several times a year (A.F.D.)**   ENTRY REQ.: **a>20, short essay**
AWARD: **ITEC Certificate in MAP**

COURSE NO.: **255**   COURSE NAME: **Deep Relaxation Massage**
SCHOOL: **BEAUTIFORM TRAINING COLLEGE**
TYPE: **P/T**   PERIOD: **3 months**
ATTENDANCE: **1 day per week for 10 weeks, OR 3 full weekends**
VENUES: **West Midlands (Birmingham)**
FEES: **£450**   OTHER COSTS: **£35 exam fee, accomodation £25/2 nights**
COMMENCE: **January, April/September**   ENTRY REQ.: **a=>18**
AWARD: **ITEC Massage Certificate**

COURSE NO.: **256**   COURSE NAME: **MAP**
SCHOOL: **BERKSHIRE SCHOOL OF NATURAL THERAPY**
TYPE: **P/T**   PERIOD: **2 months**
ATTENDANCE: **5 weekends (Saturday & Sunday)**
VENUES: **Berkshire (Crowthorne)**
FEES: **£350**   OTHER COSTS: **Nil**
COMMENCE: **May**   ENTRY REQ.: **a=>18**
AWARD: **ITEC Certificate in MAP**
NOTES: **This course is also a foundation for other therapies such as aromatherapy and reflexology**

MASSAGE (Including MAP)

COURSE NO.: **257**   COURSE NAME: **MAP**

SCHOOL: **BERKSHIRE SCHOOL OF NATURAL THERAPY**

TYPE: **P/T**   PERIOD: **2 months**

ATTENDANCE: **10 days (2 blocks of Monday - Friday)**

VENUES: **Berkshire (Crowthorne)**

FEES: **£350**   OTHER COSTS: **Nil**

COMMENCE: **Jan, March, May, July, Sept, Oct**   ENTRY REQ.: **a=>18**

AWARD: **ITEC Certificate in MAP**

NOTES: **This course is also a foundation for other therapies such as aromatherapy and reflexology**

COURSE NO.: **258**   COURSE NAME: **MAP**

SCHOOL: **BOURNEMOUTH SCHOOL OF MASSAGE**

TYPE: **P/T**   PERIOD: **10 - 14 weeks**

ATTENDANCE: **12 consecutive Tuesdays, OR 8 consecutive Sundays + 2 eve weekly for 3 weeks then 1 eve weekly**

VENUES: **Dorset (Bournemouth)**

FEES: **£445**   OTHER COSTS: **Nil**

COMMENCE: **Feb, Oct (Sundays) / Feb, July (Tuesdays)**   ENTRY REQ.: **b, c, f, i**

AWARD: **ITEC Diploma/Certificate in MAP**

NOTES: **Includes holistic facial & body massage with aromatic blends. Aromatherapy & sports therapy avail. afterwards.**

COURSE NO.: **259**   COURSE NAME: **Professional ITEC in MAP**

SCHOOL: **CARLISLE MASSAGE SCHOOL**

TYPE: **P/T**   PERIOD: **2 months**

ATTENDANCE: **4 weekends + 1/2 day + evening clinic sessions of 2 hours**

VENUES: **Cumbria (Carlisle)**

FEES: **£250**   OTHER COSTS: **Nil**

COMMENCE: **Varies (A.F.D.)**   ENTRY REQ.: **b, c**

AWARD: **ITEC Certificate in MAP**

COURSE NO.: **260**   COURSE NAME: **Advanced Massage Training Programme (ITEC MAP)**

SCHOOL: **THE CHALICE FOUNDATION**

TYPE: **P/T**   PERIOD: **6 months (flexible)**

ATTENDANCE: **4 weekends**

VENUES: **London**

FEES: **£365**   OTHER COSTS: **£28**

COMMENCE: **Monthly**   ENTRY REQ.: **Foundation 5/6-intensive massage course**

AWARD: **ITEC in MAP**

NOTES: **Students can go on to the Art of Aromatherapy Diploma course leading to the ISPA certificate**

COURSE NO.: **261**   COURSE NAME: **ITEC MAP**

SCHOOL: **CHAMPNEYS COLLEGE OF HEALTH & BEAUTY**

TYPE: **P/T**   PERIOD: **14 weeks (including break for case study)**

ATTENDANCE: **3 hours Friday evening + 6 hours Saturday for 10 weeks**

VENUES: **Hertfordshire (Tring)**

FEES: **£488**   OTHER COSTS: **Nil**

COMMENCE: **Spring, Autumn**   ENTRY REQ.: **None**

AWARD: **ITEC Diploma/Certificate in MAP**

MASSAGE (Including MAP)

COURSE NO.: **262**   COURSE NAME: **Massage Training Course (MAP)**

SCHOOL: **CLARE MAXWELL-HUDSON SCHOOL OF MASSAGE**

TYPE: **P/T**   PERIOD: **Depending on period between stages**

ATTENDANCE: **S1 = 5 weekends OR 11 Mondays, S2 = 4 weekends**

VENUES: **London**

FEES: **£1,203**   OTHER COSTS: **A.F.D.**

COMMENCE: **Continuous (A.F.D.)**   ENTRY REQ.:

AWARD: **The School Certificate in Massage**

NOTES: **Advanced course is available afterwards**

COURSE NO.: **263**   COURSE NAME: **Therapeutic Massage**

SCHOOL: **COLLEGE OF HOLISTIC MEDICINE**

TYPE: **P/T**   PERIOD: **9 months**

ATTENDANCE: **10 weekends (approx. one per month)**

VENUES: **London, Strathclyde (Glasgow)**

FEES: **£645 London, £595 Glasgow**   OTHER COSTS: **£200**

COMMENCE: **September**   ENTRY REQ.: **a>18**

AWARD: **Diploma in Therapeutic Massage**

NOTES: **10 hours homework per week out of which 4 hours practical**

COURSE NO.: **264**   COURSE NAME: **Swedish Massage**

SCHOOL: **THE COMMUNITY HEALTH FOUNDATION**

TYPE: **P/T**   PERIOD: **12 weeks**

ATTENDANCE: **12 x 3-hour evenings (Tuesdays or Thursdays)**

VENUES: **London**

FEES: **£250**   OTHER COSTS: **Books £50**

COMMENCE: **Throughout the year (A.F.D.)**   ENTRY REQ.: **None**

AWARD: **ITEC Certificate in MAP**

COURSE NO.: **265**   COURSE NAME: **A, P and Basic Massage**

SCHOOL: **THE EDINBURGH SCHOOL OF NATURAL THERAPY**

TYPE: **Short**   PERIOD: **2 weeks**

ATTENDANCE: **10 days**

VENUES: **Lothian (Edinburgh)**

FEES: **£260**   OTHER COSTS: **£40 reg. fee**

COMMENCE: **Throughout the year (A.F.D.)**   ENTRY REQ.: **5 b's for a<30, 2 b's for a>30**

AWARD: **ITEC Certificate in MAP**

NOTES: **Reg. fee is waived for those continuing from the Basic Massage course**

COURSE NO.: **266**   COURSE NAME: **MAP**

SCHOOL: **THE EDINBURGH SCHOOL OF NATURAL THERAPY**

TYPE: **F/T**   PERIOD: **6 weeks**

ATTENDANCE: **30 days**

VENUES: **Lothian (Edinburgh)**

FEES: **£780**   OTHER COSTS: **£40 reg. (see NOTES), £35 exams (ITEC & pract.)**

COMMENCE: **Throught the year (A.F.D.)**   ENTRY REQ.: **5 b's for a<30, 2 b's for a>30**

AWARD: **The School Certificate in Massage**

NOTES: **Graduates can enter Adv. Massage leading to ITEC qualif., and aromatherapy reflexology courses.**

MASSAGE (Including MAP)

COURSE NO.: **267**   COURSE NAME: **MAP**

SCHOOL: **ESSEX SCHOOL OF MASSAGE**

TYPE: **P/T**   PERIOD: **3 months**

ATTENDANCE: **6 day intensive followed by practice sessions and exam**

VENUES: **Essex (Nazeing)**

FEES: **£249**   OTHER COSTS: **Exam fee £10**

COMMENCE: **Monthly**   ENTRY REQ.: **b, c, i with b or c**

AWARD: **ITEC Certificate in MAP**

NOTES: **The school specialises in teaching small groups. Max. number of students in any one course is 4 only.**

COURSE NO.: **268**   COURSE NAME: **Remedial Massage**

SCHOOL: **THE FACULTY OF OSTEOPATHY**

TYPE: **P/T**   PERIOD: **Open**

ATTENDANCE: **Practical weekend seminars**

VENUES: **Manchester, Merseyside (Southport)**

FEES: **A.F.D.**   OTHER COSTS:

COMMENCE: **On - going**   ENTRY REQ.: **None**

AWARD: **Diploma in Remedial Massage from the Faculty of Osteopathy**

COURSE NO.: **269**   COURSE NAME: **Therpeutic Massage**

SCHOOL: **FRANCES FEWELL (GEMINI INSTITUTE)**

TYPE: **P/T**   PERIOD: **35 hours**

ATTENDANCE: **1 weekend a month**

VENUES: **Essex (Chelmsford)**

FEES: **£350**   OTHER COSTS: **Exam fees**

COMMENCE: **January, March, June, September**   ENTRY REQ.: **None**

AWARD: **Association of Natural Medicines Diploma in MAP**

NOTES: **Advanced training available afterwards**

COURSE NO.: **270**   COURSE NAME: **Professional Massage / Healthcare**

SCHOOL: **GABLECROFT COLLEGE**

TYPE: **P/T**   PERIOD: **5 - 6 months approx.**

ATTENDANCE: **1 weekend per month (4 weekends in all)**

VENUES: **Shropshire (Oswestry)**

FEES: **A.F.D.**   OTHER COSTS: **A.F.D.**

COMMENCE: **Variable (A.F.D.)**   ENTRY REQ.: **None**

AWARD: **ITEC Certificate**

COURSE NO.: **271**   COURSE NAME: **Biorelease and MAP**

SCHOOL: **GERDA BOYESEN CENTRE**

TYPE: **P/T**   PERIOD: **10 weeks**

ATTENDANCE: **5 weekends + 10 evenings (100 hours total)**

VENUES: **London**

FEES: **£525**   OTHER COSTS: **Books £25**

COMMENCE: **Jan, April, Sep**   ENTRY REQ.: **a=>18 at completion, b, c, i**

AWARD: **ITEC Diploma/Certificate in MAP**

NOTES: **Graduates are eligible to enter to the training in Biodynamic Physiatry & Counselling (see under Counselling)**

MASSAGE (Including MAP)

COURSE NO.: **272**	COURSE NAME: **Massage**
SCHOOL: **GOOD SCENTS SCHOOL OF NATURAL THERAPIES**	
TYPE: **P/T**	PERIOD: **3 - 6 months**
ATTENDANCE: **1 day per week for 3 months, OR alternate weekends for 6 months**	
VENUES: **West Sussex (Pulborough)**	
FEES: **£300**	OTHER COSTS: **Massage couch (optional)**
COMMENCE: **Jan, April, Sep**	ENTRY REQ.: **A & P**
AWARD: **Diploma in Massage**	
NOTES: **Students must sit the School Anatomy exam.**	

COURSE NO.: **273**	COURSE NAME: **Remedial and Holistic Massage**
SCHOOL: **JANE HIDER SCHOOL OF NATURAL THERAPIES**	
TYPE: **P/T**	PERIOD: **8 months**
ATTENDANCE: **1 weekend per month**	
VENUES: **Gloucestershire (Gloucester), Hereford & Worcester (Hereford)**	
FEES: **£560**	OTHER COSTS: **Books, exams.**
COMMENCE: **April, September**	ENTRY REQ.: **a=>20, b, i**
AWARD: **ITEC Certificate in MAP**	
NOTES: **Visually handicapped students accepted. Course includes advanced techniques suitable for nurses/those in caring.**	

COURSE NO.: **274**	COURSE NAME: **Holistic Body Massage**
SCHOOL: **LANCASHIRE HOLISTIC COLLEGE**	
TYPE: **P/T**	PERIOD: **9 months**
ATTENDANCE: **Approx. 1 weekend per month**	
VENUES: **Lancashire (Preston)**	
FEES: **£720 approx.**	OTHER COSTS: **Books, exams.**
COMMENCE: **January, July**	ENTRY REQ.: **a=>18, b, i**
AWARD: **ITEC Certificate in MAP and College Diploma**	
NOTES: **You can attend any part of the course, but exams. can only be passed upon attendance of all parts**	

COURSE NO.: **275**	COURSE NAME: **Holistic Massage**
SCHOOL: **LA ROSA SCHOOL OF HEALTH & BEAUTY**	
TYPE: **P/T**	PERIOD: **3 terms**
ATTENDANCE: **1 evening per week over 3 terms**	
VENUES: **Devon (Brixham)**	
FEES: **£400**	OTHER COSTS: **Nil**
COMMENCE: **September**	ENTRY REQ.: **b + f for a<30, f for i**
AWARD: **ITEC Certificate in MAP (Category 24)**	
NOTES: **Fees may be paid in instalments**	

COURSE NO.: **276**	COURSE NAME: **MAP**
SCHOOL: **LA ROSA SCHOOL OF HEALTH & BEAUTY**	
TYPE: **P/T**	PERIOD: **3 terms**
ATTENDANCE: **1 evening per week over 3 terms**	
VENUES: **Devon (Brixham)**	
FEES: **£400**	OTHER COSTS: **Nil**
COMMENCE: **September**	ENTRY REQ.: **b + f for a<30, f for i**
AWARD: **ITEC Certificate in MAP (Category 7)**	
NOTES: **Fees may be paid in instalments**	

MASSAGE (Including MAP and Biodynamic Physiatry)

COURSE NO.: **277** COURSE NAME: **MAP**
SCHOOL: **THE LEAVES INTERNATIONAL SCHOOL OF AROMATHERAPY, MASSAGE AND NATURAL THERAPY**
TYPE: **P/T** PERIOD: **3 months**
ATTENDANCE: **4-day intensive**
VENUES: **Avon (Nr. Bath), Dorset, Wiltshire (Trowbridge)**
FEES: **£247** OTHER COSTS: **Exam fee £41**
COMMENCE: **Twice yearly (A.F.D.)** ENTRY REQ.: **ITEC MAP**
AWARD: **ITEC Diploma in MAP, and the School Diploma in Holistic Massage**

COURSE NO.: **278** COURSE NAME: **Massage**
SCHOOL: **LONDON COLLEGE OF MASSAGE**
TYPE: **P/T** PERIOD: **7 - 9 months (Sea NOTES below)**
ATTENDANCE: **Beginners =eve, wkday or wknds over 10 wks, Advanced =3 hrs/wk for 12 weeks OR 4 wknds over 4 months**
VENUES: **London, Ireland (Cork)**
FEES: **£580** OTHER COSTS:
COMMENCE: **Begin.= once/month, Adv=once/2 months** ENTRY REQ.: **Begin.=None, Adv.=Beginners course**
AWARD: **The College Foundation Practitioner Certificate**
NOTES: **Two courses. Period from start to finish will depend on your commencement of the Advanced Course.**

COURSE NO.: **279** COURSE NAME: **Massage Clinical Supervision Course**
SCHOOL: **LONDON COLLEGE OF MASSAGE**
TYPE: **P/T** PERIOD: **3 months**
ATTENDANCE: **1 weekend + 1 tutorial per month**
VENUES: **London, Ireland (Cork)**
FEES: **£300** OTHER COSTS: **Nil**
COMMENCE: **Throughout the year** ENTRY REQ.: **The Foundation Certif. (above) or equivalent**
AWARD: **The College Clinical Supervision Certificate**
NOTES: **Aims to place newly graduated practitioners in clinical setting**

COURSE NO.: **280** COURSE NAME: **Bio-release & MAP**
SCHOOL: **THE LONDON SCHOOL OF BIODYNAMIC PHYSIATRY**
TYPE: **P/T** PERIOD: **10 weeks**
ATTENDANCE: **5 weekends + 10 evenings = 100 hours**
VENUES: **London**
FEES: **£580** OTHER COSTS: **£25**
COMMENCE: **January, April, September** ENTRY REQ.: **a=>18 at completion, b or c, i**
AWARD: **ITEC in MAP**
NOTES: **Graduates are eligible to enter the Biodynamic Physiatry course (see below)**

COURSE NO.: **281** COURSE NAME: **Biodynamic Physiatry**
SCHOOL: **THE LONDON SCHOOL OF BIODYNAMIC PHYSIATRY - in ass. with THE BOYESEN TRAINING CENTRE**
TYPE: **P/T** PERIOD: **2 years**
ATTENDANCE: **1 eve/wk + 1 eve /fortnight for 30 wks/yr + 5-10 hr/ wk clinic for 36 wk/yr + weekly psychotherapy + 120 hours weekend psychotherapy per year**
VENUES: **London**
FEES: **£1,800** OTHER COSTS: **£70 + psychotherapy @ £20 per session**
COMMENCE: **April 1992** ENTRY REQ.: **a>21, Bio-release & MAP course**
AWARD: **Certificate in Biodynamic Physiatry**
NOTES: **The course consists of 2 parts, one by the school, and the other by the Boyesen Training Centre (A.F.D.)**

MASSAGE (including MAP)

COURSE NO.: **282**	COURSE NAME: **Massage Diploma Course**
SCHOOL: **LONDON SCHOOL OF SPORTS MASSAGE LTD**	
TYPE: **P/T**	PERIOD: **6 months**
ATTENDANCE: **8 weekends**	
VENUES: **London**	
FEES: **£969**	OTHER COSTS: **Nil**
COMMENCE: **March, Sep, Nov**	ENTRY REQ.: **d, basic massage, sport experience preferable**
AWARD: **LSSM (The School) Diploma (Validated by the RSA)**	
NOTES: **Basic massage (entry req.) avail. Advanced Cert. (1 year of workshops) open to graduates and other therapists.**	

COURSE NO.: **283**	COURSE NAME: **MAP**
SCHOOL: **LONDON THERAPY CENTRE**	
TYPE: **Short**	PERIOD: **6 days**
ATTENDANCE: **6 days**	
VENUES: **London**	
FEES: **£325**	OTHER COSTS: **A.F.D.**
COMMENCE: **A.F.D.**	ENTRY REQ.: **A.F.D.**
AWARD: **ITEC Certificate in MAP**	
NOTES: **ITEC courses in aromatherapy, lymph drainage, nutrition & diet and reflexology are available**	

COURSE NO.: **284**	COURSE NAME: **Holistic Massage**
SCHOOL: **LYN GORLEY SCHOOL OF MASSAGE & AROMATHERAPY**	
TYPE: **P/T**	PERIOD: **3 months**
ATTENDANCE: **2 - 3 days per month (usually Thursday, Friday, Saturday)**	
VENUES: **Berkshire (Newbury)**	
FEES: **£350**	OTHER COSTS: **£25 exam fee, book £7**
COMMENCE: **Varies, but around April, October usually**	ENTRY REQ.: **b, i**
AWARD: **ITEC MAP - Holistic**	
NOTES: **Specialised in courses for health care professionals**	

COURSE NO.: **285**	COURSE NAME: **MAP**
SCHOOL: **MAGGIE NICHOL**	
TYPE: **P/T**	PERIOD: **4 months**
ATTENDANCE: **4 weekends**	
VENUES: **Hampshire (Petersfield and Portsmouth)**	
FEES: **£320**	OTHER COSTS: **Exam fee**
COMMENCE: **On - going**	ENTRY REQ.: **None**
AWARD: **ITEC Certificate in MAP**	

COURSE NO.: **286**	COURSE NAME: **Therapeutic Massage**
SCHOOL: **MARYLEBONE CENTRE TRUST - EDUCATION & TRAINING UNIT**	
TYPE: **P/T**	PERIOD: **6 months**
ATTENDANCE: **6 weekends + 4 practice evenings + 40 hour clinical placement**	
VENUES: **London**	
FEES: **£600**	OTHER COSTS:
COMMENCE: **February, September**	ENTRY REQ.: **A&P (a module run by the Trust=2 wknds)**
AWARD: **Diploma in Therapeutic Massage**	
NOTES: **Modular course; 1-A&P, 2-Theory & Practice, 3-Clinical placement arranged by MCT**	

MASSAGE (Including MAP)

COURSE NO.: 287 COURSE NAME: **Massage and Manipulative Therapy (Basic and Advanced)**

SCHOOL: **THE MIDLANDS SCHOOL OF MASSAGE**

TYPE: **P/T** PERIOD: **2 years**

ATTENDANCE: **Basic = 1 weekend a month for 6 months, Advanced = 1 weekend a month for 18 months**

VENUES: **Nottinghamshire (Nottingham)**

FEES: **£1,290** OTHER COSTS: **Reg. fee = £40 Basic + £45 Advanced**

COMMENCE: **Basic: Feb, Sep, Advanced: any month** ENTRY REQ.: **a>18**

AWARD: **Certificates in Remedial Massage & Advanced Massage and Manipulative Therapy**

NOTES: **18 self-contained modules. Graduates can enter Oxford & Northern Counties Schools of Osteopathy.**

COURSE NO.: 288 COURSE NAME: **MAP**

SCHOOL: **THE MILLFIELD SCHOOL OF BEAUTY THERAPY**

TYPE: **P/T** PERIOD: **3 months**

ATTENDANCE: **Weekends**

VENUES: **West Sussex (Rusper)**

FEES: **£600** OTHER COSTS: **Nil**

COMMENCE: **January, April, September** ENTRY REQ.: **None**

AWARD: **ITEC Diploma in MAP (massage, anatomy and physiology)**

COURSE NO.: 289 COURSE NAME: **MAP**

SCHOOL: **THE MILLFIELD SCHOOL OF BEAUTY THERAPY**

TYPE: **Short** PERIOD: **1 month**

ATTENDANCE: **5 days a week**

VENUES: **West Sussex (Rusper)**

FEES: **£600** OTHER COSTS: **Nil**

COMMENCE: **January, April, September** ENTRY REQ.: **None**

AWARD: **ITEC Diploma in MAP (massage, anatomy and physiology)**

COURSE NO.: 290 COURSE NAME: **Physical Therapies/Massage**

SCHOOL: **NATIONAL SCHOOL OF MASSAGE**

TYPE: **P/T** PERIOD: **1 - 2 years**

ATTENDANCE: **1 weekend per month (10 weekends in all)**

VENUES: **Lancashire (Southport)**

FEES: **£390 + £400 for the weekends** OTHER COSTS: **Basic Body massage £120 over 3 weekends**

COMMENCE: **Anytime** ENTRY REQ.: **a=>18, i**

AWARD: **Diploma in Physical Therapies/Massage**

NOTES: **After practising for 2 years you may apply for the 2 year Osteopathy with Northern Counties School of Osteopathy**

COURSE NO.: 291 COURSE NAME: **M.T.M. Core (Magic Touch Management)**

SCHOOL: **NEW LIFE COLLEGE**

TYPE: **P/T** PERIOD: **24 weeks**

ATTENDANCE: **2 evenings a week for 23 weeks + 2 x 1-day intensive**

VENUES: **London**

FEES: **£560** OTHER COSTS: **£25 Exam fee**

COMMENCE: **On - going** ENTRY REQ.: **b (desirable), f**

AWARD: **Certificate in MTM**

NOTES: **This course is similar to a MAP course**

MASSAGE (Including MAP)

COURSE NO.: **292** COURSE NAME: **M.T.M. Advanced (Magic Touch Management)**

SCHOOL: **NEW LIFE COLLEGE**

TYPE: **P/T**   PERIOD: **24 weeks**

ATTENDANCE: **Min. 36 hours taken in day intensives and evening/day classes (mostly weekends)**

VENUES: **London**

FEES: **£160**   OTHER COSTS: **Nil**

COMMENCE: **On - going**   ENTRY REQ.: **MTM Core or massage cert.**

AWARD: **Diploma in MTM**

NOTES: **This course is structured to acompany the core course and runs parallel to it**

COURSE NO.: **293** COURSE NAME: **Remedial Massage & Allied Therapies**

SCHOOL: **NORTHERN INSTITUTE OF MASSAGE**

TYPE: **P/T**   PERIOD: **Average 12 - 15 months**

ATTENDANCE: **Minimum of 7 x 2-day lecture/practical instruction classes**

VENUES: **Lancashire (Blackpool), some optional London classes**

FEES: **£840**   OTHER COSTS: **Nil**

COMMENCE: **Open enrollment basis**   ENTRY REQ.: **f, i**

AWARD: **College Diploma in Remedial Massage**

NOTES: **PG Adv. Remedial Mass. & Manipulative Therapy avail. to suitably qualified therapists with experience**

COURSE NO.: **294** COURSE NAME: **Healing Touch**

SCHOOL: **ON COURSE - PERSONAL AND PROFESSIONAL DEVELOPMENT CONSULTANCY**

TYPE: **P/T**   PERIOD: **4 months**

ATTENDANCE: **Basic = 4 alternate weekends, Advanced = 2 alternate intensive long weekends + exam day**

VENUES: **Hertfordshire (St. Albans)**

FEES: **£380**   OTHER COSTS: **B & B= £8/night (Optional)**

COMMENCE: **February, September**   ENTRY REQ.: **a=18, b**

AWARD: **ITEC Certificate in MAP**

NOTES: **Graduates eligible for Reg. Practitioner Membership of the Healing Touch Network**

COURSE NO.: **295** COURSE NAME: **Massage, Theory and Practical**

SCHOOL: **OXFORD HOUSE CLINIC FOR COMPLEMENTARY MEDICINE**

TYPE: **P/T**   PERIOD: **10 weeks**

ATTENDANCE: **1 evening (3 hours) per week**

VENUES: **Berkshire (Reading)**

FEES: **£200**   OTHER COSTS:

COMMENCE: **June, October**   ENTRY REQ.: **None**

AWARD: **Certificate in Massage**

COURSE NO.: **296** COURSE NAME: **MAP**

SCHOOL: **PARK SCHOOL OF BEAUTY THERAPY**

TYPE: **F/T or P/T**   PERIOD: **2 weeks minimum**

ATTENDANCE: **10 days minimum**

VENUES: **Nottinghamshire (Retford)**

FEES: **£411**   OTHER COSTS: **Overall etc £30**

COMMENCE: **Every month**   ENTRY REQ.:

AWARD: **ITEC Diploma in MAP**

MASSAGE (Including MAP)

COURSE NO.: **297**   COURSE NAME: **Anatomy, Physiology & Holistic Massage**

SCHOOL: **RAWORTH COLLEGE FOR SPORTS THERAPY AND NATURAL MEDICINE**

TYPE: **P/T**   PERIOD: **11 weeks**

ATTENDANCE: **2 days a week**

VENUES: **Surrey (Dorking)**

FEES: **£675**   OTHER COSTS: **£75**

COMMENCE: **Jan, April, July, Sep**   ENTRY REQ.: **f**

AWARD: **Certificate in Holistic Massage and ITEC**

COURSE NO.: **298**   COURSE NAME: **Diploma in Therapeutic Remedial Massage**

SCHOOL: **RAWORTH COLLEGE FOR SPORTS THERAPY AND NATURAL MEDICINE**

TYPE: **P/T**   PERIOD: **3 months**

ATTENDANCE: **1 day a week for 11 weeks OR 2 weekends a month for 3 months (commencing September)**

VENUES: **Surrey (Dorking)**

FEES: **£385**   OTHER COSTS: **£60**

COMMENCE: **Jan, Sep (weekends only)**   ENTRY REQ.: **e**

AWARD: **Diploma in Advanced Therpeutic Massage**

NOTES: **Candidates should have basic knowledge of MAP to ITEC standard. Course designed to upgrade existing skills.**

COURSE NO.: **299**   COURSE NAME: **Massage Certificate Training Course**

SCHOOL: **ROGER WORTHINGTON**

TYPE: **P/T**   PERIOD: **6 months**

ATTENDANCE: **1 half day in 2 x 10 week terms**

VENUES: **Kent (West Kingsdown)**

FEES: **£285 per term**   OTHER COSTS: **£30**

COMMENCE: **October**   ENTRY REQ.: **f**

AWARD: **ITEC Diploma in MAP**

NOTES: **Those with medical training are exempted from A&P, and so pay less fees**

COURSE NO.: **300**   COURSE NAME: **MAP**

SCHOOL: **ROYAL NATIONAL COLLEGE FOR THE BLIND**

TYPE: **F/T**   PERIOD: **1 year**

ATTENDANCE: **1 academic year (3 terms)**

VENUES: **Herefordshire (Hereford)**

FEES: **Students are funded**   OTHER COSTS: **Nil**

COMMENCE: **September**   ENTRY REQ.: **Reg. blind or partially sighted, b**

AWARD: **ITEC Diploma in MAP (massage, anatomy and physiology)**

NOTES: **Students attending are expected to spend part of their time doing business studies**

COURSE NO.: **301**   COURSE NAME: **Swedish Massage**

SCHOOL: **SCHOOL OF NATURAL THERAPIES AND ORIENTAL STUDIES**

TYPE: **P/T**   PERIOD: **4 months**

ATTENDANCE: **3 weekends**

VENUES: **Hampshire, London**

FEES: **£240**   OTHER COSTS: **£30**

COMMENCE: **A.F.D.**   ENTRY REQ.: **A&P Certificate**

AWARD: **The School Certificate in Swedish Massage**

NOTES: **ITEC Certificate available. Those with A&P are exempt from their part in the course.**

MASSAGE (Including MAP and Thai Massage)

COURSE NO.: **302**   COURSE NAME: **Dip. in Traditional Thai Healing Massage**

SCHOOL: **SCHOOL OF ORIENTAL MASSAGE**

TYPE: **P/T**   PERIOD: **6 months**

ATTENDANCE: **6 weekends + 6 practice supervision days**

VENUES: **London**

FEES: **£695**   OTHER COSTS:

COMMENCE: **November**   ENTRY REQ.: **Nil**

AWARD: **Diploma in Traditional Thai Healing Massage**

NOTES: **Thai massage differs from Swedish massage. This is the only course in Thai mas. in the UK, accredited in Bangkok.**

COURSE NO.: **303**   COURSE NAME: **Therapeutic Massage, Anatomy & Physiology**

SCHOOL: **SCHOOL OF PHYSICAL THERAPIES - BASINGSTOKE**

TYPE: **P/T**   PERIOD: **4 months**

ATTENDANCE: **8 day intensive + clinical practice**

VENUES: **Hampshire (Basingstoke)**

FEES: **£280**   OTHER COSTS: **£10**

COMMENCE: **Jan, March, June, Sept, Nov**   ENTRY REQ.: **a>21**

AWARD: **ITEC Certificate in MAP**

NOTES: **Leading to PG courses in aromatherapy, reflexology, sports therapy, nutrition and advanced massage**

COURSE NO.: **304**   COURSE NAME: **Advanced Massage Techniques Diploma**

SCHOOL: **SCHOOL OF PHYSICAL THERAPIES - BASINGSTOKE**

TYPE: **P/T**   PERIOD: **2 months**

ATTENDANCE: **4 day intensive + 50 hours clinical**

VENUES: **Hampshire (Basingstoke)**

FEES: **£160**   OTHER COSTS: **£15**

COMMENCE: **Jan, March, June, Sept, Nov**   ENTRY REQ.: **ITEC MAP**

AWARD: **Diploma in Advanced Massage Techniques**

NOTES: **A must for Massage & Sports therapists with soft tissue release, basic acupressure, polarity balance etc.**

COURSE NO.: **305**   COURSE NAME: **MAP**

SCHOOL: **THE SCHOOL OF PHYSICAL THERAPIES (GUILDFORD)**

TYPE: **P/T**   PERIOD: **4 months**

ATTENDANCE: **8-day intensive + clinical practice**

VENUES: **Surrey (Guildford)**

FEES: **£320**   OTHER COSTS: **£10**

COMMENCE: **Jan, Sept, Oct**   ENTRY REQ.: **a>21**

AWARD: **ITEC Certificate in MAP**

NOTES: **ITEC PG adv. massage, aromatherapy, nutrition, reflexology and sports therapy avail. afterwards**

COURSE NO.: **306**   COURSE NAME: **Therapeutic Massage, Anatomy & Physiology**

SCHOOL: **SCHOOL OF PHYSICAL THERAPIES (KINGSTON)**

TYPE: **P/T**   PERIOD: **4 months**

ATTENDANCE: **8-day intensive + clinical practice**

VENUES: **Surrey (Kingston)**

FEES: **£280**   OTHER COSTS: **£45 exam, £8 books**

COMMENCE: **Jan, March, June, Sept, Nov**   ENTRY REQ.: **a>21**

AWARD: **ITEC Certificate in MAP**

NOTES: **Leading to PG courses in aromatherapy, reflexology, sports therapy, nutrition and advanced massage**

MASSAGE (Including MAP)

COURSE NO.: **307**   COURSE NAME: **Training in Holistic Massage**
SCHOOL: **SCHOOL OF THE DANCING DRAGON**
TYPE: **P/T**   PERIOD: **6 months**
ATTENDANCE: **6 weekends + 50 hours practice + 3 supervision evenings**
VENUES: **London**
FEES: **£400**   OTHER COSTS:
COMMENCE: **January, October**   ENTRY REQ.: **f**
AWARD: **Association of Massage Practitioners Certificate in Holistic Massage**

COURSE NO.: **308**   COURSE NAME: **MAP**
SCHOOL: **SHIRLEY GOLDSTEIN HOLISTIC THERAPIES**
TYPE: **P/T**   PERIOD: **3 - 6 months**
ATTENDANCE: **Various combinations (A.F.D.)**
VENUES: **Devon, London**
FEES: **£385**   OTHER COSTS: **Book £7**
COMMENCE: **Throughout the year (A.F.D.)**   ENTRY REQ.: **a=18**
AWARD: **MAP Certificate**
NOTES: **Courses in Polarity, Chakra balancing & Healing, Breathing/Meditation work available**

COURSE NO.: **309**   COURSE NAME: **MAP**
SCHOOL: **SOUTH WEST SCHOOL OF HOLISTIC TOUCH**
TYPE: **P/T**   PERIOD: **6 months**
ATTENDANCE: **1 weekend per month**
VENUES: **Devon (Exeter)**
FEES: **£330**   OTHER COSTS: **Nil**
COMMENCE: **Twice yearly (A.F.D.)**   ENTRY REQ.: **None**
AWARD: **ITEC Certificate in MAP**

COURSE NO.: **310**   COURSE NAME: **Massage Therapy**
SCHOOL: **STEWART MITCHELL MASSAGE PRACTICE & TRAINING SCHOOL**
TYPE: **P/T**   PERIOD: **4 months basic**
ATTENDANCE: **Weekend seminars & weekly classes (150 hours in all)**
VENUES: **Devon (Exeter)**
FEES: **£350 - £500**   OTHER COSTS: **Nil**
COMMENCE: **Spring, Summer, Autumn**   ENTRY REQ.: **Basic education and life experience**
AWARD: **ITEC Diploma in MAP**

COURSE NO.: **311**   COURSE NAME: **Massage**
SCHOOL: **WENDOVER HOUSE COLLEGE**
TYPE: **P/T**   PERIOD: **12 weeks approx.**
ATTENDANCE: **1 evening a week (6pm - 10pm)**
VENUES: **London**
FEES: **£600**   OTHER COSTS: **£50**
COMMENCE: **January, September**   ENTRY REQ.: **b*g, i**
AWARD: **ITEC Swedish Certificate in Massage**
NOTES: **An indepth course (2 days/week for 12 weeks) @£1000 available**

MASSAGE (Including MAP) . NATUROPATHY

COURSE NO.: 312	COURSE NAME: Therapeutic Massage
SCHOOL: WENDY LORENS SCHOOL OF COMPLEMENTARY THERAPIES	
TYPE: P/T	PERIOD: 3 - 4 months (minimum)
ATTENDANCE: Minimum of 9 days, usually over weekends + practice	
VENUES: Cornwall (Penzance), Other counties by arrangement	
FEES: £275	OTHER COSTS: Exam fee = £35
COMMENCE: Twice a year (A.F.D.)	ENTRY REQ.: a=>18
AWARD: Diploma from the Association of Natural Medicine (Essex)	
NOTES: Includes A&P as well as massage	

COURSE NO.: 313	COURSE NAME: MAP
SCHOOL: THE WEST LONDON SCHOOLS OF THERAPEUTIC MASSAGE, REFLEXOLOGY & SPORTS THERAPY	
TYPE: P/T	PERIOD: 2 - 4 months
ATTENDANCE: 6 days + some Thursday evening practice sessions (7pm - 10pm) + 1 exam day	
VENUES: London	
FEES: £398	OTHER COSTS: £55 reg. fee
COMMENCE: Monthly	ENTRY REQ.: f
AWARD: ITEC Certificate in MAP	
NOTES: The course includes unlimited practice evenings. Advanced course available afterwards.	

COURSE NO.: 314	COURSE NAME: Traditional Chinese Massage Certificate Course
SCHOOL: THE WEST LONDON SCHOOLS OF THERAPEUTIC MASSAGE, REFLEXOLOGY & SPORTS THERAPY	
TYPE: P/T	PERIOD: 9 months
ATTENDANCE: 8 weekends	
VENUES: London	
FEES: A.F.D.	OTHER COSTS:
COMMENCE: Monthly	ENTRY REQ.: MAP & paramedic support
AWARD: Certificate in Traditional Chinese Massage	

COURSE NO.: 315	OURSE NAME: MAP
SCHOOL: THE WILBURY SCHOOL OF NATURAL THERAPY	
TYPE: P/T	PERIOD: Varies
ATTENDANCE: 5 days, OR 10 x 1/2 days, OR 5-day intensive + min. 7 (3 hour) practice sessions	
VENUES: East Sussex (Hove)	
FEES: £282	OTHER COSTS:
COMMENCE: A.F.D.	ENTRY REQ.: a>18
AWARD: ITEC Certificate in MAP	

COURSE NO.: 3 (C)	COURSE NAME: Acupuncture, Homoeopathy and Naturopathy
SCHOOL: ASSOCIATION OF NATURAL MEDICINES	
TYPE: P/T	PERIOD: 3 years
ATTENDANCE: Y1 & Y2 = 1 weekend per month, Y3 = 1 weekend per month + 4 Saturdays + 10 days clinical	
VENUES: Essex (Witham)	
FEES: £640 per year	OTHER COSTS: Books
COMMENCE: September	ENTRY REQ.: f
AWARD: Certificate in Acupuncture OR Homoeopathy OR Naturopathy	

NATUROPATHY . NEURO-LINGUISTIC PROGRAMMING (NLP)

COURSE NO.: **316**	COURSE NAME: **Naturopathy**
SCHOOL: **BRANTRIDGE FOREST SCHOOL**	
TYPE: **Correspondence**	PERIOD: **Open**
ATTENDANCE: **Nil**	
VENUES: **N/A**	
FEES: **£270**	OTHER COSTS: **Nil**
COMMENCE: **N/A**	ENTRY REQ.: **None**
AWARD: **Diploma in Naturopathy**	
NOTES: **Higher studies available afterwards**	

COURSE NO.: **317**	COURSE NAME: **Drugless Therapy**
SCHOOL: **BRANTRIDGE FOREST SCHOOL**	
TYPE: **Correspondence**	PERIOD: **Open**
ATTENDANCE: **Nil**	
VENUES: **N/A**	
FEES: **£270**	OTHER COSTS: **Nil**
COMMENCE: **N/A**	ENTRY REQ.: **None**
AWARD: **Diploma in Drugless Therapy**	
NOTES: **Similar to the Naturopathy course above. Higher studies available afterwards.**	

COURSE NO.: **318 (C)**	COURSE NAME: **Naturopathy** and Osteopathy
SCHOOL: **BRITISH COLLEGE OF NATUROPATHY & OSTEOPATHY**	
TYPE: **F/T**	PERIOD: **4 years**
ATTENDANCE: **5 days per week for 36 weeks per year**	
VENUES: **London**	
FEES: **£3,750 per year**	OTHER COSTS: **£500**
COMMENCE: **September**	ENTRY REQ.: **a=>18, d, f, i**
AWARD: **Diplomas in Naturopathy and Osteopathy**	

COURSE NO.: **213 (C)**	COURSE NAME: Ericksonian Hypnosis, NLP and Cognitive Psychotherapy
SCHOOL: **BRITISH HYPNOSIS RESEARCH**	
TYPE: **P/T**	PERIOD: **6 months**
ATTENDANCE: **6 weekends training + 6 days clinical supervision with hospital patients**	
VENUES: **London**	
FEES: **£1,225**	OTHER COSTS: **Nil**
COMMENCE: **March, October**	ENTRY REQ.: **Employm. in caring prof., 1st degree (see NOTES)**
AWARD: **Diploma (recognised by health authorities and social services). Leading to Membership of BHR.**	
NOTES: **Those without formal entry req. are sometimes considered**	

COURSE NO.: **319**	COURSE NAME: **NLP Diploma**
SCHOOL: **JOHN SEYMOUR ASSOCIATES**	
TYPE: **P/T**	PERIOD: **7 months**
ATTENDANCE: **1 weekend per month (non-residential)**	
VENUES: **Avon (Bristol), London**	
FEES: **£700**	OTHER COSTS:
COMMENCE: **A.F.D.**	ENTRY REQ.: **Completion of NLP Introductory (A.F.D.)**
AWARD: **Diploma in NLP**	
NOTES: **Solutions to any financial problems around paying the fees are offered. Higher studies avail. afterwards (see below)**	

NEURO-LINGUISTIC PROGRAMMING (NLP) . NUTRITION

COURSE NO.: **320**   COURSE NAME: **NLP Practitioner Course**

SCHOOL: **JOHN SEYMOUR ASSOCIATES**

TYPE: **P/T**   PERIOD: **4 months**

ATTENDANCE: **1 weekend per month (non-residential)**

VENUES: **Avon (Bristol), London (alternately)**

FEES: **£400**   OTHER COSTS:

COMMENCE: **Once yearly (A.F.D.)**   ENTRY REQ.: **Completion of their Diploma course (above)**

AWARD: **Certificate**

NOTES: **Solutions to any financial problems around paying the fees are offered**

COURSE NO.: **321**   COURSE NAME: **NLP Trainer Training**

SCHOOL: **JOHN SEYMOUR ASSOCIATES**

TYPE: **P/T**   PERIOD: **3 months**

ATTENDANCE: **1 weekend per month (non-residential)**

VENUES: **Avon (Bristol)**

FEES: **£300**   OTHER COSTS:

COMMENCE: **Once yearly (A.F.D.)**   ENTRY REQ.: **An NLP Diploma course, or working in training**

AWARD: **Certificate**

NOTES: **Solutions to any financial problems around paying the fees are offered**

COURSE NO.: **221 (C)**   COURSE NAME: **Diploma in Ericksonian Hypnosis, Psychotherapy & NLP**

SCHOOL: **NATIONAL SCHOOL OF HYPNOSIS & ADVANCED PSYCHOTHERAPY**

TYPE: **P/T**   PERIOD: **1 year followed by 1 year clinical supervision**

ATTENDANCE: **12 weekends during the year + clinical supervision to follow**

VENUES: **London (clinical supervision is not confined to London)**

FEES: **£1,269**   OTHER COSTS: **Exam fee, informal assessment £30**

COMMENCE: **April, October**   ENTRY REQ.: **PG background in the caring profession, i**

AWARD: **Diploma in Ericksonian Hypnosis, Psychotherapy & Neuro-Linguistic Programming**

NOTES: **Post-Diploma clinical supervision and advanced training available**

COURSE NO.: **322**   COURSE NAME: **N.L.P.**

SCHOOL: **PROUDFOOT SCHOOL OF HYPNOSIS & PSYCHOTHERAPY**

TYPE: **Short**   PERIOD: **6 days**

ATTENDANCE: **6-day intensive**

VENUES: **North Yorkshire (Scarborough)**

FEES: **£395**   OTHER COSTS: **Books**

COMMENCE: **Feb, June, Oct**   ENTRY REQ.: **Hypnotherapists**

AWARD: **Diploma in N.L.P.**

COURSE NO.: **323**   COURSE NAME: **Short Course in Nutrition**

SCHOOL: **THE COLLEGE OF NUTRITIONAL MEDICINE**

TYPE: **Correspondence**   PERIOD: **Variable**

ATTENDANCE: **N/A**

VENUES: **N/A**

FEES: **£125**   OTHER COSTS: **Books about £15**

COMMENCE: **N/A**   ENTRY REQ.: **None**

AWARD: **Certificate in Nutrition**

NOTES: **Correspondence Diploma course in Nutrtion is available (see below)**

NUTRITION

COURSE NO.: **324**   COURSE NAME: **Correspondence Course in Nutrition**

SCHOOL: **THE COLLEGE OF NUTRITIONAL MEDICINE**

TYPE: **Correspondence**   PERIOD: **Variable (15 sessions)**

ATTENDANCE: **N/A**

VENUES: **N/A**

FEES: **£628**   OTHER COSTS: **Books**

COMMENCE: **N/A**   ENTRY REQ.: **None**

AWARD: **Diploma in Nutrition (D.N.)**

COURSE NO.: **325**   COURSE NAME: **Basic Nutrition**

SCHOOL: **THE HOWELL COLLEGE OF HOLISTIC HEALTH**

TYPE: **Correspondence**   PERIOD: **Open**

ATTENDANCE: **N/A**

VENUES: **N/A**

FEES: **£353**   OTHER COSTS: **£10 registration fee**

COMMENCE: **N/A**   ENTRY REQ.: **a=18**

AWARD: **Certificate in Basic Nutrition**

NOTES: **Fees can be paid monthly. Scholarship available.**

COURSE NO.: **326**   COURSE NAME: **Basic Nutrition**

SCHOOL: **THE HOWELL COLLEGE OF HOLISTIC HEALTH**

TYPE: **P/T**   PERIOD: **1 year**

ATTENDANCE: **1 Saturday morning every month**

VENUES: **London**

FEES: **£353**   OTHER COSTS: **£10 registration fee**

COMMENCE: **Jan, June, Aug, Nov**   ENTRY REQ.: **a=18**

AWARD: **Certificate in Basic Nutrition**

NOTES: **Fees can be paid monthly. Scholarship available.**

COURSE NO.: **327**   COURSE NAME: **Nutrition Consultant's Certificate**

SCHOOL: **THE INSTITUTE FOR OPTIMUM NUTRITION**

TYPE: **P/T**   PERIOD: **2 years**

ATTENDANCE: **5 weekends per year (36 lectures, can be sent tapes if preferred) + 15 seminars**

VENUES: **London**

FEES: **£1,950**   OTHER COSTS: **Books £150 approx.**

COMMENCE: **September**   ENTRY REQ.: **c (see NOTES below)**

AWARD: **Institute's Diploma in Nutrition (Dip ION)**

NOTES: **2 wknd foundation course @£150 for those without Biology and Chemistry 'A' levels**

COURSE NO.: **328**   COURSE NAME: **Diploma in Nutrition and Health**

SCHOOL: **INTERNATIONAL INSTITUTE OF VITAMIN AND MINERAL THERAPISTS (IIVMT)**

TYPE: **Correspondence**   PERIOD: **12 months**

ATTENDANCE: **N/A**

VENUES: **N/A**

FEES: **£600**   OTHER COSTS: **£40 books**

COMMENCE: **Anytime**   ENTRY REQ.: **None, but b or c helpful**

AWARD: **Diploma in Nutrition and Health (USA University recognised)**

NOTES: **Course also available, on demand, as personal daily tuition for 1 month in Southern France**

NUTRITION

COURSE NO.: **329**	COURSE NAME: **Certificate in Vitamin and Mineral Therapy**
SCHOOL: **INTERNATIONAL INSTITUTE OF VITAMIN AND MINERAL THERAPISTS (IIVMT)**	
TYPE: **Correspondenc**	PERIOD: **6 - 12 months**
ATTENDANCE: **N/A**	
VENUES: **N/A**	
FEES: **£250**	OTHER COSTS: **£25 books**
COMMENCE: **Anytime**	ENTRY REQ.: **None**
AWARD: **Certificate IIVMT (USA University recognised)**	
NOTES: **Course also available, on demand, as personal daily tuition for 10 days in Southern France**	

COURSE NO.: **330**	COURSE NAME: **Nutrition & Diet**
SCHOOL: **LA ROSA SCHOOL OF HEALTH & BEAUTY**	
TYPE: **Correspondence**	PERIOD: **2 terms**
ATTENDANCE: **N/A**	
VENUES: **N/A**	
FEES: **£250**	OTHER COSTS: **Nil**
COMMENCE: **September**	ENTRY REQ.: **None**
AWARD: **Diet & Nutrition ITEC Category 23**	
NOTES: **Fees may be paid by instalments**	

COURSE NO.: **331**	COURSE NAME: **Nutrition & Diet**
SCHOOL: **LA ROSA SCHOOL OF HEALTH & BEAUTY**	
TYPE: **P/T**	PERIOD: **2 terms**
ATTENDANCE: **1 evening per week**	
VENUES: **Devon (Brixham)**	
FEES: **£250**	OTHER COSTS: **Nil**
COMMENCE: **September**	ENTRY REQ.: **None**
AWARD: **Diet & Nutrition ITEC Category 23**	
NOTES: **Fees may be paid by instalments**	

COURSE NO.: **332**	COURSE NAME: **Nutrition Consultants Diploma Course**
SCHOOL: **RAWORTH COLLEGE FOR SPORTS THERAPY AND NATURAL MEDICINE**	
TYPE: **F/T**	PERIOD: **11 weeks**
ATTENDANCE: **4 days a week**	
VENUES: **Surrey (Dorking)**	
FEES: **£1320**	OTHER COSTS:
COMMENCE: **January, September**	ENTRY REQ.: **b**
AWARD: **Nurtition Consultants Certificate and ITEC Nutrition and Diet Certificate**	
NOTES: **Includes A&P, TFH, iridology & counselling**	

COURSE NO.: **333**	COURSE NAME: **Nutrition Consultant's Certificate**
SCHOOL: **RAWORTH COLLEGE FOR SPORTS THERAPY AND NATURAL MEDICINE**	
TYPE: **P/T**	PERIOD: **11 weeks**
ATTENDANCE: **2 days a week**	
VENUES: **Surrey (Dorking)**	
FEES: **£1320**	OTHER COSTS:
COMMENCE: **January, September**	ENTRY REQ.: **b**
AWARD: **Nutrition Consultants Certificate and ITEC Nutrition and Diet Certificate**	
NOTES: **Includes A&P, TFH, iridology & counselling**	

NUTRITION

COURSE NO.: **334** COURSE NAME: **Nutrition Consultant's Diploma**

SCHOOL: **RAWORTH COLLEGE FOR SPORTS THERAPY AND NATURAL MEDICINE**

TYPE: **P/T** PERIOD: **2 terms**

ATTENDANCE: **3 days a week for 2 terms - each 11 weeks long**

VENUES: **Surrey (Dorking)**

FEES: **£1750** OTHER COSTS: **£50**

COMMENCE: **January** ENTRY REQ.: **e**

AWARD: **Nurtition Consultants Diploma**

NOTES: **Practising therapists may take individual modules only. Open to those graduated from the Cert. course.**

COURSE NO.: **335** COURSE NAME: **ITEC Nutrition Certificate**

SCHOOL: **SCHOOL OF PHYSICAL THERAPIES - BASINGSTOKE**

TYPE: **P/T** PERIOD: **3 months**

ATTENDANCE: **4 day intensive + project work**

VENUES: **Hampshire (Basingstoke)**

FEES: **£160** OTHER COSTS: **Nil**

COMMENCE: **January, July** ENTRY REQ.: **ITEC MAP or A&P**

AWARD: **ITEC Certificate in Nutrition**

NOTES: **Advanced course is available afterwards**

COURSE NO.: **336** COURSE NAME: **Nutrition Advisors Course**

SCHOOL: **SCHOOL OF PHYSICAL THERAPIES - BASINGSTOKE**

TYPE: **P/T** PERIOD: **4 months**

ATTENDANCE: **6 day intensive + clinical**

VENUES: **Hampshire (Basingstoke)**

FEES: **£240** OTHER COSTS: **Nil**

COMMENCE: **February, August** ENTRY REQ.: **ITEC Nutrition Certificate**

AWARD: **Nutrition Advisors Diploma**

COURSE NO.: **337** COURSE NAME: **ITEC Nutrition Certificate**

SCHOOL: **THE SCHOOL OF PHYSICAL THERAPIES (KINGSTON)**

TYPE: **P/T** PERIOD: **3 months**

ATTENDANCE: **4-day intensive**

VENUES: **Surrey (Kingston)**

FEES: **£160** OTHER COSTS: **£55**

COMMENCE: **August** ENTRY REQ.: **ITEC MAP or A&P qualification**

AWARD: **ITEC Certificate in Nutrition**

NOTES: **Successful completion leads on to entry to Nutrition Advisors Course**

COURSE NO.: **338** COURSE NAME: **Nutrition and Diet (ITEC)**

SCHOOL: **THE WEST LONDON SCHOOLS OF THERAPEUTIC MASSAGE, REFLEXOLOGY & SPORTS THERAPY**

TYPE: **P/T** PERIOD: **10 weeks**

ATTENDANCE: **8 evenings**

VENUES: **London**

FEES: **£79** OTHER COSTS:

COMMENCE: **A.F.D.** ENTRY REQ.:

AWARD: **ITEC Certificate in Nutrition and Diet**

ORIENTAL THERAPY & MOVEMENT . OSTEOPATHY

COURSE NO.: **339**   COURSE NAME: **The British School of Oriental Therapy & Movement**

SCHOOL: **THE BRITISH SCHOOL OF ORIENTAL THERAPY & MOVEMENT**

TYPE: **P/T**   PERIOD: **4 terms**

ATTENDANCE: **Sundays for 12 weeks per term**

VENUES: **London**

FEES: **£800**   OTHER COSTS: **£20 exam fee**

COMMENCE: **January, September**   ENTRY REQ.: **None**

AWARD: **BSOTM Certificate**

NOTES: **The school teaches oriental medicine, Ki-development, ZEN shiatsu**

COURSE NO.: **318 (C)**   COURSE NAME: **Naturopathy and Osteopathy**

SCHOOL: **BRITISH COLLEGE OF NATUROPATHY & OSTEOPATHY**

TYPE: **F/T**   PERIOD: **4 years**

ATTENDANCE: **5 days per week for 36 weeks per year**

VENUES: **London**

FEES: **£3,750 per year**   OTHER COSTS: **£500**

COMMENCE: **September**   ENTRY REQ.: **a=>18, d, f, i**

AWARD: **Diplomas in Naturopathy and Osteopathy**

COURSE NO.: **340**   COURSE NAME: **Osteopathy**

SCHOOL: **THE BRITISH SCHOOL OF OSTEOPATHY**

TYPE: **F/T**   PERIOD: **4 years**

ATTENDANCE: **Full time on weekdays. Attendance is required in vacations for clinical training for 3-6 weeks.**

VENUES: **London**

FEES: **£4,600 per year**   OTHER COSTS: **£600 for clinical equipment and books**

COMMENCE: **September**   ENTRY REQ.: **c , f**

AWARD: **B.Sc. in Osteopathy**

COURSE NO.: **86 (C)**   COURSE NAME: **Osteopathy and Chiropractic**

SCHOOL: **THE COLLEGE OF NATURAL MEDICINE-LONDON**

TYPE: **F/T - P/T**   PERIOD: **4 years**

ATTENDANCE: **Y1 = 3 days a week for 40 weeks, Y2 - Y4 = 15 hours a week for 40 weeks per year**

VENUES: **London**

FEES: **£1,800 for Y1, for rest A.F.D.**   OTHER COSTS: **Nil**

COMMENCE: **September**   ENTRY REQ.: **b*, f**

AWARD: **Diploma in Osteopathy and Chiropractic**

NOTES: **1st year is foundation course. Cranio-Sacral Osteopathy course avail. afterwards.**

COURSE NO.: **341**   COURSE NAME: **Osteopathy**

SCHOOL: **THE COLLEGE OF OSTEOPATHS EDUCATIONAL TRUST**

TYPE: **P/T**   PERIOD: **6 years**

ATTENDANCE: **Y1 to Y5 = 14 wknds per year + clinical, Y6 = 2 wknds + practice (student is licensed to practice after Y5)**

VENUES: **London (clinical in London and Hertfordshire (Borehamwood))**

FEES: **£6,600**   OTHER COSTS: **A.F.D.**

COMMENCE: **October**   ENTRY REQ.: **d (see NOTES), f, i**

AWARD: **Diploma in Osteopathy**

NOTES: **Osteopathic Science Preparatory Course £710 for those who do not hold the specified entrance qualif.**

OSTEOPATHY . POLARITY THERAPY

COURSE NO.: **342**   COURSE NAME: **Osteopathy**

SCHOOL: **EUROPEAN SCHOOL OF OSTEOPATHY**

TYPE: **F/T**   PERIOD: **4 years**

ATTENDANCE: **Y1&Y2=4 days/wk, Y3&Y4=4 days/wk+clinic hours (36 wks per year+1/2 the holidays in Y3&Y4)**

VENUES: **Kent (Maidstone)**

FEES: **£3,850**   OTHER COSTS: **£600**

COMMENCE: **September**   ENTRY REQ.: **c * science review course, f**

AWARD: **Diploma in Osteopathy**

COURSE NO.: **343**   COURSE NAME: **Osteopathy**

SCHOOL: **THE LONDON SCHOOL OF OSTEOPATHY**

TYPE: **A.F.D.**   PERIOD: **5 years**

ATTENDANCE: **2 weekends every month (18 weekends every year) + clinical work**

VENUES: **London**

FEES: **£1,800 per year**   OTHER COSTS: **A.F.D.**

COMMENCE: **October**   ENTRY REQ.: **d, f**

AWARD: **Diploma in Osteopathy**

COURSE NO.: **344**   COURSE NAME: **Diploma in Osteopathy**

SCHOOL: **MAIDSTONE COLLEGE OF OSTEOPATHY**

TYPE: **F/T**   PERIOD: **4 years**

ATTENDANCE: **4 - 5 days per week for 3 terms (11 weeks each) a year. From Y2 some holiday clinics as well.**

VENUES: **Kent (Maidstone)**

FEES: **£1,800 per year**   OTHER COSTS: **Books & equipment approx. £100 per year**

COMMENCE: **September**   ENTRY REQ.: **b, c * science review course**

AWARD: **Diploma in Osteopathy**

NOTES: **Graduates eligibe to register with the College of Osteopaths Practitioners Ass. (MCO)**

COURSE NO.: **345**   COURSE NAME: **Diploma in Osteopathy**

SCHOOL: **THE OXFORD SCHOOL OF OSTEOPATHY (OSO)**

TYPE: **P/T**   PERIOD: **2 years**

ATTENDANCE: **2 weekends per month for 36 weeks per year (Y1=March-June + Sep-Dec, Y2=Jan-June + Sep-Dec)**

VENUES: **Oxfordshire (Oxford)**

FEES: **£180 per month inclusive of meals**   OTHER COSTS:

COMMENCE: **March**   ENTRY REQ.: **h, students qualif. in aligned subject (see NOTES)**

AWARD: **Diploma in Osteopathy**

NOTES: **Restricted to SRN, SR Physiotherapists & students qualified in aligned subject, e.g., physiology, remedial massage**

COURSE NO.: **346**   COURSE NAME: **Polarity Therapist Training**

SCHOOL: **THE INTERNATIONAL SCHOOL OF POLARITY THERAPY**

TYPE: **P/T**   PERIOD: **20 months**

ATTENDANCE: **4 days every other month (40 days in all)**

VENUES: **Devon (Honiton), Dorset**

FEES: **£2,000**   OTHER COSTS: **£1,250 accommodation**

COMMENCE: **October**   ENTRY REQ.: **Had a basic course or knowledge of the system**

AWARD: **Certification as a Polarity Therapist**

NOTES: **An intensive course. Students required to work evenings of the workshops and complete home study assignments.**

POLARITY THERAPY . PSYCHOTHERAPY

COURSE NO.: **347**   COURSE NAME: **Polarity Therapy Foundation Course**

SCHOOL: **POLARITY THERAPY EDUCATIONAL TRUST**

TYPE: **P/T**   PERIOD: **4 - 5 months**

ATTENDANCE: **3 - 4 weekends + 5-day residential**

VENUES: **Cambridgshire (Cambridge), Devon, London, Lothian (Edinburgh), West Yorkshire (Leeds)**

FEES: **£480 - £580**   OTHER COSTS:

COMMENCE: **Spring, Autumn**   ENTRY REQ.: **Introductory day £25 - £45**

AWARD: **Certificate of completion**

NOTES: **Fees and dates vary depending on venue, so A.F.D. Individual therapy is part of the course.**

COURSE NO.: **348**   COURSE NAME: **Polarity Therapy Professional Training**

SCHOOL: **POLARITY THERAPY EDUCATIONAL TRUST**

TYPE: **P/T**   PERIOD: **3 years**

ATTENDANCE: **Y1&Y2 = 10 wknds + 5-day resid. , Y3 = 2 wknds + 5-day resid. + monthly supervision**

VENUES: **Cambridgshire (Cambridge), Devon, London, Lothian (Edinburgh), West Yorkshire (Leeds)**

FEES: **Up to £1,300 per year**   OTHER COSTS:

COMMENCE: **September**   ENTRY REQ.: **Foundation Course (see above)**

AWARD: **Diploma in Polarity Therapy (Membership of the Polarity Therapy Association)**

NOTES: **Fees and dates vary depending on venue, so A.F.D. Individual therapy is part of the course.**

COURSE NO.: **349**   COURSE NAME: **Polarity Healing Course**

SCHOOL: **THE SCOTTISH SCHOOL OF REFLEXOLOGY**

TYPE: **P/T**   PERIOD: **3 days, OR 6 - 8 weeks**

ATTENDANCE: **Monthly or weekly depending on the venue**

VENUES: **Depending on number of students assembling for the course (14 minimum)**

FEES: **£115**   OTHER COSTS: **Nil**

COMMENCE: **Arranged on demand**   ENTRY REQ.: **e, h**

AWARD: **Certificate in Polarity Healing**

NOTES: **Professional insurance available**

COURSE NO.: **207 (C)**   COURSE NAME: Hypnotherapy & **Psychologist Training**

SCHOOL: **ACADEMY OF HYPNOTHERAPY**

TYPE: **P/T**   PERIOD: **Depends on frequency (A.F.D.)**

ATTENDANCE: **Once a week for 5 months (or shorter period if required) + 6 test revision lessons**

VENUES: **London**

FEES: **£840 (can be paid in instalments)**   OTHER COSTS: **£256 for the revision lessons**

COMMENCE: **Anytime, continuous**   ENTRY REQ.: **i**

AWARD: **M.P.H.C. Diploma in Psycho. & Hypnotherapy**

COURSE NO.: **350**   COURSE NAME: **Training Programme in Psychotherapy**

SCHOOL: **ARBOURS ASSOCIATION**

TYPE: **P/T**   PERIOD: **4 - 5 years**

ATTENDANCE: **Approx. Y1=1 eve per wk, Following years=3 evenings per wk + 2 placements of 6 months each**

VENUES: **London**

FEES: **£525 (Y1), £1,200 per year (following years)**   OTHER COSTS: **Individual therapy & supervision**

COMMENCE: **January**   ENTRY REQ.: **f**

AWARD: **Certificate in Psychotherapy**

PSYCHOTHERAPY

COURSE NO.: **208 (C)**   COURSE NAME: **Hypnotherapy & Psychotherapy Certificate**

SCHOOL: **ARK COURSES IN HYPNOTHERAPY & PSYCHOTHERAPY**

TYPE: **P/T**   PERIOD: **1 year**

ATTENDANCE: **1 weekend per month**

VENUES: **Surry (Guildford)**

FEES: **£750**   OTHER COSTS: **Exam fee = £20**

COMMENCE: **February, July, October**   ENTRY REQ.: **a=21**

AWARD: **Certificate in Hypnotherapy/Psychotherapy**

NOTES: **Emphasis placed on supervised practical work. Diploma course avail. afterwards (see below).**

COURSE NO.: **209 (C)**   COURSE NAME: **Hypnotherapy & Psychotherapy Diploma**

SCHOOL: **ARK COURSES IN HYPNOTHERAPY & PSYCHOTHERAPY**

TYPE: **P/T**   PERIOD: **2 years**

ATTENDANCE: **1 weekend per month**

VENUES: **Surry (Guildford)**

FEES: **£950**   OTHER COSTS: **Exam fee = £20**

COMMENCE: **February, July, October**   ENTRY REQ.: **a=21, Certificate in Hypnotherapy**

AWARD: **Certificate in Hypnotherapy/Psychotherapy**

NOTES: **Emphasis placed on supervised practical work. Diploma Y2 can be started at any time of the year.**

COURSE NO.: **105 (C)**   COURSE NAME: **Counselling, Hypnotherapy and Psychotherapy**

SCHOOL: **ASSOCIATION FOR BODYMIND THERAPY AND TRAINING (AABTT)**

TYPE: **P/T**   PERIOD: **2 years**

ATTENDANCE: **1 evening (2 hours) per week + bi-monthly weekends + 6-day residential in the country**

VENUES: **London**

FEES: **£1,920**   OTHER COSTS: **Individual therapy**

COMMENCE: **January, April, September**   ENTRY REQ.: **i, some experience preferable**

AWARD: **Diploma of AABTT**

NOTES: **Completion entitles practice in counselling, hypnotherapy, psychotherapy and group facilitation**

COURSE NO.: **351**   COURSE NAME: **Psychotherapy**

SCHOOL: **BRANTRIDGE FOREST SCHOOL**

TYPE: **Correspondence**   PERIOD: **Open**

ATTENDANCE: **Nil**

VENUES: **N/A**

FEES: **£270**   OTHER COSTS: **Nil**

COMMENCE: **N/A**   ENTRY REQ.: **None**

AWARD: **Diploma in Psychotherapy**

NOTES: **Higher studies available afterwards**

COURSE NO.: **352**   COURSE NAME: **Body Oriented Psychotherapy**

SCHOOL: **BRITISH ASSOCIATION OF ANALYTICAL BODY PSYCHOTHERAPISTS**

TYPE: **P/T**   PERIOD: **5 years**

ATTENDANCE: **4 x 4-day workshops + 30 hrs theoretical seminars + 12 hrs group process + 32 hrs group sessions (Y3 only) + 96 hrs supervision group**

VENUES: **London, Sussex, other venues may also be possible**

FEES: **£1,020 per year**   OTHER COSTS: **Personal therapy, books, supervision, resid.**

COMMENCE: **A.F.D.**   ENTRY REQ.: **a=>27, f, g, degree, relevant experience**

AWARD: **Diploma in Body Oriented Psychotherapy**

PSYCHOTHERAPY (Including Gestalt)

COURSE NO.: **353**	COURSE NAME: **Individual Psychoanalytic & Analytical Psychotherapy with Adults**

SCHOOL: **BRITISH ASSOCIATION OF PSYCHOTHERAPISTS**

TYPE: **P/T** PERIOD: **4 - 5 years**

ATTENDANCE: **1 weekly theoretical seminar for 3 years + clinical seminars fortnightly**

VENUES: **London**

FEES: **£2,066** OTHER COSTS: **Personal analysis throughout training**

COMMENCE: **October** ENTRY REQ.: **Related degree and experience in working with disturbed people in a psychotherapeutic capacity**

AWARD: **Associate Member B.A.P.**

COURSE NO.: **213 (C)** COURSE NAME: **Ericksonian Hypnosis, NLP and Cognitive Psychotherapy**

SCHOOL: **BRITISH HYPNOSIS RESEARCH**

TYPE: **P/T** PERIOD: **6 months**

ATTENDANCE: **6 weekends training + 6 days clinical supervision with hospital patients**

VENUES: **London**

FEES: **£1,225** OTHER COSTS: **Nil**

COMMENCE: **March, October** ENTRY REQ.: **Employm. in caring prof., 1st degree (see NOTES)**

AWARD: **Diploma (recognised by health authorities and social services). Leading to Membership of BHR.**

NOTES: **Those without formal entry req. are sometimes considered**

COURSE NO.: **108 (C)** COURSE NAME: **Diploma in Counselling and Psychotherapy**

SCHOOL: **CENTRE FOR COUNSELLING AND PSYCHOTHERAPY EDUCATION**

TYPE: **P/T** PERIOD: **4 years**

ATTENDANCE: **1 evening per week (7pm - 10pm) + 6 weekend training per year + 4 extra training days in Y1**

VENUES: **London**

FEES: **£950 per year** OTHER COSTS: **Personal therapy**

COMMENCE: **January** ENTRY REQ.: **Counselling Skills training + previous therapy**

AWARD: **Diploma in Counselling and Psychotherapy (accredited by British Association for Counselling BAC)**

COURSE NO.: **354** COURSE NAME: **Holistic Psychotherapy**

SCHOOL: **CHIRON CENTRE FOR PSYCHOTHERAPY**

TYPE: **P/T** PERIOD: **3 years**

ATTENDANCE: **Evenings and weekends (11 hours per week)**

VENUES: **London**

FEES: **£2,000 per year** OTHER COSTS: **Nil**

COMMENCE: **September** ENTRY REQ.: **a>25, degree * life or professional experience**

AWARD: **Certificate in Holistic Psychotherapy**

NOTES: **It is body psychotherapy. Accredited by the UK standing conference for psychotherapy. Adv. course avail. after.**

COURSE NO.: **355** COURSE NAME: **Practitioner Training Gestalt Psychotherapy**

SCHOOL: **GESTALT CENTRE LONDON**

TYPE: **P/T** PERIOD: **2 years**

ATTENDANCE: **12 evenings + 1 weekend + 4-day residential per term for 6 terms**

VENUES: **London**

FEES: **£2,400** OTHER COSTS: **Individual therapy £20-£30 per hour**

COMMENCE: **January OR September** ENTRY REQ.: **Completion of advanced training**

AWARD: **Diploma in Gestalt Psychotherapy**

NOTES: **Trainee will run therapy groups and give individual therapy under supervision**

PSYCHOTHERAPY (Including Psychodrama)

COURSE NO.: **356** COURSE NAME: **Psychodrama Experience and Training**
SCHOOL: **HOLWELL CENTRE FOR PSYCHODRAMA AND SOCIODRAMA**
TYPE: **P/T** PERIOD: **3-4 years**
ATTENDANCE: **Various (16 weeks in all) (A.F.D.)**
VENUEs: **Devon (Barnstaple), London, Oxfordshire (Oxford)**
FEES: **A.F.D.** OTHER COSTS: **Nil**
COMMENCE: **All year round** ENTRY REQ.: **A.F.D.**
AWARD: **Diploma in Advanced Competence in Psychodrama**

COURSE NO.: **214 (C)** COURSE NAME: Hypnotherapy / Psychotherapy
SCHOOL: **THE HOWELL COLLEGE OF HOLISTIC HEALTH**
TYPE: **P/T** PERIOD: **1 - 2 years**
ATTENDANCE: **1 Sunday morning per month**
VENUES: **London**
FEES: **£353 per year** OTHER COSTS: **£10 reg. fee**
COMMENCE: **Jan, June, Aug, Nov** ENTRY REQ.: **a=>18**
AWARD: **Certificate (1 year, Diploma (2 years) in Hypnotherapy / Psychotherapy)**
NOTES: **Fees can be paid on monthly basis in advance**

COURSE NO.: **357** COURSE NAME: **Group Analysis**
SCHOOL: **THE INSTITUTE OF GROUP ANALYSIS**
TYPE: **P/T** PERIOD: **3 1/2 - 4 years**
ATTENDANCE: **Introd. = Once/wk (3 terms), Y1 = Twice/wk personal group analysis (min. 1 year) , Rest of period =Monday eve + Thursday afternoons + once/wk supervised group analysis**
VENUES: **London**
FEES: **Introd=£530 + £2,800 p.a. (instalments possible)** OTHER COSTS: **Selection fee £75, Indemnity insurance £45**
COMMENCE: **October** ENTRY REQ.: **Degree or exceptional experience, f**
AWARD: **Certificate of Qualification in Group Analysis & Membership of The Institiute of Group Analysis**
NOTES: **Interest-free bursary loan up to £500 avail. and to be repaid within 4 years of qualification**

COURSE NO.: **358** COURSE NAME: **Psychotherapy**
SCHOOL: **MINSTER CENTRE**
TYPE: **P/T** PERIOD: **Approx. 4 years**
ATTENDANCE: **1 day per weekl + weekends**
VENUES: **London**
FEES: **From £1,700 per year** OTHER COSTS: **A.F.D.**
COMMENCE: **October** ENTRY REQ.: **f**
AWARD: **Diploma in Psychotherapy**

COURSE NO.: **219 (C)** COURSE NAME: The National Association of Hypnotists & Psychotherapists: Training Faculty
SCHOOL: **THE NATIONAL ASSOCIATION OF HYPNOTISTS & PSYCHOTHERAPISTS: TRAINING FACULTY**
TYPE: **P/T** PERIOD: **15 months**
ATTENDANCE: **1 - 2 weekends per month (18 weekends in all) + 2 exam. days + supervision after qualification**
VENUES: **London**
FEES: **£70 - £85 per weekend** OTHER COSTS: **Books, exam fee, supervision costs**
COMMENCE: **September** ENTRY REQ.: **a=>25, d, i**
AWARD: **Diploma in Hypnosis and Psychotherapy**
NOTES: **Entitles Membership of the National Association of Hypnotists & Psychotherapists @£50**

PSYCHOTHERAPY

COURSE NO.: **220 (C)**   COURSE NAME: Hypnotherapy and **Psychotherapy**

SCHOOL: **THE NATIONAL COLLEGE OF HYPNOSIS AND PSYCHOTHERAPY**

TYPE: **P/T**   PERIOD:

ATTENDANCE: **S1 = 4 weekends, S2 = 6 weekends, S3 = 4 weekends**

VENUES: **Cheshire (Cheadle), London, Strathclyde (Glasgow)**

FEES: **£1,575**   OTHER COSTS: **£75 exam fee**

COMMENCE: **A.F.D.**   ENTRY REQ.: **a=>25, d, e, i**

AWARD: **Diploma in Hypnosis and Psychotherapy**

NOTES: **A Certificate in Hypnosis and Psychotherapy is given upon completion of Stage 2**

COURSE NO.: **221 (C)**   COURSE NAME: **Diploma in** Ericksonian Hypnosis, **Psychotherapy** & NLP

SCHOOL: **NATIONAL SCHOOL OF HYPNOSIS & ADVANCED PSYCHOTHERAPY**

TYPE: **P/T**   PERIOD: **1 year followed by 1 year clinical supervision**

ATTENDANCE: **12 weekends during the year + clinical supervision to follow**

VENUES: **London (clinical supervision is not confined to London)**

FEES: **£1,269**   OTHER COSTS: **Exam fee, informal assessment £30**

COMMENCE: **April, October**   ENTRY REQ.: **PG background in the caring profession, i**

AWARD: **Diploma in Ericksonian Hypnosis, Psychotherapy & Neuro-Linguistic Programming**

NOTES: **Post-Diploma clinical supervision and advanced training available**

COURSE NO.: **222 (C)**   COURSE NAME: Hypnotherapy and **Psychotherapy Diploma Course**

SCHOOL: **'NEW LIFE' COURSES**

TYPE: **P/T**   PERIOD: **6 months**

ATTENDANCE: **1 full weekend per month**

VENUES: **Essex (Harlow)**

FEES: **£525**   OTHER COSTS: **£20 books, £30 exam**

COMMENCE: **March, August**   ENTRY REQ.: **a>25, reasonable education background**

AWARD: **Diploma in Hypnotherapy and Psychotherapy**

NOTES: **Entitles registration with the Association of Ethical and Professional Hypnotherapists**

PSYCHOTHERAPY

COURSE NO.: **122 (C)** COURSE NAME: **Pellin Diploma Course**

SCHOOL: **PELLIN TRAINING COURSES**

TYPE: **P/T** PERIOD: **3 years**

ATTENDANCE: **Weekly 4-hour group for 3 terms of 10 weeks each + 3 weekend workshops**

VENUES: **London**

FEES: **£950 per year** OTHER COSTS: **Nil**

COMMENCE: **January, September, October** ENTRY REQ.: **Appropriate work, prof. exper. preferred**

AWARD: **Pellin Diploma in Gestalt Therapy and Contribution Training**

NOTES: **Contribution Training is a counselling + therapeutic method**

COURSE NO.: **359** COURSE NAME: **Professional Training in Regression & Integration**

SCHOOL: **PRAXIS**

TYPE: **P/T** PERIOD: **9 months**

ATTENDANCE: **5 x 4-day blocks**

VENUES: **London**

FEES: **£1,050** OTHER COSTS: **£20 the Institute Membership fee**

COMMENCE: **October** ENTRY REQ.: **2 yrs counselling training, facilitator training, Gestalt, Psychosynthesis or equivalent**

AWARD: **Certificate of the Institute of Regression and Integration**

COURSE NO.: **226 (C)** COURSE NAME: Hypnosis and **Psychotherapy**

SCHOOL: **PSYCHOTHERAPY AND HYPNOSIS TRAINING ASSOCIATION**

TYPE: **P/T** PERIOD: **2 years (or less A.F.D.)**

ATTENDANCE: **1 Sunday a month**

VENUES: **London**

FEES: **£1,500** OTHER COSTS: **Course texts £40**

COMMENCE: **On-going, start anytime** ENTRY REQ.: **None**

AWARD: **Diploma in Psychotherapy and Hypnotherapy**

COURSE NO.: **360** COURSE NAME: **Training in Wholistic Psychotherapy**

SCHOOL: **THE PSYCHOTHERAPY CENTRE**

TYPE: **P/T** PERIOD: **Min. 4 years**

ATTENDANCE: **Min. 1000 x 50-minute sessions of wholistic psychotherapy yourself + lectures and practical**

VENUES: **London**

FEES: **£500 per year for lectures & practical** OTHER COSTS: **Wholistic psychotherapy (A.F.D.)**

COMMENCE: **Anytime** ENTRY REQ.: **University/polytechnic degree, excep. intelligence**

AWARD: **Diploma in Psychotherapy**

NOTES: **Qualifying depends on output rather than input in accordance with Government guidelines**

COURSE NO.: **361** COURSE NAME: **Diploma in Humanistic Psychotherapy**

SCHOOL: **SHEFFIELD BIRTH & HEALING CENTRE**

TYPE: **P/T** PERIOD: **2 years**

ATTENDANCE: **2 evenings per week + 1 weekend per month + 1 residential week at end of year**

VENUES: **South Yorkshire (Sheffield)**

FEES: **£2,000 (or £1,750 if in advance)** OTHER COSTS: **Books & materials**

COMMENCE: **September** ENTRY REQ.: **f, relevant experience**

AWARD: **Diploma in Humanistic Psychotherapy**

NOTES: **The training is for highly self-motivated people from any walk of life**

PSYCHOTHERAPY . RADIONICS

COURSE NO.: **131 (C)**   COURSE NAME: Counselling, Hypnotherapy and **Psychotherapy**

SCHOOL: **THE UK TRAINING COLLEGE**

TYPE: **P/T**   PERIOD: **3 years**

ATTENDANCE: **1 wknd/month for 12 months per year+personal therapy 20hrs in each of Y2&Y3+St. John's Ambul. course**

VENUES: **London, Eire (Dublin)**

FEES: **£5, 450**   OTHER COSTS: **£176 exam + St. John's Ambulance course**

COMMENCE: **May, September**   ENTRY REQ.: **Y1 = None, Y2 = Y1 completion, f**

AWARD: **Diploma in Counselling, Hypnotherapy and Psychotherapy**

NOTES: **Year 1 is a foundation course ending in Certificate of Attendance**

COURSE NO.: **362**   COURSE NAME: **Advanced Certificate in Psychotherapy**

SCHOOL: **UNIVERSITY OF LEICESTER - DEPT. OF ADULT EDUCATION**

TYPE: **P/T**   PERIOD: **2 years**

ATTENDANCE: **1 day per week for 6 terms + 1 day per week clinical (which may be at students' place of work)**

VENUES: **Leicestershire (Leicester)**

FEES: **£1,200 per year**   OTHER COSTS: **Personal therapy if not already received**

COMMENCE: **September 1993 (and every 2 years)**   ENTRY REQ.: **e, experience of counselling and therapy**

AWARD: **Advanced Certificate in Psychotherapy**

COURSE NO.: **363**   COURSE NAME: **Body Centred Psychotherapy**

SCHOOL: **THE WEST LONDON SCHOOLS OF THERAPEUTIC MASSAGE, REFLEXOLOGY & SPORTS THERAPY**

TYPE: **P/T**   PERIOD: **1 year**

ATTENDANCE: **Weekends + some evenings**

VENUES: **London**

FEES: **£976**   OTHER COSTS:

COMMENCE: **October**   ENTRY REQ.: **MAP**

AWARD: **Certificate in Body Centred Psychotherapy**

COURSE NO.: **364**   COURSE NAME: **Radiesthesia and Radionics**

SCHOOL: **BRANTRIDGE FOREST SCHOOL**

TYPE: **Correspondence**   PERIOD: **Open**

ATTENDANCE: **Nil**

VENUES: **N/A**

FEES: **£270**   OTHER COSTS: **Nil**

COMMENCE: **N/A**   ENTRY REQ.: **None**

AWARD: **Diploma in Radiesthesia and Radionics**

NOTES: **Higher studies available afterwards**

COURSE NO.: **365**   COURSE NAME: **Practitioner of Radionics**

SCHOOL: **DELAWARR SOCIETY OF RADIONICS**

TYPE: **P/T**   PERIOD: **3 - 4 years**

ATTENDANCE: **Y1= 3 x 1-day+Corres., Y2=60 hour tutorial, Y3=2 seminars+30 hr tutorial, Y4=1 of 3 courses**

VENUES: **London, Oxfordshire (Oxford)**

FEES: **£1,540**   OTHER COSTS: **A.F.D.**

COMMENCE: **Twice yearly**   ENTRY REQ.: **A.F.D.**

AWARD: **Licentiate after Y2 then Membership of Delawarr Society for Radionics (LicDSRad then MDSRad)**

NOTES: **In Y4 student choose one of: Treating adverse earth energies, treatment of animals or the Ray analysis**

RADIONICS . REFLEXOLOGY

COURSE NO.: **366**   COURSE NAME: **Radionics**
SCHOOL: **ENERMED INSTITUTE OF RADIONICS AND RADIESTHESIA**
TYPE: **P/T**   PERIOD: **1 year**
ATTENDANCE: **1 day every 2 months (6 in all)**
VENUES: **Dorset (Sturminster Newton)**
FEES: **£500**   OTHER COSTS: **Books £75, instruments £250 approx.**
COMMENCE: **March, September**   ENTRY REQ.: **f**
AWARD: **Certification plus Diploma (for final examination) in Radionics**

COURSE NO.: **367**   COURSE NAME: **PG RAY Analysis for Radionic and Other Health Care**
SCHOOL: **THE MAPERTON TRUST**
TYPE: **P/T**   PERIOD: **10 months**
ATTENDANCE: **1 tutorial per month**
VENUES: **East Sussex (Brighton)**
FEES: **£1,000**   OTHER COSTS: **Books and instruments**
COMMENCE: **Anytime (individual tuition)**   ENTRY REQ.: **e**
AWARD: **Certification of Attendance**

COURSE NO.: **368**   COURSE NAME: **Radionic Training**
SCHOOL: **THE PHOENIX OF RADIONICS**
TYPE: **P/T**   PERIOD: **1 1/2 years**
ATTENDANCE: **9 sessions (weekends)**
VENUES: **Hertfordshire**
FEES: **£702**   OTHER COSTS: **A.F.D.**
COMMENCE: **September**   ENTRY REQ.: **b, f, g**
AWARD: **Licentiate in Radionics**
NOTES: **Further 1 1/2 years of study leeds to Membership**

COURSE NO.: **369**   COURSE NAME: **Advanced Course in Radionic Homoeopathy**
SCHOOL: **SCHOOL OF PHYSICAL THERAPIES - BASINGSTOKE**
TYPE: **P/T**   PERIOD: **4 months**
ATTENDANCE: **8 day intensive + clinical**
VENUES: **Hampshire (Basingstoke)**
FEES: **£320**   OTHER COSTS: **Nil**
COMMENCE: **March, July, November**   ENTRY REQ.: **A&P + dowsing for health**
AWARD: **Diploma in Radionic Homoeopathy**
NOTES: **Graduation leeds to Membership of the Society of Radionic Homoeopaths**

COURSE NO.: **370**   COURSE NAME: **Reflexology Diploma Course**
SCHOOL: **THE ASSOCIATION OF MEDICAL AROMATHERAPISTS**
TYPE: **P/T**   PERIOD: **10 weeks**
ATTENDANCE: **3 weekends**
VENUES: **Strathclyde (Glasgow)**
FEES: **£250**   OTHER COSTS:
COMMENCE: **March, October**   ENTRY REQ.: **A&P**
AWARD: **Post Graduate Diploma in Reflexology**

REFLEXOLOGY

COURSE NO.: **371**   COURSE NAME: **Reflexology**

SCHOOL: **ASSOCIATION OF NATURAL MEDICINES**

TYPE: **P/T**   PERIOD: **6 months**

ATTENDANCE: **Weekends, OR days, OR evenings**

VENUES: **Essex (Witham), Hertfordshire, London**

FEES: **A.F.D.**   OTHER COSTS:

COMMENCE: **Throughout the year (A.F.D.)**   ENTRY REQ.: **f**

AWARD: **Certificate in Reflexology**

COURSE NO.: **372**   COURSE NAME: **Reflexology**

SCHOOL: **THE BAYLY SCHOOL OF REFLEXOLOGY**

TYPE: **P/T**   PERIOD: **8 months (minimum)**

ATTENDANCE: **3 weekends + examination day**

VENUES: **Hereford & Worcester (Malvern), London, Lothian (Edinburgh), West Midlands (Birmingham), West Yorkshire (Leeds), Eire (Dublin)**

FEES: **£279**   OTHER COSTS: **Books & charts < £50**

COMMENCE: **Every month**   ENTRY REQ.: **None**

AWARD: **The School Certificate in Reflexology**

COURSE NO.: **373**   COURSE NAME: **Post Graduate Course in Reflexology**

SCHOOL: **BEAUMONT COLLEGE OF NATURAL MEDICINE**

TYPE: **F/T**   PERIOD: **6 months**

ATTENDANCE: **3 days for 8 weeks + 2 days for 16 weeks + 1 day**

VENUES: **East Sussex (Eastbourne)**

FEES: **£350**   OTHER COSTS: **£40 exam fee**

COMMENCE: **Feb, Oct, Nov**   ENTRY REQ.: **A&P Certificate (avail. with the college)**

AWARD: **The College Diploma in Reflexology and accreditation to International Federation of Reflexologists (IFR)**

NOTES: **B & B from £10 / night can be arranged**

COURSE NO.: **374**   COURSE NAME: **Reflexology**

SCHOOL: **BERKSHIRE SCHOOL OF NATURAL THERAPY**

TYPE: **P/T**   PERIOD: **2 months**

ATTENDANCE: **3 x 2-day period (6 days in total)**

VENUES: **Berkshire (Crowthorne)**

FEES: **£245**   OTHER COSTS: **Nil**

COMMENCE: **February, April, July, October**   ENTRY REQ.: **ITEC in MAP or equivalent**

AWARD: **ITEC Certificate in Reflex-Zone Therapy**

COURSE NO.: **375**   COURSE NAME: **Reflex Zone Therapy**

SCHOOL: **BOURNEMOUTH SCHOOL OF MASSAGE**

TYPE: **P/T**   PERIOD: **8 - 12 weeks**

ATTENDANCE: **5 days over approx. 8 weeks**

VENUES: **Dorset (Bournemouth)**

FEES: **£195**   OTHER COSTS: **Nil**

COMMENCE: **January, May, October**   ENTRY REQ.: **ITEC in A&P**

AWARD: **ITEC Diploma/Certificate in Reflexology**

NOTES: **Students may take this course as a post graduate course OR in conjunction with A&P course**

REFLEXOLOGY

COURSE NO.: **376**   COURSE NAME: **Reflexology**

SCHOOL: **THE BRITISH SCHOOL OF REFLEXOLOGY**

TYPE: **P/T**   PERIOD: **8 months approx.**

ATTENDANCE: **Total of 4 weekends, OR midweek**

VENUES: **Essex (Harlow), London, Nottinghamshire (Nottingham)**

FEES: **£570**   OTHER COSTS:

COMMENCE: **Every month**   ENTRY REQ.: **None**

AWARD: **The School Diploma in Reflexology**

COURSE NO.: **377**   COURSE NAME: **Reflex Zone Therapy of the Feet**

SCHOOL: **BRITISH SCHOOL - REFLEX ZONE THERAPY**

TYPE: **P/T**   PERIOD: **2 - 12 months (depending on gap between courses)**

ATTENDANCE: **2 x 3-day course (Introductory and Advanced, with a minimum of 8 weeks and max. of 1 year gap)**

VENUES: **Lancashire (Lancaster), London, Middlesex (Wembley Park)**

FEES: **£300**   OTHER COSTS:

COMMENCE: **A.F.D.**   ENTRY REQ.: **e, h**

AWARD: **Certificate in Reflexology**

NOTES: **Advanced training in reflexology and lymphatic drainage is available**

COURSE NO.: **378**   COURSE NAME: **Reflexology**

SCHOOL: **CRANE SCHOOL OF REFLEXOLOGY**

TYPE: **P/T**   PERIOD: **7 - 8 months approx.**

ATTENDANCE: **3 weekends bi-monthly + exam. day**

VENUES: **Avon (Bristol), London, Manchester, West Midlands (Birmingham), North Yorkshire (York)**

FEES: **£525**   OTHER COSTS: **Nil**

COMMENCE: **A.F.D.**   ENTRY REQ.: **a>18**

AWARD: **ITEC Certificate in A&P and Reflexology**

NOTES: **Diploma Practitioners Course available afterwards**

COURSE NO.: **379**   COURSE NAME: **Reflexology Seminar**

SCHOOL: **THE DALLAMORE COLLEGE OF ADVANCED REFLEXOLOGY**

TYPE: **P/T**   PERIOD: **6 months**

ATTENDANCE: **1 Saturday per month for 6 months (might change in the autumn to 1 weekend per month for 3 months)**

VENUES: **London, Norfolk (Norwich), West Midlands (Birmingham)**

FEES: **£300 approx.**   OTHER COSTS: **Books and charts**

COMMENCE: **Continuous**   ENTRY REQ.: **None**

AWARD: **Certificate in Reflexology, Intermediate and advanced**

COURSE NO.: **380**   COURSE NAME: **Reflexology**

SCHOOL: **DILWORTH SCHOOL OF REFLEXOLOGY**

TYPE: **P/T**   PERIOD: **10 - 12 months**

ATTENDANCE: **2 weekends + 4 days (Saturdays or Sundays) + assessment weekend**

VENUES: **Bukinghamshire (Aylesbury)**

FEES: **£380**   OTHER COSTS: **Nil**

COMMENCE: **Feb, April, June, Oct**   ENTRY REQ.: **a>21**

AWARD: **Practitioners Certificate in Reflexology**

NOTES: **Graduates eligible for Membership of the Association of Reflexologists**

REFLEXOLOGY

COURSE NO.: **381**   COURSE NAME: **Reflexology**

SCHOOL: **THE EDINBURGH SCHOOL OF NATURAL THERAPY**

TYPE: **Short**   PERIOD: **1 week**

ATTENDANCE: **5 days**

VENUES: **Lothian (Edinburgh)**

FEES: **£130**   OTHER COSTS: **£40 reg. fee**

COMMENCE: **Throughout the year (A.F.D.)**   ENTRY REQ.: **Basic Massage (See under Massage) or ITEC MAP**

AWARD: **Certificate in Reflexology**

COURSE NO.: **382**   COURSE NAME: **Reflexology**

SCHOOL: **GABLECROFT COLLEGE**

TYPE: **P/T**   PERIOD: **5 - 6 months**

ATTENDANCE: **1 weekend per month (4 weekends in all)**

VENUES: **Shropshire (Oswestry)**

FEES: **A.F.D.**   OTHER COSTS: **A.F.D.**

COMMENCE: **Variable (A.F.D.)**   ENTRY REQ.: **None**

AWARD: **Certificate in Reflexology, recognised by The Association of Reflexologists**

COURSE NO.: **383**   COURSE NAME: **Reflexology**

SCHOOL: **GOOD SCENTS SCHOOL OF NATURAL THERAPIES**

TYPE: **P/T**   PERIOD: **5 weeks**

ATTENDANCE: **1 day per week**

VENUES: **West Sussex (Pulborough)**

FEES: **£150**   OTHER COSTS: **Nil**

COMMENCE: **January, April, Sep**   ENTRY REQ.: **A&P**

AWARD: **Reflexology Certificate**

NOTES: **Students must sit the school anatomy exam.**

COURSE NO.: **384**   COURSE NAME: **Reflexology**

SCHOOL: **GREENHILL COLLEGE**

TYPE: **P/T**   PERIOD: **22 weeks**

ATTENDANCE: **3 hours per week (10am - 1pm) over 2 academic terms**

VENUES: **Middlesex (Harrow)**

FEES: **£240**   OTHER COSTS: **£5 text book**

COMMENCE: **A.F.D.**   ENTRY REQ.: **Human Biology, A or P or Beauty therapy**

AWARD: **ITEC Category 16 Reflex Zone Therapy**

COURSE NO.: **385**   COURSE NAME: **Reflexology**

SCHOOL: **HOTHS SCHOOL FOR HOLISTIC THERAPIES**

TYPE: **P/T**   PERIOD: **9-12 months**

ATTENDANCE: **6 weekends**

VENUES: **Gloucestershire (Cheltenham), Leicestershire (Leicester)**

FEES: **£435**   OTHER COSTS: **Exam**

COMMENCE: **March, September**   ENTRY REQ.: **a>18, b**

AWARD: **Practitioners Certificate in Reflexology**

NOTES: **Membership of Reflexologists' Society, Ass. of Holistic Therapists and National Register of ICM**

REFLEXOLOGY

COURSE NO.: **386** COURSE NAME: **Reflex-Zone Therapy**

SCHOOL: **JANE HIDER SCHOOL OF NATURAL THERAPIES**

TYPE: **P/T** PERIOD: **2 days**

ATTENDANCE: **1 weekend**

VENUES: **Hereford & Worcester (Hereford)**

FEES: **£70** OTHER COSTS: **Exam fee £25**

COMMENCE: **A.F.D.** ENTRY REQ.: **A.F.D.**

AWARD: **ITEC Certificate in Reflex-Zone Therapy**

NOTES: **Visually handicapped students accepted. Course includes advanced techniques suitable for nurses/those in caring.**

COURSE NO.: **387** COURSE NAME: **Reflexology**

SCHOOL: **JANICE ELLICOT SCHOOL OF REFLEXOLOGY**

TYPE: **P/T** PERIOD: **2 months**

ATTENDANCE: **2 long weekends (Friday, Saturday and Sunday)**

VENUES: **London**

FEES: **£225** OTHER COSTS: **Anatomy book £5**

COMMENCE: **Jan, March, May, July, Sep, Nov** ENTRY REQ.: **None**

AWARD: **Certificate in Reflexology**

NOTES: **Advanced course (2-day) @£50 in May and November is available afterwards**

COURSE NO.: **388** COURSE NAME: **Reflexology**

SCHOOL: **LANCASHIRE HOLISTIC COLLEGE**

TYPE: **P/T** PERIOD: **9 months**

ATTENDANCE: **Approx. 1 weekend per month**

VENUES: **Lancashire (Preston)**

FEES: **Approx. £90 per weekend** OTHER COSTS: **Books, charts, exams.**

COMMENCE: **January, July** ENTRY REQ.: **a=>18, b, i**

AWARD: **College Certificate, ITEC Certificate and Ass. of Reflexologists Certificate**

NOTES: **Any part of reflexology course can be taken ad lib., but exam. can only be passed upon attendance of all**

COURSE NO.: **389** COURSE NAME: **Reflexology**

SCHOOL: **THE LEAVES INTERNATIONAL SCHOOL OF AROMATHERAPY, MASSAGE AND NATURAL THERAPY**

TYPE: **P/T** PERIOD: **9 months**

ATTENDANCE: **3 weekends + exam day**

VENUES: **Avon (Nr. Bath), Dorset, Wiltshire (Trowbridge)**

FEES: **£411** OTHER COSTS:

COMMENCE: **Twice yearly (A.F.D.)** ENTRY REQ.: **ITEC A&P**

AWARD: **ITEC Diploma in Reflexology**

COURSE NO.: **390** COURSE NAME: **Practitioner Course in Reflexology - Certificated**

SCHOOL: **MARY MARTIN SCHOOL OF REFLEXOLOGY**

TYPE: **P/T** PERIOD: **9 months**

ATTENDANCE: **Selected Saturdays (10am - 5.30pm)**

VENUES: **London**

FEES: **£750** OTHER COSTS: **£40 exam fee**

COMMENCE: **June, October** ENTRY REQ.: **a=>21, f**

AWARD: **Practitioners Certificate in Reflexology**

NOTES: **School is affiliated to the Reflexologists' Society and Institute for Complementary Medicine**

REFLEXOLOGY

COURSE NO.: **391**   COURSE NAME: **Reflexology**

SCHOOL: **THE MILLFIELD SCHOOL OF BEAUTY THERAPY**

TYPE: **P/T**   PERIOD: **3 months**

ATTENDANCE: **7 - 8 days**

VENUES: **West Sussex (Rusper)**

FEES: **£350**   OTHER COSTS: **Nil**

COMMENCE: **January, April, September**   ENTRY REQ.: **A&P**

AWARD: **ITEC Certificate in Reflexology**

COURSE NO.: **392**   COURSE NAME: **Reflexology**

SCHOOL: **THE NATURAL CLINIC AROMATHERAPY SCHOOL**

TYPE: **P/T**   PERIOD: **9 months**

ATTENDANCE: **4 blocks of 2 week day sessions (total = 8 days)**

VENUES: **Kent (Tunbridge Wells)**

FEES: **£458**   OTHER COSTS: **Books £20**

COMMENCE: **3 courses throughout the year (A.F.D.)**   ENTRY REQ.:

AWARD: **Certificate in Reflexology**

NOTES: **Entitles registration with The Association of Reflexologists (M.A.R. initials)**

COURSE NO.: **393**   COURSE NAME: **Reflexology Certificate Course**

SCHOOL: **'NEW LIFE' COURSES**

TYPE: **P/T**   PERIOD: **6 months**

ATTENDANCE: **1 day (at weekends) per month**

VENUES: **Essex (Harlow), Nottinghamshire (Nottingham)**

FEES: **£206**   OTHER COSTS: **Books £10, Exam fee £30**

COMMENCE: **Feb, June, Sep**   ENTRY REQ.: **a>21 with reasonable educational background**

AWARD: **Certificate in Reflexology**

NOTES: **Entitles registration with The Association of Holistic Reflexologists**

COURSE NO.: **394**   COURSE NAME: **Reflexology Theory and Practical**

SCHOOL: **OXFORD HOUSE CLINIC FOR COMPLEMENTARY MEDICINE**

TYPE: **P/T**   PERIOD: **10 weeks**

ATTENDANCE: **1 evening (3 hours) per week**

VENUES: **Berkshire (Reading)**

FEES: **£200**   OTHER COSTS:

COMMENCE: **June, October**   ENTRY REQ.: **None**

AWARD: **Certificate in Reflexology**

COURSE NO.: **55 (C)**   COURSE NAME: Aromatherapy and **Reflexology**

SCHOOL: **THE RADIX COLLEGE OF BEAUTY CULTURE**

TYPE: **Short**   PERIOD: **1 week**

ATTENDANCE: **5 consecutive days + 1 exam. day**

VENUES: **Strathclyde (Ayr)**

FEES: **£353**   OTHER COSTS: **Exam fee**

COMMENCE: **Throughout the year (A.F.D. & see NOTES)** ENTRY REQ.: **e, or allied professional with massage experience**

AWARD: **ITEC Diplomas in Aromatherapy and Reflexology (2 diplomas)**

NOTES: **Running a course depends on no. of candidates, but two definite commenc. dates are May and October**

REFLEXOLOGY

COURSE NO.: **395**	COURSE NAME: **Certificate in Reflexology**

SCHOOL: **RAWORTH COLLEGE FOR SPORTS THERAPY AND NATURAL MEDICINE**

TYPE: **P/T**	PERIOD: **1 term**

ATTENDANCE: **2 days per week for 11 weeks**

VENUES: **Surrey (Dorking)**

FEES: **£675**	OTHER COSTS: **£30**
COMMENCE: **Jan, April, July, Sep**	ENTRY REQ.: **f**

AWARD: **Certificate in Reflexology**

NOTES: **Fees are £475 only if without A&P**

COURSE NO.: **396**	COURSE NAME: **Diploma in Clinical Reflexology**

SCHOOL: **RAWORTH COLLEGE FOR SPORTS THERAPY AND NATURAL MEDICINE**

TYPE: **P/T**	PERIOD: **1 term**

ATTENDANCE: **2 days per week for 11 weeks**

VENUES: **Surrey (Dorking)**

FEES: **£675**	OTHER COSTS:
COMMENCE: **Jan, April, July**	ENTRY REQ.: **e**

AWARD: **Diploma in Clinical Reflexology**

NOTES: **Includes pathology, nutrition, intro. chinese med., supervised clinical and further techniques**

COURSE NO.: **397**	COURSE NAME: **Reflex Zone Therapy**

SCHOOL: **SCHOOL OF NATURAL THERAPIES AND ORIENTAL STUDIES**

TYPE: **P/T**	PERIOD: **6 months**

ATTENDANCE: **2 weekends + 4 seminar days + practice days**

VENUES: **Hampshire, London**

FEES: **£240**	OTHER COSTS: **£30**
COMMENCE: **A.F.D.**	ENTRY REQ.: **A&P**

AWARD: **Certificate in Reflex Zone Therapy**

COURSE NO.: **398**	COURSE NAME: **ITEC Reflexology**

SCHOOL: **SCHOOL OF PHYSICAL THERAPIES - BASINGSTOKE**

TYPE: **P/T**	PERIOD: **3 months**

ATTENDANCE: **4 day intensive + 100 hours clinical**

VENUES: **Hampshire (Basingstoke)**

FEES: **£160**	OTHER COSTS: **£12**
COMMENCE: **July, September**	ENTRY REQ.: **ITEC MAP**

AWARD: **ITEC Certificate in Reflexology**

NOTES: **Graduates eligible for application for membership of the International Federation of Reflexologists**

COURSE NO.: **399**	COURSE NAME: **ITEC Reflexology**

SCHOOL: **THE SCHOOL OF PHYSICAL THERAPIES (KINGSTON)**

TYPE: **P/T**	PERIOD: **3 months**

ATTENDANCE: **4-day intensive + 100 hours clinical practice**

VENUES: **Surrey (Kingston)**

FEES: **£160**	OTHER COSTS: **£52**
COMMENCE: **May**	ENTRY REQ.: **ITEC MAP or A&P qualification**

AWARD: **ITEC Certificate in Reflexology**

NOTES: **Completion allowing students to apply for Membership of the International Federation of Reflexologists**

REFLEXOLOGY

COURSE NO.: **400**   COURSE NAME: **Classical Reflexology**

SCHOOL: **THE SCOTTISH SCHOOL OF REFLEXOLOGY**

TYPE: **P/T**   PERIOD: **9 months**

ATTENDANCE: **2 hours weekly OR 1 day per month (weekly or monthly depending on venue)**

VENUES: **Grampian (Aberdeen), Lothian (Edinburgh), Strathclyde (Glasgow), Tayside (Dundee), Tyne & Wear (Newcastle)**

FEES: **£560**   OTHER COSTS:

COMMENCE: **September**   ENTRY REQ.: **a>18**

AWARD: **The School Certificate in Reflexology (G.S.S.R.)**

NOTES: **Early starter option. Postal study in advance of course £32.**

COURSE NO.: **401**   COURSE NAME: **Facial and Abdominal Reflexology**

SCHOOL: **THE SCOTTISH SCHOOL OF REFLEXOLOGY**

TYPE: **P/T or Short**   PERIOD: **4 weeks OR 1 day**

ATTENDANCE: **2 hours weekly for 4 weeks, OR 1 day only**

VENUES: **Grampian (Aberdeen), Lothian (Edinburgh), Strathclyde (Glasgow), Tayside (Dundee), Tyne & Wear (Newcastle)**

FEES: **£55**   OTHER COSTS: **Nil**

COMMENCE: **4 wks after Reflexology Cert. course exam.**   ENTRY REQ.: **Reflexologist**

AWARD: **The School Certificate**

NOTES: **The course open to qualified reflexologists**

COURSE NO.: **402**   COURSE NAME: **Reflexology**

SCHOOL: **SOUTH WEST SCHOOL OF HOLISTIC TOUCH**

TYPE: **P/T**   PERIOD: **3 months**

ATTENDANCE: **1 weekend monthly**

VENUES: **Devon (Exeter)**

FEES: **£150**   OTHER COSTS: **Nil**

COMMENCE: **Twice yearly (A.F.D.)**   ENTRY REQ.: **None**

AWARD: **ITEC Certificate in Reflexology**

COURSE NO.: **403**   COURSE NAME: **Reflexology**

SCHOOL: **WENDY LORENS SCHOOL OF COMPLEMENTARY THERAPIES**

TYPE: **P/T**   PERIOD: **6 months (minimum)**

ATTENDANCE: **9 days usually weekends**

VENUES: **Cornwall (Penzance)**

FEES: **£350**   OTHER COSTS: **£35**

COMMENCE: **A.F.D.**   ENTRY REQ.: **a>18, A&P preferable**

AWARD: **Diploma in Reflexology from the Association of Natural Medicine (Essex)**

COURSE NO.: **404**   COURSE NAME: **Foot Reflex Therapy**

SCHOOL: **THE WEST LONDON SCHOOL OF FOOT REFLEX THERAPY (REFLEXOLOGY)**

TYPE: **P/T**   PERIOD: **9 months**

ATTENDANCE: **Foundation=2 days + 2 wknds + 1 eve, Professional=1 day (5 months to prepare case histories separate the two)**

VENUES: **London**

FEES: **£450**   OTHER COSTS:

COMMENCE: **Monthly**   ENTRY REQ.: **MAP or A&P (even if concurrent)**

AWARD: **ITEC Certificate in Foot Reflex Therapy**

AWARD: **Advanced course available afterwards**

REFLEXOLOGY . SHIATSU

COURSE NO.: **405**   COURSE NAME: **Reflexology**

SCHOOL: **THE WHITE ROSE SCHOOL OF BEAUTY**

TYPE: **P/T**   PERIOD: **10 weeks**

ATTENDANCE: **1 day per week for 5 weeks + 1 evening per week for 10 weeks**

VENUES: **West Yorkshire (Huddersfield)**

FEES: **£300**   OTHER COSTS: **Book £10, Exam fee £59**

COMMENCE: **A.F.D.**   ENTRY REQ.: **a=>17, h, MAP**

AWARD: **ITEC Diploma in Reflexology**

COURSE NO.: **406**   COURSE NAME: **Reflextherapy**

SCHOOL: **THE WILBURY SCHOOL OF NATURAL THERAPY**

TYPE: **P/T**   PERIOD: **10 months**

ATTENDANCE: **S1 = 4 days, S2 & S3 = 2 days each + min. 12 indiv. or group coaching sessions + revision day**

VENUES: **East Sussex (Hove)**

FEES: **£423**   OTHER COSTS:

COMMENCE: **A.F.D.**   ENTRY REQ.: **A.F.D.**

AWARD: **ITEC Diploma in Reflexology**

COURSE NO.: **407**   COURSE NAME: **I.F.R. Registered Reflexology Course**

SCHOOL: **THE YORKSHIRE COLLEGE OF BEAUTY THERAPY**

TYPE: **P/T**   PERIOD: **6 months**

ATTENDANCE: **3 weekends**

VENUES: **West Yorkshire (Leeds)**

FEES: **£411**   OTHER COSTS:

COMMENCE: **September**   ENTRY REQ.: **A&P Qualification**

AWARD: **I.F.R. Diploma in Reflexology**

COURSE NO.: **408**   COURSE NAME: **Professional Shiatsu Practitioner Training**

SCHOOL: **BRISTOL SCHOOL OF SHIATSU AND ORIENTAL MEDICINE**

TYPE: **P/T**   PERIOD: **3 years**

ATTENDANCE: **Y1 = 12 wknds, Y2 = 7 wknds + 5-day residential, Y3 = 7 wknds + 5-day residential + 4 days clinical**

VENUES: **Avon (Bristol)**

FEES: **£817 per year**   OTHER COSTS: **£80 books**

COMMENCE: **February, September, November**   ENTRY REQ.: **a=>18**

AWARD: **Diploma in Shiatsu**

NOTES: **Post Graduate training available**

COURSE NO.: **409**   COURSE NAME: **Diploma Course in Shiatsu - Do**

SCHOOL: **BRITISH SCHOOL OF SHIATSU - DO**

TYPE: **P/T**   PERIOD: **3 years**

ATTENDANCE: **Varies: options of weekends, evenings and weekends or daytime course (A.F.D.)**

VENUES: **London**

FEES: **£3,000 approx.**   OTHER COSTS:

COMMENCE: **Throughout the year (A.F.D.)**   ENTRY REQ.: **None**

AWARD: **Diploma in Shiatsu - Do**

NOTES: **After Y2 Certificate is awarded entitling practice. Y3 is probationary year.**

SHIATSU

COURSE NO.: 410   **COURSE NAME: Shiatsu Practitioner Training Course**

SCHOOL: **THE DEVON SCHOOL OF SHIATSU**

TYPE: **P/T**   PERIOD: **2 1/2 - 3 years**

ATTENDANCE: **Y1 = 8 wknds + 3 days, Y2 = 13 wknds, Y3 = 4 wknds + 6 long weekends + 5-day residential**

VENUES: **Devon (Totnes)**

FEES: **£1,870**   OTHER COSTS: **£100 books**

COMMENCE: **February, October**   ENTRY REQ.: **f**

AWARD: **Diploma in Shiatsu**

COURSE NO.: 411   **COURSE NAME: Shiatsu Diploma Course**

SCHOOL: **EAST ANGLIAN SCHOOL OF SHIATSU**

TYPE: **P/T**   PERIOD: **1 year**

ATTENDANCE: **1 weekend per month (12 weekends)**

VENUES: **Suffolk (Ipswich)**

FEES: **£595**   OTHER COSTS: **Approx. £40 books**

COMMENCE: **September**   ENTRY REQ.:

AWARD: **Intermediate Shiatsu Diploma**

NOTES: **This is the first year of a 3-year course professional training**

COURSE NO.: 412   **COURSE NAME: The European Shiatsu School - Shiatsu Diploma Course**

SCHOOL: **THE EUROPEAN SHIATSU SCHOOL**

TYPE: **P/T**   PERIOD: **3 years**

ATTENDANCE: **1 wknd every 3 wks (14 wknds per year) for 3 years + 1 wknd for adv. pathology + 1 assess. wknd**

VENUES: **London, Avon (Bath), Berks. (Reading), Devon (Totnes), Dorset (B'mouth), E.Sussex (Brighton), Kent (Canterbury), Oxfordshire (Oxford), Surrey (Redhill), W. Midlands (Birmingham), Wiltshire (Marlborough)**

FEES: **£555 (£777 incl. Foundation Course- see NOTES)** OTHER COSTS: **Books £35, pathology wknd £45, assess. £40**

COMMENCE: **January Or May Or November (A.F.D.)**   ENTRY REQ.: **Completion of Foundation Course or equiv.**

AWARD: **Diploma in Shiatsu**

NOTES: **Foundation Course:4 wknds (1 every 3 wks) or 5-day resid. or 1 eve./wk for 24 wks @£222 held in all venues**

COURSE NO.: 413   **COURSE NAME: Shiatsu Certificate Course**

SCHOOL: **GLASGOW SCHOOL OF SHIATSU**

TYPE: **P/T**   PERIOD: **3 years**

ATTENDANCE: **Introductory = 1 wknd/month for 4 months, Intermediate = 1 wknd/month for 11 months, Advanced = 11 wknds, Probationer = 4 wknds + 4-day residential + 4 days clinical**

VENUES: **Strathclyde (Glasgow)**

FEES: **£1,272 + residential**   OTHER COSTS: **£15 member. of Society, books (optional)**

COMMENCE: **Introductory: March, rest: August** ENTRY REQ.: **None**

AWARD: **Certificate in Shiatsu Therapy (to the standard of The Shiatsu Society's Practitioner Assessment Panel)**

COURSE NO.: 414   **COURSE NAME: Healing - Shiatsu Professional Training**

SCHOOL: **HEALING - SHIATSU EDUCATION CENTRE**

TYPE: **P/T**   PERIOD: **3 years**

ATTENDANCE: **1 non-residential weekend + 3 x 5-day residential each year**

VENUES: **Avon (Bristol) for the non-residential, and Dyfed (Llandeilo) for the residential**

FEES: **£809**   OTHER COSTS: **£100 max.**

COMMENCE: **Autumn**   ENTRY REQ.: **1 introductory weekend**

AWARD: **Diploma in Healing - Shiatsu**

SHIATSU

COURSE NO.: **415**   COURSE NAME: **Diploma Course in Shiatsu and Oriental Medicine**

SCHOOL: **KI KAI SHIATSU CENTRE**

TYPE: **P/T**   PERIOD: **3 years**

ATTENDANCE: **12 weekends per year. The April intake involve 9 weekends and Thursday evenings.**

VENUES: **London**

FEES: **£660 per year**   OTHER COSTS: **Books £20 approx.**

COMMENCE: **April, October**   ENTRY REQ.: **None, interview for those wanting to join Y2&Y3**

AWARD: **Centre's Diploma in Shiatsu**

NOTES: **Y1 entitles a Certificate. Completing the whole course entitles reg. with The Shiatsu Society (U.K.).**

COURSE NO.: **416 (C)**   COURSE NAME: Yoga, **Shiatsu** and Traditional Chinese Medicine

SCHOOL: **LONDON CENTRE FOR YOGA AND SHIATSU**

TYPE: **P/T**   PERIOD: **2 1/2 - 3 years**

ATTENDANCE: **Y1 & Y2=16 wknds each, Y3=16 wknds + clinical: EITHER 1 month in China, OR 6 months P/T**

VENUES: **London**

FEES: **£1,500 per year**   OTHER COSTS: **Clinical, personal therapy**

COMMENCE: **March, October**   ENTRY REQ.: **None**

AWARD: **Diploma in Yoga, Shiatsu and Traditional Chinese Medicine**

COURSE NO.: **417**   COURSE NAME: **Shiatsu Practitioner Certificate**

SCHOOL: **THE LONDON COLLEGE OF SHIATSU**

TYPE: **P/T**   PERIOD: **2 1/2 - 3 years**

ATTENDANCE: **Evenings and weekends (500 hours in total)**

VENUES: **London**

FEES: **£2,000**   OTHER COSTS:

COMMENCE: **Jan, April, July, Sep**   ENTRY REQ.: **To be fit and well**

AWARD: **Certificate in Shiatsu**

COURSE NO.: **418**   COURSE NAME: **Shiatsu Practitioner Training**

SCHOOL: **THE SHIATSU COLLEGE**

TYPE: **P/T**   PERIOD: **3 years**

ATTENDANCE: **Y1 & Y2 = 12 weekends, Y3 = 9 weekends + 5-day residential**

VENUES: **London, Norfolk (Norwich) up to Y2**

FEES: **£950 per year**   OTHER COSTS: **Nil**

COMMENCE: **September**   ENTRY REQ.: **f**

AWARD: **Shiatsu College Certificate**

NOTES: **A 600 hour course well within current Shiatsu Society Reg. requirements (MRSS)**

COURSE NO.: **419**   COURSE NAME: **Shiatsu Practitioner Training (Intensive)**

SCHOOL: **THE SHIATSU COLLEGE**

TYPE: **P/T**   PERIOD: **2 years**

ATTENDANCE: **Y1 = 2 days per week for 3 x 8-week terms, Y3 = 9 weekends + 5-day residential**

VENUES: **London**

FEES: **£2,792**   OTHER COSTS: **Nil**

COMMENCE: **September**   ENTRY REQ.: **f**

AWARD: **Shiatsu College Certificate**

NOTES: **600 hour course well within current Shiatsu Society Reg. requirements (MRSS). Resid. outside London.**

SHIATSU . SPORTS THERAPY

COURSE NO.: **420**   COURSE NAME: **Shiatsu and Traditional Oriental Medicine**
SCHOOL: **THE SHIATSU COLLEGE**
TYPE: **P/T**   PERIOD: **1 year**
ATTENDANCE: **3 x 4-day residential**
VENUES: **Outside London**
FEES: **£660**   OTHER COSTS: **Nil**
COMMENCE: **November**   ENTRY REQ.: **Shiatsu College Certificate**
AWARD: **Post Graduate Diploma**

COURSE NO.: **421**   COURSE NAME: **Sports Massage Course**
SCHOOL: **CLARE MAXWELL-HUDSON SCHOOL OF MASSAGE**
TYPE: **P/T**   PERIOD: **7 weeks**
ATTENDANCE: **2 x 4-day blocks**
VENUES: **London**
FEES: **£532**   OTHER COSTS: **A.F.D.**
COMMENCE: **Continuous (A.F.D.)**   ENTRY REQ.: **MAP**
AWARD: **The School Certificate in Sports Massage**

COURSE NO.: **422**   COURSE NAME: **Sports Therapy**
SCHOOL: **LA ROSA SCHOOL OF HEALTH & BEAUTY**
TYPE: **P/T**   PERIOD: **7 - 8 months**
ATTENDANCE: **One evening per week over two terms (Sept - April)**
VENUES: **Devon (Brixham)**
FEES: **£250**   OTHER COSTS: **Nil**
COMMENCE: **September**   ENTRY REQ.: **ITEC MAP (Category 7)**
AWARD: **ITEC Category 11 Sports Therapy**
NOTES: **Fees may be paid in instalments**

COURSE NO.: **423**   COURSE NAME: **Sports Therapy**
SCHOOL: **THE LEAVES INTERNATIONAL SCHOOL OF AROMATHERAPY, MASSAGE AND NATURAL THERAPY**
TYPE: **P/T**   PERIOD: **3 days**
ATTENDANCE: **3 days**
VENUES: **Avon (Nr. Bath), Dorset, Wiltshire (Trowbridge)**
FEES: **£259**   OTHER COSTS: **Exam fee £33**
COMMENCE: **A.F.D.**   ENTRY REQ.: **e**
AWARD: **ITEC Diploma in Sports Therapy**
NOTES: **Open to qualified massage therapists and aromatherapists**

COURSE NO.: **424**   COURSE NAME: **Sports Injuries**
SCHOOL: **NATIONAL SCHOOL OF MASSAGE**
TYPE: **P/T**   PERIOD:
ATTENDANCE: **2 weekends**
VENUES: **Lancashire (Southport)**
FEES: **£100**   OTHER COSTS: **Nil**
COMMENCE: **A.F.D.**   ENTRY REQ.: **A course in Physical Therapy**
AWARD: **Post Graduate**
NOTES: **Advanced weekend @£50 is available afterwards**

SPORTS THERAPY

COURSE NO.: **425**   COURSE NAME: **Diploma in Sports Therapy**

SCHOOL: **RAWORTH COLLEGE FOR SPORTS THERAPY AND NATURAL MEDICINE**

TYPE: **F/T (for P/T A.F.D.)**   PERIOD: **1 year**

ATTENDANCE: **4-5 days a week for 3 terms (11 weeks long each)**

VENUES: **London, Surrey (Dorking)**

FEES: **£3,960**   OTHER COSTS: **£250**

COMMENCE: **September**   ENTRY REQ.: **b, f**

AWARD: **Diploma in Sports Therapy (International Institute for Sports Therapy)**

NOTES: **Includes sports massage, gym instructions, diet & nutrition, fitness techniques & injury rehabilitation**

COURSE NO.: **426**   COURSE NAME: **Diploma Sports Massage & Injury Rehabilitaion**

SCHOOL: **RAWORTH COLLEGE FOR SPORTS THERAPY AND NATURAL MEDICINE**

TYPE: **P/T**   PERIOD: **1 year**

ATTENDANCE: **2 1/2 days a week for 3 terms (11 weeks long each)**

VENUES: **London**

FEES: **£2,250**   OTHER COSTS: **£100**

COMMENCE: **September**   ENTRY REQ.: **f**

AWARD: **Diploma in Sports Massage & Injury Rehabilitation**

NOTES: **May be taken over a longer period (longer than 1 year)**

COURSE NO.: **427**   COURSE NAME: **Sports Therapy**

SCHOOL: **SCHOOL OF NATURAL THERAPIES AND ORIENTAL STUDIES**

TYPE: **P/T**   PERIOD: **2 months**

ATTENDANCE: **2 weekends**

VENUES: **Hampshire, London**

FEES: **£180**   OTHER COSTS: **£10**

COMMENCE: **A.F.D.**   ENTRY REQ.: **A&P Certificate**

AWARD: **The School Certificate in Sports Therapy**

COURSE NO.: **428**   COURSE NAME: **ITEC Sports Therapy Certificate**

SCHOOL: **SCHOOL OF PHYSICAL THERAPIES - BASINGSTOKE**

TYPE: **P/T**   PERIOD: **3 months**

ATTENDANCE: **4 day intensive + 40 hours clinical**

VENUES: **Hampshire (Basingstoke)**

FEES: **£160**   OTHER COSTS: **Nil**

COMMENCE: **March**   ENTRY REQ.: **ITEC MAP**

AWARD: **ITEC Certificate in Sports Therapy**

NOTES: **Completion of this + First Aid course can lead to Membership of Fellowship of Sports Masseurs**

COURSE NO.: **429**   COURSE NAME: **ITEC Sports Therapy Certificate**

SCHOOL: **THE SCHOOL OF PHYSICAL THERAPIES (KINGSTON)**

TYPE: **P/T**   PERIOD: **3 months**

ATTENDANCE: **4-day intensive + 40 hours clinical practice**

VENUES: **Surrey (Kingston)**

FEES: **£160**   OTHER COSTS: **£55**

COMMENCE: **July**   ENTRY REQ.: **ITEC MAP**

AWARD: **ITEC Certificate in Sports Therapy**

NOTES: **Completion of this, PLUS a First Aid course leads to Membership of the Fellowship of Sports Masseurs**

SPORTS THERAPY . STRESS MANAGEMENT

COURSE NO.: **430**　　　　COURSE NAME: **Sports Therapy**

SCHOOL: **THE WEST LONDON SCHOOLS OF THERAPEUTIC MASSAGE, REFLEXOLOGY & SPORTS THERAPY**

TYPE: **P/T**　　　　　　　　　　PERIOD: **4 - 5 months**

ATTENDANCE: **5 days**

VENUES: **London**

FEES: **£250**　　　　　　　　OTHER COSTS:

COMMENCE: **A.F.D.**　　　　　ENTRY REQ.: **MAP**

AWARD: **ITEC Certificate in Sports Therapy**

COURSE NO.: **431**　　　　COURSE NAME: **Certificate in Rational-Emotive Therapy (R.E.T.)**

SCHOOL: **CENTRE FOR STRESS MANAGEMENT**

TYPE: **Short**　　　　　　　　PERIOD: **1 weekend**

ATTENDANCE: **Friday evening + all day Saturday & Sunday + 1 1/2 exam day**

VENUES: **London**

FEES: **£176**　　　　　　　　OTHER COSTS:

COMMENCE: **January, March, May**　　ENTRY REQ.: **None**

AWARD: **Certificate in R.E.T.**

COURSE NO.: **432**　　　　COURSE NAME: **Diploma in Rational-Emotive Therapy (R.E.T.)**

SCHOOL: **CENTRE FOR STRESS MANAGEMENT**

TYPE: **P/T**　　　　　　　　　　PERIOD: **1 year**

ATTENDANCE: **12 evening workshops + 12 x 1-day supervision workshops (132 hours)**

VENUES: **London**

FEES: **£1,175**　　　　　　　OTHER COSTS:

COMMENCE: **A.F.D.**　　　　　ENTRY REQ.: **The Centre's Certificate in R.E.T. (see above)**

AWARD: **Diploma in R.E.T.**

URSE NO.: **433**　　　　COURSE NAME: **Certificate in Stress Management**

SCHOOL: **CENTRE FOR STRESS MANAGEMENT**

TYPE: **P/T**　　　　　　　　　　PERIOD: **(modular)**

ATTENDANCE: **1 day workshops**

VENUES: **London**

FEES: **£400 approx.**　　　　OTHER COSTS: **Reg. fee £50**

COMMENCE: **Anytime**　　　　ENTRY REQ.: **Cert. in Counselling of the Centre's R.E.T.**

AWARD: **Certificate in Stress Management**

URSE NO.: **434**　　　　COURSE NAME: **Diploma in Stress Management**

SCHOOL: **CENTRE FOR STRESS MANAGEMENT**

TYPE: **P/T**　　　　　　　　　　PERIOD: **(modular)**

ATTENDANCE: **1 day and 2 day workshops**

VENUES: **London**

FEES: **£350 approx.**　　　　OTHER COSTS: **Reg. fee £30**

COMMENCE: **Anytime**　　　　ENTRY REQ.: **The Centre's Cert. in Stress Management**

AWARD: **Diploma in Stress Management**

STRESS MANAGEMENT . T'AI-CHI CH'UAN . TIBB . TRADITIONAL CHINESE MEDICINE

COURSE NO.: **435**   COURSE NAME: **Stress Management**

SCHOOL: **HOTHS SCHOOL OF HOLISTIC THERAPY**

TYPE: **P/T**   PERIOD: **4 months**

ATTENDANCE: **Seminars and 2 weekend workshops**

VENUES: **Gloucestershire (Cheltenham), Leicestershire (Leicester)**

FEES: **£300**   OTHER COSTS: **Nil**

COMMENCE: **On - going**   ENTRY REQ.: **b**

AWARD: **Practitioners Certificate in Stress Management**

NOTES: **Leads to Membership of Association of Holistic Therapists**

COURSE NO.: **436**   COURSE NAME: **Training Teachers of Relaxation and Stress Management**

SCHOOL: **RELAXATION FOR LIVING (Reg. Charity)**

TYPE: **P/T**   PERIOD:

ATTENDANCE: **2 long weekends**

VENUES: **Middlesex (Uxbridge), other venues in Midlands, North and West**

FEES: **A.F.D.**   OTHER COSTS: **£50 + books**

COMMENCE: **April**   ENTRY REQ.: **f, i, Introd. course**

AWARD: **Under review**

NOTES: **Residential courses. Pre-course and post-course study and written work essential.**

COURSE NO.: **437**   COURSE NAME: **T'ai - Chi Ch'uan Basic Training**

SCHOOL: **SCHOOL OF T'AI - CHI CH'UAN - CENTRE FOR HEALING**

TYPE: **P/T**   PERIOD: **3 years**

ATTENDANCE: **1 evening per week for 3 terms per year, OR once a week for 6 weeks for short courses**

VENUES: **London and residential places**

FEES: **Average £110 per term**   OTHER COSTS:

COMMENCE: **Feb, April, June, Sep**   ENTRY REQ.:

AWARD: **T'ai - Chi & Spiritual Studies Certificate**

NOTES: **Self-healing, meditation and self-growth approach to T'ai - Chi**

COURSE NO.: **438**   COURSE NAME: **Diploma in Phytotherapy - Tibb**

SCHOOL: **MOHSIN INTERNATIONAL FOR HIGHER EDUCATION - TIBB FOUNDATION**

TYPE: **Correspondence + Clinical**   PERIOD: **Open**

ATTENDANCE: **Flexible**

VENUES: **Leicestershire (Leicester), Pakistan (Islamabad)**

FEES: **£1,650**   OTHER COSTS: **Nil**

COMMENCE: **Continuous**   ENTRY REQ.: **a>18, f**

AWARD: **Diploma in Phytotherapy - Tibb**

NOTES: **Clinical practice available in Pakistan. Higher studies available.**

COURSE NO.: **416 (C)**   COURSE NAME: **Yoga, Shiatsu and Traditional Chinese Medicine**

SCHOOL: **LONDON CENTRE FOR YOGA AND SHIATSU STUDIES**

TYPE: **P/T**   PERIOD: **2 1/2 - 3 years**

ATTENDANCE: **Y1 & Y2=16 wknds each, Y3=16 wknds + clinical: EITHER 1 month in China, OR 6 months P/T**

VENUES: **London**

FEES: **£1,500 per year**   OTHER COSTS: **Clinical, personal therapy**

COMMENCE: **March, October**   ENTRY REQ.: **None**

AWARD: **Diploma in Yoga, Shiatsu and Traditional Chinese Medicine**

VEGATESTING . YOGA THERAPY

COURSE NO.: **439**   COURSE NAME: **Vega Test**

SCHOOL: **THE CENTRE FOR THE STUDY OF COMPLEMENTARY MEDICINE**

TYPE: **P/T**   PERIOD: **A.F.D.**

ATTENDANCE: **Beginners = 3 days, Intermediate & Advanced = 2 - 3 days each**

VENUES: **Hampshire (Southampton)**

FEES: **Beginners = £358, rest A.F.D.**   OTHER COSTS:

COMMENCE: **Twice yearly, but A.F.D.**   ENTRY REQ.: **Medically qualified or paramedics**

AWARD:

COURSE NO.: **440**   COURSE NAME: **Bioenergetic Medicine - Vega Test**

SCHOOL: **RICHARDSON CLINIC**

TYPE: **P/T**   PERIOD: **5 weeks or more (see ATTENDANCE)**

ATTENDANCE: **5 weekends, consecutive or split over several weeks**

VENUES: **West Yorkshire (Heckmondwicke)**

FEES: **£500**   OTHER COSTS: **Nil**

COMMENCE: **By arrangement**   ENTRY REQ.: **e, f, h**

AWARD: **None (see NOTES below)**

NOTES: **Upon completion students may be considered for entry to National Bioenergetic Society**

COURSE NO.: **441**   COURSE NAME: **Teacher Diploma Course - Hatha Yoga**

SCHOOL: **THE BRITISH SCHOOL OF YOGA**

TYPE: **Correspondence**   PERIOD: **12 months**

ATTENDANCE: **N/A**

VENUES: **N/A**

FEES: **£195**   OTHER COSTS:

COMMENCE: **Anytime**   ENTRY REQ.: **None**

AWARD: **BSY Diploma and Associate Membership (BSYA(T))**

NOTES: **For Full Membership a written proof of having taught Hatha Yoga at not less than 20 classes**

COURSE NO.: **442**   COURSE NAME: **The BWY Teaching Diploma (Route 3)**

SCHOOL: **THE BRITISH WHEEL OF YOGA**

TYPE: **Correspondence**   PERIOD: **3 years**

ATTENDANCE: **3 teaching practices**

VENUES: **A.F.D.**

FEES: **A.F.D.**   OTHER COSTS: **Reg. fee £15**

COMMENCE: **A.F.D.**   ENTRY REQ.: **2 yr regular attendance with approved teacher, f**

AWARD: **British Wheel of Yoga Teachers' Diploma**

NOTES: **For those who cannot attend because living far away**

COURSE NO.: **443**   COURSE NAME: **The BWY Teaching Diploma (Route 1)**

SCHOOL: **THE BRITISH WHEEL OF YOGA**

TYPE: **P/T**   PERIOD: **2 years minimum**

ATTENDANCE: **2 - 2 1/2 hours per week, OR 1 full day per month. Also min. 2 supervised teaching practices.**

VENUES: **All over England & Wales (A.F.D. & see GEOGRAPHICAL index)**

FEES: **A.F.D.**   OTHER COSTS: **Reg. fee £15**

COMMENCE: **A.F.D.**   ENTRY REQ.: **2 yr regular attendance with approved teacher, f**

AWARD: **British Wheel of Yoga Teachers' Diploma**

YOGA THERAPY

COURSE NO.: **444**   COURSE NAME: **Viniyoga Practitioner Programme**

SCHOOL: **CENTRE FOR YOGA STUDIES**

TYPE: **P/T**   PERIOD: **4 years**

ATTENDANCE: **Each year: 6 weekends + 6-day residential retreat + 12 hours individual lessons**

VENUES: **Avon (Bath), London**

FEES: **£650 per year**   OTHER COSTS: **Residential fees £200**

COMMENCE: **January (held every 2 years)**   ENTRY REQ.: **50 hrs in approved courses, OR indiv. lessons**

AWARD: **Diploma for Ability to Teach Individual Lessons & Group Classes**

NOTES: **Next course will commence in January 1993**

COURSE NO.: **445**   COURSE NAME: **Chinese Buddhist Yoga**

SCHOOL: **CHINESE YOGA FEDERATION**

TYPE: **P/T**   PERIOD: **2 years**

ATTENDANCE: **2 classes per week**

VENUES: **London, Norfolk (Norwich), Oxfordshire (Oxford)**

FEES: **£3 per class approx.**   OTHER COSTS: **Reg. fee, books**

COMMENCE: **October (held every 2 years)**   ENTRY REQ.: **Yoga Teachers Diploma, OR e**

AWARD: **Teaching Diploma of the Chinese Yoga Federation**

NOTES: **2 annual residential seminars per year. Equivalent training avail. in European centres and East Europe.**

COURSE NO.: **446**   COURSE NAME: **Yoga Teacher Training Course**

SCHOOL: **IYENGAR YOGA INSTITUTE**

TYPE: **P/T**   PERIOD: **2 years**

ATTENDANCE: **1 class per week for 60 weeks + apprenticeship in another class**

VENUES: **London, other major cities**

FEES: **£480**   OTHER COSTS: **£180 approx. for other classes**

COMMENCE: **September**   ENTRY REQ.: **2 years study with a qualified teacher**

AWARD: **BKS Iyengar Yoga Teachers' Association: Yoga Teaching Certificate (Introductory Level)**

NOTES: **Further training for higher grades of certificate available afterwards**

YOGA THERAPY

COURSE NO.: **447**   COURSE NAME: **Dru Yoga Therapeutics**
SCHOOL: **LIFE FOUNDATION SCHOOL OF THERAPEUTICS**
TYPE: **P/T**   PERIOD: **3 years**
ATTENDANCE: **4 residential weekends per year**
VENUES: **West Midlands (Wolverhampton)**
FEES: **£775**   OTHER COSTS: **£40 full board residential per weekend**
COMMENCE: **January**   ENTRY REQ.: **Nil**
AWARD: **Diploma in Dru Yoga Therapy and Teaching**

COURSE NO.: **416 (C)**   COURSE NAME: **Yoga**, Shiatsu and Traditional Chinese Medicine
SCHOOL: **LONDON CENTRE FOR YOGA AND SHIATSU**
TYPE: **P/T**   PERIOD: **2 1/2 - 3 years**
ATTENDANCE: **Y1 & Y2=16 wknds each, Y3=16 wknds + clinical: EITHER 1 month in China, OR 6 months P/T**
VENUES: **London**
FEES: **£1,500 per year**   OTHER COSTS: **Clinical, personal therapy**
COMMENCE: **March, October**   ENTRY REQ.: **None**
AWARD: **Diploma in Yoga, Shiatsu and Traditional Chinese Medicine**

COURSE NO.: **448**   COURSE NAME: **Kundalini Yoga**
SCHOOL: **KUNDALINI YOGA FOUNDATION**
TYPE: **P/T**   PERIOD: **1 - 2 years**
ATTENDANCE: **Minimum one evening per week except holidays**
VENUES: **Avon (Bristol), Cumbria (Carlisle), London, West Midlands (Birmingham)**
FEES: **£250 for teacher (excluding adv. course)**   OTHER COSTS: **Around £30 - £40**
COMMENCE: **A.F.D.**   ENTRY REQ.: **See NOTES below**
AWARD: **Kundalini Yoga Foundation Teaching certificate**
NOTES: **Candidates are required to attend and participate in a minimum of 40 yoga classes**

LATE ENTRIES

COURSE NO.: **449**　　　　COURSE NAME: **Anatomy and Physiology**

SCHOOL: **THE TISSERAND INSTITUTE**

TYPE: **P/T**　　　　　　　　　　PERIOD: **6 weeks**

ATTENDANCE: **2 class days**

VENUES: **London**

FEES: **£229**　　　　　　　　　OTHER COSTS:

COMMENCE: **March, September**　　ENTRY REQ.: **None**

AWARD: **Certificate in A&P**

COURSE NO.: **450**　　　　COURSE NAME: **Advanced Aromatherapy**

SCHOOL: **AYLESBURY COLLEGE**

TYPE: **P/T**　　　　　　　　　　PERIOD: **15 weeks**

ATTENDANCE: **3 hours once a week**

VENUES: **Buckinghamshire (Aylesbury)**

FEES: **£211**　　　　　　　　　OTHER COSTS:

COMMENCE: **Spring, Autumn**　　ENTRY REQ.: **Beauty therapy, or facial & body massage qualif.**

AWARD: **ITEC Certificate in Advanced Aromatherapy**

COURSE NO.: **451**　　　　COURSE NAME: **Holistic Aromatherapy**

SCHOOL: **SIMPLY HERBAL COLLEGE OF HOLISTIC THERAPIES**

TYPE: **F/T**　　　　　　　　　　PERIOD: **3 months**

ATTENDANCE: **5 days a week (9am-3.30pm) for 12 weeks Monday to Friday**

VENUES: **Wiltshire (Salisbury)**

FEES: **£1,469**　　　　　　　　OTHER COSTS: **Nil**

COMMENCE: **January, April, September**　　ENTRY REQ.: **21<a<55, b, g for i**

AWARD: **ITEC Diploma in Aromatherapy, Simply Herbal Diploma in Holistic Aromatherapy**

NOTES: **College is accredited I.S.P.A. and I.T.E.C.**

COURSE NO.: **452**　　　　COURSE NAME: **Holistic Aromatherapy**

SCHOOL: **SIMPLY HERBAL COLLEGE OF HOLISTIC THERAPIES**

TYPE: **P/T**　　　　　　　　　　PERIOD: **6 months**

ATTENDANCE: **12 alternate long weekends (Friday = 6pm-9pm, Saturday & Sunday = 9am-6pm)**

VENUES: **Wiltshire (Salisbury)**

FEES: **£135 per weekend**　　　OTHER COSTS: **Nil**

COMMENCE: **January, July**　　ENTRY REQ.: **21<a<55, b, g for i**

AWARD: **ITEC Diploma in Aromatherapy, Simply Herbal Diploma in Holistic Aromatherapy**

NOTES: **College is accredited I.S.P.A. and I.T.E.C.**

CRYSTAL THERAPY . HOMOEOPATHY . HYPNOTHERAPY . MASSAGE . OSTEOPATHY

COURSE NO.: **453**	COURSE NAME: **Certificated Crystal Healing Course**

SCHOOL: **ACADEMY OF CRYSTAL AND NATURAL AWARENESS**

TYPE: **P/T**	PERIOD: **2 years**

ATTENDANCE: **1 weekend every 2 months**

VENUES:: **London, North and West**

FEES: **A.F.D.**	OTHER COSTS: **Books & crystals**
COMMENCE: **January (also A.F.D.)**	ENTRY REQ.: **None**

AWARD: **Certificate in Crystal Healing**

NOTES: **After Y1 students can practice, after 2nd year become Members of Affiliation of Crystal Healing Organisations**

COURSE NO.: **454**	COURSE NAME: **Homoeopathy**

SCHOOL: **THE COLLEGE OF CLASSICAL HOMOEOPATHY**

TYPE: **P/T**	PERIOD: **4 years**

ATTENDANCE: **1 weekend a month in September to June (12 weekends in all) per year + 1 day per wk clinical in Y3 & Y4**

VENUES: **Avon (Bristol), Cumbria (Carlisle), London, West Midlands (Birmingham)**

FEES: **£700 approx. per year**	OTHER COSTS: **Books**
COMMENCE: **September**	ENTRY REQ.: **a>21, f**

AWARD: **Licentiate of The College of Classical Homoeopathy (L.C.C.H.)**

NOTES: **Membership (M.C.C.P.) after minimum 12 months PG supervised clinical work**

COURSE NO.: **455**	COURSE NAME: **Diploma in Hypnotherapy**

SCHOOL: **HOLISTIC HYPNOTHERAPY**

TYPE: **Correspondence**	PERIOD: **N/A**

ATTENDANCE: **2 x 1/2 day, OR 1 day**

VENUES: **Middlesex (Feltham)**

FEES: **£500**	OTHER COSTS: **Books**
COMMENCE: **N/A**	ENTRY REQ.: **a>25**

AWARD: **Diploma in Hypnotherapy**

NOTES: **Graduates become eligible for membership of .240professional organisation**

COURSE NO.: **456**	COURSE NAME: **MAP**

SCHOOL: **AYLESBURY COLLEGE**

TYPE: **P/T**	PERIOD: **14 weeks**

ATTENDANCE: **3 hours once a week**

VENUES: **Buckinghamshire (Aylesbury)**

FEES: **£164**	OTHER COSTS:
COMMENCE: **Spring, Autumn**	ENTRY REQ.: **Some practical massage, or a knowledge of A&P**

AWARD: **ITEC Certificate in MAP**

COURSE NO.: **457**	COURSE NAME: **Osteopathy Course**

SCHOOL: **NORTHERN COUNTIES SCHOOL OF OSTEOPATHY**

TYPE: **P/T**	PERIOD: **2 years**

ATTENDANCE: **1 weekend per month**

VENUES:: **Durham (Durham)**

FEES: **£1,656**	OTHER COSTS: **None**
COMMENCE: **January (also A.F.D.)**	ENTRY REQ.: **2 year background in healing (practitioner)**

AWARD: **Diploma in Osteopathy**

REFLEXOLOGY . SPORTS THERAPY

COURSE NO.: **458** COURSE NAME: **Reflexology**
SCHOOL: **AYLESBURY COLLEGE**
TYPE: **P/T** PERIOD: **11 weeks**
ATTENDANCE: **3 hours once a week**
VENUES: **Buckinghamshire (Aylesbury)**
FEES: **£136** OTHER COSTS:
COMMENCE: **Summer** ENTRY REQ.: **Massage qualification**
AWARD: **ITEC Certificate in Reflexology**

COURSE NO.: **459** COURSE NAME: **Reflexology**
SCHOOL: **THE TISSERAND INSTITUTE**
TYPE: **P/T** PERIOD: **6 months**
ATTENDANCE: **10 class days**
VENUES: **London**
FEES: **£582** OTHER COSTS:
COMMENCE: **March, November** ENTRY REQ.: **None**
AWARD: **Certificate in Reflexology**

COURSE NO.: **460** COURSE NAME: **Sports Therapy**
SCHOOL: **AYLESBURY COLLEGE**
TYPE: **P/T** PERIOD: **36 weeks**
ATTENDANCE: **9 hours two days a week**
VENUES: **Buckinghamshire (Aylesbury)**
FEES: **A.F.D.** OTHER COSTS:
COMMENCE: **September** ENTRY REQ.:
AWARD: **IIST**

When Replying To Any Advertisement
Please Mention

START A CAREER
IN
COMPLEMENTARY MEDICINE

SCHOOLS

ACADEMY OF CRYSTAL AND NATURAL AWARENESS, THE
Crystal House, 4 Bridgwater Road, Bleadon, Weston-Super-Mare, Avon, BS24 0BG
0934-815083
Courses: 453

ACADEMY OF HYPNOTHERAPY
28 Lakeside Crescent, Cockfosters, Hertfordshire, EN4 8QJ
081-441 9685
Courses: 207 (C)

ACADEMY OF NATURAL HEALTH
7A Clapham Common South Side, London, SW4 7AA
071-720 9506
Courses: 248

ACADEMY OF ON-SITE MASSAGE, THE
14 Brunswick Square, Hove, BN3 1EH
0273-207508
Courses: 249

ACADEMY OF SYSTEMATIC KINESIOLOGY, THE
39 Browns Road, Surbiton, Surrey, KT5 8ST
081-399 3215
Courses: 236

ACUPUNCTURE & CHINESE HERBAL PRACTITIONERS TRAINING COLLEGE
1037B Finchley Road, Golders Green, London, NW11 7ES
081-455 5508
Courses: 2

ALEXANDER TECHNIQUE - THE NORTH LONDON TEACHERS TRAINING COURSE
16 Rodborough Road, London, NW11
081-455 3938
Courses: 15

ALLIED SCHOOL OF REMEDIAL MASSAGE, THE
37 Barnfield Close, Galmpton, Brixham, Devon, TQ5 0LY
0803-843492
Courses: 250

ALTERNATIVE TRAINING
8 Kiln Road, Llanfoist, Abergavenny, Gwent, NP7 9NS
0873-6872
Courses: 158

ANGLO-EUROPEAN COLLEGE OF CHIROPRACTIC
13-15 Parkwood Road, Bournemouth, Dorset, BH5 2DF
0202-431021
Courses: 85

ANGLO-EUROPEAN SCHOOL OF
HERBALISM
40 Stokewood Road, Bournemouth, BH3 7NE
0202-529793
Courses: 173

ANGLO-EUROPEAN SCHOOL OF
IRIDOLOGY
40 Stokewood Road, Bournemouth, BH3 7NE
0202-529793
Courses: 231

APPLIED SCIENCE-LEEDS POLYTECHNIC
Calverley Street, Leeds, LS1 3HE
0532-832600 Ext. 3847
Courses: 147

ARBOURS ASSOCIATION
6 Church Lane, London, N8 7BU
081-340 7646
Courses: 350

ARK COURSES
Honeymead, Grafham Grange, Grafham, Nr.
Bramley, Guildford, GU5 0LH
0483-893675
Courses: 208 (C), 209 (C)

AROMATHERAPY ASSOCIATES LTD.
68 Maltings Place, Bagleys Lane, Fulham,
London, SW6 2BY
071-371 9878
Courses: 20

AROMATHERAPY SCHOOL, THE
c/o Natural by Nature Oils, 27 Vivian Avenue,
Hendon Central, London, NW4 3UX
081-202 5718
Courses: 21

ASHTANGA CENTRE
9 Vallis Way, Frome, Somerset, BA11 3BD
0373-72205
Courses: 237, 251

ASSOCIATION FOR BODYMIND
THERAPY/TRAINING
Princes House, 8 Princes Avenue, Muswell
Hill, London, N10 3LR
081-883 5418
Courses: 105 (C)

ASSOCIATION OF AURICULOTHERAPY
GREAT BRITAIN LTD, THE
11 Level Lane, Buxton, Derbyshire, SK17 6TJ
0298-25467
Courses: 77

ASSOCIATION OF MEDICAL
AROMATHERAPISTS, THE
17 Queen's Crescent, Glasgow, G4 9BL
041-357 2557
Courses: 22, 252, 370

ASSOCIATION OF NATURAL MEDICINES
27 Braintree Road, Witham, Essex, CM8 2DD
0376-511069
Courses: 3(C), 23, 106, 210, 253, 371

AVON HYPNOTHERAPY (A.H.T.) CENTRE
114 Green Lane, Derby, DE1 1RY
0850-327701
Courses: 211, 212

AYLESBURY COLLEGE
Oxford Road, Aylesbury, Buckinghamshire,
HP21 8PD
0296-434111
Courses: 24, 450, 456, 458, 460

AYURVEDA - (Science of Life) INDIAN
MEDICAL SCIENCE
121 Coral Street, Leicester, Leicestershire, LE4
5BG
0533 -662475
Courses: 82

BATES COLLEGE, THE
Friars Court, 11, Tarmount Lane, Shoreham-by-
Sea, West Sussex, BN43 6RQ
0273-452623
Courses: 83

BAYLY SCHOOL OF REFLEXOLOGY, THE
Monks Orchard, Whitbourne, Worcester, WR6
5RB
0886-21207
Courses: 372

BEAUMONT COLLEGE OF NATURAL
MEDICINE
16 Dittons Road, Eastbourne, East Sussex, BN21
1DW
0323-24855
Courses: 25, 26, 254, 373

BEAUTIFORM TRAINING COLLEGE
10 Balaclava Road, Kings Heath,
Birmingham, B14 7SG
021-444 5435
Courses: 255

BERKELEY COLLEGE OF NATURAL
THERAPIES
47 Oxbarn Avenue, Bradmore,
Wolverhampton, WV3 7HD
0902-336823
Courses: 4, 5

BERKSHIRE SCHOOL OF NATURAL
THERAPY
Conifers, 21 Dukes Wood, Crowthorne,
Berkshire, RG11 6NF
0344-761715
Courses: 27, 28, 29, 256, 257, 374

BILSTON COMMUNITY COLLEGE
West Field Road, Bilston, West Midlands,
WV14 6ER
0902-492498 (Contact: Mrs Polly Gabriel)
Courses: 107

BOURNEMOUTH SCHOOL OF MASSAGE
14 Greenwood Road, Bournemouth, Dorset,
BH9 2LH
0202-513838
Courses: 30, 31, 258, 375

BRANTRIDGE FOREST SCHOOL
Highfield, Dane Hill, Haywards Heath, West
Sussex, RH17 7EX
0825-790214/0860-320566/7
Courses: 91, 148, 174, 184, 316, 317, 351, 364

BRETLANDS BEAUTY TRAINING CENTRE
Baden Powell Place, Langton Road, Tunbridge
Wells, Kent, TN4 8XD
0892-33161/37569
Courses: 32, 241

BRISTOL SCHOOL OF SHIATSU AND
ORIENTAL MEDICINE
81 Cornwall Road, Bishopston, Bristol, Avon,
BS7 8LJ
0272-425680
Courses: 408

BRITISH ASSOCIATION OF ANALYTICAL
BODY PSYCHOTHERAPISTS
47 Dean Court Road, Rottingdean, Brighton,
BN2 7DH
0273-303382
Courses: 352

BRITISH ASSOCIATION OF
PSYCHOTHERAPISTS
37 Mapesbury Road, London, NW2
081-346 1747
Courses: 353

BRITISH BIOMAGNETIC ASSOCIATION
The Williams Clinic, 31 St. Marychurch Road,
Torquay, Devon, TQ1 3JF
0803-293346
Courses: 84

BRITISH COLLEGE OF ACUPUNCTURE,
THE
8 Hunter Street, London, WC1N 1BN
071-833 8164
Courses: 6

BRITISH COLLEGE OF COMPLEMENTARY
MEDICAL PRACTICES
Oak House, Grosvenor Square, Sale, Cheshire,
M33 1RW
061-969 1051
Courses: 99

BRITISH COLLEGE OF NATUROPATHY
AND OSTEOPATHY
Frazer House, 6 Netherhall Gardens, London,
NW3 5RR
071-435 7830/6464
Courses: 318 (C)

BRITISH HYPNOSIS RESEARCH
8 Paston Place, Brighton, East Sussex, BN2
1EG
0273-693622
Courses: 213 (C)

BRITISH INSTITUTE OF HOMOEOPATHY,
THE
427 Great West Road, Hounslow, Middlesex,
TW5 0BY
081-577 7781
Courses: 187

BRITISH SCHOOL OF HOMOEOPATHY
23 Sarum Avenue, Melksham, Wiltshire, SN12
6BN
0225-790051
Courses: 185, 186

BRITISH SCHOOL OF ORIENTAL
THERAPY AND MOVEMENT, THE
46 Whitton Road, Twickenham, Middlesex,
TW1 1BS
081-744 1974
Courses: 339

BRITISH SCHOOL OF OSTEOPATHY, THE
1 - 4 Suffolk Street, London, SW1Y 4HG
071-930 9254
Courses: 340

BRITISH SCHOOL OF REFLEXOLOGY,
THE
The Holistic Healing Centre, 92 Sheering Road,
Old Harlow, Essex, CM17 0JW
0279-429060
Courses: 376

BRITISH SCHOOL OF SHIATSU-DO
East West Centre, 188 Old Street, London,
EC1V 9BP
071-251 0831
Courses: 409

BRITISH SCHOOL OF YOGA, THE
46 Hagley Road, Stourbridge, West Midlands,
DY8 1QD
0384-371320
Courses: 100, 441

BRITISH SCHOOL - REFLEX ZONE
THERAPY
87 Oakington Avenue, Wembley Park,
Middlesex, HA9 8HY
081-908 2201
Courses: 377

BRITISH WHEEL OF YOGA, THE
1 Hamilton Place, Boston
Road, Sleaford, Lincolnshire, NG34 7ES
0529-306851
Courses: 442, 443

CAMBRIDGE SCHOOL OF BEAUTY
THERAPY
94 High Street, Sawston, Cambridge
0223-832228
Courses: 33

CARLISLE MASSAGE SCHOOL
176 Lansdowne Crescent, Carlisle, CA3 9ER
0228-511819
Courses: 259

CENTRE FOR AUTOGENIC TRAINING
101 Harley Street, London, W1N 1DF
071-935 1811
Courses: 81

CENTRE FOR COUNSELLING AND
PSYCHOTHERAPY EDUCATION
21 Lancaster Road, London, W11 1QL
071-221 3215
Courses: 108 (C)

CENTRE FOR INTEGRATIVE
PSYCHOTHERAPY & COUNSELLING
38 Belvedere Road, Taunton, Somerset, TA1
1HD
0823-337049
Courses: 109

CENTRE FOR STRESS MANAGEMENT
156 Westcombe Hill, Blackheath, London, SE3
7DH
081-293 4114
Courses: 110, 431, 432, 433, 434

CENTRE FOR THE STUDY OF
COMPLEMENTARY MEDICINE, THE
51 Bedford Place, Southampton, SO1 2DG
0703-334752/071-935 7848
Courses: 439

CENTRE FOR TRAINING IN ALEXANDER
TECHNIQUE, THE
142 Thorpedale Road, London, N4 3BS
071-281 7639
Courses: 16

CENTRE FOR YOGA STUDIES
P.O.Box 158, Bath, BA1 2YG
0225-426327
Courses: 444

CHALICE FOUNDATION, THE
P.O.Box 684, London, E17 3JP
0803-834406
Courses: 34, 260

CHAMPNEYS COLLEGE OF HEALTH AND
BEAUTY
Chesham Road, Wigginton, Nr. Tring,
Hertfordshire, HP23 6HY
0442-873326/863351
Courses: 35, 261

CHINESE YOGA FEDERATION
Kongoryuji Temple, East Dergham, Norfolk,
NR19 1AS
0362-693962
Courses: 445

CHIRON CENTRE FOR HOLISTIC
PSYCHOTHERAPY
26 Eaton Rise, Ealing, London, W5 2ER
081-997 5219
Courses: 354

CLARE MAXWELL-HUDSON SCHOOL OF
MASSAGE
P.O.Box 457, London, NW2 4ER
081-450 6494
Courses: 242, 262, 421

COLLEGE OF CLASSICAL
HOMOEOPATHY, THE
45 Barrington Street, Tiverton, Devon, EX16
6QP
0884-258143
Courses: 454

COLLEGE OF DIETARY HEALING
52 Roman Way, Honiton, Devon, EX14 8PT
0404-44714
Courses: 149

COLLEGE OF HEALING
Runnings Park, Croft Bank, West Malvern,
Worcestershire, WR14 8BR
0684-565253/573868
Courses: 169

COLLEGE OF HERBS AND NATURAL
HEALING
25 Curzon Street, Basford, Newcastle-under-
Lyme, Staffordshire, ST5 0PD
0782-717383 (Fax 0782-713274)
Courses: 175

COLLEGE OF HOLISTIC MEDICINE
4 Craigpark, Glasgow, G31 2NA
Courses: 111, 263

COLLEGE OF HOMOEOPATHY, THE
Regent's College, Inner Circle, Regent's Park,
London, NW1 4NS
071-487 7416
Courses: 188, 189

COLLEGE OF NATURAL MEDICINE -
LONDON, THE
38 Nigel House, Portpool Lane, London, EC1N
7UR
071-405 2781
Courses: 7, 78, 86 (C), 137, 190

COLLEGE OF NUTRITIONAL MEDICINE,
THE
'East Bank', New Church Road, Smithills,
Bolton, BL1 5QP
0204-492550
Courses: 150, 151, 152, 232, 233, 323, 324

COLLEGE OF OPTHALMIC
SOMATOLOGY
24 Chapel Market, London, N1 9EZ
071-278 4610/1212
Courses: 234, 235

COLLEGE OF OSTEOPATHS
EDUCATIONAL TRUST, THE
1 Furzehill Road, Borehamwood,
Hertfordshire, WD6 2DG
081-905 1937
Courses: 341

COLLEGE OF PRACTICAL
HOMOEOPATHY, THE
186 Wolverhampton Street, Dudley, West
Midlands, DY1 3AD
0384-233664
Courses: 191

COLLEGE OF TRADITIONAL CHINESE
ACUPUNCTURE UK, THE
Tao House, Queensway, Royal Leamington
Spa, Warwickshire, CV31 3LZ
0926-422121
Courses: 8

COMMUNITY HEALTH FOUNDATION,
THE
188 Old Street, London, EC1V 9BP
071-251 4076
Courses: 264

CONSTRUCTIVE TEACHING CENTRE
LTD., THE
18 Landsdowne Road, Holland Park, London,
W11 3LL
071-727 7222
Courses: 17

CRANE SCHOOL OF REFLEXOLOGY
135 Collins Meadow, Harlow, Essex, CM19
4EJ
0279-21682
Courses: 378

CRANIAL OSTEOPATHIC ASSOCIATION
478 Baker Street, Enfield, Middlesex, EN1 3QS
081-367 5561
Courses: 138

CRANIOSACRAL THERAPY
EDUCATIONAL TRUST
29 Dollis Park, Finchley, London, N3 1HJ
081-349 0297
Courses: 139

CRYSTAL 2000
37 Bromley Road, St. Annes-on-Sea,
Lancashire, FY8 1PQ
0253-723735
Courses: 141

DALLAMORE COLLEGE OF ADVANCED
REFLEXOLOGY,THE
50 Sydney Dye Court, Sporle, Kings Lynn,
Norfolk, PE32 2EE
0760-725437
Courses: 379

DELAWARR SOCIETY OF RADIONICS
Delawarr Laboratories, Raleigh Park Road,
Oxford, OX2 9BB
0865-248572
Courses: 365

DEV AURA ACADEMY
Little London, Tetford, Lincolnshire, LN9 6QL
0507-533781
Courses: 92

DEVON SCHOOL OF SHIATSU, THE
The Coach House, Buckyette Farm,
Littlehempston, Totnes, Devon, TQ9 6ND
080426-593
Courses: 410

DILWORTH SCHOOL OF REFLEXOLOGY
193 Tring Road, Aylesbury, Buckinghamshire,
HP20 1JH
0296-24854
Courses: 380

DONCASTER COLLEGE
High Melton, Doncaster, DN5 7SZ
0709-582427
Courses: 112

EAST ANGLIAN SCHOOL OF SHIATSU
2 Capondale Cottages, New Lane, Holbrook,
Ispswich, IP9 2RB
0473-328061
Courses: 411

EDINBURGH SCHOOL OF NATURAL
THERAPY, THE
2 London Street, Edinburgh, EH3 6NA
031-557 3901
Courses: 36, 265, 266, 381

ENERMED INSTITUTE OF RADIONICS
AND RADIESTHESIA
4A The Parade, Station Road, Sturminster
Newton, Dorset, DT10 1BA
0258-73986
Courses: 366

ESSEX SCHOOL OF MASSAGE
Hadleigh Rise, Middle
Street, Nazeing, Essex, EN9 2LH
STD - 2110
Courses: 267

EUROPEAN SCHOOL OF OSTEOPATHY
104 Tonbridge Road, Maidstone, Kent, ME16
8SL
0622-671558
Courses: 342

EUROPEAN SHIATSU SCHOOL, THE
Highbanks, Lockeridge, Marlborough, Wiltshire,
SN8 4EQ
0672-86362
Courses: 412

FACULTY OF HERBAL MEDICINE (General
Council & Register of Consultant Herbalists)
Grosvenor House, 40 SeaWay, Middleton-on-
Sea, West Sussex, PA22 7AA
0243-586012
Courses: 176

FACULTY OF OSTEOPATHY, THE
Newsham House, 103 Manchester Road, Bury,
Lancashire, BL9 0TD
061-797 7770 Ext. 9
Courses: 268

FRANCES FEWELL (GEMINI INSTITUTE)
70 Readers Court, Gt. Baddow, Chelmsford,
Essex, CM2 8HA
0245-265527/74678
Courses: 37, 269

GABLECROFT COLLEGE
Church Street, Whittington, Nr. Oswestry,
Shropshire, SY11 4DT
0691-659631
Courses: 38, 270, 382

GERDA BOYESEN CENTRE
Acacia House, Centre Avenue, Acton Park,
London, W3 7JX
081-743 2437
Courses: 113, 271

GESTALT CENTRE LONDON
64 Warwick Road, St. Albans, Hertfordshire,
AL1 4DL
0727-864806
Courses: 114, 355

GLASGOW SCHOOL OF SHIATSU
19 Langside Park, Kilbarchan, Renfrewshire,
PA10 2EP
05057-4657
Courses: 413

GOOD SCENTS SCHOOL OF NATURAL
THERAPIES
Rock Lodge, The Hollow, Washington,
Pulborough, West Sussex, RH20 3DA
0903-893098
Courses: 1, 39, 159, 272, 383

GREENHILL COLLEGE
Lowlands Road, Harrow, Middlesex, HA1 3AQ
081-422 2388
Courses: 40, 384

HAHNEMANN COLLEGE OF
HOMOEOPATHY, THE
243 The Broadway, Southall, Middlesex, UB1
1NF
081-843 9220/574 4281/476 7263
Courses: 192

HALEY COLLEGE FOR COUNSELLING
AND PSYCHOTHERAPY
Effingham Road, Burstow, Surrey, RH6 9RP
0342-712393
Courses: 115, 116

HEALING-SHIATSU EDUCATION CENTRE
"The Orchard", Lower - Maescoed,
Herefordshire, HR2 0HP
087-387207
Courses: 414

HOLISTIC HYPNOTHERAPY
17 Sycamore Close, Feltham, Middlesex, TW13 7HN
081-751 5907
Courses: 455

HOLWELL CENTRE FOR PSYCHODRAMA AND SOCIODRAMA
East Down, Barnstaple, North Devon, EX31 4NZ
0271-850267/597
Courses: 356

HOMOEOPATHIC FOUNDATION, THE
Grosvenor House, 40 Sea Way, Middleton-on-Sea, West Sussex, PA22 7AA
0243-586012
Courses: 193

HOTHS SCHOOL OF HOLISTIC THERAPY
39 Prestbury Road, Pittville, Cheltenham, Gloucestershire, GL52 2PT
0242-512601/0533-837305
Courses: 41, 93, 142, 247, 385, 435

HOWELL COLLEGE OF HOLISTIC HEALTH, THE
93 Cheap Street, Sherborne, Dorset, DT9 3LS
0935-813257
Courses: 101, 153, 154, 160, 214 (C), 238, 325, 326

HOWELL COLLEGE OF LYMPH & COLON THERAPISTS, THE
93 Cheap Street, Sherborne, Dorset, DT9 3LS
0935-813257
Courses: 90, 243

HYGEIA COLLEGE OF COLOUR THERAPY, THE
Hygeia Studios, Brook House, Avening, Tetbury, Gloucestershire, GL8 8NS
0453-832150
Courses: 94

HYPNOTHINK FOUNDATION, THE
P.O.Box 154, Cheltenham, Gloucestershire, GL53 9EG
0242-242101
Courses: 215, 216

INSTITUTE FOR OPTIMUM NUTRITION, THE
5 Jerdan Place, London, SW6 1BE
071-385 7984
Courses: 327

INSTITUTE OF ALLERGY THERAPISTS
Ffynnonwen, Llangwyryfon, Aberystwyth, Dyfed, SY23 4EY
09747-376
Courses: 19

INSTITUTE OF CLINICAL AROMATHERAPY, THE
22 Bromley Road, London, SE6 2TP
081-690 2149/690 6681
Courses: 42, 43

INSTITUTE OF CRYSTAL AND GEM THERAPISTS
Anubis House, Creswell Drive, Ravenstone, Leicestershire, LE6 2AG
0530-510864
Courses: 143

INSTITUTE OF EMOTIO-SOMATIC THERAPY
52 Bishopsthorpe Road, London, SE26 4PA
081-659 0021
Courses: 117

INSTITUTE OF GROUP ANALYSIS, THE
1 Daleham Gardens, London, NW3 5BY
071-431 2693
Courses: 357

INSTITUTE OF TRADITIONAL HERBAL MEDICINE AND AROMATHERAPY, THE
152 Tufnell Park Road, London, N7 0DZ
071-272 7403
Courses: 44

INTERNATIONAL COLLEGE OF ORIENTAL MEDICINE UK, THE
Green Hedges House, Green Hedges Avenue, East Grinstead, West Sussex, RH19 1SU
0342-313107
Courses: 9

INTERNATIONAL INSTITUTE OF VITAMIN AND MINERAL THERAPISTS
3 Ryde Mews, Binstead Road, Ryde, Isle of Wight, PO33 3NG
Courses: 328, 329

INTERNATIONAL SCHOOL OF POLARITY THERAPY, THE
12-14 Dowell Street, Honiton, Devon, EX14 8LT
0404-44330
Courses: 346

IYENGAR YOGA INSTITUTE
223A Randolph Avenue, London, W9 1NL
071-624 3080
Courses: 446

JANE HIDER SCHOOL OF NATURAL
THERAPIES
48 Park Street, Hereford, Hereford and
Worcester, HR1 2RD
0432-271866
Courses: 273, 386

JANICE ELLICOT SCHOOL OF
REFLEXOLOGY
42 Alder Lodge, Stevenage Road, London, SW6
6NP
071-386 9914
Courses: 387

JOHN SEYMOUR ASSOCIATES
17 Boyce Drive, St. Werburghs, Bristol, BS2
9XQ
0272-557827
Courses: 319, 320, 321

KI KAI SHIATSU CENTRE
8 Willow Road, Hampstead, London, NW3
081-368 9050
Courses: 415

KINESIOLOGY SCHOOL, THE
8 Railey Mews, London, NW5 2PA
071-482 0698
Courses: 239

KUNDALINI YOGA FOUNDATION
Satya Kaur & Shiv Charan Singh
61 Sladedale Road, London, SE18 1PY
081-854 8748
Courses: 448

KUNDALINI YOGA FOUNDATION
Kartar Kaur
55 Sunny Gardens Road, London, NW4 1SJ
081-203 7302
Courses: 448

KUNDALINI YOGA FOUNDATION
Sat Nam Kaur & Guru Dharam Singh
Lotus Healing Centre, 129 Queens Crescent,
London, NW5 4HE
071-284 4614
Courses: 448

KUNDALINI YOGA FOUNDATION
Guru Singh
39b Fitzroy Street, London, W1
071-388 4776
Courses: 448

KUNDALINI YOGA FOUNDATION
Inderpal Kaur
16 Homefield, N. Yates, Bristol
0454-314755
Courses: 448

KUNDALINI YOGA FOUNDATION
Guru Jiwan Singh
6 Chad Road, Birmingham, B15 3EN
Courses: 448

KUNDALINI YOGA FOUNDATION
Tom Brett
Laburnam Cottage, Scotby Road, Cumwhiton,
Carlisle, CA4 8DL
0228-60352
Courses: 448

LA ROSA SCHOOL OF HEALTH AND
BEAUTY
17 Southdown Close, Brixham, Devon, TQ5
0AQ
0803-858571
Courses: 45, 275, 276, 330, 331, 422

LANCASHIRE HOLISTIC COLLEGE
"Greenbank House", 65A Adelphi Street,
Preston, Lancashire, PR1 7BH
0772-825177
Courses: 46, 274, 388

LE PLAN INTERNATIONAL SCHOOL OF
HEALING, THE
10 Irene Road, London, SW6 4AL
Courses: 170

LEAVES INTERNATIONAL SCHOOL OF
AROMATHERAPY, MASSAGE & NATURAL
THERAPY, THE
Court Mills House, Court Street, Trowbridge,
Wiltshire, BA14 8BR
0225-753643
Courses: 47, 161, 277, 389, 423

LEICESTER UNIVERSITY
Dept. of Adult Education, Vaughan College, St.
Nicholas Circle, Leicester, LE1 4LB
0533-517368
Courses: 134, 135, 362

LIFE FOUNDATION SCHOOL OF
THERAPEUTICS (UK)
Maristowe House, Dover Street, Bilston, West
Midlands, WV14 6AL
0902-409164
Courses: 102, 447

LIFE FOUNDATION SCHOOL OF
THERAPEUTICS (UK)
15 Holyhead Road, Bangor, Gwynedd LL57
2EG
0248-370076
Courses: 102, 447

LIVING COLOUR
33 Lancaster Grove, Belsize Park,
Hampstead, London, NW3 4EX
071-794 1371
Courses: 95

LONDON CENTRE FOR YOGA AND
SHIATSU
49B Onslow Gardens, London, N10 3JY
081-444 0103
Courses: 416 (C)

LONDON COLLEGE OF CHINESE HERBAL
MEDICINE & ACUPUNCTURE
127 Queens Crescent, London, NW5 4HE
071-284 4614
Courses: 10

LONDON COLLEGE OF CLASSICAL
HOMOEOPATHY, THE
Morely College, 61 Westminster Bridge Road,
London, SE1 7HT
071-928 6199
Courses: 194, 195, 196

LONDON COLLEGE OF CLINICAL
HYPNOSIS
229A Sussex Gardens, Lancaster Gate, London,
W2 2RL
071-402 9037
Courses: 217

LONDON COLLEGE OF MASSAGE
146 Great Portland Street, London, W1N 5TA
071-323 3574
Courses: 162, 278, 279

LONDON COLLEGE OF SHIATSU, THE
1 Central Park Lodge, 54 - 58 Bolsover Street,
London, W1P 7HL
071-383 2619
Courses: 417

LONDON SCHOOL FOR BIODYNAMIC
PHYSIATRY, THE
178 Acton High Street, Acton, London, W3
9NN
081-993 6351
Courses: 280, 281

LONDON SCHOOL OF ACUPUNCTURE &
TRADITIONAL CHINESE MEDICINE
3rd Floor, 36 Featherstone Street, London,
EC1Y 8QX
071-490 0513
Courses: 11, 12, 177

LONDON SCHOOL OF HOMOEOPATHY
57 Wise Lane, Mill Hill, London, NW7 2RN
081-959 2968
Courses: 197

LONDON SCHOOL OF MACROBIOTICS
188-194 Old Street, London, EC1V 9BP
071-251 4076
Courses: 246

LONDON SCHOOL OF OSTEOPATHY, THE
Whitelands College, West Hill, London, SW15
3SN
081-785 2267
Courses: 343

LONDON SCHOOL OF SPORTS MASSAGE
LTD.
88 Cambridge Street, London, SW1V 4QG
071-233 5962
Courses: 282

LONDON THERAPY CENTRE
109 Ebury Street, London, SW1W 9QU
071-823 4955
Courses: 283

LYN GORLEY SCHOOL OF MASSAGE AND
AROMATHERAPY
The Vicarage, Church Road, Shaw, Newbury,
Berkshire, RG13 2DR
0635-34365
Courses: 284

MAGGIE NICHOL
35B Worthing Road, Southsea, Hampshire, PO5
2RJ
0705-733089
Courses: 285

MAIDSTONE COLLEGE OF OSTEOPATHY
30 Tonbridge Road, Maidstone, Kent, ME16
8RT
0622-752375
Courses: 344

MAITRYA SCHOOL OF HEALING
(Camberley Branch),
9 Tekels Park, Camberley, Surrey, GU15 2LE
0276-23300/081-546 5793
Courses: 96

MAPERTON TRUST, THE
Wincanton, Somerset, BA9 8EH
0963-32651
Courses: 163, 367

MARY MARTIN SCHOOL OF
REFLEXOLOGY
37 Standale Grove, Ruislip, Middlesex, HA4
7UA
0895-635621
Courses: 390

MARYLEBONE CENTRE TRUST -
EDUCATION & TRAINING UNIT
Regent's College, Regent's Park, London, NW1
4NS
071-487 7415
Courses: 286

McTIMONEY CHIROPRACTIC SCHOOL
14 Park End Street, Oxford, Oxon, OX1 1HH
0865-246786
Courses: 87

MERCURIAN SCHOOL OF HYPNOSIS AND
RADICAL HYPNOTHERAPY
243 Great Clowes Street, Salford, M7 9DZ
061-792 6565
Courses: 218

MICHELINE ARCIER ARMOMATHERAPY
7 William Street, Knightsbridge, London, SW1X
9HL
071-235 3545
Courses: 48

MIDLANDS COLLEGE OF
HOMOEOPATHY, THE
186 Wolverhampton Street, Dudley, West
Midlands, DY1 3AD
0384-233664
Courses: 198

MIDLANDS SCHOOL OF MASSAGE, THE
The Castle Clinic, 16 The Ropewalk,
Nottingham, NG1 7DT
0602-472263
Courses: 287

MILLFIELD SCHOOL OF BEAUTY
THERAPY, THE
Millfields, Rusper, Nr. Horsham, Sussex, RH12
4PR
0293-871406/0293-22491
Courses: 49, 288, 289, 391

MINSTER CENTRE
53-57 Minster Road, London, NW2 3SH
071-431 4151
Courses: 358

MODERN TUTORIAL SCHOOL OF
AURICULAR ACUPUNCTURE, THE
59 Telford Crescent, Leigh, Lancashire, WN7
5LY
0942-678092
Courses: 79

MOHSIN INTERNATIONAL FOR HIGHER
EDUCATION - TIBB FOUNDATION
446 East Park Road, Leicester, Leicestershire,
LE5 5HH
0533-734633
Courses: 438

**NATIONAL ASSOCIATION OF
HYPNOTISTS AND
PSYCHOTHERAPISTS, THE
145 Coleridge Road, Cambridge, CB1 3PN
0223-247893
Courses: 219 (C)**

NATIONAL COLLEGE OF HYPNOSIS AND
PSYCHOTHERAPY, THE
12 Cross Street, Nelson, Lancashire, BB9 7EN
0282-699378
Courses: 220 (C)

NATIONAL COLLEGE OF PSYCHIC
COUNSELLING, THE
3 Broadfield, Harlow, Essex, CM20 3PR
0279-425284
Courses: 118, 119

NATIONAL SCHOOL OF HYPNOSIS AND
ADVANCED PSYCHOTHERAPY
28 Finsbury Park Road, London, N4 2JX
071-359 6991
Courses: 221 (C)

NATIONAL SCHOOL OF MASSAGE
72 Portland Street, Southport, Lancashire
0704-543532
Courses: 80, 290, 424

NATURAL CLINIC AROMATHERAPY
SCHOOL, THE
Bretland House, Bretland Road, Rusthall,
Tunbridge Wells, Kent, TN4 8PB
0892-548840
Courses: 50, 51, 392

NEW BEGINNINGS
237 Empire Road, Greenford, Middlesex, UB6
7HB
081-991 9117
Courses: A.F.D. and see advertisement in PART
I - Assertiveness

NEW LIFE COLLEGE
86 Old Brompton Road, London, SW7 3LQ
071-584 7580
Courses: 291, 292

NEW LIFE COURSES
3 Broadfield, Harlow, Essex, CM20 3PR
0279-425284
Courses: 222 (C), 393

NORMAN VAUGHTON SCHOOL OF
HYPNOSIS AND PSYCHOTHERAPY
8 Fairway Drive, Chilwell, Nottingham, NG9
4BN
0602-255025
Courses: 223

NORTH WEST COLLEGE OF
HOMOEOPATHY
23 Wilbraham Road, Fallowfield, Manchester,
M14 6FB
061-257 2445
Courses: 200

NORTHERN COLLEGE OF ACUPUNCTURE
124 Acomb Road, York, YO2 4EY
0904-785120/784828
Courses: 13

NORTHERN COLLEGE OF
HOMOEOPATHIC MEDICINE, THE
Swinburne House, Swinburne Street,
Gateshead, NE8 1AX
091-490 0276
Courses: 199

NORTHERN COUNTIES SCHOOL OF
OSTEOPATHY
112 Grange Road, Hartlepool, Cleveland, TS26
8JJ
0429-236310
Courses: 457

NORTHERN INSTITUTE OF MASSAGE
100 Waterloo Road, Blackpool, Lancashire, FY4
1AW
0253-403548
Courses: 293

When Contacting Any School Please Mention
START A CAREER IN COMPLEMENTARY MEDICINE

ON COURSE

Personal & Professional Development Consultancy

56, North Avenue, Shenley, Radlett, HERTS WD7 9DG   Telephone: 0923 858232

'ON COURSE' aims:

- to provide learning and resources for personal and professional growth
- to promote an integrative approach to learning that encompases effective development as well as skills and knowledge
- to support individuals in managing personal and professional change and integration

To this end our facilities offer:

- An adult learning environment that values individual autonomy and responsibility, collaboration in determining learning goals, assessment and monitoring of learning experiences
- An experiential mode of enquiry for the reflective and creative development of the professional
- Empowerement of the individual within a collaborative context in encouraging a healthy reverberation within the helping relationship

SERVICES

Consultancy
In -house courses/workshops
Supervision of councellors/groupworkers
Staff support groups
Individual/group counselling
Training trainers
Certificate & Diploma courses
Regular workshops

CERTIFICATE & DIPLOMA COURSES

ITEC Certificate in Anatomy, Physiology and Holistic Massage
Starts Febraury 1992 and September 1992

ITEC Diploma in Aromatherapy
Starts September 1992

Certificate in Holistic Counselling Skills
Starts May 1992

Certificate in Counselling
Starts September 1992

Certificate for Trainers of Assertiveness
Starts October 1992

WORKSHOPS

* **Aura Sensing**
* **Tai Chi Qigong**
* **Creative Visualisation**
* **Stress Management**
* **Supervision Skills**

* **Assertion Training**
* **Sexuality**
* **Crisis Counselling**
* **Leadership Training**
* **Dramatherapy**

Director: Alex Chew, RMN, PGCEA, Dip Counselling, Dip Dramatherapy, Cert Assertiveness and Stress Management Trainers (HPRG Surrey Univ), ITEC registered tutor

ON COURSE - PERSONAL AND
PROFESSIONAL DEVELOPMENT
CONSULTANCY
56 North Avenue, Shenley, Radlett,
Hertfordshire, WD7 9DG
0923-858232
Courses: 52, 76, 120, 121, 294

OSHO SCHOOL OF HERBAL MEDICINE &
NATURE CARE
2 Bridge Farm Cottage, Station Road, Pulham
Market, Nr. Diss, Norfolk, IP21 4SJ
0379-608201
Courses: 178

OXFORD HOUSE CLINIC FOR
COMPLEMENTARY MEDICINE
2 Cheapside, Reading, Berkshire, RG1 7AA
0734-391361
Courses: 295, 394

OXFORD SCHOOL OF OSTEOPATHY, THE
Doyle Croft, P.O.Box 67, Banbury,
Oxfordshire, OX16 8LE
0869-35383
Courses: 345

PARK SCHOOL OF BEAUTY THERAPY
Storcroft House, London Road, Retford,
Nottinghamshire, DN22 7EB
0777-860377
Courses: 53, 296

PEARL HEALING CENTRE, THE
37 Carew Road, Thornton Heath, Surrey, CR7
7RF
081-689 1771
Courses: 97, 144

PELLIN TRAINING COURSES
15 Killyon Road, London, SW8 2XS
071-720 4499
Courses: 122 (C)

PHOENIX COLLEGE OF RADIONICS, THE
62 Alexandra Road, Hemel Hempstead,
Hertfordshire, HP2 4AQ
0442-243333
Courses: 368

POLARITY THERAPY EDUCATIONAL
TRUST
11 The Lea, Allesley Park, Coventry,
CV5 9HY
0203-670847
Courses: 347, 348

PRAXIS
132 Weston Park, London, N8 9PN
081-341 1756
Courses: 359

PROFESSIONAL ASSOCIATION FOR
ALEXANDER TEACHERS, THE
14 Kingsland, Jesmond, Newcastle-upon-Tyne,
Tyne & Wear, NE2 3AL
091-281 8032
Courses: 18

PROFESSIONAL DEVELOPMENT
FOUNDATION
21 Lime House Court, Morris Road, London,
E14 6NQ
071-987 2805
Courses: 123, 124

PROMETHEUS SCHOOL OF HEALING
152 Penistone Road, Shelley, Huddersfield,
Yorkshire, HD8 8JH
0484-602993
Courses: 171

PROUDFOOT SCHOOL OF HYPNOSIS &
PSYCHOTHERAPY, THE
9 Belvedere Place, Scarborough
0723-363638
Courses: 224, 225, 322

PSYCHOTHERAPY CENTRE, THE
1 Wythburn Place, London, W1H 5WL
071-723 6173
Courses: 360

PSYCHOTHERAPY AND HYPNOSIS
TRAINING ASSOCIATION
Hillier House, 509 Upper Richmond Road,
London, SW14 7EE
081-878 3227
Courses: 226 (C)

PURPLE FLAME SCHOOL OF
AROMATHEARAPY STRESS
MANAGEMENT
61 Clinton Lane, Kenilworth, Warwickshire,
CV8 1AM
0926-55980
Courses: 54, 164, 244, 245

PURTON HOUSE SCHOOL OF
HOMOEOPATHY
Purton House, Purton Lane, Farnham Royal,
Buckinghamshire, SL2 3LY
0753-646625
Courses: 201

RADIX COLLEGE OF BEAUTY CULTURE, THE
West Sanquhar Road, Ayr, KA8 9HP
0292-289374
Courses: 55 (C)

RAWORTH COLLEGE FOR SPORTS THERAPY & NATURAL MEDICINE
20-26 South Street, Dorking, Surrey, RH4 2HQ
0306-742150
Courses: 56, 57, 103, 104, 297, 298, 332, 333, 334, 395, 396, 425, 426

RELAXATION FOR LIVING
29 Burwood Park Road, Walton-on-Thames, Surrey, KT12 5LH
Courses: 436

RICHARDSON CLINIC
Westgate, Heckmondwike, West Yorkshire, WF16 0HE
0924-402763/4
Courses: 440

ROGER WORTHINGTON
Alternative Therapy Clinic, 187A Worlds End Lane, Orpington, Kent, BR6 6AU
0689-860001/831211
Courses: 299

ROYAL NATIONAL COLLEGE FOR THE BLIND
College Road, Hereford, HR1 1EB
0432-265725
Courses: 300

SCHOOL OF ELECTRO-CRYSTAL THERAPY
117 Long Drive, South Ruislip, Middlesex, HA4 0HL
081-841 1716
Courses: 145

SCHOOL OF HOMOEOPATHIC MEDICINE (DARLINGTION)
29 Manor Street, Otley, West Yorkshire, LS21 1AX
0943-461784
Courses: 202

SCHOOL OF HOMOEOPATHY, THE
Yondercott House, Uffculme, Devon, EX15 3DR
0873-856872/0884-840270
Courses: 203

SCHOOL OF NATURAL THERAPIES AND ORIENTAL STUDIES
28 Longmead, Liss, Hampshire, GU33 7JX
0730-893591
Courses: 58, 155, 165, 301, 397, 427

SCHOOL OF ORIENTAL MASSAGE
8 Paston Place, Brighton, East Sussex, BN2 1EG
0273-693622
Courses: 302

SCHOOL OF PHYSICAL THERAPIES - BASINGSTOKE, THE
Lauriston House, London Road, Basingstoke, Hampshire, RG21 2AA
0256-475728
Courses: 59, 60, 156, 240, 303, 304, 335, 336, 369, 398, 428

SCHOOL OF PHYSICAL THERAPIES - GUILDFORD, THE
62 Blackdown Close, Basingstoke, Hampshire, RG22 5BW
0256-470727
Courses: 61, 305

SCHOOL OF PHYSICAL THERAPIES - KINGSTON,THE
51 Villiers Road, Kingston Upon Thames, KT1 3AP
081-546 0290
Courses: 62, 63, 157, 306, 337, 399, 429

SCHOOL OF PHYTOTHERAPY (HERBAL MEDICINE)
Bucksteep Manor, Bodle Street Green, Nr. Hailsham, East Sussex, BN27 4RJ
0323-833812/4
Courses: 179, 180, 181, 182

SCHOOL OF PLANETARY HERBALISM
5 Turnpike Road, Red Lodge, Bury Street, Edmunds, Suffolk, IP28 8JZ
0638-750140
Courses: 183

SCHOOL OF PSYCHOTHERAPY AND
COUNSELLING
Regent's College, Inner Circle, Regent's Park,
London, NW1 4NS
071-487 7406
Courses: 125, 126

SCHOOL OF T'AI-CHI CH'UAN-CENTRE
FOR HEALING
5 Tavistock Place, London, WC1H 9SS
081-444 6445
Courses: 437

SCHOOL OF THE DANCING DRAGON
50 Burma Road, London, N16 9BJ
071-275 8002
Courses: 307

SCOTTISH COLLEGE OF HOMOEOPATHY
17 Queens Crescent, Glasgow, G4 9BL
041-332 3917
Courses: 204, 205

SCOTTISH SCHOOL OF REFLEXOLOGY,
THE
2 Wheatfield Road, Ayr, KA7 2XB
0292-280494
Courses: 349, 400, 401

SHEFFIELD BIRTH & HEALING CENTRE
71 Crescent Road, Nether Edge, Sheffield, South
Yorkshire
0742-509759
Courses: 361

SHIATSU COLLEGE, THE
20A Lower Goat Lane, Norwich, NR2 1EL
0603-632555
Courses: 418, 419, 420

SHIRLEY GOLDSTEIN HOLISTIC
THERAPIES
30 Gloucester Crescent, London, NW1 7DL
071-267 2552/580 6358
Courses: 308

SHIRLEY PRICE AROMATHERAPY
SCHOOL
Wesley House, Stockwell Head, Hinckley,
Leicestershire, LE10 1RD
0455-6154666/615436
Courses: 64, 65, 66, 166

SIMPLY HERBAL COLLEGE OF HOLISTIC
THERAPIES
22 West Street, Wilton, Salisbury, Wiltshire,
SP2 0DF
0722-743995
Courses: 451, 452

SKILLS WITH PEOPLE LTD.
15 Liberia Road, London, N5 1JP
071-359 2370
Courses: 127

SOCIETY FOR PRIMARY CAUSE
ANALYSIS BY HYPNOSIS, THE
13 Beechwood Road, Sanderstead, South
Croydon, Surrey, CR2 0AE
081-657 3624
Courses: 227

SOCIETY OF ELECTRO-ACUPUNCTURE &
PHOTONIC MEDICINE, THE
21 Hazelmere Road, Petts Wood, Orpington,
Kent, BR5 1PA
0689-831211
Courses: 14

SOCIETY OF TEACHERS OF THE
ALEXANDER TECHNIQUE
10 London House, 266 Fulham Road, London,
SW10 9EL
071-351 0828
Courses: Not listed. A.F.D.

SOUTH WEST SCHOOL OF HOLISTIC
TOUCH
117 Fore Street, Exeter, Devon, EX4 3JQ
0392-410759
Courses: 69, 309, 402

SOUTH WORCESTERSHIRE
HYPNOTHERAPY CENTRE
16 Sansome Walk, Worcester, WR1 1NN
0905-612846
Courses: 228, 229

STEWART MITCHELL MASSAGE
PRACTICE AND TRAINING SCHOOL
PRACTICE
38 South Street, Exeter, EX4 1ED
0392-410855
Courses: 310

SYMPHYSIS FOR THE STUDY OF
HOLISTIC HEALTH
160 Upper Fant Road, Maidstone, Kent, ME16
8DJ
0622-729231
Courses: 140

TAMESIDE COLLEGE OF TECHNOLOGY
Dept. of Caring & Personal Services
Beaufort Road, Ashton-under-Lyne, Tameside,
Greater Manchester
061-330 6911
Courses: 128, 129

THERAPY TRAINING COLLEGE
8 & 10 Balaclava Road, Kings Heath,
Birmingham, B14 7SG
021-444 5435
Courses: 230

TILE HILL COLLEGE OF FURTHER
EDUCATION
Tile Hill, Coventry, West Midlands, CV4 9SU
0203-694200
Courses: 130

TISSERAND INSTITUTE, THE
Linkline House, 65 Church Road, Hove, East
Sussex, BN3 2BD
0273-206640
Courses:

UK TRAINING COLLEGE, THE
10 Alexander Street, Bayswater, London, W2
5NT
071-221 1796/727 2006
Courses: 131 (C), 167

UNIVERSAL COLOUR HEALERS
RESEARCH FOUNDATION
67 Farm Crescent, Wrexham Court, Slough,
Buckinghamshire, SL2 5TQ
0753-76913
Courses: 98

UNIVERSITY OF DURHAM
Dept. of Adult Education
32 Old Elvet, Durham, DH1 3HN
091-374 3724
Courses: 132, 133

UNIVERSITY OF MANCHESTER
Dept. of Extra-Mural Studies
Humanistics Building, Oxford Road,
Manchester, M13 9PL
061-273 3307
Courses: 136

UNIVERSITY OF SEVEN RAYS
(Healing Faculty)
Whiteways, 13 Cowper Road, Bournemouth,
Dorset, BH9 2UJ
0202-512382/0923-282834
Courses: 172

WENDOVER HOUSE COLLEGE
Wendover House, 2 Beaconsfield Road, Friern
Barnet, London, N11 3AB
081-361 8161
Courses: 70, 311

WENDY LORENS SCHOOL OF
COMPLEMENTARY THERAPIES
Penmarric Lodge, Penare Terrace, Penzance,
Cornwall, TR18 2DT
0736-62068
Courses: 71, 312, 403

WEST LONDON SCHOOL OF FOOT
REFLEX THERAPY, THE
41 St. Luke's Road, London, W11 1DD
071-474 7212
Courses: 404

WEST LONDON SCHOOLS OF
THERAPEUTIC MASSAGE,
REFLEXOLOLGY AND SPORTS THERAPY,
THE
41 St. Luke's Road, London, W11 1DD
071-229 4672/7411
Courses: 72, 168, 313, 314, 338, 363, 430

WHALE WHOLISTIC HEALTH AND LIFE
EXTENSION
290 Hanworth Road, Hampton, Middlesex,
TW12 3EP
081-979 7841
Courses: 146

WHITE ROSE SCHOOL OF BEAUTY, THE
2nd Floor, Standard House, George Street,
Huddersfield, West Yorkshire, HD1 4AD
0484-510625
Courses: 73, 405

WILBURY SCHOOL OF NATURAL
THERAPY, THE
64 Wilbury Road, Hove, East Sussex, BN3 3PY
0273-24420/26777
Courses: 315, 406

WITNEY SCHOOL OF CHIROPRACTIC
P.O. Box 69, Witney, Oxon, OX8 5YD
0367-20181
Courses: 88, 89

YORKSHIRE COLLEGE OF BEAUTY
THERAPY, THE
31-32 Park Row, Leeds, West Yorkshire, LS1
5JT
0532-453676
Courses: 74, 407

YORKSHIRE SCHOOL OF HOMOEOPATHY
9 Franklins Yard, York, YO1 2TN
0904-641981
Courses: 206

ZIVA BELIC AROMATHERAPY
INTERNATIONAL SCHOOL
20 Darwin Road, South Ealing, London, W5
4BD
081-568 0415/7
Courses: 75

When Contacting Any School
Please Mention

START A CAREER

IN

COMPLEMENTARY MEDICINE

GEOGRAPHICAL

AVON

ALLERGY THERAPY
19

AROMATHERAPY
47

GENERAL
161

HYPNOTHERAPY
211, 212, 223

MASSAGE
249, 250, 277

NEURO-LINGUISTIC
PROGRAMMING
319, 320, 321

REFLEXOLOGY
378, 389

SHIATSU
408, 412, 414

SPORTS THERAPY
423

YOGA
443, 444, 448

BEDFORDSHIRE

AURICULAR THERAPY
77, 79

YOGA
443

BERKSHIRE

ACUPUNCTURE
2

AROMATHERAPY
27, 28, 29

COLOUR THERAPY
98

MASSAGE
256, 257, 284, 295

REFLEXOLOGY
374, 394

SHIATSU
412

YOGA
443

BUCKINGHAMSHIRE

AROMATHERAPY
24, 450

COLOUR THERAPY
98

HOMOEOPATHY
201

MASSAGE
456

REFLEXOLOGY
380, 458

SPORTS THERAPY
460

YOGA
443

CAMBRIDGESHIRE

AROMATHERAPY
33

POLARITY THERAPY
347, 348

YOGA
443

CHESHIRE

AROMATHERAPY
64

HYPNOTHERAPY
220 (C)

PSYCHOTHERAPY
220 (C)

YOGA
443

CLEVELAND

YOGA 443

CORNWALL

AROMATHERAPY
71

MASSAGE
253, 312

REFLEXOLOGY
403

YOGA
443

CUMBRIA

MASSAGE
259

YOGA
443, 448

DERBYSHIRE

HERBALISM
175

HYPNOTHERAPY
211, 212

YOGA
443

DEVON

AROMATHERAPY
45, 69, 71

CRANIO-SACRAL THERA-
PY
139

DIETARY THERAPY
150

HOMOEOPATHY
194, 203, 454

IRIDOLOGY
232, 233

MASSAGE
253, 275, 276, 308, 309, 310

NUTRITION
331

POLARITY THERAPY
346, 347, 348

PSYCHOTHERAPY
356

REFLEXOLOGY
402

SHIATSU
410, 412

SPORTS THERAPY
422

YOGA
443

DORSET

AROMATHERAPY
30, 31, 47

CHIROPRACTIC
85

COLON HYDROTHERAPY
90

CRYSTAL THERAPY
143

GENERAL
161

HEALING
172

HERBALISM
173

IRIDOLOGY
231

MASSAGE
258, 277

POLARITY THERAPY
346

RADIONICS
366

REFLEXOLOGY
375, 389

SHIATSU
412

SPORTS THERAPY
423

YOGA
443

DURHAM

COUNSELLING
132, 133

HOMOEOPATHY
202

OSTEOPATHY
457

YOGA 443

DYFED

ALLERGY THERAPY
19

SHIATSU
414

YOGA
443

EAST SUSSEX

AROMATHERAPY
25, 26

HERBALISM
180, 181, 182

MASSAGE
249, 254, 315

PSYCHOTHERAPY
352

RADIONICS
367

REFLEXOLOGY
373, 406

SHIATSU
412

YOGA
443

ESSEX

ACUPUNCTURE
3 (C)

AROMATHERAPY
23, 37

COUNSELLING
106

HOMOEOPATHY
3 (C)

HYPNOTHERAPY
210, 222 (C)

MASSAGE
253, 267, 269

NATUROPATHY
3 (C)

PSYCHIC COUNSELLING
118, 119

PSYCHOTHERAPY
222 (C)

REFLEXOLOGY
371, 376, 393

ORIENTAL THERAPY
AND MOVEMENT
339

OSTEOPATHY
86 (C), 318 (C), 340, 341, 343

POLARITY THERAPY
347, 348

PSYCHOTHERAPY
105 (C), 108 (C), 122 (C),
131 (C), 207 (C), 213 (C),
214 (C), 219 (C), 220 (C),
221 (C), 226 (C), 350, 352,
353, 354, 355, 356, 357,
358, 359, 360, 363

RADIONICS
365

REFLEXOLOGY
371, 372, 376, 377, 378,
379, 387, 390, 397, 404, 459

SHIATSU
409, 415, 416 (C),
417, 418, 419

SPORTS THERAPY
421, 425, 426, 427, 430

STRESS MANAGEMENT
431, 432, 433, 434

T'AI-CHI CH'UAN
437

TRADITIONAL
CHINESE MEDICINE
416 (C)

YOGA
416 (C), 443, 444,
445, 446, 448

LOTHIAN

AROMATHERAPY
36

MASSAGE
265, 266

POLARITY THERAPY
347, 348

REFLEXOLOGY
372, 381, 400, 401

MERSEYSIDE

MASSAGE
268

YOGA
443

MIDDLESEX

AROMATHERAPY
40

CRYSTAL THERAPY
146

HYPNOTHERAPY
228, 452

REFLEOXOLOGY
377, 384

STRESS MANAGEMENT
436

MID GLAMORGAN

MASSAGE
249

YOGA
443

NORFOLK

AROMATHERAPY
64

REFLEXOLOGY
379

SHIATSU
418

YOGA
443, 445

NORTH YORKSHIRE

ACUPUNCTURE
13

HOMOEOPATHY
206

HYPNOTHERAPY
224, 225

NEURO-LINGUISTIC
PROGRAMMING
322

REFLEXOLOGY
378

YOGA
443

NORTHAMPTONSHIRE

COUNSELLING
134, 135

YOGA
443

NORTHERN IRELAND*

AROMATHERAPY
64

NORTHUMBERLAND

YOGA
443

NOTTINGHAMSHIRE

AROMATHERAPY
53

HYPNOTHERAPY
211, 212, 223

MASSAGE
287, 296

REFLEXOLOGY
376, 393

YOGA
443

OXFORDSHIRE

CHIROPRACTIC
87, 88, 89
OSTEOPATHY
345

PSYCHOTHERAPY
356

RADIONICS
365

SHIATSU
412

YOGA
443, 445

SCOTLAND (Central)*

AURICULAR THERAPY
77, 79

SHROPSHIRE

ALEXANDER TECHNIQUE
18

AROMATHERAPY
38

MASSAGE
270

REFLEXOLOGY
382

YOGA
443

SOMERSET

COUNSELLING
109

DIETARY THERAPY
150

IRIDOLOGY
233

KINESIOLOGY
237

MASSAGE
251

YOGA
443

SOUTH YORKSHIRE

COUNSELLING
112

STAFFORDSHIRE

YOGA
443

STRATHCLYDE

AROMATHERAPY
22, 55 (C), 64

COUNSELLING
111

HOMOEOPATHY
204, 205

HYPNOTHERAPY
220 (C)

MASSAGE
252, 263

PSYCHOTHERAPY
220 (C)

REFLEXOLOGY
55 (C), 370, 400, 401

SHIATSU
413

YOGA
443

SUFFOLK

HERBALISM
178, 183

SHIATSU
411

YOGA
443

SURREY

AROMATHERAPY
56, 57, 61, 62, 63

COLOUR THERAPY
96, 97

COMPLEMENTARY
MEDICINE
103, 104

COUNSELLING
116

CRYSTAL THERAPY
144

DOWSING
157

HYPNOTHERAPY
208 (C), 209 (C), 227

KINESIOLOGY
236

MASSAGE
297, 298, 305, 306

NUTRITION
332, 333, 334, 337

PSYCHOTHERAPY
208 (C), 209 (C)

REFLEXOLOGY
395, 396, 399

SHIATSU
412

SPORTS THERAPY
425, 429

YOGA
443

SOUTH GLAMORGAN

HOMOEOPATHY
193

MASSAGE
249

YOGA
443

SOUTH YORKSHIRE

PSYCHOTHERAPY
361

OVERSEAS*

AROMATHERAPY
64

PAKISTAN*

TIBB
438

**UNITED ARAB
EMIRATES***

AROMATHERAPY
75

**A.F.D.
(Ask For Details)**

*For the following courses ask
the schools for the venues in
which they are held. These
courses may also be held in
other named venues, so check
with the rest of venues
(counties) in this index.*

ACUPUNCTURE
5

ALEXANDER TECHNIQUE
17

COMPLEMENTARY
MEDICINE
100

COUNSELLING
117

CRYSTAL THERAPY
146, 453

HERBALISM
176

HOMOEOPATHY
193

HYPNOTHERAPY
221

KINESIOLOGY
236, 239

MASSAGE
249, 312

POLARITY THERAPY
349

PSYCHIC COUNSELLING
118, 119

PSYCHOTHERAPY
352

SHIATSU
420

STRESS MANAGEMENT
436

T'AI-CHI CH'UAN
437

YOGA
446

** For all these courses ask the
schools running them for the
exact locations of the venues.*

TYPE OF COURSE

CORRESPONDENCE

ACUPUNCTURE 4	HERBALISM 174, 179	NUTRITION 323, 324, 325, 328, 329, 330
COLOUR THERAPY 91	HOMOEOPATHY 184, 187	PSYCHOTHERAPY 351
DIETARY THERAPY 148, 150, 151, 153	HYPNOTHERAPY 215, 216, 218, 228, 455	RADIONICS 364
GENERAL 158, 160, 163, 164, 166	NATUROPATHY 316, 317	YOGA 441, 442

CORRESPONDENCE + CLINICAL

COMPLEMENTARY MEDICINE 102	HERBALISM 176	TIBB 438
	HOMOEOPATHY 185, 193, 201	

CORRESPONDENCE + SHORT

COMPLEMENTARY
MEDICINE
100

FULL TIME

ACUPUNCTURE
9, 11, 12

ALEXANDER TECHNIQUE
15, 16, 17, 18

AROMATHERAPY
21, 26, 56, 67

CHIROPRACTIC
86

**COMPLEMENTARY
MEDICINE**
103

DIETARY THERAPY
147

HERBALISM
180

HOMOEOPATHY
188, 191, 195, 204

MASSAGE
254, 266, 296, 300

NATUROPATHY
318 (C)

NUTRITION
332

OSTEOPATHY
318 (C), 340, 342, 344

REFLEXOLOGY
373

SPORTS THERAPY
425

FULL TIME + PART TIME

ACUPUNCTURE
7

CHIROPRACTIC
86 (C)

HOMOEOPATHY
190

OSTEOPATHY
86 (C)

PART TIME

ACUPRESSURE
1

ACUPUNCTURE
2, 3 (C), 5, 6, 8, 10, 13, 14

ALEXANDER TECHNIQUE
18

AROMATHERAPY
20, 22, 23, 24, 25, 27, 28, 29,
30, 31, 33, 37, 38, 39, 40, 41,
44, 45, 46, 47, 49, 50, 52, 54,
57, 58, 59, 60, 61, 62, 63, 64,
65, 68, 69, 70, 71, 450

ASSERTIVENESS
76

AURICULAR THERAPY
77, 78, 79, 80

AUTOGENIC TRAINING
81

AYURVEDA
82

SHORT

ALLERGY THERAPY
19

AROMATHERAPY
32, 34, 35, 36, 42, 43, 48, 51,
53, 55 (C), 66, 72, 73, 74, 75

COLOUR THERAPY
92

CRANIO-SACRAL THERAPY
138

CRYSTAL THERAPY
146

DOWSING
156, 157

HYPNOTHERAPY
212, 224, 225

IRIDOLOGY
232

KINESIOLOGY
246

LYMPH DRAINAGE
241, 242, 244, 245

MASSAGE
249, 265, 283, 289

NEURO LINGUISTIC PROGRAMMING
322

REFLEXOLOGY
55 (C), 381, 401

STRESS MANAGEMENT
431

When Contacting Any School
Please Mention

START A CAREER

IN

COMPLEMENTARY MEDICINE

INDEX BY PAGE NUMBER

Course No.	Page No.	Course No.	Page No.	Course No.	Page No.
1, 2	143	150-154	173	297-301	204
3 (C)	143, 179, 207	155-159	174	302-306	205
4	143	160-164	175	307-311	206
5-9	144	165-169	176	312-315	207
10-14	145	170-174	177	316, 317	208
15-19	146	175-179	178	318 (C)	208, 213
20-24	147	180-183	179	319	208
25-29	148	184-188	180	320-323	209
30-34	149	189-193	181	324-328	210
35-39	150	194-198	182	329-333	211
40-44	151	199-203	183	334-338	212
45-49	152	204-206	184	339-341	213
50-54	153	207 (C)	184, 215	342-346	214
55 (C)	154, 227	208 (C)	184, 216	347-350	215
56-59	154	209 (C)	185, 216	351, 352	216
60-64	155	210-212	185	353-355	217
65-69	156	213 (C)	186, 208, 217	356-358	218
70-74	157	214 (C)	186, 218	359-361	220
75-79	158	215-217	186	362-365	221
80-84	159	218	187	366-370	222
85	160	219 (C)	187, 218	371-375	223
86 (C)	160, 213	220 (C)	187, 219	376-380	224
87-89	160	221 (C)	187, 209, 219	381-385	225
90-94	161	222 (C)	187, 219	386-390	226
95-99	162	223-225	188	391-394	227
100-104	163	226 (C)	188, 220	395-399	228
105 (C)	164, 185, 216	227	188	400-404	229
106, 107	164	228-230	189	405-409	230
108 (C)	164, 217	231	189	410-414	231
109	164	232-236	190	415	232
110-114	165	237-241	191	416 (C)	232, 236, 240
115-119	166	242-246	192	417-419	232
120, 121	167	247-251	193	420-424	233
122 (C)	167, 220	252-256	195	425-429	234
123, 124	167	257-261	196	430-434	235
125-129	168	262-266	197	435-438	236
130	169	267-271	198	439-443	237
131 (C)	169, 189, 221	272-276	199	444-446	238
132-134	169	277-281	200	447, 448	239
135-139	170	282-286	201	449-452	240
140-144	171	287-291	202	453-457	241
145-149	172	292-296	203	458-460	242

V   COMBINING THERAPIES

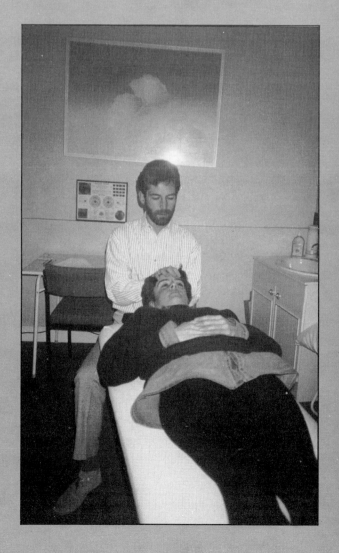

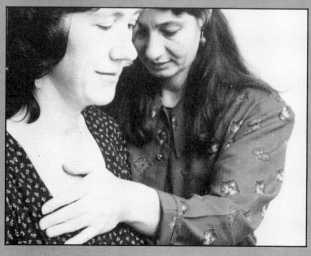

COMBINING THERAPIES

It is becoming increasingly common nowadays for therapists to practise more than one therapy in their clinics. The availability of courses that can be attended outside the normal clinic hours may be the most important factor encouraging this trend.

But why?

Some people cannot undergo certain therapies, either because of their intolerance to the way it is performed, or because their condition does not allow the therapist to give them proper treatment. For example, somebody who cannot tolerate needles cannot be treated by acupuncture; equally, certain patients may be handicapped in a way that makes osteopathy inappropriate.

Others may have tried a certain therapy but with no success. It would be very hard to persuade such people to try the same therapy with a different therapist, even if it could be shown that earlier failure was due to the incompetence of the therapist.

For some patients, their condition calls for the application of more than one therapy. For example, if the patient is too tense or does not feel at ease during treatment to really benefit from osteopathic treatment, the therapist may get better results if this tension and discomfort can be reduced through a Bach flower remedy or relaxation exercises.

Away from the patients, practitioners themselves may become interested in other therapies and so study them and then incorporate them into their practices. This could be very beneficial to the community as a whole, especially if this practitioner is the only practitioner - or one of only a handful of practitioners - in that community.

For all these reasons, and others, combining therapies could be most useful. However, it should be stressed that you should master any therapy you practise. If you cannot master more than one therapy, then apply yourself to that one alone, and give your community the best help you can offer in that field. But, if you have already mastered the therapy you are practising, and feel that you are able to attain a good standard of performance in a second therapy, nothing should stop you from doing so.

COMMON COMBINATIONS

Acupuncture and auricular therapy are obviously a very good combination since they are identical in everything except in the place of application. Acupuncturists insert needles in certain points that are selected from hundreds of points scattered all over the body, while auricular therapists use the points on the ears only. Both can also work well in combination with all the other therapies. However, some therapies - such as shiatsu or, to a lesser extent, reflexology - may work in a way that is so similar that their use by the same therapist would be pointless.

Alexander Technique is an educational method that can be used by any therapist if he/she so desires. Since people nowadays do not use their bodies correctly, this technique can prove beneficial to any patient, even if he/she has originally visited the practitioner to seek the latter's services in another therapy. Indeed, the Technique could prove to be the answer to the problem.

Allergy therapy, being a combination of diagnosis and treatment, is a very good tool for any therapist, who might use just the diagnosis part of it, or just the treatment part of it (advice on diet and nutrition plus desensetisation).

Aromatherapy works well in combination with other therapies. Many reflexologists and masseurs and masseuses study aromatherapy in order to give their patients the added benefit of essential oils.

Bach flower remedies are wonderful healers and could be used by any therapist. While in some cases they may be the only remedy that is needed, in others they can be combined with other forms of treatment to help in clearing away the negative states of mind and spirit that have caused the problem or those that accompany it. In any case, they do not require lengthy courses and tuition, although the practitioner has to be an understanding person with strong feelings towards fellow human beings, and have a reasonable ability to diagnose.

The Bates eye therapy (method) may be unique in complementary medicine in that it is used for the treatment of one organ of the body only, whereas all other therapies and methods, and indeed the wholistic approach of alternative and complementary medicine, usually involoves the whole body. In fact, Bates Method practitioners never claim to cure diseased people, eventhough the method they practise can do so and has done so. That said, the Method is non-invasive and in line with the approach of alternative and complementary medicine. Moreover, like alternative therapies, it is not in general of interest to orthodox medical circles (opticians, optometrists and ophthalmologists in this case).

Biochemic tissue salts therapy is part of any homoeopathic course, and so is part of any homoeopathy practice. It can be used by other therapists after obtaining the necessary knowledge and qualifications.

Biomagnetic therapy and **magnetotherapy** are again very powerful therapies and could be used in combination with other therapies. The short time required for any biomagnetic therapy session offers the therapist the opportunity to apply another form of treatment in addition to it, if that is appropriate. This also applies to magnetotherapy, especially if the main part of the treatment is carried out by the patient at home.

Chiropractic is not normally practised with **osteopathy** by the same therapist. There are many differences between the two, but the main difficulty is that both require training of several years' duration. However, there are one or two courses in which both are taught at the same time. But combining either of them with other non-manual therapies, such as homoeopathy or herbalism, may be very beneficial.

Colonic hydrotherapy is a different matter because it uses a machine, and the patient's privacy is an important factor. Because of this some therapists are deliberately selective to avoid problems. The way this therapy works, and the machinery involved, affects the way the clinic is furnished and designed, and so it may be difficult to mix it with other therapies requiring other sorts of space, unless perhaps it is incorporated into a multi-disciplined clinic or one where space is not a problem. However, giving advice or dietary, nutritional, herbal or other such treatment is quite possible within a limited space.

Colour therapy, crystal therapy and electro-crystal therapy involve some equipment or instruments. They can be practised alongside other therapies, although each uses a concept which is totally different to other therapies.

Dietary therapy, herbalism, homoeopathy, nutrition and tibb are all non-manual methods of treatment. They could well be used alongside other manual therapies, whether for the same patient or for different patients in the same clinic.

Hypnotherapy is something different and should not be combined with any other therapy. However, if a patient suffers from stress, insomnia, lack of vitality or the like, he or she could benefit from vitamins and minerals, dietary advice, some naturopathic measures, or any other treatment that would back up the hypnotherapy treatment. Bach flower remedies are obvious candidates for use in combination with hypnotherapy as the aim of both, in many cases, is one.

The same applies to a different extent to **assertiveness, counselling, healing, NLP, psychic counselling, psychotherapy and stress management.** However, for any therapist it might be worth training in counselling and stress management, as both are important to either as a tool for the therapist in the case of the former, or as a beneficial treatment (or co-treatment) in the case of the latter - for most patients suffer from stress.

Lymph drainage (or lymphatic irrigation) is now practised by therapists of other disciplines, and can be incorporated within any manual therapy. Masseurs, reflexologists and aromatherapists may practise it following training in it either in a separate course or as part of their original training.

Kinesiology combines diagnosis and treatment. It could be practised alongside many other therapies, especially where diet and nutritional advice is to be given. Some sports teams use kinesiologists to work on the muscles of their athletes, so one can safely say that it would help the work of a sports therapist.

Polarity therapy uses various aspects of alternative health care and so should be compatible with many other therapies.

Sports therapy is normally practised in locations different to those where other therapies operate. None the less, more knowledge about diet, nutrition, muscle tone, stress management and many other disciplines - whether acquired through short or long courses - should enhance the ability of the sports therapists.

Yoga is another therapy that is not normally possible to incorporate in a clinic which offers other forms of therapy. It is a philosophy, a way of life and of thinking which the patient must learn first from a yoga teacher, and then through daily practice. However, some institutes that use yoga therapy also rely heavily - in addition to yoga movements - on good diet in treating a variety of conditions.

All therapists have to have a way of diagnosing a case, and their college or school should have taught them effective techniques of diagnosis. In some therapies, such as homoeopathy, osteopathy, and reflexology, diagnosing represents an inseparable part of the therapy itself. In others any diagnostic technique is welcomed, as it helps the therapist to trace the real cause of disease.

Chinese diagnosis (pulses, tongue, physiognomy etc) is taught in all acupuncture courses, while iridology is normally taught on its own in special courses. Many therapists nowadays enhance their diagnosing power by learning a variety of diagnostic techniques. For homoeopaths, the choice of medicine which they prescribe will depend on the overall picture of the case after a dialogue with the patient; however, many homoeopaths now attend **iridology** courses to acquire this powerful tool. The ICM Report on Trends in Complementary Medicine showed that 50% of the whole sample of therapists in the survey who used iridology were homoeopaths. The fact that the other 50% represented other kinds of therapists shows that any practitioner could be better off with iridology.

Dowsing, radionics and vegatesting are other diagnostic techniques, using a range of equipment from a simple pendulum costing few pounds to expensive electronic analysers and other machines. Training in one or more of these techniques would enhance the practitioner's ability to deal with any case.

Although not the most known aspect of it, the diagnosing methods of **reflexology** are very powerful: if anything is wrong with an organ, this is likely to manifest itself in its reflex point. Therapists who have trained in the diagnosing techniques of reflexology have the added benefit of being able to offer reflexology as a complete and potent treatment in its own right.

How practical?

From a purely practical point of view, it should not be forgotten that any therapist - manual or non-manual - who spends a long time with any patient because of the very nature of the therapy practised will not be able to give that patient any additional treatment without extending yet further the normal session time. Of course, we are talking here about thorough treatment, not some simple temporary measures that any practitioner could offer to patients if he or she has the proper knowledge.

COORDINATING TRAINING

There is no doubt that people differ in their learning abilities. Some have the ability to grasp a subject immediately, while others need more time. Some can go on studying for hours, while others become restless after only half an hour. And some have better memorizing power than others.

Personal circumstances also have an effect on learning. Time available, physical ability, jobs, household duties, financial circumstances, levels of interest and enthusiasm are all factors which play a part. Such matters will undoubtedly dictate to some extent which course you enrol in, and whether you can enrol in more than one course.

Full-time courses are very demanding, and will take most of your time. If you have important duties, such as caring for a child, full-time courses will definitely take all of your remaining time. You should be sure that you can get the maximum possible from any course that you attend. Do not jeopardize this by trying to do too much: if you are doing a full-time course it may be counter-productive to enrol in another course at the same time, unless you are very keen and a particularly hard worker. This is not intended as discouraging advice, merely that I want to make it clear that enrolling in another course alongside a full-time course could result in satisfaction in neither.

If, however, the full-time course requires an attendance of only a few days every week, then a part-time course - for instance at weekends - may well be possible. The same applies for correspondence courses, which may be even easier to fit in alongside a full-time course.

You could attend more than one part-time course at once, providing that timetables permit this. Part-time courses are less demanding from the point of view of attendance, but not necessarily in terms of workload, and you should beware of this. In fact, some part-time courses require considerable amounts of homework from the student to compensate for less tuition time. You may find it easier to combine a part-time course with a correspondence course. Correspondence courses have no time limit for completion. If you have a full-time job, you may well be able to fit a combination of part-time and correspondence courses around this, especially if the part-time courses are held at weekends.

Short courses require an attendance of just a few days and so can be made to fit in with any other commitment you might have. Even if you are a full-time employee, you can still use part of your holiday, or even take unpaid leave, to attend a short course.

Of course, it is easier to attend courses if you are self-employed. This obviously applies to many practitioners of complementary therapies who wish to learn other disciplines, and so broaden their knowledge and increase their professional potential. You can also study during any spare time that you have between sessions with patients, as well as using your time outside normal clinic hours.

Remember that, if you are already a therapist, all the cost of additional training is tax-deductible on the grounds that the course is updating your skills. This may also apply to people working in fields other than complementary therapy: a professional accountant should be able to tell you if you are eligible or not.

VI   WHICH COURSE?

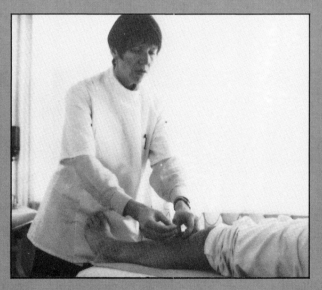
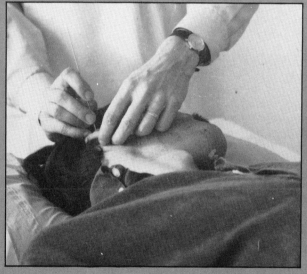
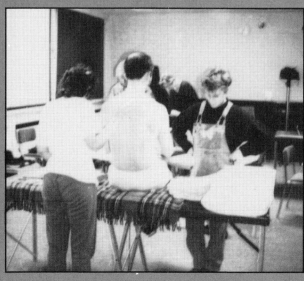
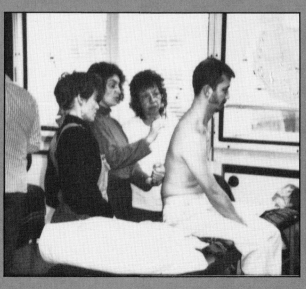

WHICH COURSE?

If, after having gone through the directory, you are still not sure what is the most suitable course for you, then the following information and suggestions will perhaps be helpful. Even if you have already made up your mind and decided to enrol in a certain course, you may still benefit from these suggestions.

CRITERIA

Many factors will affect the choice of courses that you want to enrol in. These include your own interests, the type of course, its structure and syllabus, the costs, location, the time required to complete the course, the value of the qualifications awarded, and how the course in question can be combined with another course that you might be interested in attending, simultaneously or at a later date.

Where applicable, I shall refer you to the relevant part and section of this book, and give you some hints on how to formulate your criteria for choosing the course that is most suitable for you.

1. Interest

You will find it valuable to browse through the descriptions of each therapy given in PART I. These descriptions, although brief, will perhaps give you information that you did not know about the therapy that particularly interests you, or excite your interest in another therapy, which you could study in addition to the first one. If that is the case, you should turn to PART V to see how you could combine studies of the two courses.

2. The type of course

This is one of the most important factors in deciding which course to enrol in. Your present employment or responsibilities may prevent you from attending at certain times of the month, week or day, and so you will need to look for a course that can fit in with your other commitments. However, if you are employed, and perhaps thinking of changing your career, then you should turn to PART III ('Financing your training'), and see whether you could abandon your present employment to enrol in a full-time course, if such a course suits you best.

As for correspondence courses, you will see from the directory that some offer clinical training at the end of the course, while others do not. If this is your first course, you should think of enrolling in one that includes a training period, so that you can gain the practical experience and confidence needed to start your own practice. But if you are already a practising therapist, and want to learn some other form of therapy, then a course with no training period may be more relevant. Obviously some therapies are easier to learn by correspondence than others. Manual therapies cannot be learnt by correspondence at all.

Some institutions will give the therapist who has studied by correspondence a chance to sit their examinations if he or she has had good practical experience after completing the course. The Society of Homoeopaths, for instance, does not consider correspondence courses in homoeopathy to be adequate training for those who wish to practise professionally. However, they told me that they would give any homoeopath who had practised for several years after a correspondence course the chance to sit their examination, which would lead to his or her entry into the Society's Register.

One point to note about full-time and part-time courses: full-time courses are not necessarily better than part-time courses. In fact, some people think that the longer period of training covered by a part-time course gives you more time to grasp the philosophy, ideas, treatment methods and other aspects of the therapy. However, this would also depend on your learning abilities, circumstances, the course structure and syllabus, and of course the lecturers.

3. Structure and syllabus

Most courses have different structures for the different stages or years of the course. If you are able to allocate all your time to the course, then this has no significance for you. But, if you have to struggle to schedule all your responsibilities in with the course, then the structure of the course is important. You will have to reschedule your activities every time the course enters a new stage where its structure changes.

The structure includes the number of tuition hours, the days on which they are held, the times of the day, the schedule of practical instruction, and the working hours of the clinic, if you are beginning your practical training at the end of the course. The structure also takes account of what part of the course is by correspondence, and when the examinations and tests are held which will allow you to move on to the next stage or year of the course.

The syllabus will be another important factor when you decide to enrol in a certain course, and there are a variety of issues at stake here. The first concerns the contents of the course, and whether they match the standard that you require. For instance, whoever passes the examinations set by the International Therapy Examination Council (ITEC), whether in aromatherapy, massage or reflexology is considered to have attained an internationally recognized standard. This does not mean that you have to sit an ITEC examination after passing your school or college examination in order to attain this standard. But if you would like to get an extra qualification which is internationally recognized, then this is an obvious way to do it. The same applies to the Society of Homoeopaths, as mentioned above. Until now there have been no regulatory standards for any therapy, but for the sake of the profession this is bound to change in the future, and work is being done in this regard.

You should check the syllabus of your chosen course to see if it contains anything that you have already studied, so that you can be exempted from it if you wish. This especially applies to anatomy and physiology, which you may have studied as part of a reflexology course, for instance; if you then enrolled in a course in aromatherapy, you could be excused from the anatomy and physiology part of it. Some schools exempt you from the tuition only, but not the examinations, while others exempt you from both.

The third important point concerns the clinical training. How many hours of the total do they represent, and where does such training take place - in the college's own clinic, or some appointed clinic?

4. Cost

You should not reject any course on the grounds that the cost exceeds your budget without first referring to PART III ('Financing your training'). In that section we discussed the various ways by which you can raise the money to cover your costs during training. It is a great shame if somebody is prevented from fulfilling an ambition because of financial difficulties.

So, do turn to that section of PART III and investigate the possibilities of raising more money if the best route to training requires a larger budget than you expected.

There are many ways of paying the course fees other than in one single payment. Ask for details from the school or college running the course, and refer to PART TIII ('The cost of training').

5. Location

The importance of the location where the course is held depends not only on the distance from your home, but also on the type of the course and how often you have to attend. If the course is held every weekend, or every other weekend, and is far away from home, then you have to bear in mind the high travelling costs that you will incur: this could be a deciding factor. The cost will rise even higher if you have to spend nights in a hotel or bed-and-breakfast while you attend the course.

Obviously, we are talking here about part-time and short courses; full-time courses need to be relatively near the place where you live, and correspondence courses need no attendance at all. However, if there is a clinical training period that follows the correspondence part of the course, then you should check out in advance where this is to be held. If you are in employment and you live far away from the place where clinical training is held, there may be a possibility of condensing the total period of this training into a short period, so that you can attend by using holiday or leave. There are numerous other such possibilities here, and each case is different; it is worth keeping an open mind.

6. Time

The period of time needed to cover the whole course is especially important if you are starting your professional life after this course, or if you have dropped out of your employment in order to start a new career in alternative therapy. In other words, if the course is meant to train you in the career that you will practise to make a living, then the period of time needed to finish the course and get your qualifications is more important to you than it is to the person who is training while in employment, or who is already practising another alternative therapy. Again, you should not rule out the idea of enrolling in any course that you are interested in simply on financial grounds without looking through the various ways of getting finance that were discussed in PART III ('Financing your training').

However, there are other reasons why the time factor may be important, such as if you cannot shelve your other duties for a long time, or simply cannot tolerate a long period of training - if you no longer have the mental ability and stamina, for instance.

7. The value of the qualification

Up until now, there has been no system of official bodies representing each therapy to apply a unified structure to the qualifications awarded by the various colleges or schools. Every college or school gives its own awards to the students who pass its examinations, and hence the value of any award is dependent upon the syllabus, the teaching standards, the level of clinical training, and the way that the college or school assesses its students. So it is obvious that the value of the qualifications differs from one school to another.

However, things are improving, and colleges and schools running courses in the same discipline are beginning to get their act together by creating umbrella organisations, such as The Council of Acupuncture in which most of the schools of acupuncture are represented. Britain's chiropractic associations have formed the Chiropractic Registration Steering Group for the purpose of adopting common training standards. Schools and organisations of homoeopathy and of other disciplines are expected to follow suit.

Recommendations, therefore, are still one of the main deciding factors in choosing which college or school to enrol in. The best people to approach for recommendations are associations or societies that are not affiliated to any college or school, such as the Institute for Complementary Medicine (ICM), the Council for Complementary and Alternative Medicine (CCAM), the Society of Homoeopaths, the National Consultative Council (NCC), the British Association for Counselling (BAC) and others mentioned in Part VII. In addition, anybody who has been trained in a certain school could give you useful advice about it regarding the teaching methods, assessments, homework and whatever other information you may wish to know.

8. Combining therapies

If you think that you may decide to enrol in another course while doing the course that you are most interested in, then you should look at the possibility of combining the two. You should check whether their schedules clash, whether it will be hard for you to fulfil the requirements of both at the same time, or if part of one course is duplicated in the other (in which case you may be able to avoid repeating it). At any rate, you should refer to PART V, where we have discussed the different combinations, and any potential difficulties arising from them.

9. Other aspects

After you have decided which course to enrol in, you can still double-check your decision by asking the school or college running the course for any additional information you may need.

Here are some suggestions:

What affiliations does the course have with professional bodies?

What is the average size of the classes? (The fewer students there are to a class, the better.)

Is the resulting qualification recognized internationally, or nationally? If the answer is "yes", this is an added bonus, but remember that there is no single board representing any of the therapies that can give an official stamp to these qualifications.

How many students have graduated at the school in the past? How many of them are practising now? Ask for a register of those currently in practice.

How many lecturers are there, and what are their professional and educational qualifications and experience?

VII   ORGANISATIONS

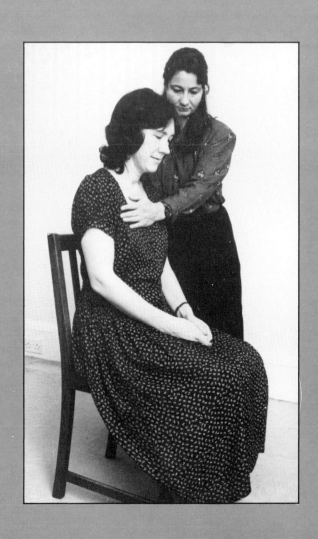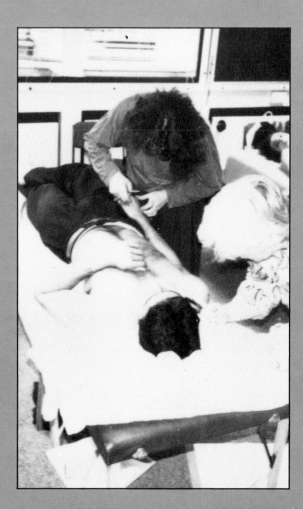

Selection Criteria

The organisations included below are independent (not affiliated to any school) and/or they are open for membership to anybody who is eligible (provided he/she meets the conditions of acceptance) and who is, normally, a practitioner of one of the alternative disciplines. Any organisation that is the association or society of graduates of a particular school is not included in this book.

THE ASSOCIATION OF HOLISTIC THERAPISTS

The Association of Holistic Therapists was formed in 1984 to further the cause of natural therapy conceptualised in the holistic principle as a common bond in a multidisciplinary environment, ultimately to aspire to the status of 'Holistic Practitioner'.

AIMS AND OBJECTIVES

The objective is to foster the holistic concept within the framework of a professional multidisciplinary organisation for lay complementary and alternative practitioners and for those health-care persons engaged in the 'Professions Supplementary to Medicine'.

The opinion is that a multidisciplinary platform would reinforce the adoption of the holistic principle and lead to the practice of preventive medicine and to the establishment of the lay 'Holistic Practitioner' through the avenue of the therapies.

The Association of Holistic Therapists aims to provide a professional standing for all qualified and experienced lay practitioners; and, in particular considers it has a role to play in providing a unifying platform for the range of qualifying standards against eventual 'registration' moves within the UK and within the European framework.

The primary objective of the Association is to be a learned body, furthering and studying the cause of the natural method and the holistic concept. In particular to encourage the membership to establish controlled frameworks and conditions within which to determine the methods and analyse results of the therapeutic technique employed, above all to record all events. The charge is often made from the orthodox viewpoint that the complementary and alternative therapeutic methods are not scientifically evaluated.

As indicated above, the Association aims to represent its membership at the various meetings which have and will be held to discuss the achievement of common and unifying qualification standards for the wide range of therapies which fall under the complementary and alternative umbrella.

The deliberations concerning common qualifying standards for the UK and those to be established for the European Community by 1992 for practicing within its geographical framework; each of these are independent of each other, it appears that negotiations will be mutually exclusive but in practice there is sure to be some spill-over interactively. The Association of Holistic Therapists see its role in this context as that of acting as a professional 'union', striving to safeguard the status of its members, unifying under the common bond of 'holistic therapists/practitioners'.

REGISTER

The Association is run and administered through the Hoths School for Holistic Therapy, this provides the means for the running of the Association. The Hoths School is a separate body.

The Association of Holistic Therapists has a Constitution and a Code of Ethics; and it provides a Register of Holistic Practitioners with specializations annotated.

MEMBERSHIP

The Association has three categories of membership:

i) Corporate Membership for practitioners who are qualified and have at least two years practice experience; or who have a practice experience rating of at least 5 years and have presented a paper acceptable to the Membership Committee.

ii) Associate Membership for all qualified persons but who have not completed the practical experience period; or, if satisfying the practical experience requirement are undertaking the presentation of a written paper for the upgrading to Corporate member.

iii) Student Membership for those undertaking a course of study with the Hoths School of Holistic Therapy or other acceptable course of study.

For more details write to: The Association of Holistic Therapies, 1 Hall Lane, Aylestone, Leicester, LE2 8SF.

THE BRITISH ASSOCIATION FOR COUNSELLING

The British Association for Counselling represents counselling at a national and international level and aims to promote the understanding, awareness and availability of counselling throughout society and to raise standards of training and practice. The organisation provides support for counsellors and those using counselling skills as part of their job and gives opportunities for personal growth, education and training. To these ends BAC has developed excellent Codes of Ethics and Practice for counsellors, trainers, the supervision of counsellors and counselling skills. BAC expects practitioners to have appropriate training for the type of counselling they undertake and to work towards accreditation. It also has Recognition Schemes for training courses, trainers and supervisors in addition to individual accreditation.

Counselling has close links with medicine and is becoming more and more acceptable as a complementary resource in General Practice as well as an alternative means of help in the private sector.

The British Association for Counselling runs an Information & Publications Office which produces unique directories on counselling and training resources and will provide information on these and other subjects. Publications include a quarterly journal called 'Counselling' with news and features on a variety of topics concerned with counselling, a comprehensive series of Information Sheets, a selection of booklets on careers and training and on specific subjects such as HIV, Sexual Problems, Counselling in General Practice and selected books published in association with other organisations.

BAC has a network of local branches and contact groups for the support of counsellors. There are seven Divisions concerned with particular areas of interest eg, Education, Medical Settings, Pastoral Care, Personal/Sexual/Marital/Family, Race and Cultural Education, Students and Work.

For more information write to: The British Association for Counselling, 1 Regent Place, Rugby, CV21 2PJ. Tel: 0788 578328.

THE BRITISH REGISTER
OF
COMPLEMENTARY PRACTITIONERS

British Register of Complementary Practitioners is a partnership between practitioners, training organisations, specialist groups and the ICM.

At present over 100 training organisations are associated with the ICM and we expect this number to continue to increase.

OBJECTIVES

To create a national Registration scheme which would work to agreed standards and recognise externally accredited awards at degree, diploma and certificate levels. This, we think will protect the future of all branches of complementary medicine.

WORK

For nine years the ICM has held the registers of a number of professional associations. These registers contain the names of qualified practitioners which historically and empirically have offered a suitable service to the public. We expect these practitioners to transfer to the British Register when the appropriate Division is opened.

Relations with other organisations:

British Medical Association

Institute of Advanced Nursing Education

Local Education Authorities

Media

National Council for Vocational Qualifications

Care Sector Consortium

Government

Health Authorities

Student Nurses

Conferences

Other professional registers and associations.

WORKING FOR THE FUTURE

The next logical step is a British Council of Complementary Medicine. The British Council will have a position similar to that of the General Medical Council and its formation will follow the establishment of all the Divisions of the British Register.

THE REGISTER

Practitioners who have not trained on a recognised course may apply under the Grandparent clause. They will be asked to show evidence of professional practice as specified by the Registration Panel of the particular Division. The Registration Panel may request an interview. The Register will supply further information on request.

WE INVITE YOU TO JOIN US.

AS A QUALIFIED COMPLEMENTARY PRACTITIONER YOUR SKILLS WILL BE WELCOMED BY THE BRITISH REGISTER AND YOU ARE ENTERING A PARTNERSHIP OF THOSE WHO SEEK TO SERVE THE PUBLIC NEED AT ALL LEVELS OF CONSCIOUNESS.

For further details, please contact: The British Register of Complementary Practitioners, P.O. Box 194, London SE16 1QZ. Tel: 071-237 5165.

COUNCIL
FOR COMPLEMENTARY AND
ALTERNATIVE MEDICINE

The Council, formed in 1984 and officially launched in the House of Commons in 1985, provides a forum for communication and cooperation between professional bodies representing acupuncture, herbal medicine, homoeopathy and osteopathy.

The objects of the Council include the following:

1. To establish and maintain a forum for determining standards of education, training, qualification, ethics and discipline for practitioners of complementary and alternative medicine for the protection and benefit of the public;

2. To seek statutory registration for all or any of the member bodies of the Council who may be desirous of such registration as and when appropriate; and

3. To preserve freedom of choice for members of the public to select their means of health care.

The Council's intention is to promote and maintain the highest standards of training, qualification and treatment in complementary and alternative medicine and to facilitate the dissemination of information relating to it. The Council is deeply concerned with the safety of the public and committed to the principle that all those who practise non-orthodox medicine are ethically controlled and bound by codes of conduct.

While these therapies differ in approach from conventional medicine, each has a sound theoretical basis resting on years, or even centuries, of experience. In the hands of trained practitioners these therapies are intrinsically safe, since they emphasise holistic, natural principles and preventive medicine.

The individual members of the professional bodies represented within CCAM have all undergone a minimum of 3 years training in their chosen therapy. All are bound by strict codes of conduct enforced by the professional bodies. All practitioners carry full professional indemnity and public liability insurance.

Countless people have derived great benefit from these forms of treatment and the Council seeks that they play a vital role in enhancing the overall provision of health care in this country.

For further information contact: CCAM, 179 Gloucester Place, London NW1 4DX. Tel: 071-724 9103.

THE HEALTH
PRACTITIONERS' ASSOCIATION

At the time, in the 1930's, Parliament was discussing a Bill which related to the practice of medicine in this country. The wording of the bill was such that if it had become law the practice of all health care would have been confined only to those who were on the Medical Register, and so thousands of unregistered practitioners throughout the country would have been outlawed and their hundreds and thousands of patients would have lost the right to have the treatment of their choice.

Seeing the dangers contained in the Bill, Dr. Joseph Bridges, a lawyer, gathered together a steadfast group of osteopaths, naturopaths, pharmacists, chiropracters, herbalists etc. and formed the Health Practitioners'

Association in 1935. This became the collective voice of unregistered practitioners together with their patients and played a distinguished part in the successful campaign which resulted in the alteration of the wording of the Bill.

From the beginning HPA membership reflected a broad spectrum of practices and membership was drawn from osteopaths, herbalists, chiropracters and naturopaths. Today these groups are still represented with the addition of acupuncturists, homoeopaths, reflexologists and others to make it a multidisciplinary organisation. Membership of the HPA is granted only to those who satisfy the Council that their training, conduct and ability are of a sufficiently high standard.

The HPA has affiliations with many professional bodies both in the UK and overseas and it maintains close links with Westminster and Brussels to ensure political representation for the interests of the members of the association and their patients and for everyone in the field of Natural Medicine.

AIMS AND OBJECTIVES

The aims and objectives of the Association are simple.

1. To advance the art of healing and its application to the maintenance of Human Well Being.

2. To preserve the right of the public to use its own judgement and choice in seeking advice and treatment outside conventional practice.

3. To provide facilities for the education of students and for further research and training in methods of healing practice by Health Practitioners and to provide a central office, clinics and lecture rooms for lectures and debates.

4. To circulate by means of a journal, information and articles on matters of interest to Health Practitioners and their methods of training and healing.

5. To protect the public by maintaining a high standard of proficiency among exponents on non-allopathic and Natural Methods of Healing.

6. To encourage the collaboration of Medical Practitioners and Health Practitioners in the best interests of the patients.

7. To give advice and assistance in a choice of Health Consultant.

8. To seek to obtain Statutory recognition of all Health Practitioners who conform to standards recognised by this Association.

9. To do all such lawful things as may be incidental or conducive to the promotion or carrying out of the foregoing aims and objects.

The remit of the HPA is therefore wide but nonetheless well defined.

The Association has no paid officers but is able to survive on the strength of the goodwill amongst its members and its income is derived solely from members' subscriptions, which is sufficient to meet the ongoing expenses in running the Association.

REGISTER

The HPA maintains a nationwide register of practitioners which gives details of all therapies offered by members of the register. This is advertised in national publications and sent out to any member of the public who writes to the Asssociation's secretary and it is compiled on a region by region basis. It is designed to help the practitioner in promoting his or her own practice, but is also designed as a service to the public in helping them to find a practitioner of their choice in the area in which they live.

MEMBERSHIP

The HPA welcomes applications for membership from any practitioner qualified and trained in his or her own chosen therapies, provided they are able to meet the requirements of the rules of membership which include the carrying of public indemnity insurance and agreement with the Code of Ethics, approved by the Office of Fair Trading which is binding on all members.

Full members of the HPA are entitled to use the initials MHPA after their names. Students of natural medicine are welcome to write to the Secretary of the HPA for consideration for associate membership.

For further information about the Association write to: The Secretary, (HPA) 187a Worlds End Lane, Chelsfield Park, Orpington, Kent BR6 6AU.

THE INSTITUTE
FOR
COMPLEMENTARY MEDICINE

A SHORT HISTORY

The ICM was established as an independent charity in 1982, to ensure that high standards of practice and training in natural health care were available to the public.

To help people who wish to use complementary health care, the I.C.M. has:

Opened a library of books, journals and research documents for public, media and official use; this has recently been augmented by the gift of the Tertius Boswall Watson collection;

Established 72 volunteer-manned Public Information Points for local referrals;

Founded an Association for Complementary Medicine to keep supporters abreast of our activities and developments nationally and internationally;

Provided educational expertise through the Education Committee of the Institute to help Associations and Training bodies towards accreditation;

Presented introductory courses for nurses and doctors to facilitate their work with complementary therapy practitioners;

Founded the Journal of Complementary Medicine as a forum for research and review of advances in complementary medicine.

WORKING FOR THE FUTURE

Looking ahead the I.C.M. has set itself a programme of five years' work the prime purpose of which will be to safeguard the standards set by British practitioners and assure their future in Europe. This will build on work already done and is designed to be formally accredited with the Training Agency, NCVQ and CNAA.

The I.C.M. has now been granted the right to the title BRITISH REGISTER OF COMPLEMENTARY PRACTITIONERS (Discipline). Within the structure of this register, it will be possible to offer all types of practitioner independence and autonomy and a voice in the future of the whole movement. Different disciplines will move through the administrative steps at rates to suit their own needs. The I.C.M. are currently inviting organisations that wish to begin this process to enter a loose affiliation as a guarantee of serious intent.

The College to be founded in the Docklands will provide the possibility for therapy Training Organisations to play a central part in the international movement towards gentler health care. They will also be able to share core facilities beyond their individual reach.

There is an urgent need for a College of Complementary Medicine to act as the focal point for complementary medicine and to offer courses at degree, diploma and certificate level. This is the next major activity of the ICM and the focus of its attention for the coming decade.

For further details of these and other initiatives, please ring 071-237 5165 or send a large S.A.E. to: The Institute for Complementary Medicine, P.O. Box 194, London SE16 1QZ.

THE
NATIONAL CONSULTATIVE COUNCIL

The National Consultative Council was formed in January 1990 to provide a consultative body for alternative and complementary medicine.

Today the National Consultative Council for alternative and complementary medicine represents approximately 40 organisations comprising around 60,000 practitioners.

AIMS AND OBJECTIVES

The principal reasons for establishing the NCC are:

1. To facilitate the process of getting individual therapies' houses in order, i.e. moving towards compliance with suggested guidelines which would be acceptable to Government.

The N.C.C. is working with the Department of Employment's Directorate of Training, Enterprise and Education to establish adequate machinery as well as competencies for an N.C.V.Q. qualification. Organisations within a particular therapy are meeting and beginning the process of establishing points of agreements, and identifying those areas which need to be bridged.

The Training and Education and Therapy Groups sub-committees, have set out guidelines for each step in the process towards the formation of Associations, (or its equivalent), and to facilitate the process towards setting their own standards.

On Therapy Groups we are committed to assisting all therapy organisations to co-ordinate their actions within each single therapy group (ie umbrella groups where appropriate). As a consultative body we are able to assist them to meet the requirements of Government and to provide the best service for the public.

2. To act as a national organisation for all the therapies, one with which both Government and the public can easily relate.

3. To enable the member organisations to speak with one voice, as and when this is appropriate.

4. To forge and maintain links with the relevant authorities in Whitehall and Brussels.

5. To use the NCC's consultative structure to create draft policies for the role of the therapies in a much wider national health-care provision.

It is of our objectives to become recognised by Government and the medical profession as providing therapies suitable for use within the N.H.S. and therefore paid for appropriately by N.H.S. funds. It is not our objective to become incorporated within the N.H.S.

In the latter case, the N.C.C. will then have its own Register of Practitioners; with each member organisation registered with the N.C.C. adminstering its own Register of individual practitioners. Each Association or Confiferation, once formed under the aegis of the N.C.C. will then set their own minimum standards.

6. To look after the overall interests of its members and to co-operate with other organisations as far as possible.

On Co-operation we seek to build good solid relationships with all organisations interested in health-care. This may be difficult in some areas but we need the tenacity to stay with the overall aim of creating unity in natural care.

By doing this, the therapies are likely to become more established and secure and they will therefore:

be more widely available to the public;

attract resources for development, student training and research;

pre-empt the imposition of any unwanted order from without (eg from Brussels);

stimulate new therapeutic ideas.

POLICY AND WORK

We aim to cooperate with, rather than confront, the medical profession. The aim of the N.C.C. is to achieve a ruling from the G.M.C. that Doctors may prescribe (refer to the Code of Conduct) alternative and/or complementary therapies providing they remain in charge of their patients.

Our policy is that medical diagnosis is the prerogative of the registered medical practitioner and must be restricted to those trained to the level of, or equivalent to, the medical profession; and that those therapies capable of medical diagnosis and identifying something that is either missed by the G.P. or that the G.P. has not had the opportunity to consider, have a responsibility to advise patients to refer to their doctor.

The N.C.C. recognises the importance of research if wider use of natural therapies are to take their rightful place alongside allopathic approaches in future health care. Under the guidance of the N.C.C., a Research sub-committee has taken on the role of assessing how best to further this aim and how funding might be made available.

The N.C.C. work falls in three main areas:

1. Helping therapy organisations to meet acceptable levels of training, professional structuring and other essential elements of efficiency and credibility.

2. Advising on and promoting alternative and complementary medicine at all levels, from Westminster and Brussels to the man in the street.

On Westminster and Brussels our personal contact with MPs, members of the House of Lords, MEPs and the E.C. will continue to be developed. This is already at a high level with Lord Ennels as our President, and the close contact with the Parliamentary Group for Alternative and Complementary Medicine.

3. To build an organisation which can professionally handle the mass of work that will come its way as a leading authority in the alternative and complementary medicine field. This is an essential element in the early development of the N.C.C.

MEMBERSHIP

Membership of the N.C.C. falls into two main groups:

(a) Category 1 - Therapist associations and training establishments.

(b) Category 2 - Remainder of members: individuals, commercial, charitable trusts, research groups, other health-care organisations, clinics and centres.

For more details write to:

Hon Secretary, John Hopson, 39 Prestbury Road, Cheltenham, Glos. GL52 2PT. Tel: 0242-512601

THE RESEARCH COUNCIL FOR COMPLEMENTARY MEDICINE

The Research Council for Complementary Medicine (RCCM) is dedicated to rigorous examination of therapies which lie outside, but complement, orthodox medicine. We have gained an international reputation for being the first in the field to encourage high standards of research through properly structured clinical trials. We also have the added advantage of not being associated with any particular therapy and are thus seen to be free of a lot of the 'lobbying' and 'in-fighting' so often associated with 'alternative' medicine.

The administration of the RCCM achieved Government support for its first three years. Further recognition has been received from the Medical Research Council which shared sponsorship with us of a university fellowship, recently completed at Glasgow. This has helped to establish our credibility in political, medical and public perceptions.

Such official backing does not guarantee sufficient income through donations and grants to enable us to fulfil our long-term aims. We have set up an independent financial Trust to administer the long-term research projects we have in mind and help raise the required funds.

In the forefront of our thinking is research into non-invasive methods of health-care and the management of illness. The public are increasingly conscious of 'green' issues and are demanding 'natural' solutions. The RCCM believes that corporate and private support of its activities, especially the clinical trials, is essential if the efficacy of the complementary therapies is to be determined.

The real and lasting gain for any potential benefactor would be the knowledge of having helped sponsor what may well prove to be vitally important advances in the health care of the community.

For further information, write to: Jonathan Monckton, Director, The Research Council for Complementary Medicine, 60 Great Ormond Street, London WC1N 3JF. Tel: 071 833 8897.

THE SOCIETY OF HOLISTIC MEDICINE PRACTITIONERS

OBJECTIVES

The Society is established for charitable purposes only. The objectives of the Society in particular are as following:-

1. To promote the advancement of the science and art of all natural medicines and healings and to encourage the natural and healthy way of life.

2. To unite all qualified practitioners of Natural Medicine and healings by maintaining a register/registers both in this country and overseas.

3. To raise the status as well as to protect the interest of the practitioners in this field and to help as well as protect the public by setting a high standard of professional competence amongst practitioners of Natural Medicines and healings.

In furtherance of the objects, the Society also aims to achieve as following:

1. To produce, maintain and keep register/registers of Practitioners and their therapies for the benefit of the public and to circulate to Health Authorities and other such bodies as well as to the public if necessary.

2. To provide the practitioners post graduate courses and to provide the beginners other such courses in the field of Natural Medicine.

3. To build or hire teaching premises.

4. To organise exhibitions, conferences, seminars, meetings, conventions, film shows and related functions.

5. To establish and maintain advisory and information points. And to publish and circulate professional journals and literature to members, libraries, authorities and public.

6. Organise discussion groups for mutual understanding to conduct study and research classes, to hold Yoga classes for relief and to conduct various other classes in this field.

7. To co-operate with, or to affiliate, or to accept affiliation with, or to dis-affiliate from anyone, or more bodies or organisation with similar objectives in anyway convenient for the promotion of the Society.

MEMBERSHIP

Individual Membership is open to all bona fide practitioners of Natural Medicines and Healers, who are interested in furthering the objects of the Society.

For further details write to: 54 Cardington Square, Hounslow West, Middlesex 4TW 6AJ.